Ancient Peoples and Places

WESSEX

General Editor

DR GLYN DANIEL

Ancient Peoples and Places

WESSEX

BEFORE THE CELTS

J. F. S. Stone

72 PHOTOGRAPHS
17 LINE DRAWINGS
AND 5 MAPS

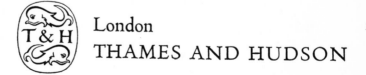

London
THAMES AND HUDSON

THIS IS VOLUME NINE IN THE SERIES
Ancient Peoples and Places
GENERAL EDITOR: DR GLYN DANIEL

© THAMES AND HUDSON LONDON 1958
PRINTED IN GREAT BRITAIN
BY THOMAS FORMAN AND SONS LTD
NOTTINGHAM

CONTENTS

ILLUSTRATIONS

7

8

Foreword

SHORTLY BEFORE his sudden and unexpected death in June 1957, J. F. S. Stone had completed the draft text of a book for the *Ancient Peoples and Places* series. As close personal friends of long standing, we had agreed that I should read his first draft and that we would then discuss such modifications or alterations as might be thought necessary. A typescript ready to be sent to me was among his papers at his death, and following our original plan, and with Mrs. Stone's warm approval, I took over the MS. and such illustrations as he had collected for the book to prepare it for the press. Originally conceived as a *Prehistoric Wessex,* the book had evidently developed in the author's mind as a study of somewhat more restricted scope for which the title *Wessex Before the Celts* was more appropriate. The book therefore appears under this title, and my part in its preparation has been limited, so far as the text is concerned, to certain modifications of archæological interpretation and emphasis which in any event would have resulted from our joint revision, and the inevitable tidying-up of a draft not yet in its final version. Essentially, however, the book which now appears represents the volume planned and written by J. F. S. Stone.

STUART PIGGOTT

Author's Preface

THIS BOOK ON PRE-CELTIC WESSEX does not attempt to deal in detail with the archæology of the region which has been covered very adequately by L. V. Grinsell in his recent *Archæology of Wessex*. Its aim instead is to present in small compass a summary of its earlier prehistory, of man's gradual control of his environment in this most vital region of Britain that in later centuries was to witness the birth of English history. But even though a coherent picture of continuity of life and endeavour is slowly emerging as a result of relatively recent excavations and study, it cannot be denied that the task of writing the book has proved a formidable one. The very richness of the region in prehistoric remains has of necessity imposed limitations and has called for rigorous selection from vast quantities of material accumulated by numerous students whose work it has been impossible to acknowledge individually in the text though it has been included as far as practicable in the reasonably full bibliography appended.

Some may feel that clarity has been sacrificed by the inclusion of too much detail. I cannot hope to escape this criticism. Others may justifiably consider many of the statements made to be too dogmatic. Here I can only beg the reader to bear in mind that future work is bound to modify many of the inferences drawn from present inadequate data. We are still only on the threshold of a true appreciation of man's past, and I would therefore wish this short essay to be viewed in the light of an introductory chapter written to stimulate interest in, and further study of, so momentous a region. It is indeed no exaggeration to say that Wessex has acted as a seed- or hotbed for a very long time, receiving the full impact of Continental and foreign stimuli, invasive and otherwise, that have in the sequel shaped in no small measure the course of British history. The emergence and growth of the character of the rural population with their strongly marked conservatism, stubbornness, common sense and love of freedom can be dimly discerned in these early pages, and it is on such characters that much of British history rests.

I have been fortified in the attempt to sketch the rhythmic ebb and flow of early Wessex fortunes by a personal background of some thirty-six years of excavation experience in the region. This, however, might have proved relatively sterile but for the most generous help and encouragement of Professor Stuart Piggott who has not only allowed me to peruse his relevant chapters of the forthcoming monumental *Victoria County History of Wiltshire* but has also accepted the onerous task of reading through and criticizing the manuscript.

J.F.S.S.

CHAPTER I

Savage Wessex

FEW CAN VISIT WESSEX without at some place or another being impressed by the very large tracts of open chalk downland that dominate much of the landscape and which are centred on Salisbury Plain. So large are they that they comprise major parts of Wiltshire, Hampshire and Dorset, counties which, with the addition of the eastern part of Somerset and the chalk escarpment of Berkshire, are usually regarded as falling within the general term of 'Wessex'.

Fig. 1

The characteristic features of these chalk-lands are undulating stretches of softly-rounded contours intersected by combes and valleys, with steep slopes towards their edges rising sometimes to heights above 900 feet. The thin layer of soil that covers the chalk rock is not likely to have supported more than a sparse covering of vegetation with local patches of scrub or gorse which would tend to thicken in the damper watered valleys. Isolated clumps of trees and small woods no doubt relieved the somewhat monotonous scenery on certain restricted and local areas that still retained their capping of Tertiary clay-with-flints. Thus these chalk areas would prove ideal for primitive agriculturalists and stock-breeders, and could relatively easily have been brought under control with a minimum of effort and with the help of grazing beasts.

But heavily wooded country almost completely surrounded these comparatively open and desirable downs, the varied underlying geological deposits favouring the growth of timber. Nevertheless, access to them was not difficult; in fact, their ready accessibility was later to become the major cause of the gradual rise of this part of Wessex to European eminence during the early Bronze Age of these islands. As will appear in the sequel, the Christchurch Avon through the New Forest

Fig. 1

gave access to the English Channel and northern France; the Bristol Avon to the Bristol Channel and so to South Wales and Ireland; and the Thames, with its tributary the Kennet, to the North Sea and northern Europe. Coupled with these three major river routes were certain overland ways equally suitable for relatively unimpeded movement; one wide chalk belt ran through Cranborne Chase to the Dorset Downs and so to Weymouth; another across the Hampshire Downs to the South Downs and the Sussex coast; and yet a third along the Icknield Way to East Anglia. On the west, a thinning of the woodland near Frome, which has come to be known as the Frome Gap, gave access to the open limestone hills of Mendip. Whilst the northern part of Wiltshire could gain direct access, along the Jurassic Way, to Lincolnshire and Yorkshire, this route does not seem to have been much used until later times.

Salisbury Plain in particular thus occupied a most advan-tageous position on a natural trans-peninsular route capable of linking the rich metalliferous lands of the west of Britain and especially of Ireland with the Continent, and of receiving stimuli from a number of widely separated quarters. It would indeed have been surprising, with such potential wealth at its doors, if this region had not been at some early stage of its history exploited to the full.

Wessex, and especially the chalk areas, did indeed attract settlement, and an endeavour will be made in these pages to sketch in broad outline man's interactions with his environ-ment in this immensely important region, from the Mesolithic period to the dawn of the Iron Age. As Professor Piggott has so pertinently observed, 'Wessex has attracted the archæologist and presented him with some of the most complex problems of his study for a good three hundred years and will continue to do so. If we ever succeed in understanding the prehistory of Wiltshire in detail, we shall have gone a long way towards understanding that of Britain.'

However, long before the potentialities of the chalk-lands for settlement and agricultural purposes had been realized, man had roamed southern England in search of food. Excluding evidence of seasonal Palæolithic occupation which does not concern us here, the first glimpse we get of human activity is of groups of savages concerned solely with the quest for food; hunting, trapping and fishing as a precarious means of liveli-hood. It would seem that the coasts, rivers and woodland alone attracted them for their quarry and it is, therefore, not surprising that the chalk downlands were to a certain extent avoided. By the time of the wet Atlantic climatic phase of the Mesolithic period, when the greater part of northern Europe was still heavily forested, two main groups of such hunters and food-gatherers have been recognized, traditionally separate but later having to a certain extent coalesced through insular isolation. Their cultures are defined largely by the type of flint imple-ments they used: a very small light blade or flake industry with battered points and microburins (microliths), and a heavy core-axe industry where sharpening of the edges was carried out by transverse blows (*tranchet* axes and later, locally, 'Thames picks'). The earlier microlithic industries (related to the French Sauveterrian) and their products are scattered fairly uniformly over the greater part of Britain, and these form part of a general-ized epi-palæolithic flint industry centred in France. On the other hand, the Forest Cultures of northern Europe of Magle-mosean tradition (a name derived from the settlement-site of Maglemose in Denmark) had developed their characteristic *tranchet* axes, transverse arrow-heads and bone tools recognizable as harpoons, and perforated antler hammers.

These Forest Cultures, in Britain classified as the Lower Halstow forest culture, occur for the most part on our eastern coasts, and by way of the Thames settlement was made over the sandy areas of Surrey, Sussex and Hampshire, in time intermingling with the older microlithic tradition. In Wessex evidence of occupation is found along the Thames and Kennet to Thatcham, Hackpen Hill and Windmill Hill on the Marl-borough Downs, and thence to Chippenham, Bath and Wraxall, all on the Bristol Avon and suggesting that this major riverine route, to become of such importance later, had already become a recognized trackway to the West. Further west still, microlithic industries are known along the southern Welsh coast; and at Nab Head in western Pembrokeshire they included *tranchet* axes comparable with one from Penwith in Cornwall. The Mendips, the North Somerset coast around Porlock, and inland at Middlezoy near Bridgwater, have also yielded chipping sites including *tranchet* axes.

Fig. 1

Even the clay-with-flints capping of the South Downs between Butser and Winchester was not shunned, though so far in this region only Oakhanger near Selborne on the Hamp-shire greensand has yielded extensive chipping floors. The high concentration of chipping sites and *tranchet* axes on the Isle of Wight and on the banks of the Solent are considered by W. F. Rankine to be connected with the ancient, but now submerged Solent River system with its Frome, Stour and Lower Avon tributaries. Riverine penetration to Salisbury Plain is attested by finds along the Nadder, Wylye, Upper Avon and Bourne valleys; and of the Lower Avon to Armsley near Fording-bridge and possibly Downton. A very important chipping site has been discovered at Iwerne Minster on the River Stour.

Although no dwellings similar to the shallow scooped wind-shelters excavated at Farnham in Surrey have yet been found in Wessex, there is no reason to doubt the probability of their existence. Pits associated with microliths have been recorded from Beaulieu, and have recently been found by P. A. Rahtz at Downton, though these need further examina-tion; and the extensive chipping floors at Oakhanger and Iwerne Minster are at least suggestive of their possible presence. Very much more work needs to be done on the identification and the distribution of these Mesolithic hunters in Wessex.

The opening-up of trackways, mainly riverine, by these hunters and their acquired knowledge of the coastline was later to become of supreme importance, and we must include also their tentative recognition of the properties of certain stones other than flint. In their seasonal movements to Devon and Cornwall they seem to have been attracted by certain siltstone pebbles which they collected and brought back with them to their Farnham and other camping grounds. So too the Green-sand Chert of the Blackdown Hills in Somerset and the Haldons in Devon appears to have been utilized and dispersed as implements mainly to the West. Portland Chert from Dorset, on the other hand, though less extensively used, was neverthe-less carried to the Isle of Wight and to the Farnham settlement.

Certain quartzite 'maceheads' with hour-glass perforations must also have been included in their equipment. One, made of fine-grained sarsen, was found in 1883 in peat 20 feet below the estuarine mud of the Ocean Dock at Southampton, whilst another came from the Mesolithic site at Thatcham. Many such 'maceheads' or small club-heads have been found in Britain in less satisfactory associations and these are mainly concentrated in East Anglia and in the Western Weald though a few are known from Wessex. W. F. Rankine has suggested that some may have been derived from the Bunter Pebble Beds and seem carefully selected for symmetry and suitability for perforation.

The hunting population can at no time have been large; and of their spiritual aspirations we have no inkling in southern Britain. No graves have yet come to light; and the only objects found, other than their hunting equipment, have been a num-ber of small perforated shale discs as if for a necklace, and an object, possibly a phallus or a degenerate figurine, from Nab Head near St. Bride's in Pembrokeshire, all of which may have been derived from contemporary Neolithic settlers in the district and are suggestive of cultural and chronological overlap.

B

CHAPTER II

First Farmers

THUS FOR THE GREATER PART of his existence man as savage had been entirely dependent upon his skill in hunting or fishing, with his food supply eked out no doubt with roots and berries. Constant movement and a total absence of husbandry would have limited population increase and inhibited any incentive or desire for an alternative mode of life.

However, during the eighth and seventh millenniums B.C., observations by a few appreciative minds in the Near East that seeds could be collected, grown and stored for future use, that animals could be domesticated, selected and bred for special purposes, and, subsequently, that vessels could be artificially made of fired clay for the storage of food and drink, caused an unparalleled revolution in human domestic economy. Freed at last from the uncertainties of the chase and of their effects on the well/being of his immediate family, man could begin to learn to co/operate with his fellows, to specialize in certain pursuits, and to find time to speculate on his existence. Present indica/ tions are that the Natufians of Palestine were the first to appreci/ ate the potentialities of primitive cereals, and that at very early levels at Jericho primitive stone/built villages were developing even at the pre/pottery stage about 7000 B.C. The resulting Neolithic agricultural economy, with nature at last coming under partial control, very gradually spread from these Near Eastern centres over the steppes from South Russia to the Baltic, up the Danube to Central Europe, and along the Mediter/ ranean coasts to Iberia and southern France, where by the middle of the third millennium B.C. agricultural communities were still scattered over the countryside with high concentra/ tions around the Swiss lakes and down the Rhine.

About 2000 B.C., with at least one thousand years of literate urbanized civilization behind it, Egypt had already entered upon her Middle Empire, and the XIth Dynasty ushered in a period of great prosperity in art, sculpture, architecture and literature. Crete, too, had entered her Middle Minoan phase with a stone-built palace at Knossos. Both of these urbanized centres needed ever-increasing supplies of raw materials and by one means or another sent out expeditions to trade with less civilized societies, to open up sources of supply, chiefly metalliferous, and to exploit them when found. New waves of more advanced technological culture were thus set in motion, which were shortly to overtake the last ripples of the earlier agricultural revolution that by this time were just reaching remote Britain and the North.

It is now more or less generally accepted that the first seeds of this slowly advancing Neolithic agricultural economy were implanted in southern Britain somewhere before 2000 B.C., the immigrants who brought this New Stone Age culture from France being ultimately of long-headed 'Mediterranean' stock. As yet, however, they were ignorant of, and uninfluenced by, a desire for metals such as gold, copper and tin, at that time so much sought after by the ancient civilizations of the East: a quest soon to revolutionize western European technology, and thence that of Ireland and the British Isles.

The native Mesolithic food-gatherers, no doubt sporadically at first, must have witnessed and viewed with suspicion the canoe-loads of farmers, their families and livestock coasting along our southern shores and seeking likely landing places. Opposition can have been but slight in view of the low population density and of the totally different economies of the two societies. In any event we know that landings and consolidation proved successful from Devon to Sussex, and that this immigration was almost certainly dictated by the necessity for new grazing grounds and less impoverished land. Burning down scrub and light woodland can for a few years maintain fertility of the soil for small-scale garden hoe-culture, but gradual movement to fresh sites is essential. So, also, fresh pastures have to be found for cattle when the vegetation grows sparse.

The relatively unoccupied and open chalk downlands naturally attracted attention and were in fact deliberately chosen for their easily available pasturage. On them we have consider-able evidence of the colonists' activities. The primary area of settlement was thought to be on Windmill Hill, near Avebury on the Marlborough Downs which, owing possibly to the priority of modern excavation, has given its name to the earliest Neolithic culture found in these islands (in the past termed Neolithic A). But recent trial excavations in a similar enclosure at Robin Hood's Ball near Stonehenge have shown that it also belongs to the same early culture, seemingly uncontaminated by later occupation, and may represent an earlier phase of the gradual spread of the immigrants to the North.

At any rate, in the deepest levels of the ditched enclosure crowning Windmill Hill the characteristic forms of round-bottomed, bag-shaped, leathery, mainly unornamented pottery found there are now recognized as belonging to the great Western Neolithic series of ceramics, the nearest comparable material being that of the Early Cortaillod Culture found round the shores of Lake Neuchâtel and elsewhere in Switzer-land. Generalized forms of this ware occur in many parts of France, but regional variants, and our lack of knowledge of comparable sites along the northern coast-line, make it ex-tremely difficult to identify any specific region of embarkation for the makers of the particular forms found at Windmill Hill and in comparable sites on the Sussex Downs. Similar wares occur in enclosures at Maiden Castle in Dorset and at Hembury Fort in Devon, but these often possess 'trumpet lugs' which are unknown at Windmill Hill and in the Cortaillod Culture. Hence it seems most probable that the immigrants who

Plates 1–4

built these two western ditched enclosures must have come
from farther west in Brittany, where similar lugs are found;
whilst the immigrants to the Sussex coast seem more closely
connected with north-eastern France and Belgium. The answer
to the problem will no doubt be clearer when we know more
of the archæology of northern France, but we should not
underrate the conscious absorption of new ideas and equipment
gleaned from the native Mesolithic population on both sides of
the Channel with whom the peasants must occasionally have
come into contact. As Professor Toynbee has emphasized,
regional variants in equipment and the development of new
institutions are inherent in the special stimulus imparted to
immigrants by transmarine colonization; cleavage from old
traditions and absorption of new ideas not infrequently accompany such migrations.

These ditched enclosures, also known as causewayed camps,
are one of the chief manifestations of the Windmill Hill
Culture in southern England though exact parallels are not
encountered on the Continent. It is true that somewhat similar
earthworks of the interrupted-ditch type form part of the
Michelsberg Culture in Germany, but this culture is of later
date and cannot be considered as ancestral to that of Windmill
Hill. But there may be ancestral elements shared in common by
the cultures of Michelsberg and that of Windmill Hill, with
origins in the north European plain; in Britain these traditions
may have mingled with those of Cortaillod or French derivation. On Combe Hill near Eastbourne a causewayed camp is
known to have been dug and occupied by a group of people
whose pottery may have North European affiliations.

Of the thirteen examples of such earthwork enclosures
known, six lie in Wessex and all crown well-defined chalk
hill-tops commanding extensive views. Others, no doubt, still
await discovery. They consist of single or multiple, more or less
concentric, lines of discontinuous ditches with undug cause-

Fig. 1

21

ways separating them, and these ditches appear to have been originally dug as quarries to form embanked enclosures within. Owing to long-continued weathering and silting-up they are not easy to see on the ground except at Knap Hill near Alton Priors and at Windmill Hill itself, where the excavations by A. Keiller in 1924-29 have until recently been preserved in approximately their excavated state. Here we have triple lines of ditches, the outer as much as 8 feet deep, and enclosing an area about 1200 by 1000 feet. On the other hand, Maiden Castle and Robin Hood's Ball have two only, whereas those on Hambledon Hill, Whitesheet Hill and Knap Hill possess single circles apiece. All have been tested by excavation, though only Maiden Castle and Windmill Hill extensively.

The contents of the ditches at these last two sites, which are flat-bottomed with vertical sides, proved illuminating and enable us to form a reasonably clear picture of life at the time and of succeeding, but otherwise unrelated, Stone Age peoples who settled in the same areas soon after the enclosures had fallen into disuse and had become derelict. Although never intended for permanent occupation, the refuse in the lowest primary levels shows that seasonal squatting by small groups of people had caused much of the accumulation as in corresponding sites on the Sussex Downs. Besides numerous fragments of the characteristic pottery vessels already noted, temporary hearths were encountered, as well as quantities of animal bones, and stone and bone tools. It is the presence of these very numerous bones of domesticated animals that gives us a possible key to an understanding of the basic economy of the culture, that of stock-breeding. There is no evidence that these earthworks with their interrupted ditches were constructed for defensive purposes, or for permanent settlement, but they are explicable as cattle-kraals for easy sorting and herding.

The bones, often split for marrow, of oxen, sheep, goats and pigs are represented; but it is the number of slaughtered cattle, frequently killed by pole-axing, and especially of calves, that gives us the clue. The absence of cultivated roots and winter feeding-stuffs necessitated an annual round-up of the herds and the slaughter of excess stock; the latter practice continued until a couple of centuries ago in these islands. One can picture the intense seasonal activity centred in and around these enclosures; with dogs barking, cattle being driven in for selection of future breeding-stock and slaughtering of the unwanted, the dis-memberment of the carcasses for food, and the feasting. The women no doubt prepared the skins for new leather clothing for the winter and for making into ropes, since no evidence exists of any form of spinning or weaving. Flax was grown, but probably for its nutritious oily seeds rather than for its fibres. Leather-working almost certainly formed an essential part of every woman's occupation; the presence of numerous flint scrapers for preparing the hides, and of antler-combs for re-moving the coarse hair from the skins, and still used for a somewhat similar purpose by the Esquimaux, are evidence not only of skill in leather-craft but also of another instance of a normal Mesolithic hunter-fisher art having been taken over by the immigrants to cope with the rigours of a British winter.

The species of domesticated animals first introduced into these islands are of considerable interest. They must have been brought over the Channel in canoes, presumably as young livestock only in the first instance, as a full-grown cow or bull would hardly have commended itself as a voyage companion. The cattle appear to have been of the small, long-horned type related to the primitive *Bos primigenius,* but this calls for more research. The sheep seem to have been the same as the 'Turbary Sheep' of the Swiss Neolithic (*Ovis familiaris palustris* Rut.), and the pig a small form agreeing also with the Swiss Neolithic breed (*Sus scrofa palustris* Rut.). The dog, of which complete specimens have been found at both Maiden Castle and Wind-mill Hill, was of a large fox-terrier type and identical with the

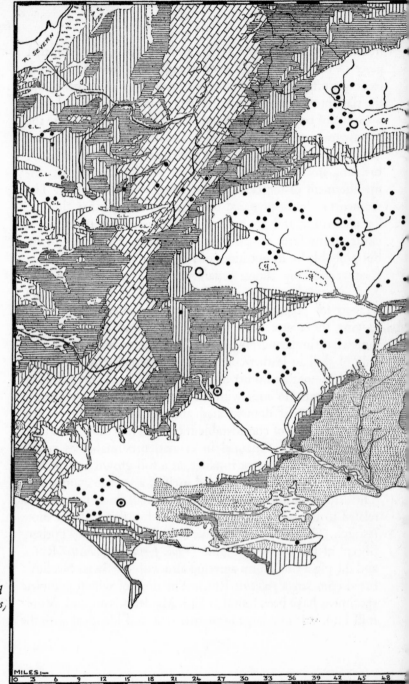

Fig. 1 The natural background of Wessex, and the distribution of long barrows (dots) and causewayed camps (circles)

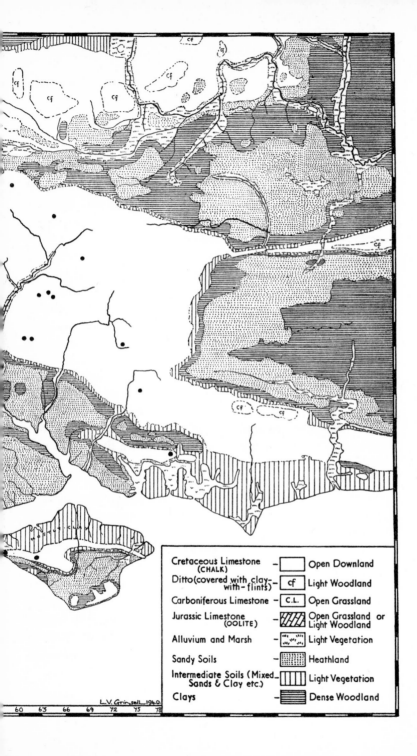

Cretaceous Limestone (CHALK)	–	[ ]	Open Downland
Ditto (covered with clay-with-flints)	–	cf	Light Woodland
Carboniferous Limestone	–	C.L.	Open Grassland
Jurassic Limestone (OOLITE)	–	////	Open Grassland or Light Woodland
Alluvium and Marsh	–		Light Vegetation
Sandy Soils	–		Heathland
Intermediate Soils (Mixed Sands & Clay etc.)	–	||||	Light Vegetation
Clays	–		Dense Woodland

L.V. Grinsell 1940

60 63 66 69 72 75 78

Swiss *Canis familiaris palustris* Rut. No evidence exists for the domestication of the horse in the Windmill Hill Culture.

Our evidence for corn-growing and for the introduction of cereals comes from the presence of a few grain rubbers of sand-stone and from an examination of grain impressions on pottery; Windmill Hill has produced so far the greatest number of identifiable impressions—one hundred and twenty-seven in all—from sites of the culture. Wheat appears to have been the principal product, amounting to more than nine-tenths of the cereal total, with Emmer (*Triticum dicoccum*) the commonest, Einkorn (*T. monococcum*) a very modest second, and probably a contaminant of the former. Barley amounted to only ten per cent of the cereals, naked barley being commoner than the hulled form. Two large flax seed impressions have suggested comparison with similar seeds grown in the Swiss Neolithic and indicate its cultivation, probably for food; apple-pip impressions suggest that crab-apples were included in the diet.

No signs of permanent occupation have been found in these enclosures, and no large rectangular timber structures, similar to those at Köln-Lindenthal and elsewhere on the Rhine, have been located except in the case of the fragmentary remains of a possible one on the edge of the Easton Down flint mines near Salisbury, which we shall note later.

More significant, however, are proved contacts with the West. On the Mendips, there was a temporary cave shelter at Chelm's Combe, and the post-holes of some form of structure at Chew Park are clearly linked with the timber-built oval and rectangular houses at Clegyr Boia near St. David's, Pembroke-shire almost in the shadow of the Prescelly Mountains, whose significance for Stonehenge will be apparent later. Even then these mountains must have loomed large as a landmark or potent magic beacon to those venturesome enough to brave a sea passage, since similar settlement sites and house types are known in Devon and Cornwall and even at Lough Gur, Co.

Limerick, which indicate that the southern shores of the Irish Sea were by no means unknown or unfrequented by Neolithic colonists and voyagers at the time.

Timber for the construction of canoes, stockades, buildings and other purposes was at all times obtainable provided that felling equipment was easily and continuously made available; and we must not forget the obvious necessity of forest and scrub clearance. Raw material in the form of flint lay ready to hand in seams in the chalk, but it is not now clear that the specialized industry of flint-mining for the purpose of satisfying the demand for flint axes was initiated by the Windmill Hill people and as the industry was certainly greatly expanded by succeeding Stone Age cultures, we may defer further comment for the moment. At all events, flint alone was used for the manufacture of axes at Windmill Hill itself and in the causewayed camps of Sussex, whereas at Maiden Castle and Hembury Fort in Devon polished stone axes of igneous rocks also make their appear-ance, again suggestive of west, rather than north-east, French influence. But the wide use of leaf-shaped arrow-heads on all contemporary British sites and their absence in Brittany implies derivation from eastern France and Belgium where they were freely used, as was also the practice of flint-mining. It is clear, as we have already noted, that our local primary Neolithic phase resulted from the combination of a number of cultural traits. The Windmill Hill Culture may well embody the elements derived, on the one hand from the 'Western' Neo-lithic cultures represented in France and Switzerland, and on the other from the early 'Northern' cultures of the North European plain. Nor can we ignore the potential contributions of the older hunting cultures of Mesolithic origin.

CHAPTER III

Family Tombs

THE SPIRITUAL BELIEFS and magico-religious practices of the Windmill Hill people, though somewhat
meagre and contradictory, are of considerable interest. The
disposal of the dead is a case in point. Here we have to balance
the seemingly callous and casual way in which a few bodies
were interred amongst the accumulating refuse of the ditches of
the causewayed camps, against the very careful preservation
of many of their dead and subsequent burial in specially constructed and laboriously built tombs. Cannibalism also seems
to have entered into their primitive beliefs, though this is
difficult to prove. Signs of fertility cults, natural to pastoral
stock-breeding societies, are not infrequently encountered.

Besides the burial of a dwarf in the primary silting of the
outer ditch of Windmill Hill, a number of human bones were
found there scattered throughout the occupational debris.
Cranial fragments predominated in many of the camps,
especially at Whitehawk in Sussex where a number were
found with animal bones, pottery and burnt flints close to a
hearth and charred by fire. One cannot escape the conclusion
that some form of head-hunting must have been practised and
formed part of the Western Neolithic Culture since similar
cranial fragments, including cranial amulets, have also been
recorded from France and Switzerland; and later we shall note
the disproportionate number of skulls to lower jaws in the
West Kennet long barrow. Fragmentary skulls and broken
human bones have even been found in the British flint mines;
at Grime's Graves in Norfolk a human femur had been used as
a pick to lever out the chalk.

Probably the best authenticated example of apparent cannibalism comes from Maiden Castle. Here, under the eastern
end of an enormously long and aberrant mound 1790 feet in

length and 65 feet wide, overlying the ditches of the cause⁄
wayed camp but generally contemporary with it, Sir Mortimer
Wheeler in 1937 found three burials; two of children and
another of a young man 'who had been systematically dis⁄
membered immediately after death. The bones bore many axe
marks, and the whole body had been cut up as by a butcher
for the stew⁄pot. The skull had been hacked into pieces as
though for the extraction of the brain . . . all the parts were
present. Save where they had been hacked off, the limbs were
still in articulation, as were the divided halves of the spine.
The impression given at the time of discovery . . . was that the
body had been cooked and eaten.' Subsequent anatomical
examination confirmed that a number of unsuccessful attempts
had been made to extract the brain until finally this was
accomplished through the base of the skull.

Such, then, are the scanty indications of practices that have
suggested head⁄hunting and cannibalism, though clearly it
would be unwise to be too dogmatic until we know more. So
let us turn to the more normal methods of burial of the Wind⁄
mill Hill Culture.

In contrast to the inconspicuous seasonal cattle⁄kraals, long
barrows form the most numerous and prominent landmarks of
the downland scenery. Compared with Sussex, which possesses
some twelve examples only, Wessex can boast at least one
hundred and sixty scattered from the Dorset Downs to the
north of Wiltshire with a few outliers on the Mendips intro⁄
duced no doubt from this primary area of settlement through
the Frome Gap. A solitary long barrow at Holdenhurst, near
Christchurch, which O. G. S. Crawford long ago pointed
out must have been the port for the Dorset and Wiltshire
Downs, and one on the Purbeck Hills, serve to emphasize the
remarkable concentration on the chalk downlands. A few
small isolated groups in Lincolnshire and Yorkshire are the
only others known in Britain.

Fig. 1

Fig. 10

Yet ten of these barrows are sited within a radius of 2 miles of Stonehenge, suggesting that even at this early date the region had acquired a measure of sanctity. Now, excavations in 1953 round the undressed monolith at Stonehenge, known as the Heel Stone, proved that this had been erected in Beaker or even pre-Beaker times; three years later a sherd probably of Windmill Hill ware was found at the base of a disturbed area close to the same stone and could be taken as suggesting that this monolith antedated the first phase of Stonehenge, until recently known as Stonehenge I. The implications of this most remarkable fact are not only that the site may already have been selected for some ritual purpose by the Windmill Hill colonists with their cause-wayed camp 2½ miles away, but that even at this early date they may have seen fit to undertake the laborious task of trans-porting a huge natural block of sarsen from the Marlborough Downs, a feat to be repeated much later on a more grandiose scale but one which was well within their grasp from the experience they had gained in the building of the West Kennet chambered long barrow near Avebury, which we shall shortly describe.

In Wessex we have to draw a sharp distinction between the chambered and unchambered varieties of long barrow, which, in the absence of excavation, are not always easy to distinguish from external features alone. The former, in general a small minority, are confined to the Marlborough Downs especially round Avebury, while the latter cover a very large part of the remainder of the chalk downlands to the south, the two groups being separated by the dry greensand Vale of Pewsey, a by no means insurmountable barrier, yet one that accounts for many differences between the two regions.

Let us first consider the more numerous unchambered group which consists of long mounds with flanking ditches that sometimes continue round one end, and from which the material of the mound was obtained. Some may be nearly 500 feet in length, others less than 100 feet, whilst most are higher and broader at one end than the other. Often they are sited on conspicuous crests, less often on lower, flatter ground. Though normally isolated, some are intimately associated with earthen structures of the Cursus type, and others, especially round Stonehenge, with later round-barrow groups suggesting that the sanctity of these areas continued into Bronze Age times, as in the Normanton, Lake and Winterbourne Stoke groups.

Fig. 9

Our knowledge of their internal features is derived mainly from South Wiltshire where thirty-seven were excavated early last century by Colt Hoare and later by Thurnam, in a some-what rough-and-ready manner. Nevertheless, their results, analysed by Thurnam, are of value and can be interpreted in the light of more recent work especially by Pitt-Rivers's total excavation of Wor Barrow, and later in barrows at Thick-thorn, Holdenhurst and elsewhere. But further scientific work is needed in this field, and more comparative material.

A distinctive internal feature appears to be a thick layer of decayed turf or humus piled along the axis at ground level or, as at West Kennet, a similarly placed ridge or spine of stone boulders. In Bowl's Barrow near Heytesbury a similar ridge of stone boulders included the very remarkable block of Pem-brokeshire 'preselite' weighing upwards of 5 cwt and now in the Salisbury Museum, petrologically identical with many of the 'bluestones' at Stonehenge and implying that it was locally available for incorporation in the barrow during its construc-tion. Pits in the barrow floors, interpreted as fulfilling some ritual purpose, have been found in a number of them, whilst in one at Warminster a standing stone 5 feet high had been erected.

Communal burial of anything from two to twenty-four individuals on the floor and under the higher end appears to have been the normal practice, though at Winterbourne Stoke one inhumation alone was found in a mound 240 feet long.

Very frequently the bodies appear to have been mixed up together, a large proportion of the bones being disarticulated. Colt Hoare noted that many were 'strangely huddled' or 'lying in a confused and irregular manner', whilst in Bowl's Barrow Thurnam recorded a heap of disarticulated bones representing some twenty-four individuals, some of which were without flesh when buried.

This mode of collective burial of articulated and disarticulated bones together, of people of all ages and sexes, can best be explained on the assumption that the burial rites involved a two-stage process; the gradual accumulation of the dead of a tribe or family in temporary mortuary houses, and their subsequent final burial with elaborate funeral ritual under a long barrow. The completion of the barrow can be considered as the final rite, the denial for ever of further access to the dead. What determined this final act we do not know; seemingly it could take place with feasting after a single death, or not until a whole generation at least had died. In any event, the recent recognition of these mortuary houses or enclosures has added appreciably to our knowledge of contemporary ritual. The houses themselves appear to have been long rectangular wooden structures, or ditched and banked enclosures, which were sometimes buried under the mound itself as at Wor Barrow on Cranborne Chase. Here, Pitt-Rivers found an enclosure of small posts set in a bedding trench and enclosing an area 90 feet by 35 feet with an entrance to the south-east.

At other times the ritual seems to have involved the partial cremation of the bones or temporary contact with purificatory fires. This has been noted in five Wiltshire barrows, the heaps of bones having been placed on platforms of flints. Grave-goods were rarely placed with the dead, fragments of broken pottery, presumably scattered during some ritual act, are found on occasion, and these belong consistently to the Windmill Hill Culture. Nevertheless, it still remains a moot point whether communal burial in long barrows formed part of the originally introduced culture. The origin of the unchambered barrows remains obscure. There is no reason to suppose that they were derived from the Severn-Cotswold chambered cairns, and few have as yet been recognized in northern France except in the Morbihan region of Brittany. Here, especially at Manio near Carnac, long, low mounds cover rectangular-shaped enclosures within which are numerous burials in stone cists with pottery of the undecorated Western Neolithic type and comparable with Windmill Hill ware. These and other features inclined Professor Piggott at one time to the view that these mounds must in some way be connected with the un-chambered long barrows of England. But he has recently pointed to similarly comparable barrows in the early Neolithic cultures of the North European plain.

Plates 1–4

However, while the colonists were infiltrating along our southern shores, related groups were moving up the Atlantic coasts and, coming from the Loire estuary, they settled in the Severn-Cotswold region. With them they brought the ele-ments of a Megalithic religion, a cult involving the use of massive stones for the construction of collective chambered tombs, for the burial of their dead. These so-called 'long barrows of the Cotswolds' are very well documented and have received most careful attention in recent years. They are built mainly of local oolite or other Jurassic rocks and in form ap-proach the trapezoid or rectangle with the wider end incurved to form a forecourt, behind the centre of which is the burial chamber in the typologically early forms, or a 'false portal' in the later. The edges of the cairns are usually delimited by dry stone walling or peristaliths, whilst the chambers themselves are built of orthostats, with dry-walling between, to carry cap-stones or a corbelled roof. As in unchambered barrows, burial was collective, bones of as many as forty-eight persons having been found in one cairn at Tinkinswood. Whilst grave-goods

Plate 5

C

are scarce, the pottery is again consistently Western Neolithic and related to that of Windmill Hill.

The main concentration of these chambered cairns lies outside Wessex to the north of Tetbury, but a fine example of a southern outlier exists at Stoney Littleton, near Wellow, into which access is still possible. In spite of extensive restoration in the nineteenth century this tomb gives a very good impression of the type. The gallery is here nearly 50 feet long with three pairs of transeptal chambers, the roof being a corbelled barrel vault.

Before their final closure and elaborate ritual blocking, the interiors of these tombs must have been readily accessible. Successive burials took place in them and, when full, the bones of previous occupants were pushed aside. Thus in one small chamber ($4\frac{3}{4}$ by $3\frac{3}{4}$ by $2\frac{1}{2}$ feet) at Lanhill near Chippenham, nine individuals of a single family, and ranging from one to seventy years in age, had been packed away at the rear, whilst an articulated skeleton, the last burial, occupied the front half of the chamber.

At a very early period this new cult involving the use of collective chambered tombs impinged on, and coalesced with, the practice of burial in unchambered long barrows to form the chambered variety around Avebury, on the headwaters of the river Kennet, where suitably large blocks of sarsen sandstone lay promiscuously on the surface of the downs. Here we have a compact group of some nine surviving or recorded barrows built of chalk rubble from the flanking ditches, as in the south, but embodying stone-built chambers in the Cotswold style.

The West Kennet barrow is one of the largest and most famous examples. Although partly explored by Thurnam in 1859, it was not carefully excavated by modern standards until 1955-56, when it was found that four chambers fortunately still remained completely intact and undisturbed. This excavation by Professor Piggott and R. J. C. Atkinson, has in fact proved to be one of the most interesting and informative of recent years; and the Ministry of Works, in whose hands the guardianship rests, has restored most admirably the impressive gallery and chambers for inspection by visitors.

The mound itself is 340 feet long, built of chalk quarried from the two parallel flanking ditches which are separated from it by a wide 'berm', and possesses a spine of rounded sarsen boulders running along its length. From the centre of a façade of massive upright stones at the east end, a gallery nearly 8 feet high runs below the capstones inwards for some 40 feet and is terminated by the end chamber excavated by Thurnam. On either side of the gallery four separate chambers, forming double transepts, were found to be filled almost to the cap/ stone roofing with humanly inserted deposits, the stratigraphi/ cal relationships of which confirmed similar but naturally occurring cultural deposits observed elsewhere, especially at Windmill Hill nearby.

The floor of each chamber was covered with a jumbled mass of human bones, often with skulls pushed into the back recess; and potsherds of early Windmill Hill types, including a bowl of developed Abingdon style with shell grit, accom/ panied them. Thirty disarticulated skeletons were found in the four chambers and, surprisingly, more lower jaws were present than skulls, suggesting that some of the latter had been re/ moved, possibly for ritual purposes. Over these lay successive layers of occupational refuse, apparently placed as a ritual act and derived from outside the tomb. These had apparently been inserted intentionally, as each was separated by layers of com/ paratively clean sterile chalk rubble which could not have silted in naturally in the quantities observed. Pottery of the later Secondary Neolithic Cultures of both Peterborough and Rinyo/Clacton types, including Bell/Beaker sherds, some with cord/zoned ornament, were fairly plentifully strewn in these

Plates 6–8

Plate 6

Plate 7

Plate 8

Fig. 5
Plate 11

Plate 14

later layers with charcoal, animal bones, beads, bone pins and spatulæ; whilst an almost complete Bell-Beaker lay on the topmost layer under the corbelled roof of the north-west chamber. In the absence of natural agencies, these distinct and separate layers are only explicable on the assumption that the tomb retained a degree of sanctity for some years and that later peoples occupying the district saw fit to perpetuate the memory of the dead by scattering token remains of their feasts in the chambers. In any event, the important feature is the relationship of the early Windmill Hill pottery with a tomb of the Severn-Cotswold type, a relationship that is not yet susceptible of exact solution.

At a late date in its history the final rite involved the closure of the entrance to the tomb. This consisted in the erection of two further massive stones in the forecourt, continuing the line of the passage, and the emplacement transversely across and in front of them of colossal blocks weighing upwards of 20 tons apiece, to form a sort of false entrance. Owing to the shallowness of the holes into which the latter were placed, and the thrust of the mound behind, some fell outwards at an early date. However, the experience gained by the builders in this complex operation, and in the emplacement of massive capstones on vertical uprights, may well have contributed to the tradition of skill involved in the setting up of the stones of Avebury itself, later to culminate in the erection of Stonehenge—to which, as we have seen, the Heel Stone may already have been taken. But such operations needed much timber for packing and leverage, and it is of interest to observe on some of the West Kennet orthostats the highly polished markings and grooves where flint or stone axes had been sharpened and reground.

But the effort involved in terms of man-power was not confined solely to the construction of these laboriously built tombs for collective burial. The cult of the dead occasionally demanded very much greater effort, the burden of digging immensely elongated enclosures with which certain long barrows are intimately associated. The Stonehenge 'Cursus', discovered and so called in 1723 by Stukeley, who likened it to a racecourse and so gave it the name now used for this type of structure, lies about half a mile to the north of Stonehenge. This banked and ditched enclosure, nearly 1¾ miles long, 110 yards wide and enclosing 70 acres, lies on undulating ground and is terminated at its eastern end by a long barrow. A small trial excavation in 1947 showed that the ditch had been dug by gangs of workers with deer's-antler picks to form a continuous inner bank, causeways having been left here and there, confirming indications on aerial photographs. The remains of a flint chipping floor were also found on the bottom.

Fig. 9

This enclosure pales into insignificance, however, when compared with that of the Dorset Cursus which runs from Bokerly Down to Thickthorn Down, a distance of fully 6 miles, and encloses 220 acres. Here, too, the ditches and banks are separated by about 100 yards and run parallel, though much of it is now ploughed out. The labour and tribal organization involved must have been immense; it has been calculated that a volume of some 6½ million cubic feet was extracted for the banks and this may be compared with the 3½ million dug from the Avebury ditch. One striking feature of this cursus is that it is bipartite; at some stage it must have been decided to double its length from Bottlebush Down, where parts of the earthwork can still be seen. Four long barrows are included in it: one at each end, that on Bokerly Down being the longest on record (490 feet); one at right angles on the crest of Gussage Down; and a fourth included in one of the banks. This intimate association of long barrows with cursus earthworks, known also in Oxfordshire, is strong presumptive evidence of contemporaneity. Their purpose we can only guess at; possibly some form of processional way, a conception later to be translated into avenues of stones. But we can be certain that they were used for religious ceremonial rather than for domestic or agricultural purposes.

We can also be sure that the same impelling religious urge occasionally called for more personal objects. Chalk figurines, rather crudely carved and possibly representing the Mother or Earth Goddess, have been found at Windmill Hill and Maiden Castle, though they are rare in the Western Neolithic Culture. Carved chalk phalli, probably connected with ferti/ lity cults, are also rare but have been recorded from Windmill Hill and from the Thickthorn long barrow. Small chalk 'cups' and pottery 'spoons' or 'ladles' are not infrequently found in both this and the immediately succeeding cultures; it has been suggested that these also may belong to the same class of ritualistic objects as the phallic carvings.

CHAPTER IV

Flint and Stone

THE OLD DEFINITION of man as a toolmaker is an apt one, for by his tools we can distinguish him from his fellows and gauge his reactions with his environment. In her own words, Professor D. A. E. Garrod has wisely said, 'Man's tools are the instruments of his response to the world in which he lives, but they are much more—they are the weapons of his conquest of that world . . . this is the true drama of prehistory, the clue to its interpretation.'

As the name implies, Western Neolithic man's response to his forest environment was not continued acquiescence in its presence but the conscious introduction of ground and polished *Plates 10, 12, 13* stone axes for its control, of types superior to the *tranchet* axes of the Forest Cultures and capable of more effective use. But these axes needed raw materials from which to make them, and in quantities that could satisfy the ever-increasing demand. Flint had been used from time immemorial for the chipping of tools, the special characters of which serve to distinguish one culture from another, though it is not yet possible to distinguish the source of origin of each type of flint with any degree of precision. It occurs fairly abundantly in various regions weathered out on the surface and sometimes, as at Little Somborne in Hampshire, it is obtainable from natural outcrops. Some years ago the remains of a surface workshop was found here, extending over two acres, which turned out 'Thames picks', a type of implement of Mesolithic ancestry not infrequently found on the chalk downs, and contemporary but unconnected with the Western Neolithic Culture.

But such surface flint is of poor quality and flakes badly; the best is obtainable only from seams lying deep in the upper chalk. It is almost certainly to the credit of the Neolithic

39

colonists of North and West Europe, and not to the Forest Cultures, that the properties of these deep flint seams were recognized and exploited, even though traditionally in most of Europe the normal axe was of igneous rock. In their settlement of the chalk regions of Belgium, northern France and southern England, the only raw material immediately available was flint; and it is in these areas that we find flint-mining developed practically for the sole production of axes. Nevertheless, the bone tools used in the mining process, many of the axe forms produced, and certain naturalistic carvings of deer on flint crust as at Grime's Graves in Norfolk, all imply that the colonists were not averse—as we have already seen—to absorb-ing certain useful Mesolithic traits and benefiting from their acquired knowledge. Further, the very existence of these new mining activities and the specialization entailed clearly shows that at last it had become possible to divert surplus foodstuffs, at least temporarily and seasonally, to skilled workers other than those engaged exclusively on farming and intermittent barrow-building.

No fewer than nine mining sites were known on the Sussex Downs before the discovery in 1929 of the first mines in Wessex on Easton Down 7 miles north-east of Salisbury, to be followed three years later by another large group of 100 shafts or so at Martin's Clump in Hampshire 2 miles to the north-east and on the same ridge of downland. The Easton Down mines have been the more extensively examined; they cover some 40 acres (mainly of unploughed downland), and on the surface appear as hollows surrounded by low banks almost touching each other; the filled-in shafts of the mines lie below.

The process of mining consisted in digging vertical shafts down to a seam of suitable flint nodules by means of deer's-antler picks used as wedges rather than as picks in the modern sense, all the tines but for the brow tine having been removed from either shed antlers or those obtained from hunted and

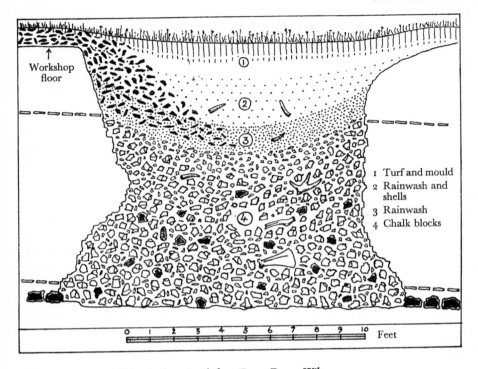

Fig. 2   Section of the filling of a flint-mine shaft on Easton Down, Wilts

slaughtered beasts. To judge by the numbers used and discarded, deer must have been very numerous. The crowns from such
antlers were not infrequently used as rakes, and for shovels the
shoulder blades of large wild oxen *(Bos primigenius)*. Having
reached the seam from 8 to 12 feet below ground level, the base
of the pit was enlarged by undercutting to bell-shaped form at
both Easton Down and Martin's Clump, to obtain the maxi-   *Fig. 2; Plate 9*
mum yield of flint without driving galleries in all directions as
was commonly done in the Sussex mines and at Grime's
Graves. On the surface and on well defined workshop floors,
the extracted flint was then fabricated into axes; the preliminary
removal of the cortex and rough shaping would be carried out

41

in one area and then passed to another contiguous area for final and more delicate finishing. The last act of grinding and polishing seems very rarely if ever to have formed part of the process; this seems to have been left to the individual taste and requirements of the purchaser, though one such finished pro, duct was found in Floor 7 at Easton Down.

From the unweathered chalk walls of the shafts, often still bearing the imprints of the antler picks, and of the chalk blocks filling them, it is clear that the shafts were soon filled in to make room for the next pit. Pottery is not unnaturally rarely found in these industrial workings, though scraps of Windmill Hill ware were found in the rainwash silting at the top of one of them and in the nearby dwelling of a miner. Over this silting lay the workshop floor in which was found the polished axe just mentioned, and a heap of forty-five grey, red and yellow Eocene pebbles—possibly collected by miner's children for a primitive game of marbles!

The mining area is surrounded by settlement sites at Easton Down, the temporary or seasonal dwelling-quarters of the miners. Though initiated by Windmill Hill people, it is evi, dent from the types of pottery recovered that the mines con, tinued to be worked by a number of succeeding cultures including those using Peterborough and Beaker wares; in one instance a typical round-bottomed Windmill Hill pot had been decorated in the Peterborough style thus proving direct overlap of the two cultures.

A fall of a ton or so of chalk from the wall of a shaft during re-excavation rather forcibly suggested insecurity, and that the absence of galleries might here be accounted for on the grounds of safety. But in this the present writer was mistaken. The recent discovery of another small group of flint mines at Durrington, near Amesbury, which had proved relatively abortive in flint, showed that at times it was possible to cut galleries at the flint face only 4 feet below the surface. An outcrop of flint had here been exploited by the open-cast method, and higher up the hill the vein had been followed by sinking shafts and pecking out galleries in the normal manner. This group was discovered during pipe-laying operations; no doubt many others exist though now obliterated by later cultivation.

The primary layers at Windmill Hill have yielded axes of flint only; it was not until the later occupation of the same site by the Secondary Neolithic cultures we shall discuss in the next chapter that axes made from rocks foreign to the district first make their appearance. They have been found, however, in the earliest corresponding levels at Maiden Castle and Hembury Fort, again emphasizing the west French connexions of these camps.

Such axes of rocks other than flint are exceedingly numerous and form a feature of most museum collections; but it was not until the early 1920s that their potential value as trade indica-tors was appreciated, largely through the pioneer petrological work of H. H. Thomas on the source of the Stonehenge 'bluestones', and by the late Alexander Keiller's recognition of the wider potentialities of the method. As a direct result of this work a committee was formed in 1936 by the South-Western Group of Museums and Art Galleries to study their petrology and distribution in Wessex and in the adjoining counties of Gloucestershire, Devon and Cornwall, with special reference to their probable sources of origin. So productive and illumi-nating did the work become that the Council for British Archæology in 1945 raised what was virtually a regional monopoly on to a national basis with the direct result that Great Britain has now been regionalized for the purposes of this study and its development.

It has in fact proved to be a most fruitful line of research. Over a thousand specimens have been sliced and examined by the South-Western Committee, and it has been found possible to place well over four hundred of these into twenty-four

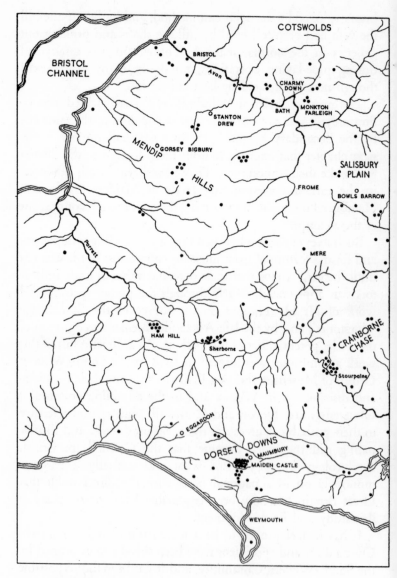

Fig. 3   Distribution of axes of stones geologically foreign to Wessex

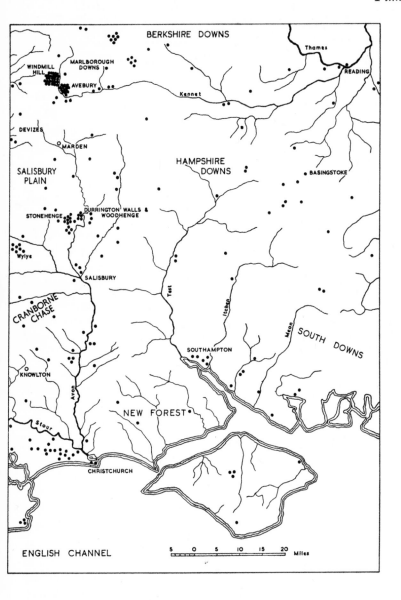

petrological groups which in many instances have been traced
to their sources of origin—sometimes well-known factory sites,
at other times to outcrops of identical rock. These igneous
outcrops and factory sites lie geologically outside Wessex and
occur mainly along our western coasts from Brittany to Cornwall and up the Irish Sea to the Lake District and Northern
Ireland. Distributional studies of their products, specimens of
all of which are to be found in Wessex, thus provide a valuable

Fig. 3

guide to the trade routes over which they were carried and to
the cultural contexts in which they are found. Mere cursory
examination of the distribution map of all foreign stone axes,
irrespective of origin and known to have been found in
Wessex, indicates that the main routes of penetration from the
primary coastal trade routes were riverine, as would be expected in densely forested country, and follows precisely the
same pattern as those of Mesolithic finds. In particular, we
should note the concentration of find spots along the rivers
Stour and Christchurch Avon, the Kennet tributary of the
Thames, and especially along the Bristol Avon, the trunk road
as it were to the west.

Trade and movement were indeed widespread and involved
even cross-Channel voyages. Certain axes from Jersey, Southampton, Bournemouth and Tewkesbury (Group VIIA)
have recently been proved by P.-R. Giot to have emanated
from Brittany, whilst it is possible that the ten ceremonial axes

Plate 10

of jade or jadeite in Wessex came from that country also; more
work is now being done on these.

On the other hand, Cornwall seems to have been the main
source of supply of certain greenstone axes. Small numbers
have been proved petrologically to have come from outcrops at
St. Ives, from Trenow near Marazion (Group III), Kenidjack
Castle near Cape Cornwall (Group XVII), Camborne
(Group XVI) and Balstone Down near Callington (Group
IV), though the actual factory sites have not yet been located.

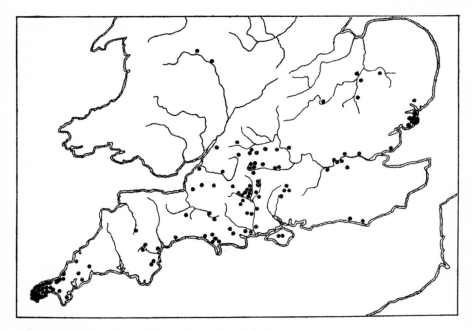

Fig. 4   Distribution of axes of Group 1 in southern England

Two Marazion specimens have been found in Stonehenge and as far afield as Bridlington in Yorkshire. Of far greater impor, tance, however, was a factory turning out the products of Group I, the largest group so far examined and comprising one hundred and six specimens. Their distribution is shown in Fig. 4 from which it will be seen that we are here dealing with a major industrial Cornish activity which found an immediate market in Wessex. Although exact identification has not yet proved possible, there is not much doubt that the factory must have existed in the Mount's Bay region between Penzance and Mousehole where very similar outcrops occur, but probably now submerged below sea-level. This area is known to have subsided (as at Er Lannic in Brittany and around Jersey), and

Fig. 4

the identification of an axe from Salisbury and of a large battle,
axe from Okehampton, Devon, as having very probably
originated from the Gear Rock, now on the 5,fathom line and
about half a mile out in the bay off Penzance, lends colour to
the supposition.

This Group I factory, wherever it was, turned out a great
variety of products, more so in fact than any other known site
or group, and this may well mean that it continued to be
worked for some years. Specimens have been found in the
secondary occupation layers at Windmill Hill, at Stonehenge,
Woodhenge and in another similar ceremonial earthwork at
Dorchester in Oxfordshire, and in a few round barrows of the
early Wessex Culture, which implies that the factory may have
been in the hands of Secondary Neolithic producers.

But Wessex was also importing the products of factories very
much farther afield; such long,range connexions may be indi,
cative of a class of trader who found lengthy journeys worth
while. Axes from such factory sites as that at Graig Lwyd in
Caernarvonshire, from the screes of the Pike of Stickle in
Langdale, and even from Tievebulliagh Hill in Co. Antrim
are all well represented, and especially so in the Avebury dis,
trict. These were not necessarily traded overland through the
Midland Gap as were most probably Graig Lwyd axes; the
high concentration of most types at Bournemouth, and
scattered finds round the coasts of Dorset, Devon and Corn,
wall are strongly in favour of a degree of coastal traffic. At
least six have come from the Whin Sill of the Teesdale area;
these are mostly of Early Bronze Age (Wessex Culture) battle,
axe form, one of which is of great interest as it came from a
round barrow at Upton Lovel in Wiltshire and was directly
associated with mullers of both Groups I and IIIA and other
early transitional Bronze Age objects.

We have seen already that both Mesolithic hunters and
Western Neolithic colonists settled in Pembrokeshire, and we

Plate 13

48

have seen too that this county is dominated by the Prescelly Mountains which have readily accessible outcrops of distinc/ tive volcanic rocks scattered along their crest. The most distinctive of these is spotted dolerite or 'preselite', which out/ crops at Carn Meini and Cerrig Marchogion and which contains well/marked white or pinkish felspathic spots of all sizes from that of a pea to that of a walnut. Something about its character must have been sufficiently impressive and signi/ ficant to warrant the laborious transport to Wiltshire of some eighty large blocks weighing anything up to 4 tons apiece, one or more blocks of which were incorporated in the spine of Bowl's Barrow. More will be said later about these 'bluestones' when we come to consider Stonehenge itself, but what is now clear is that these blocks did not come from a region renowned for megalithic monuments or stone circles. It did, however, produce ground stone axes and—of even more significance, as will appear later—battle/axes of 'preselite'; a large specimen of the latter, weighing 5 lb. 2 oz., was found at Fifield Bavant, and other axes along the south coast from Sidmouth to Bourne/ mouth.

Plate 12

Apropos dating the industry, the only axes that occur in the Western Neolithic levels of Maiden Castle and Hembury Fort belong to Groups IIA and IVA, both almost certainly from Cornwall. All other groups examined have been found in Late Neolithic contexts and must have been exploited by Secondary Neolithic people; the products are also more deve/ loped and varied, and include perforated axe/hammers, mace/ heads and battle/axes.

But before leaving the subject of axes, we must not omit to mention that originally they also possessed a ritual or votive significance, of the content of which cult we now have no inkling. In the Minoan world there was the well/known Cult of the Double Axe, and as a symbol possibly of a deity, the concept of the symbolic axe was common in Europe. In

D

Brittany, large numbers of magnificent axes made from rare and beautiful rocks were ceremonially deposited as grave-furniture in such Megalithic tombs as those of Mané-er-Hroëk, Mont Saint-Michel and Tumiac, or at the base of standing stones. And not content with burying the actual objects themselves, representations were sometimes carved on the structural stones of the tombs. In Wessex, we have little evidence of the cult except for the otherwise relatively useless but beautiful

Plate 10

imported axes of jade or jadeite, and of others made from softish sandstone or even of chalk as are two from Woodhenge. However, the concept was present and, as we shall see, later found positive expression in carvings of bronze axes on the stones of Stonehenge.

Consolidation

IN THE LAST three chapters we have considered the Primary Neolithic colonists and the indelible marks they left behind them on the Wessex landscape. Estimates of the length of their sojourn have been very varied, the most extreme being that of W. A. Sturge, President of the Prehistoric Society of East Anglia in 1909, who confidently stated and considered that he had proved 'on irrefragable evidence' that the Neolithic period had lasted well over 200,000 years—a grossly inaccurate estimate that we now know to be out by a factor of about 1000 and a measure of the distance we have travelled in understanding the chronology of prehistoric Europe since that date. Five to ten generations of men, or 100-200 years, would perhaps be nearer the mark as an estimate of time before these Neolithic peoples had inextricably mingled with the native population or had moved northwards in search of new pastures.

Estimates of vital statistics, in the absence of full information, could be equally inaccurate, and we do not propose to embark on them. However, if we take an average of ten individuals per long barrow, we have tangible evidence of some sixteen hundred burials spread over this much shorter period. This does not represent a very high population density for so scattered a community engaged as we have seen in stock-raising, cereal-growing, digging causewayed enclosures and constructing immense long barrows and colossal cursus earthworks. It is obvious that much man-power remains unaccounted for. Either burial in long barrows was accorded only to the heads of tribes and their families, which is the more probable explanation, or the native population was dragooned and exploited for such navvy tasks as digging earthworks and sinking shafts for flint. The normal estimate of a hunting population as one per square mile would undoubtedly apply to the period before the introduction of farming, and with a total area of 7290 square miles Wessex could no doubt have supported this number of individuals. But there can equally be no doubt that numbers must have greatly increased as a result of the impact of this newly introduced farming economy.

We have, therefore, now to deal with the reverse process; the results of this impact on the native population during and after the recession of the full force of the innovation. The stimulus did indeed call forth responses, varied in character, but all attributable nevertheless to this primary causative impulse. New and distinct 'cultures' suddenly make their appearance, characterized mainly by new pottery forms, and all closely linked by common usage of flint and bone tools of very distinctive but developed Mesolithic types. To these resurgent cultures, some of which were ultimately affiliated to those of what Gjessing has called the Circumpolar Stone Age of the northern hemisphere from Norway to North America, the name of Secondary Neolithic has been given; secondary in the sense that they were derived from the Primary Neolithic Culture by an admixture of peoples who still retained many of their essential Mesolithic characters and traditions.

Wessex was the common meeting ground of these diverse elements and in Wessex we witness their full interplay not only in the early stages of contact but in the later phases of amalgamation, with the subsequent impact of the new BellBeaker and SingleGrave invaders from the Continent. Here we need not enter into the minutiæ of their complex interrelationships. It will be sufficient to distinguish three main components which, in spite of regional variants, have been termed the Peterborough (formerly Neolithic B), the RinyoClacton or Grooved Ware, and the Dorchester Cultures, after typesites where their remains were first recognized. All three contributed their quota to the ensuing vigorous Bronze Age, but none are easy to define in terms of man owing to the remarkable paucity of human remains. All have been found to be consistently later in date than Western Neolithic deposits and fall therefore within the Late Neolithic phase, though some slight overlap is perceptible in Wessex itself. True Windmill Hill ware is now recognized as covering the Early and Middle phases which are both stratigraphically earlier at Windmill Hill and in the West Kennet chambered long barrow than in the overlying Peter-borough and Rinyo-Clacton occupation layers.

PETERBOROUGH CULTURE

In origin it is possible to distinguish two main strains in the Peterborough ware as developed in Britain; a combination in fact of the pit-comb ware of Scandinavia—a product of the huge province embraced in the Circumpolar Stone Age cul-tures—and of the cord-ornamented funnel-beakers charac-teristic of the great area stretching from South Russia to the Baltic. Both resulted from the impact of Neolithic peasantry on the northern Forest Cultures and both strains seem to have merged after crossing the North Sea to produce forms not characteristic in detail of either province. These folk-move-ments, for such they must have been, took place largely on our south-eastern shores, the main movement being up the Thames valley to Wessex and the headwaters of the Kennet, and from thence to the Cotswolds.

Pottery of the Mortlake bowl style, developed locally by these people through contact with the later phases of the Wind-mill Hill Culture in East Anglia and up the Thames, takes the form of thick, coarse, round-based pots with thickened rims and profuse ornament over the greater part of the vessels. This ornament usually consists of twisted or whipped cord impressions, though impressions of the articular ends of bird bones and finger-nail rustication are not infrequent.

If one infers these people to have been in the main of hunting stock, their skill in obtaining supplies of deer's antlers must have been of value in the flint-mining industry where on Easton Down we find their pottery, including a hybrid lugged vessel of Windmill Hill form decorated with whipped cord ornament, amongst the temporary dwellings of Beaker date. We have little knowledge of any permanent settlement. In three small pits surrounded by stake holes at Winterbourne Dauntsey and interpreted as dwellings, Peterborough sherds have been found with a typical flint-mine axe from the nearby mines. In these pits were the bones of oxen, pigs and sheep, which shows that by now they had assimilated the value of domesticated animals; but the remains of myriads of slugs amongst their food refuse presents a picture of unsavoury squalor. Evidence of their presence is also found in the deserted ditches of Windmill Hill, along the course of the West Kennet avenue, and as far south as Cranborne Chase, in Maiden Castle and in the ditches of the Holdenhurst long barrow. Polished stone axes of igneous rocks from the West usually accompany their remains, strongly suggesting that they were the purveyors of such commodities.

Little is known of their burial practices. We have noted their ritual deposits of domestic refuse in the West Kennet long barrow. With this refuse was found a contemporary cremation of two individuals. However, we appear to have a more elaborate burial in a barrow on Handley Down. The fragments of an inhumation were here found under a low barrow surrounded by a very irregular ditch having a wide causeway. Peterborough sherds occurred in the body of the mound and in the ditch silting.

The second component of the Secondary Neolithic cultures, the Rinyo-Clacton or Grooved Ware Culture, is almost as ill-defined in the south of Britain. Nothing comparable with the Orcadian stone-built houses at Skara Brae and Rinyo with their beds, dressers and other domestic amenities has survived. The culture, which is concentrated in the two widely separated regions of the Orkneys and the south of England with practically

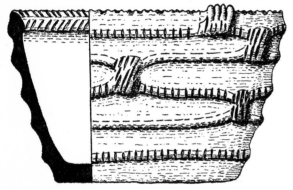

Fig. 5   Cup of Rinyo-Clacton ware from Woodlands, near Woodhenge, Wilts. 2¼ in. high

no intermediate links, was first recognized by its characteristic pottery at Woodhenge and was later seen to be closely affiliated to similar wares from the submerged Essex coast at Clacton-on-Sea near which seven Group I Cornish axes have been found. Pit-comb and cord ornament are here absent, but once again two strains can be distinguished in the pottery, the bases of both of which are flat-bottomed. One strain is decorated by shallow grooving, channelling or incision, including sometimes dotted triangles or lozenges (*pointillé* ornament); the other by a freer use of plastic ornament. The former may be derived

Fig. 5; Plate 11

55

from Late Neolithic styles in north-western France and Iberia, whilst the latter is more generalized and with its pinched-up rusticated decoration may well have come from anywhere along the European coast of the English Channel.

It seems probable that the makers of this type of pottery first settled between Weymouth and Christchurch, thence spreading northwards through Wessex; their implements were the flint and stone ones characteristic of Secondary Neolithic culture. One of their most interesting settlement sites lies in the Amesbury district on both banks of the river Avon. Some pits at Ratfyn have yielded Rinyo-Clacton sherds, transverse or *petit tranchet* derivative arrow-heads and bones of ox and pig; and—of unusual interest—the shoulder-blade of a brown bear (*Ursus arctos*).

At Woodlands, within 300 yards of Woodhenge, four pits have been excavated which can only be described as ritual in character. These had been carefully dug and contained a surprising assortment of articles mixed with wood ash and charcoal. They appeared to have been filled by tipping into them baskets of food refuse and of almost unused tools amongst which were a Graig Lwyd axe, a flint axe, a number of *petit tranchet* arrow-heads, flint saws or serrated flakes, scrapers, a flint knife and fabricator, a hammerstone and naturally formed flint balls, and bone pins or awls. The bones found showed that ox, sheep, and pig were eaten, as well as roedeer and fox. Bones of a dog were also found. Fishing activities resulted in numerous jaws of chub. Shells of scallop, common mussel and oyster show that even then these were considered delicacies and that contact with the sea was maintained. The associated pottery was also of particular interest; small highly decorated flat-based cups that may well have been the prototypes from which sprang the pygmy cups of the ensuing Bronze Age.

Fig. 5

Woodhenge itself produced much plastically ornamented pottery under the bank and in its ditch, with Beaker sherds at

higher levels; but Windmill Hill ware was also present, suggest⁄
ing cultural overlap. Allied ware has also been found under
and above the edges of the banks of the contiguous earth⁄
work known as Durrington Walls, along the southern edge of
which was a long straight line of 58 post⁄holes with offsets
suggestive of part of a building and associated with similar
occupational refuse including an unusually high proportion of
pig bones. A few sherds of grooved ware in the primary silting
of the ditch at Stonehenge have helped to date the first phase
of that monument, as does also the presence of Group I axes
here and at Woodhenge nearby. Between these two famous
monuments and also to the south of Stonehenge, the surface of
the ground still remains a prolific hunting ground for flint
implements of Secondary Neolithic date, including *tranchet*
axes, *petit tranchet* derivative arrow⁄heads and other recognized
types. The culture is also represented, along with Peterborough
pottery, in the secondary occupation layers at Windmill Hill,
in the West Kennet long barrow, and in the settlement area
along the West Kennet avenue where pits and hearths have
yielded similar material with axes from both Graig Lwyd
and Great Langdale.

Plate 11

DORCHESTER CULTURE

The third component in Wessex has been termed the Dor⁄
chester Culture, named after a number of sites examined from
1946 onwards at Dorchester⁄on⁄Thames near Oxford. This
'culture' has been tentatively defined by Professor Piggott to
embrace certain features not wholly covered by the other two
cultures, though he very clearly recognized that future work
might drastically modify its status or even discard it as a dis⁄
tinct and separate entity. It is, indeed, doubtful whether it can
be considered to exist in its own right. The future may well

show that its manifestations are but imperfectly understood facets of the two Secondary Neolithic cultures we have just considered, the full content of which has not yet been assessed.

The tenuous characters that distinguish this culture appear to be somewhat negative. For instance, no settlement sites are known, and no distinctive pottery can be claimed as an index; Peterborough, Rinyo-Clacton and late Windmill Hill ware normally accompany some of its manifestations. However, on the positive side we have, firstly, communal cremation burials in flat cemeteries often accompanied by rings of holes or pits of a ritual nature never intended to hold stone or timber uprights; these may or may not be surrounded by an enclosure of the ceremonial 'henge' type to be discussed later. Secondly, certain inhumation burials under round barrows or cairns in which single-graves have replaced the collective burial practice of the long barrows.

The recognition and implications of these cremation cemeteries and circles of ritual pits at Dorchester-on-Thames have thrown considerable light on the first phase of Stonehenge which comprises the bank and ditch, Aubrey Holes and cremation cemetery. Although consideration of the latter must be deferred for the moment, it is well to remember that both Rinyo-Clacton ware, typical Rinyo-Clacton bone 'skewer-pins' and polished stone maceheads were found at both sites. Until the recent discovery of a contemporary cremation cemetery at Ronaldsway in the Isle of Man, and of these Dorchester cemeteries, the practice of cremation was thought to have been an introduction of the Bronze Age. But it is now known to be of much greater antiquity, and its origin must be sought either in indigenous invention in these islands, in some way connected with the Ronaldsway cemetery, or elsewhere. At Er Lannic in Brittany two half-submerged stone circles exist, many of the stones having stone-lined cists at their bases in which were cremations and ritual deposits. These included stone axes and pottery vessels of the *vase-support* type ornamented with dotted triangles and lozenges of the style which we have seen may have been ancestral to our provincial Rinyo-Clacton ware. It seems not impossible that the practice of cremation, and the setting of cremations or standing stones in circles may have formed an integral part of a culture represented on both sides of the Channel.

A few anomalous round barrow burials should also be mentioned here. These may, however, have been derived partly from contact with the contemporary Bell-Beaker and Single-Grave Cultures we have yet to consider. One significant feature not encountered in later barrows of the Bronze Age appears to be the presence of an irregular, pitted, surrounding quarry ditch, sometimes with an entrance causeway as seen in barrows on Handley and Crichel Downs in Dorset, seemingly allied to the ditches of the henge and cursus type. In other instances, the inclusion of perforated antler maceheads of typical Mesolithic ancestry, such as those from barrows on Cop Head Hill, Warminster and at Collingbourne Ducis (with a Group I stone hammer), are almost certainly diagnostic; but it is only when we meet with an assemblage of objects such as those from the Upton Lovel barrow opened by W. Cunnington in 1801, that we can indeed be a little more sure of our ground. Plate 13 This barrow covered a grave in which were two inhumations associated with more than five dozen perforated bone points, very probably used as a fringe to a garment, three flint axes, some mullers of Cornish origin (Groups I and IIIA), two perforated stone battle-axes (one coming from the Whin Sill of the Teesdale area), boars' tusks, a jet ring, jet and bone beads, a bronze awl and a grooved whetstone. Such a mixed group implies an early native burial at a time when the Wessex Bronze Age was just beginning.

CHAPTER VI

Invasion

AMONGST THESE COMMUNITIES of economically self-sufficient Secondary Neolithic stock-breeders and huntsmen, who were now spreading and multiplying throughout Britain, there appeared on our eastern and southern shores a new immigration round about 1800 B.C., by infiltration no doubt at first, but later to assume considerable proportions. For many years the general characters of these predominantly round-headed invaders, the so-called Beaker-Folk, have been identified both by their characteristic physical form and by their well-made pottery of drinking-vessel or beaker shape decorated with cord or, more usually, hyphenated or fine comb-tooth ornament, and which may connote heavy drinking habits. Physically they were of Dinaric type, large-headed with rugged features, prominent brow-ridges and wide lower jaws, the result, according to Coon, of partial fusion with the Corded-ware people of the Middle Rhineland. But their chief title to fame rests on their introduction of radically different burial customs—individual burial, often under round barrows, and with grave-goods disposed around the body for use in an after-life. This insistence on individualism appears in fact to be their key-note.

Plates 14, 15, 22 Starting, it is usually thought, from Spain, the Bell-Beaker styles of pottery were adopted widely in Europe. Peoples using such pots moved up the western coasts to Brittany and the Channel Islands, and in the Rhineland and Central Europe mixed with other Late Neolithic groups. From the Rhineland and Holland they began to migrate to Britain. In spite of absorption of other traditions and admixture with other cultures, their characteristic vessels of usually bright red ware remained remarkably uniform throughout their progress and can be recognized almost anywhere. Although contacts with more advanced societies had made them familiar with the advantages of metal, it is essential to recognize in Britain, especially during the early stages of colonization, that these people were primarily a stone-using and sub-Neolithic people who, at the same time, showed no traces of a Mesolithic back-ground. In the past it has been usual to treat them as having ushered in the Early Bronze Age, but it is now very much open to question whether they can any longer command that status and whether their culture was in any way based on that of a metal economy. It cannot be denied that very occasionally they sought and acquired metal articles for ornament and use, but it would be more accurate to class them formally as Late Neolithic with the proviso that they stood on the threshold of the Bronze Age. In Wessex, their close association with, and acceptance of the ways of life of, the Peterborough and Rinyo-Clacton peoples cannot be denied. In fact, they soon seem to have assumed the position of a dominant minority capable of harnessing local resources and of imposing a measure of unifi-cation on the existing population, but not until they had contributed substantially to the mixed traditions of the Late Neolithic for several generations at least.

The Beaker invasion was no simple matter; immigrant bands from the Continent entered our eastern and southern shores at numerous points and spread rapidly inland in much the same way as the later Saxon invaders. As long ago as 1912, Lord Abercromby, following Thurnam's original classifica-tion of 1871, divided the pottery types introduced by these invaders into two main classes, his so-called A and B Beakers; but it was not until 1929-31 that Professors Childe and Clark gave substance to these two alphabetically termed forms and defined clearly the dual character of the invasion. They were able to show that whereas the A form with its globular body and straight neck was frequently associated with stone battle- Plates 16, 24

axes, flint daggers, barbed and tanged arrow-heads, V-perforated buttons and riveted metal knives or daggers, the B form
Plates 14, 15, 22 of sinuous ovoid outline was usually found with archer's
wristguards, similar flint arrow-heads and tanged metal daggers.
At the same time, a study of their distribution suggested that
the A form had been brought to our eastern shores mainly
round the Wash with subsequent penetration overland to
Wessex, and that the B form (apparently characteristic of an
earlier immigration) was concentrated mainly on our south-
eastern and southern coasts, subsequently spreading inland up
both the Thames and the Hampshire Avon valleys to the
same region. Abercromby's C type beakers can now be seen
to represent a third immigration from the Netherlands to north-
east England and east Scotland.

Although this dual invasion in its broadest aspects is still
recognized, more recent work by Professor Piggott has clarified
and at the same time emphasized its complexity. No longer can
we accept the implied priority of the A form of beaker but
must probably view it as a purely insular development associated with invaders of 'Battle-Axe' tradition who had emanated
from the Elbe district of northern Europe. Two distinct points
of departure are in fact now admitted as contributing to the
components of the Beaker Culture in southern England; an
earlier migration from the Rhineland, and a later and perhaps
more warlike invasion from the 'Battle-Axe' regions of the
Elbe. Both share the custom of Single Grave burial, usually
under a barrow.

The B Beaker is the earlier of the two components with
which we are here concerned, and most closely approximates
to the Bell-Beakers of the Continent, whereas the shape and
decoration of the A Beakers form no part of the original complex. With very good reason, therefore, an attempt is being
made to drop this somewhat non-informative terminology and,
instead, to focus attention on the primary B form by calling

it uncompromisingly a Bell-Beaker to indicate its proximate Continental origin, even though regional variants appear as a result of transmarine migration; and to call the A form a Necked Beaker, a term that is sufficiently non-committal and yet retains a clear picture of its essential shape.

BELL-BEAKERS

Bell-Beakers first make their appearance in these islands in late Windmill Hill times when, during the construction of the Giant's Hill long barrow at Skendleby in Lincolnshire, sherds were actually incorporated in the material of the mound. The ware continued in use throughout the Late Neolithic period, and in a few instances has been found to antedate Necked Beakers.

Our knowledge of the people who made them is derived largely from burials in individual graves often, but not always, under a small, circular, low mound or cairn 2 feet or less high; sometimes inserted as secondary burials in existing long bar-rows as at Thickthorn, and sometimes placed at the foot of standing stones as in the Avebury avenue. The body was in-variably placed in a fully contracted position on its side, with a beaker or other articles disposed around. Thus, on the top of Stockbridge Down two small lonely graves were found, one without covering mound but containing a flexed female skele-ton with a crudely made beaker, the other just over 100 yards away under a low flint cairn 18 inches high. A young woman whose skeleton suggested a graceful figure and who was of about 25 years of age had been buried under the latter in a grave 3 feet 6 inches deep with a beaker and small bronze awl. Interesting features of this burial were the presence of the sur-rounding causewayed ditch and of two contemporary crema-tions that had been placed in the grave whilst it was being

Fig. 6

Plates 58, 59

filled in, both indicative of local Secondary Neolithic practices. An interment which had been inserted later at the edge of the cairn belonged to the Wessex Culture.

Some score or so of such poorly furnished burials are known in Wessex, scattered generally as might befit nomadic life. Probably the most richly furnished graves of the period are those from Mere, Roundway and Winterslow, all in Wilt-

Plates 14, 15

Plate 18

shire. Each contained, besides beakers of Rhenish form, tanged metal daggers and archer's wristguards, whilst that at Mere had two Irish gold discs, and Roundway a broken metal pin of possibly central European Aunjetitz origin. The daggers are well-known types and are widely distributed from Iberia to Czechoslovakia and the Rhine; but all three possess well defined grooves along the edges of their blades which may mean that they were traded in an unfinished state for later sharpening by those acquiring them. In Britain, such daggers are most likely of Irish origin.

The practice of trepanning the human skull is an old one in prehistoric Europe, and primitive surgery saw fit to indulge in the operation for ritual purposes roughly between 1900 and 1400 B.C. The skull of the dismembered body from the Maiden Castle long mound, previously noted, was so operated upon, and another interesting case comes from a Bell-Beaker

Plate 20

grave on Crichel Down, Dorset. Here the roundel of bone had been most skilfully removed by grooving, probably by means of a flint flake, until it could be prised off, the patient meanwhile presumably having been rendered unconscious by some means or another. There is evidence that in a number of instances the patient recovered and that there was growth of new bone; but in this case the operation was unsuccessful.

This practice naturally raises another form of contemporary ritual, that of the ceremonial burial of the head alone, termed cephalotaphy, which may have been resorted to as a charm to increase productivity. In the centre of the Beaker settlement

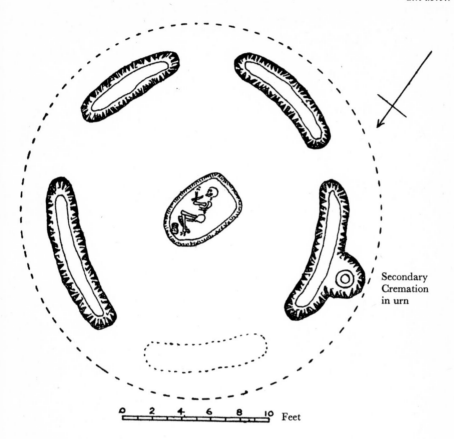

Secondary
Cremation
in urn

0   2   4   6   8   10 Feet

Fig. 6 Plan of Beaker burial under barrow on Stockbridge Down, Hants

surrounding the Easton Down flint-mines is a small barrow
23 feet in diameter and less than 2 feet high. The large grave
below was found on excavation to contain a skull only, with
atlas and axis articulated, pillowed on 6 inches of chalk dust,
and with a roughly chipped bar of flint suggestive of a phallus
standing upright against it. This remarkable burial recalls the
little altar at the bottom of one of the mine shafts at Grime's

Plate 19

E

Graves on which was seated the carved representation of a fat pregnant woman with a chalk phallus and antler picks grouped around, no doubt for the same purpose of ensuring a continued supply of good workable flint.

Permanent settlements of the period are rare, but sherds of Beaker ware turn up in many scattered places. The Easton Down flint-mines have so far produced the largest number of pits surrounded by stake holes which have been interpreted as the temporary dwellings of miners and their families who had resorted to the site to replenish their stocks of axes. Beaker sherds of both Bell and Necked varieties are here abundant, accompanied by the refuse of meals and numerous flint imple- ments including scrapers, axes and knives. Under the floor of one of the huts, and at the bottom of a circular pit filled with powdered bone ash, a pet dog had been carefully buried in an attitude of sleep. This dog is of the same large fox-terrier breed *(Canis palustris)* as those we have encountered at Windmill Hill and Maiden Castle.

Plate 23

A similar dwelling pit filled with the same sort of domestic rubbish has been recorded from Boscombe Down East, a mile to the north of the flint-mines, and numerous sherds were found in trenching operations on the Larkhill ranges during the last war. At Lymore near Milford-on-Sea, a pit containing nothing but a beaker has been probably erroneously described as a dwelling, though numbers of sherds and somewhat degenerate- looking vessels in the Bournemouth area attest occupation thereabouts.

Whether originally sepulchral or not, two vessels from Ink- pen in Berkshire call for special comment. A fine example of a tall Bell-Beaker was here accompanied by an open dish stand- ing on four small legs or feet, which is a type of contemporary

Plates 21, 22

vessel very much favoured in the central European provinces and which may well have been brought over from that region. From that region, too, came fragments of Niedermendig lava brought over possibly for use as quern stones for grinding cereals. This particular form of lava can only have come from the Andernach district of the Rhine; yet pieces have been found in Stonehenge, in the ceremonial site called the Sanctuary near Avebury, and on the line of the Avebury avenue itself.

The crops grown show a marked change from the agricul-tural habits of the Windmill Hill farmers. From grain impres-sions on pottery we find that the Beaker-Folk grew principally barley instead of wheat, which is consistent with our know-ledge of the same people's habits on the Continent. Whether this was connected with the brewing of strong liquors we do not know, but we may suspect it. The large number of flax seed impressions on a Bell-Beaker from Handley Down in Dorset is also of interest. Such a find is unparalleled in Britain and it is obvious that much seed must have been lying around when the pot was made. This again indicates connexions with the Upper or Middle Rhineland; but at Handley we do not know whether the seed was used as a cereal or for making tex-tiles. Unfortunately we know nothing of the clothing of the Beaker people.

NECKED BEAKERS

Not long after the users of Bell-Beakers from the Rhineland had established an early but firm foothold, other invaders, perhaps of a more warlike nature, from north-eastern Germany may have followed in their footsteps, whose main impact on our shores was between the Wash and Flamborough Head. The stone battle-axes of north European type which suggest the incursion of their users are spread widely from Yorkshire and East Anglia into Derbyshire and Wessex, and are found buried as 'weapons of prestige' in men's graves. Such graves contain objects which relate to the so-called Warrior Cultures of the Battle-Axe,

Single-Grave and Corded-Ware peoples of northern Germany round the Elbe; at the same time, they show insular variations due no doubt to transmarine migration and possibly also to lack or shortage of women-folk amongst the primary invading forces.

This lack can possibly be inferred in Britain from their characteristic pottery vessels, which may be termed Necked Beakers rather than 'Type A', which have no precise Continental parallels, and which are only explicable on the assumption that they were modelled on the lines of the otherwise unrelated Corded-Beakers of the invaders' homeland; for these, though ornamented with cord impressions also possess globular bodies with tall straight necks. The invaders on arrival soon found the country occupied by Bell-Beaker users, with whom they had already been in contact on the Rhineland, and it seems not unnatural that by admixture and intermarriage their insistent demand for vessels of traditional form resulted in the development of this purely insular Necked form combining both the shape and ornament of the two separate forms of Corded- and Bell-Beakers. However, both Bell and Necked Beakers seem to have co-existed since they have been found together in Wick Barrow, Stogursey in Somerset; and that their makers did not clash with the Secondary Neolithic inhabitants, but soon contrived to live with and probably dominate them, seems clear from the way in which sherds of their pottery are so frequently found associated with Peterborough and Rinyo-Clacton types. Occasional hybrid beakers possessing finger-nail or even *pointillé* ornament are evidence of fusion of traditions.

The warlike equipment of these people included stone battle-axes, flint daggers and riveted metal daggers. Sometimes, but not often, these weapons were buried with their dead together with Necked Beakers; more frequently, however, pottery vessels were excluded. It is in fact becoming more and more apparent that many other graves without beakers, but including one or more of these weapons, must represent the British counterparts of these intrusive cultures. Though nor-mally shallow, their single-graves can be very deep; thus one at Wilsford in Wiltshire and another on Crichel Down in Dorset were both nearly 10 feet below ground level. The graves were usually covered by simple bowl barrows, often

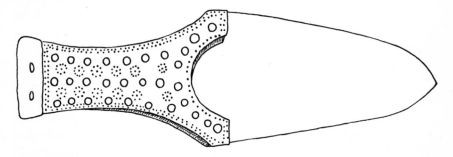

Fig. 7   Bronze knife-dagger with ornamental wooden hilt of rivets and pins of bronze, from burial at Milston, Wilts. 8¼ in. overall

much larger than those covering Bell-Beakers, being anything from 5 to 10 feet high and up to 100 feet in diameter.

The stone battle-axes, perforated to take a shaft, are usually simple but finely made with rounded butt and without ex-panded cutting edge—an insular development of the more complicated Continental forms. They were often made from highly polished and beautiful rocks such as the red tourmaline granite Cornish specimen from Woodhenge and that of olive-green quartzite from Ratfyn nearby. Another large specimen from Fifield Bavant is of preselite, as are others from South Wales, which proves contact again with Pembrokeshire. In fact, the appearance of perforated battle-axes, amongst the products of the Cornish and South Welsh axe factories only clearly shows their interest in these industries and the results of

Plate 12

69

the demands made upon them. The presence of numerous Necked Beaker sherds round the flint-mine shafts of Easton Down and Martin's Clump denotes continued dependence on flint as a raw material for domestic and other purposes; the small scrapers and knives, and barbed and tanged arrow-heads recovered from their temporary shelters are certainly most competently made by pressure flaking which we would hardly expect from any but primary stone-using communities.

The beautifully made thin flint daggers, flaked over both faces, are a case in point, though it cannot be denied that they were probably made to imitate contemporary metal types. They appear in relatively large numbers in East Anglia and the Lower Thames where metal forms are extremely scarce, whereas in Wessex the reverse is the case, which strongly suggests that trade with Irish metallurgists was adequate for their requirements. However, it must not be supposed that copper and bronze daggers of the flat round-heeled riveted type were readily available in Wessex; actually they seem to have been comparatively rare and were probably much prized when acquired. The type is widely distributed throughout Early Bronze Age Europe and it is not easy to determine whence the Wessex specimens came; some may have been brought in by the invaders, but it is more than likely that the majority were obtained through trade with Ireland and were ultimately of Iberian inspiration. Future spectrographic analysis may help to solve the problem. An example of a very rare but *Fig. 7* distinctive British dagger was found early last century at Milston in Wiltshire. Here the handle consisted of two plates of wood held together by thirty bronze rivets and strengthened at the end by a bone pommel. Further, it was decorated by dots in the form of lines and rosettes made by inserted bronze pins. This remarkable piece is clearly related to the gold-studded and gold-mounted dagger-hafts of the later Wessex Culture and can well have been ancestral to them.

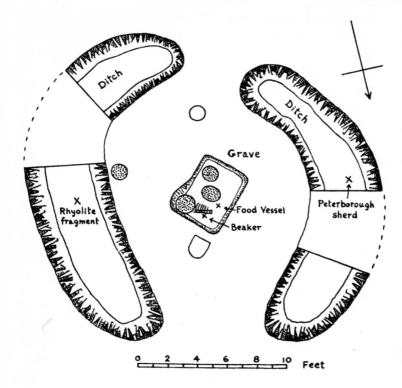

Fig. 8 Burials at Fargo Plantation, Wilts

One of the most difficult problems of this period relates to the status of the early 'Food Vessel' class of pottery occasionally found associated in graves with Necked Beakers. Do they represent a new ethnic element? Are they in their inception an integral part of the Warrior Culture? Or can they be a purely local phenomenon, a development in fact of some of the Secondary Neolithic wares we have already encountered? In the north, various forms of similar pots are relatively abundant and were probably developed from Late Neolithic ceramics with Beaker infusion. Feminine articles such as jet necklaces, copper and bronze awls and small metal knives frequently accompany them, and it has therefore not unnaturally been suggested that some of the earlier examples may represent the female counterparts of the Necked Beakers.

But in the south, and in Wessex in particular, early Food Vessels are exceedingly rare. Two specimens of much the same type have, however, been found actually with Necked Beakers in Fargo Plantation, three-quarters of a mile north-west of Stonehenge, and on Charmy Down near Bath. No barrow covered the Fargo grave, which was 3 feet deep; but in it and sealed in by a compact layer of chalk rubble were the beaker and food vessel, a partial inhumation consisting of the upper part of a body only, without head, and two cremations. All were undoubtedly contemporary. The ditch with its two wide causeways surrounding the grave presents points of consider-able interest; here we have a very small example of a type of ceremonial earthwork known technically as a 'henge', such as we associate with the Beaker-Folk, and which will be examined in the next chapter. A deep post-hole just inside the southern entrance may well have held some form of totem-pole; whilst in the ditch was a fragment of the Pembrokeshire blue-stone rhyolite and a large sherd of Peterborough pottery, the bearing of which on Blue Stonehenge we shall mention later. The Charmy Down beaker and food vessel were associated with a small bronze riveted knife-dagger and a ribbed bead of shale, a type of bead that normally accompanies the grave-goods of the immediately succeeding Wessex Culture and which clearly suggests cultural overlap.

Unfortunately we know all too little of the mode of life of these warriors. Conical shale buttons with V-perforations and grooved shale belt rings or fastenings imply more advanced forms of clothing, though traces of textiles have been recorded only once—from a Beaker burial at Kellythorpe in Yorkshire. To visualize garments from a few buttons only is, however,

Plates 24, 25

Fig. 8

beyond our capability, though we note in passing that button-fastened garments in early second millennium Europe are characteristically western, as opposed to those fastened by decorative pins which are distinctive of central and northern Europe.

CHAPTER VII

Temples

OUT OF THE COMPLEX amalgam of differing ethnic
and cultural groups we have so far considered there arose
a distinctive manifestation of the Late Neolithic period, the
construction of ritual or ceremonial circular enclosures known
as 'henges'. Their origin is shrouded in obscurity though we
do know that they are confined solely to Great Britain and have
no Continental parallels or prototypes from which they could
have sprung. The word 'henge' is, strictly speaking, applicable to Stonehenge only in its final form with superimposed
stone lintels as a name meaning 'the stone gallows'. But by
common usage, following Sir Thomas Kendrick's original
definition of this class of monument in 1932, and in the absence
of a more suitable word, the term is now generally applied to
various roughly contemporary enclosures having certain features in common. These features normally consist of a surrounding bank and ditch, with the ditch *inside* the bank as
opposed to other earthworks of clearly defensive character, and
with one or more causewayed entrances. The areas so enclosed,

Fig. 8
Fig. 15

which may vary in diameter from only 20 feet as in the Fargo
Plantation grave to over 1500 feet in the case of Durrington
Walls, may, but do not always, include circles of upright

Figs. 11, 12, 14

stones (Avebury and Stonehenge II) or timber posts (Woodhenge), or of ritual holes or pits which have been demonstrated
never to have held either (Stonehenge I), or even of one or
more burials only (Fargo Plantation).

With only a few exceptions practically all these earthworks
appear to have been carefully sited on level, often low-lying,

Fig. 9

ground frequently in relatively close proximity to streams or
rivers; the enclosed areas are clearly visible from the encircling
banks, which appear to have been the most important feature,

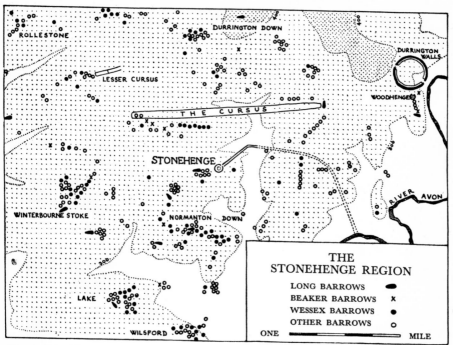

Fig. 9   Barrow-burials around Stonehenge

the ditch having been a mere quarry whence the material for
their construction was obtained. Avenues of stones or earthen
banks in some instances lead to or from them.   Plate 27

Some forty-five or fifty monuments of the class have been
recognized within recent years, distributed from Cornwall to
the Orkney Islands. Probably a good fifteen of them of every
possible combination lie in Wessex alone, though not all have
been tested by excavation. In spite, however, of very considerable variation, attempts have been made to divide them
into two classes, those with a single entrance having been
ascribed to the earlier Secondary Neolithic phase, and those
with two or more to the later Beaker Cultures. This division

75

is broadly true though it cannot be accepted yet as invariable and much more work needs to be done on these sites; cultural overlapping undoubtedly took place, whilst under Beaker domination many of our finest examples appear to have been constructed, especially those embodying standing stones as at Avebury. This is important as emphasizing the acceptance and adoption by the Beaker-Folk and Warrior Cultures of some of the ceremonial practices initiated locally by the non-Beaker elements of the population. The introduction of the single-grave under a round barrow by these intruders completely inhibited, as we have seen, the rite of communal burial under long barrows; yet for some unknown reason the ceremonial henge found favour and under Beaker influence and organization expanded to remarkable lengths. The nature of the ceremonies and rites enacted in them we shall never know, but it is certain, as R. J. C. Atkinson has pointed out, that the beliefs which found expression in such a building as that of Avebury must have been of a peculiarly compelling kind. Although it is agreed that the majority were regarded as sacred and non-utilitarian in character, there is no reason to suppose that their primary function was necessarily sepulchral or connected with acts of worship of some primitive deity. A few may have been used as tribal assembly places whilst others,

Fig. 8

like the small Fargo Plantation grave, may simply be anomalous graves built on the lines of the larger and more formal 'temples'. However, the existence of cremation cemeteries within some of them and the number of barrows that surround others both strongly argue in favour of the supposition that some at least were connected with a cult of the dead.

Stonehenge and Avebury, our two most famous examples,

Plates 26–29, 32

lie on the Wiltshire Downs at nodal points on the waterways and transpeninsular routes which were to contribute to the rise of Wessex to power. Although both are atypical, it is appropriate that we should consider them first; but it should not be forgotten that in their strategic positions they not unnaturally underwent a number of periods of reconstruction and develop' ment which have added considerably to the difficulties of archæological interpretation and masked their underlying unity.

As a result of recent excavations carried out since 1950, it has became increasingly clear that Stonehenge had a long history, which must be divided into at least three major periods of construction. In his recent book on Stonehenge, R. J. C. Atkinson has considered the monument in great detail and it is, therefore, unnecessary to recapitulate the mass of evidence and its interpretation which he has so ably assembled and reviewed. I shall endeavour here merely to confine myself to a few points of outstanding interest.

It will be recalled that Stonehenge lies in an area of Secon' dary Neolithic settlement, and that the undressed monolith, the Heel Stone, *may* represent the earliest feature on the site. This is certainly suggested by the fact that, at some date later than at the time of its erection, an Early Bronze Age beaker had been broken against it, the fragments of which were found during the excavations, having slipped down the side of the stone as it canted over due to the rotting of anti'friction stakes at its base. However, it is now generally agreed that the first major period of construction, that of Stonehenge I, consisted of the digging of the Ditch and Bank and the Aubrey Holes. These features were laid out with considerable accuracy in true circles from the same centre, the diameter of the Bank being about 320 feet. The flat'based quarry Ditch, in this in' stance on the *outside* of the Bank, has almost vertical sides and averages 5½ feet in depth. One functional causeway 35 feet wide was left as an entrance, and early excavations by Colonel

Fig. 10

77

Fig. 5

Hawley revealed numerous post-holes of unknown significance over its surface. Besides antler picks and rough flint implements, the only objects of importance so far recovered from the primary silting of the Ditch have been four or five sherds of Rinyo-Clacton ware, which are comparable with those from Woodhenge nearby and can be dated about 1900-1700 B.C.

The fifty-six Aubrey Holes, originally discovered by John Aubrey in 1666, are set in a circle just within the Bank and, when rediscovered in the early 1920s, were supposed to have held originally stone or timber uprights. Later excavations in 1950, coupled with the discovery of similar pits in other henges at Dorchester near Oxford and on Cairnpapple Hill in West Lothian, showed that they were not structural in function but must have been connected with some ritual or cult of which we now have no knowledge. The holes are roughly circular pits varying from about 2 to 4 feet in depth and contain very mixed fillings of chalk rubble, burnt material and soil. Many seem to have been deliberately refilled soon after digging; others, having been filled were redug to varying depths and fresh deposits were placed in them. Small heaps of cremated human bones have been found in most of the thirty-two that have so far been examined; but this need not imply that the holes were originally sepulchral, since other cremations have been found in the Ditch and under the turf just within the Bank.

About fifty-five cremations have been found in this flat cemetery, one of which was actually on the floor of the Ditch with no signs of disturbance above, which shows that it was contemporary. Long skewer-like bone pins, flint bars or fabricators, a small polished stone macehead and a minute pottery vessel accompanied some of them. Such objects are characteristic of the Secondary Neolithic cultures in Britain, as are also six Cornish stone axes from the site. By good fortune sufficient charcoal was obtained from Aubrey Hole 32 for a

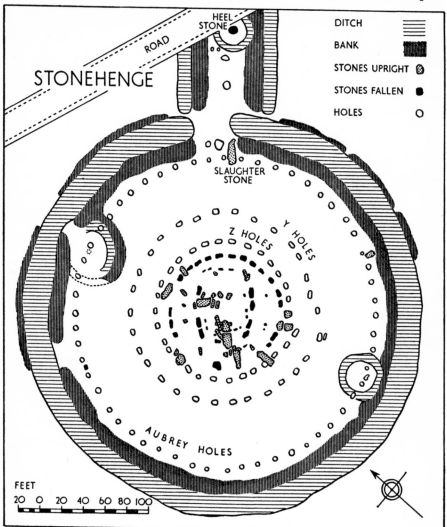

Fig. 10 Plan of Stonehenge as at present

radio-active carbon analysis of date by W. F. Libby of Chicago. This yielded 1848 B.C. ± 275 years, which means that the odds are about 2 to 1 that Stonehenge I was constructed between 2125 and 1575 B.C. Admittedly the margin of un-certainty here is great but, nevertheless, this C14 analysis does support the date of 1900-1700 B.C., arrived at independently by archæological means. It should be added that no evidence exists for any contemporary internal structure.

STONEHENGE II

This structure no longer exists and is completely invisible to the ordinary visitor. Its very presence was unsuspected until 1954, when excavations within the monument on the line of the existing but robbed and defaced bluestone circle were carried out to determine the spacing of this last and latest circle. These disclosed the settings of an earlier double circle with diameters of 74 and 86 feet respectively and of about thirty-eight stones apiece; however, the stones had been extracted at a later date for purposes of reconstruction. Each adjacent pair of 'Q' and 'R' holes formed the ends of dumb-bell-shaped hollows tightly packed with chalk rubble where the stones had once stood, with minute fragments of bluestones embedded in them. Clear evidence was thus obtained that a Blue Stone-henge had preceded the erection of the present monument. The entrance to this double circle, marked by two additional inlying pairs of stone-holes, is not aligned on the causeway of Stonehenge I, but on that of the axis of the present structure. This most important fact proves that the orientation on the midsummer sunrise was deliberate, and that very probably the *Fig. 11; Plate 31* construction of the Avenue was conceived at the same time.

The relative date of Stonehenge II has been shown to lie between the end of Stonehenge I and the erection of the sarsen

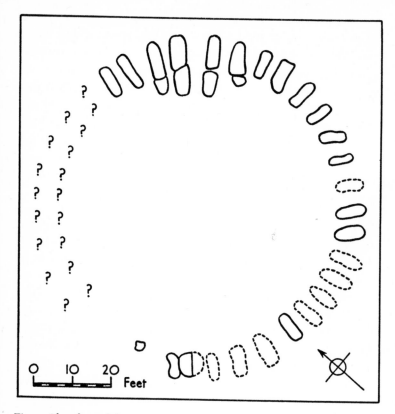

Fig. 11 Plan of stone-holes representing the monument of Stonehenge II

structure. This corresponds with the position of bluestone fragments and Beaker pottery in the Ditch on top of the secondary silting. Hence it has been inferred that the period of its construction must lie around 1700-1600 B.C.

But the building was never completed. The most surprising fact that emerged from continued excavations in 1956 was that a part of the western quadrant, as yet of unknown extent, was devoid of any traces of these double stone-holes. If, as seems likely, a double circle of undressed bluestone monoliths was

F

conceived under Beaker dominance, the project was abandoned when only threequarters completed. This may have
been due to a variety of causes; the supply of the required
number of stones from Pembrokeshire may have temporarily
stopped; the decision to dismantle another possible bluestone
circle in the vicinity (for such may have existed at the west end
of the Cursus) and to add its stones to the quota may have been
abandoned; or a new decision may have been taken under
foreign influence to build the grandiose structure we know
today. I propose to consider this later Stonehenge III phase in
a subsequent chapter.

Nevertheless, the fact remains that the stones, each weighing
upwards of 4 tons, were brought from Pembrokeshire, a distance of 135 miles as the crow flies, and from the same restricted
area of the Prescelly Mountains from which the BeakerFolk
were deriving their preselite battleaxes. It was in 1923 that H.
H. Thomas proved conclusively by petrological analysis that
the three main varieties of rocks at Stonehenge, spotted dolerite
or preselite, rhyolite and volcanic ash all came from relatively
confined areas on the Prescelly Mountains, and that the socalled Altar Stone of micaceous sandstone in all probability
came from the Cosheston Beds around Milford Haven. The
stump of a block of Cosheston greygreen sandstone and chippings have also been found more recently to have emanated
from Mill Bay on the southern shore of the same Haven.

The problem of transport must have been a heavy one; but
recent thought and experiment favours a coastal route along
the South Welsh coast, on canoes lashed together, with subsequent carriage up the Bristol Avon to Frome and thence
overland to the River Wylye at Warminster; and finally down
the Wylye to Salisbury and from there to Amesbury. From
Amesbury to Stonehenge we have the earthembanked
Avenue connecting the river with the monument; its presence
may denote some form of processional way up which the

Plate 12

Fig. 9

sacred stones were dragged on sledges. But even so, many of Plate 30 the stones must have been lost in transit and now lie sub-merged below sea- and river-level. This Bristol Avon waterway was, as we have seen, a much frequented one, and evidence is accumulating to show that Beaker movements and trade to South Wales and Ireland made use of it. Thus, we have an Irish gold disc from Monkton Farleigh similar to those from Plate 17 Mere, and Beaker graves at Charmy Down and Corston near Plate 18 Bath within easy reach of the unembanked Stanton Drew stone circles with their attendant stone avenues, which in some way were connected with the River Chew, a tributary of the Avon. Here the stones appear to have been hauled some 5 miles from nearby outcrops at Harptree on the Mendips, about 5 miles from which lies Gorsey Bigbury, a somewhat ambiguous henge. This last monument has yielded no evidence of internal features, but from the ditch nearly a hundred fragmentary Necked Beakers and much rusticated ware have been obtained; large numbers of flint implements, including microliths, accompanied them. Brean Down on the Severn has also yielded fragments of the same pottery.

AVEBURY

If sheer size and complexity are criteria, the enormous earth-works and associated stone structures at Avebury on the Marl- Plates 27, 28, 32 borough Downs are unquestionably the most impressive monuments of the period in Great Britain. The labour in-volved must have been immense when we recall that the builders had to rely for tools on wood for levers, rollers and sledges, and on antler picks and scapulæ of oxen for digging and shovelling. But now a very large part of the village of Avebury lies within the huge encircling bank and ditch, and time and the hand of man have mutilated and sadly impaired its former grandeur. It is indeed very difficult to appreciate today at a glance and from any one spot the underlying theme as a whole; yet when we recall that the bank once rose at least 50 feet above the bottom of the wide and flat-based ditch, and that the whole of the enclosed 28½ acres was once embellished with numerous massive stone circles and monoliths (now mostly demolished for building the village) we can vaguely appreciate that we stand in what must have been one of the greatest religious centres of the country.

Fig. 12; Plate 28

The organization of the necessary man-power and the under-lying resolve needed for such an astonishing project transcended by far that needed for so relatively small a structure as Stone-henge II; yet there is reason to believe that they were both constructed at about the same time and by the same people.

As long ago as 1648 John Aubrey noted that Avebury far surpassed Stonehenge 'as a cathedral doth a parish church', whilst Stukeley has for ever placed us in his debt by describing and illustrating the monument as he saw it in 1723. Although a number of excavations have since been carried out within it, nothing systematic was attempted until 1908-22 when H. St. G. Gray investigated some areas of the ditch and bank, to be followed by A. Keiller in 1934-39 who was able to throw considerable light on the stone structures themselves and to institute a policy of careful conservation and reconstruction. But it cannot be said that these investigations in so large an area have clarified the history of the monument. They have instead emphasized its complexity and made it more difficult to relate the various components involved. All that can be inferred at present is that the whole monument evolved by slow development within the period of the Secondary Neolithic-Beaker cultural overlap, and that it was not planned in its entirety as one coherent whole.

The vast internal ditch, in places 30 feet deep and as much as 17 feet at the base, is now filled with silt to about 17 feet, and

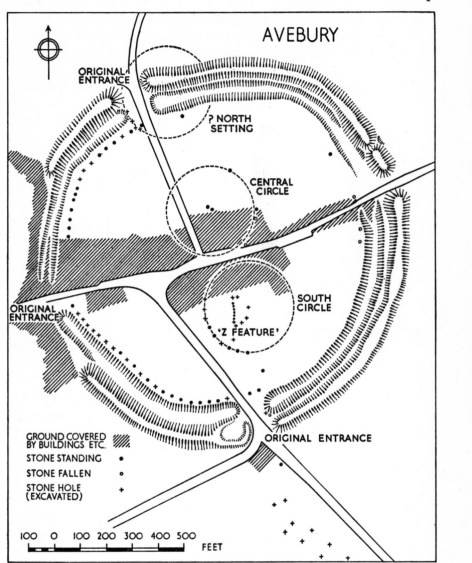

AVEBURY

ORIGINAL
ENTRANCE

? NORTH
SETTING

CENTRAL
CIRCLE

SOUTH
CIRCLE

ORIGINAL
ENTRANCE

'Z FEATURE'

ORIGINAL ENTRANCE

GROUND COVERED
BY BUILDINGS ETC.

STONE STANDING •

STONE FALLEN ◦

STONE HOLE +
(EXCAVATED)

100   0   100 200 300 400 500

FEET

Fig. 12 Plan of Avebury stone circles

Fig. 12

has three proven causeways on the north, south and west, with possibly another on the east. The bank, now about 15 feet high and ¾ mile in circumference, is composed of chalk rubble with a facing or revetment of Lower Chalk blocks which had been obtained from the bottom of the ditch, higher levels consisting of Middle Chalk only. Peterborough ware, *petit tranchet* arrow-heads, flint scrapers and serrated flakes, with blades of polished ox-ribs, have been obtained from the old ground surface beneath it; the secondary silting of the ditch yielded both Peterborough and Beaker sherds, and the burial of a female dwarf surrounded by an oval setting of sarsen blocks. No identifiable sherds have been recovered from the primary silt.

Inside the ditch, and about 30 feet from its edge, stood the Great Stone Circle consisting originally of about a hundred huge sarsen monoliths, a very large pair of which still stand at
Plate 28
the entrance to the Avenue. These blocks of sarsen, a highly silicified sedimentary sandstone, still occur in great profusion on the Marlborough Downs, the remains of a local capping of the chalk, and are here known as 'grey-wethers'. The use of packing blocks of Lower Chalk round some of these stones proves that the circle was erected at the time the ditch was dug.

Two smaller circles originally stood inside the Great Stone Circle, the central one comprising some 30 stones set on a dia-meter of 320 feet with, in the middle, a setting of three closely spaced uprights named by Stukeley a 'Cove' and similar to other settings at Stanton Drew in Somerset. The southern circle, of which only five stones remain, originally held some thirty-two stones set on a diameter of 336 feet, with a central monolith 21 feet high recorded by Stukeley but no longer present. The northern circle, or rather the presence of three stone-holes inter-preted as such during the 1934-39 excavations, is unproved and ambiguous; if it really existed before the construction of the bank, ditch and Great Stone Circle, an earlier date could be inferred for these three internal circles. But no evidence exists for

independent dating. The line of stone-holes inside the southern circle, known as the Z feature, cannot be interpreted; Lower Chalk
blocks were, however, found as packing blocks in the holes.

From the southern entrance the West Kennet Avenue of
sarsen monoliths follows a somewhat tortuous rather than
sinuous course southwards for a distance of nearly 1½ miles and
terminates at another stone and timber building on Overton

Fig. 13

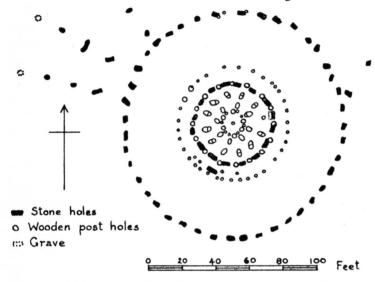

Stone holes
Wooden post holes
Grave

0   20   40   60   80   100   Feet

Fig. 13 Plan of the stone and timber circles at The Sanctuary, Avebury, Wilts

Hill known as the Sanctuary. This Avenue consisted originally of about 200 stones set in pairs spaced 80 feet apart
longitudinally and 50 feet transversely; and it has been noted
that both the Avebury and Sanctuary branches run down to
the River Kennet. This can hardly be fortuitous and, since the
avenues at Stonehenge and Stanton Drew are also linked
directly with rivers, it seems not unlikely that the West Kennet
Avenue may once have consisted of two independent parts
which later were joined together.

Plate 27

Over part of its course the Avenue has been shown to run through a Secondary Neolithic settlement which has yielded typical Peterborough, Rinyo-Clacton and Beaker sherds, as well as Cornish and Graig Lwyd axes and Niedermendig lava. At the bases of three of the stones were burials, two with Bell-Beakers and one with a Rinyo-Clacton bowl.

The Sanctuary has been totally effaced, though it partly existed in Stukeley's day. It was, however, subsequently re-discovered and excavated in 1930 by Mrs. Cunnington who, to perpetuate its memory, marked the positions of the stone and timber post-holes found with low concrete pillars. This small structure is not a simple one; clearly it had been modified and rebuilt a number of times. The earlier feature embodying six

Fig. 13

concentric timber circles with a single post at the centre very possibly represents the plan of a roofed wooden building 65 feet in diameter which, after periods of reconstruction, was demolished and replaced by the concentric stone circles. The outer one of these consisted of forty-two stones set on a dia-meter of 130 feet and the inner of thirty-two stones on a diameter of 45 feet. The Kennet Avenue, which narrows as it ap-proaches, is joined to the outer stone circle on the north-west. Peterborough and Beaker sherds were recovered from the post-holes together with *petit tranchet* arrow-heads and Niedermendig lava; the burial of a youth of long-headed, long barrow type about 14 years old, and possibly dedicatory, was found at the base of one of the stones of the inner circle together with a Bell-Beaker.

Just over a mile to the west of The Sanctuary, and also on the Bath road, lies Silbury Hill, the largest prehistoric artificial mound in Europe, whose volume is approximately $12\frac{1}{2}$ million cubic feet and which covers about $5\frac{1}{2}$ acres. It is now 130 feet high, 550 feet in diameter and has a flat top 100 feet across. Its position in the immediate vicinity of the Avebury complex suggests that it may be contemporary, but no evidence exists

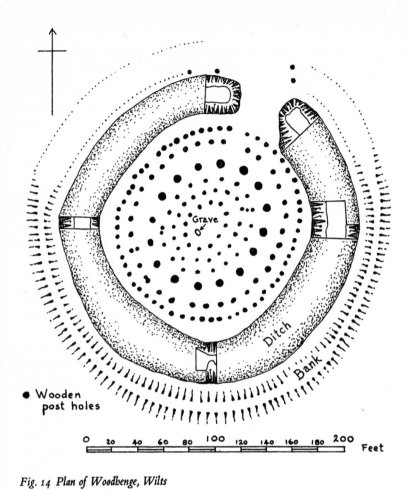

Fig. 14 Plan of Woodhenge, Wilts

whereby to date it other than by the fact that the adjacent Roman road was intentionally diverted to avoid it. A number of attempts by tunnelling and the sinking of shafts have been made to force its secret, but these have proved unsuccessful. Dean Merewether in 1849 found a conical heap of turf with many sarsen boulders near its centre on the old turf line, and records the presence of antler tines and 'fragments of a sort of string, of two strands, each twisted, composed of (as it seemed) grass, and about the size of whipcord'. If really a colossal barrow, it is certainly worthy of its setting in the metropolitan area of Avebury and must form the resting place of someone of very considerable authority and prestige.

WOODHENGE

We have already commented on the evidence of Secondary Neolithic settlement embraced within the Woodhenge-Durrington Walls district. In this relatively small area on the western bank of the River Avon, just over 1 mile north of Amesbury and within 2 miles of Stonehenge, are two con-tiguous henges of outstanding interest, the relationship of which to each other is by no means clear though both appear to have been in use at the same time.

Woodhenge was discovered from the air in 1925 by Squadron-Leader G. S. M. Insall, v.c., who noticed rings of black dots within a circular enclosure which until then had mistakenly been thought to be a ploughed-down disc barrow. Subsequent excavations by Mr. and Mrs. Cunnington in 1926-28 proved that these dots were in fact timber post-holes arranged in six concentric circles within a ditched enclosure having one entrance causeway. By analogy with Stonehenge the earthwork was jocularly termed Woodhenge even though no evidence existed for any form of lintelled structure.

This earthwork is from bank to bank 250 feet in diameter with an internal flat-based quarry ditch. In it was an inhuma-tion grave cut into the chalk base before silting began. The post-holes within vary in size, increasing inwards to the third ring which must have held massive timber uprights, the holes for which had ramps and were on an average 5 feet in diameter and 5 feet 8 inches deep. The inner three rings then decrease in

Fig. 14

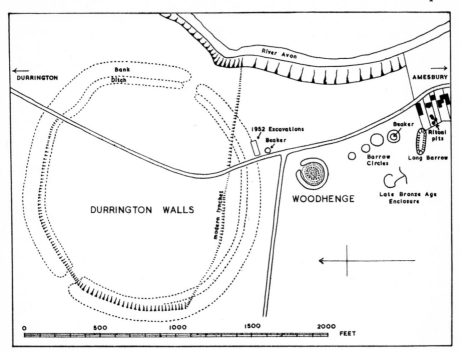

Fig. 15 Plan of Durrington Walls and adjacent monuments, Wilts

size to the centre. The plan suggests no periods of reconstruc﹍
tion; and the building may probably have been roofed with an
open centre. Just off centre was a shallow grave containing an
infant with skull cleft in half, possibly a sacrificial or dedicatory
deposit. One cremation was found in one of the large post﹍
holes. Considerable quantities of plastically ornamented Rinyo﹍
Clacton ware occurred in the ditch and under the bank. But
Windmill Hill and Beaker sherds occurred too with *petit
tranchet* arrow﹍heads, serrated flakes, scrapers and two ritual
chalk axes. This suggests that the building lay in an area of
intensive occupation, the stratification of which is by no means

clear. As at The Sanctuary, the position of the holes has been marked with concrete pillars.

DURRINGTON WALLS

Another ceremonial henge comparable in size to, and indeed larger than that at Avebury, but lacking evidence of stone or timber uprights, lies within 80 yards of Woodhenge. Durring-ton Walls unfortunately is now much defaced and almost obliterated, and its huge size is thus difficult to appreciate from the ground. It is of the double entrance type, with one entrance opening directly on to the River Avon, and has been built at the head of a combe, the whole central area of which is visible from the top of any part of the bank. Pipe-laying opera-tions in 1950 disclosed considerable Rinyo-Clacton occupa-tional refuse under the northern bank and similar refuse overlapping the tail of the southern, associated, as we have seen, with some elongated timber structure. A sherd of Beaker ware was, however, found under the western bank in 1917.

Fig. 15

OTHER HENGES

Other henges have been identified in Wessex, but it would be tedious and unnecessary to enumerate them all here. Marden in the Vale of Pewsey may lay claim to being the largest, but we know virtually nothing about it. Maumbury Rings near Dorchester has a single entrance and is remarkable in having a ditch composed of numerous huge conical pits up to 35 feet deep. The double-entrance henge at Knowlton near Cran-borne (one of a group of henge and related earthworks) is surprising in possessing, in its extremely isolated position, the ruins of a small twelfth- to sixteenth-century church within its enclosure. This act of consecration of a pagan monument, where certain unlawful acts may well have persisted, should be compared with the intentional defacement and burial of many of the stones of the Avebury circles and avenue in the thirteenth and fourteenth centuries, under one of which was found the crushed skeleton of a barber-surgeon of the time of Edward I; and of the deliberate defacement and destruction of many of the stones at Stonehenge at some unknown but probably post-Roman date.

Another possible enclosure of the Woodhenge type may exist on Silk Hill, Brigmerston, on the opposite side of the Avon and 3 miles north-east of Durrington Walls.

CHAPTER VIII

The Final Stonehenge

IN OUR SUMMARY REVIEW of ceremonial enclosures we have seen that sufficiently stable conditions existed for human resources and manpower to be devoted largely to their construction under Beaker and Warrior Culture dominance. No warrant exists, however, for assuming that any form of kingship over a large area existed; at most, local control must have been exercised by culturally related chieftains acting sometimes in competition, at other times in consort with all the resources at their disposal in the execution of some huge earthwork or stone structure. Small earthworks may conceivably have been connected with temporary halting places or local tribes, but structures of the size and complexity of Avebury point to the existence of some more centralized and permanent authority.

Both Stonehenge I and II are consistent with this general *Fig. 10;* Plate 26 class of enclosure and stone circle of Secondary Neolithic-Beaker inception, including even the transport of the bluestones which was certainly an outstanding achievement. But Stonehenge III, the last and final structure in this monument's chequered history, does not fall within the class. Instead, it stands out sharply as a completely new and unique feat in north-western Europe, built on a site that involved a very large shift in the centre of gravity from the Marlborough Downs to South Wiltshire, and involving also the transport of colossal blocks of sarsen weighing up to 50 tons apiece from that hallowed district 18 miles to the north. This shift of emphasis will become more apparent when we come to consider, in the next chapter, the Early Bronze Age Wessex Culture and its barrows; but there can be little doubt that it was mainly due to the new and competing factor of the metal trade with Europe, which arose as a direct result of the ready market offered to

Irish metallurgists by the Beaker and sub-Beaker population. Stonehenge, with its avenue to the River Avon, was certainly more advantageously placed on the natural route from the West to the English Channel than was Avebury, and few would question that this new factor proved powerful enough to efface all traces of former self-sufficiency and at the same time the venue of traditional practices; even the less distinguished Woodhenge and Durrington Walls now fell into disuse. Some might wish to connect the rise of Stonehenge with the introduction of sun-worship which we have seen may be presumed to be inherent in the orientation of the Stonehenge II structure; but such speculations are profitless in the absence of exact knowledge.

I have said that Stonehenge III is unique. This is true in that a large number of the sarsens and bluestones have been dressed to shape and finish in a building that also possesses curved lintels poised on their uprights with mortise and tenon jointing, and with tongues and grooves holding them more securely in place, a carpentry technique transferred to stone and far in advance of the mere erection of free-standing boulders. Dishing of the tops of the uprights aided stability, whilst the convexly curved taper or *entasis* on some seems purposely to have been an added refinement. The plan of the sarsen structure is symmetrical and shapely, and it must be clear that the designer was no novice. It is in fact inconceivable that such a structure could have arisen in the North out of the void without some examples of experimental development behind it. Such a unique object postulates a unique event, and I feel sure that we must look to the literate civilizations of the Mediterranean for the inspiration and indeed for the actual execution under the hands and eyes of some trader or mission from that region.

The main problem underlying Stonehenge III is that in its final form it utilized elements from two separate lintelled structures, one of sarsen and the other of bluestone, with possibly a

Plate 36

95

third of undressed bluestone boulders, which were ultimately fused into one building after a considerable amount of reshuffling of the bluestone elements. These Pembrokeshire bluestones include undressed monoliths, presumably derived from the uncompleted Stonehenge II circles, and a number of dressed stones including two lintels which *may* have formed part of the original plan, or which *may* have stood elsewhere in the vicinity, to be incorporated only at a later stage. Recent excavations have been largely concerned in attempts to unravel some of these phases, but it cannot be said that they have met as yet with complete success. It is not, as I have said, my intention to describe the monument in detail as this has been done by my colleague R. J. C. Atkinson. All that I need here emphasize are some of the problems and conclusions we have tentatively arrived at individually and collectively, the most important being that three main building phases have been distinguished, though even here it would be wrong to assume that they are firmly established.

STONEHENGE IIIA

After the total removal of the double bluestone circle from the already hallowed site, the 'Q' and 'R' holes were refilled and packed with chalk rubble. Disregarding the immense problems associated with the transport of the sarsens from the Marlborough Downs and the victualling of the hundreds of workers employed on the project, the first phase must have been concerned with the dressing and erection of the five great trilithons and the outer circle of thirty uprights with their thirty lintels. The fact that the same centre and axis were used suggests no lengthy period of discontinuity between the abortive erection of Stonehenge II and the decision to abandon it in favour of the novel design that somehow now presented itself.

This symmetrical and superlative sarsen structure may be considered to have been complete in itself. No compelling reason can be adduced to suggest that the original plan necessarily contemplated the incorporation of the undressed bluestone boulders; this may well have been an afterthought. Nevertheless, we cannot disregard the fact that other masons at the same time must have been dressing and possibly constructing a smaller imitation with lintels somewhere in the vicinity. It will be recalled that a chipping of rhyolite was found in the ditch of the Fargo Plantation grave three-quarters of a mile to the north-west. It was for that very reason that a section was cut, in 1947, through the Cursus as near as possible to the grave; this yielded another fragment of bluestone, this time of Cosheston sandstone, from the ditch. Intensive search of the ground in the neighbourhood resulted in the discovery of numerous chippings representing most of the known varieties of rocks at Stonehenge, but none in the intervening fields separating the two sites. This fact implies that a bluestone structure incorporating many Pembrokeshire varieties of stone *may* at some stage have existed near the west end of the Cursus, to be demolished and used later in the construction of the main monument.

The date of the erection of the main sarsen structure is now no longer a matter of mere speculation. The absence of contemporary domestic refuse and graves on so sacred a site is not to be wondered at, and this very fact has in the past raised numerous difficulties when efforts were made to interpret its age and history, and has been the cause of much argument. But, until recently, our only course has been to rely on certain external features, on the contents in fact of the many graves that surround the monument as does a cemetery its parish church, even though such an assumption lacked precision. To be precise one needed some internal feature, something actually attached to or forming part of the stones themselves. By great

good fortune this was forthcoming in 1953, during an inten﹣
sive photographic survey by R. J. C. Atkinson, in the form of
a number of weather﹣beaten carvings on some of the stones,
apparently contemporary with their original dressing, which
until then had remained unobserved and unrecognized in spite
of past observation and photographic zeal.

Plate 33

Stone 53 of the second trilithon was then found to have on
its inner side at eye﹣level representations of bronze axe﹣blades
and of a bronze dagger; these were subsequently confirmed by
the discovery of other axe carvings on the outsides of the up﹣
rights of the outer circle, especially on those of stones 3 and 4.
The forms here so clearly portrayed full size, belong to well﹣
known types of flat and hammer﹣flanged axes with widely
splayed cutting edges that were in current use during the Early
Bronze Age and which were probably being manufactured in,
and exported from, Ireland around 1500 B.C., though the
type, especially those with cast flanges, was fundamentally of
Central European origin. Very special interest may be attached,
therefore, to such a decorated hammer﹣flanged specimen that

Fig. 16

was actually found within 500 yards of Stonehenge during
pipe﹣laying operations in 1952. The significance of these axe
carvings on the sacred stones can hardly be dissociated from
the widespread axe﹣cult of Mediterranean origin which we
have noticed had already been transmitted in modified form
to the stone axes of the North by way of the Breton megalithic
tombs.

The carving of the hafted dagger with its long tapering
blade and slight projecting shoulders at its base is even more
informative. Since the axe carvings can be recognized as
accurate copies of current types, we are entitled to assume that
that of the dagger must be other than purely imaginative. Such
a type is, however, unknown in north﹣western Europe during
the Bronze Age when it would have been a simple matter to
copy local native forms. Only one other carving seemingly

portraying a similar type of dagger together with axes has been recorded and this comes from a grave slab of an early Bronze Age burial near Badbury Rings in Dorset. What, then, does the dagger represent? And does it provide the clue to the building of Stonehenge III we have awaited so long?

Plate 34

The writer is of the opinion that it does for the reason that the nearest parallels come from the Culture of the Shaft Graves of Mycenæ, in which a type of dagger having much the same outline as the Stonehenge carving was in use from about 1600 to 1500 B.C. Now, this would imply that some trader or other from the Greek Mainland who was familiar with such weapons had visited Britain about this time, and that it may have been under his influence and inspiration that the building was erected, the carving representing, as it were, his signature or that of a mission, on completion. Such a sophisticated structure was clearly beyond the realms of the natives' imagination, although in design and proportion it could well have represented, so far from home, a pale reflection of Ægean architecture and masonry. In our next chapter we shall be considering some of the distant trade contacts of the Wessex Culture that embraced both Continental Europe and the Mycenæan world. It is gradually becoming more and more apparent that the idea of expeditions from the Ægean to the barbarian North, and even possibly the establishment of trading posts in Wessex, is not so far-fetched as they might at first appear. As we shall see, the legendary voyages of the Argo in search of the Golden Fleece may not merely be old wives' tales, but could conceivably enshrine vague folk memories of early expeditions in search of gold, copper and amber.

Fig. 16 Decorated bronze axe-blade, found near Stonehenge. Length 4¼ in.

STONEHENGE IIIB

The next building phase appears to have been concerned with attempts to blend and incorporate *some* of the bluestones now

Fig. 17

lying idle from the dismantled and unfinished period II structure. This is certainly the most difficult phase to interpret,
since it was clearly a period of indecision and seems to have
formed no part of the originally conceived plan. Apparently
the first intention was to erect a double bluestone circle outside
the lintelled sarsen circle in the fifty-nine 'Z' and 'Y' holes, in
a manner that was both geometrically and æsthetically most un-
satisfactory. The holes for these circles were certainly dug, but
excavation has proved that they never actually held stones or
had ever been refilled. All contained an accumulation of air-
borne soil with various objects, including bluestone chippings,
disposed throughout in positions consistent with the subsequent action of earthworms. For some reason this project was
abandoned, perhaps through a human or natural catastrophe.

The problem of greatest complexity, however, involves the
shape and contents of the small internal bluestone structure
within the central space enclosed by the five trilithons, which

Plate 35

was in the last phase to contain the present bluestone horseshoe.
We know that this last IIIC phase contained dressed bluestones from an earlier structure including two very shapely
lintels worked in the very best style and clearly tooled to shape
and dressed under the eye of the original architect; and we know

Plate 36

also that these lintels had rested for a time on uprights, as
patches of polish imparted through thermal expansion and
contraction at the point of contact of upright and lintel are
unmistakably present on one. But we do not know conclusively that these lintels actually formed part of this earlier
IIIB structure in view of the possibility of the presence of
another bluestone structure at the west end of the Cursus.

Plate 31

However, excavations in 1954 and 1956 yielded the valuable
information that an oval or elliptical setting of stone-holes had
originally held stone uprights and had formerly stood within
this central area. These had been filled in with compacted
chalk rubble which in one instance had at a later date been dug

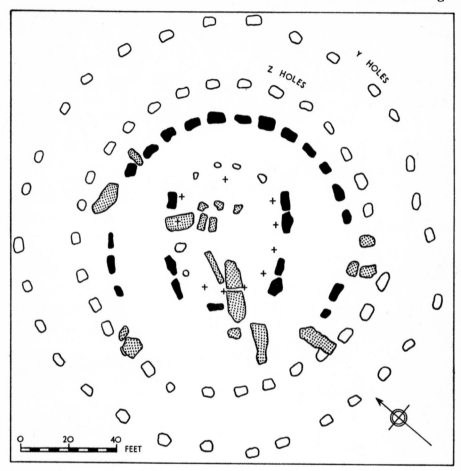

Fig. 17 Plan of Stonehenge in Phase IIIb. Standing sarsens black, fallen sarsens stippled, stone-holes for bluestones in outline, suggested positions marked by crosses

into for the purpose of erecting an upright of the last IIIC phase; but in so doing the end of the stone had been accidentally broken off and had therefore to be used as a chock stone to raise the monolith to the required height. But even more surprisingly, this particular filled-in IIIB stone-hole was found to have been dug into the filling of an even earlier trench or elongated stone-hole that had two clearly defined stone impressions on its base. Here we may well have evidence of some internal bluestone setting contemporary with the period II unfinished double circles; but future excavations alone can disentangle the details of this implied and complex sequence.

STONEHENGE IIIC

Fig. 10;
Plates 26, 29, 35

The last and final phase of reconstruction is, as might be expected, the clearest, though the manner in which the bluestones were re-used does not suggest the hand of a master-builder. It could well, in fact, have taken place a century or so after the completion of the original sarsen masterpiece, i.e., round about 1400 B.C.

The decision to remodel the bluestone elements is likely to have followed fairly rapidly after the abandonment of the 'Z' and 'Y' hole plan; and it is evident that very special care was taken to efface as far as possible memories of the former bluestone structures. The two beautifully shaped lintels were now relegated to inferior positions as mere uprights, with their mortise holes turned outwards, along with the undressed boulders in the newly planned single circle inside the sarsen circle. Excavations have shown that the sixty-odd stones of this circle, mostly now robbed or intentionally battered to below ground level, were very closely set more or less on a circle lying midway between the old 'Q' and 'R' holes of the period II double circle and not infrequently resting on the chalk rubble filling of the dumb-bell-shaped holes connecting them.

The inner bluestone horseshoe also took shape at this time. Having dismantled the older oval setting and any other exist~ ing bluestone features, nineteen of the longest and most elegant were erected in the form of a horseshoe within the area of the sarsen trilithons. All those now existing are of spotted dolerite

Fig. 18 Isometric drawing of Stonehenge central area before re~erection of stones in 1958

or preselite, and all have been most carefully dressed to obelisk~ like shape. Many are missing and a number are defaced, but amongst them are two of outstanding interest as they must have formed part of the earlier structure. One has a longitudinal groove down its length while the other, now buried below one of the fallen stones of the great trilithon, possesses a corres~ ponding tongue.

Fig. 18

The so~called Altar Stone of micaceous sandstone from the Milford Haven region lies recumbent below two of the fallen stones of the same trilithon. It is the largest bluestone at Stone-henge, being 16 feet long by $3\frac{1}{2}$ feet wide and $1\frac{3}{4}$ feet thick, and has been dressed. At present nothing is known about its original setting or whether it now rests as originally intended.

We have no evidence for any reconstruction of the sarsen features of the monument and so must consider the building as being now complete and the venerated centre of a wide and important district. So far we have discussed its bare bones, but these bones were constructed by man; by men in fact who, in the later phases at least, seem to have been dissatisfied with the way in which their sacred bluestones had or had not been incorporated into the superlative sarsen design they so fully appreciated and unquestionably revered, but who were as yet undecided as to the final form the building should take. The master-builder was no longer with them to guide them, and so they had no other choice but to revert to their old traditional practice of erecting the bluestones as a plain uninspired monolithic horseshoe and circle within, and architecturally unconnected with, the sarsen structure.

It now remains for us to examine and infer what we can of the people likely to have been implicated in its construction, and the cause of its elevation towards the southern edge of Salisbury Plain.

CHAPTER IX

Heroes and Traders

THE MEASURE OF COHERENCE and cultural unity imposed by the Beaker and Single-Grave invaders of Northern Germany and the Rhine on the previous population of the British Isles, and their genius for exploration and exploitation, was now to reap its reward. Trade contacts had been established with Irish metallurgists who had awaited the necessary stimulus and urge to develop their industrial activities already implanted in Ireland from Iberia; and connections had been maintained with their Continental kith and kin who were no doubt kept appraised of western potentialities in supplies of copper, tin and gold. Here we need but recall the Irish gold discs from Mere and Monkton Farleigh which may even in their designs copy the decoration of the heads of racquet pins of Central European Early Bronze Age type and have been made at the behest of the Beaker-Folk.

Plates 17, 18

The old transpeninsular waterways connecting the Bristol Channel with the English Channel and the Continent, which skirted the southern edge of Salisbury Plain, were now to see an ever-increasing flow of traffic. This traffic was to result in the temporary and almost fabulous enrichment of certain local members of the Secondary Neolithic society, chieftains or potential mercantile aristocrats fully prepared to enrich themselves, but unprepared and incapable of adding much to the sum of human endeavour other than by stimulating artisans and craftsmen and thus ushering in the brilliant Early Bronze Age that was destined to have so far-reaching an effect on Europe. The growth of Wessex was without question based on trade, but on a form of trade organized solely perhaps to satisfy the personal aggrandisement of a warrior aristocracy of 'heroic' outlook. It would seem that the pattern of human society was now to become a barbaric reflection of that em/bodied in the Homeric poems, with power concentrated in the hands of a chieftain class, a pattern that spread right across Europe with Mycenæ at its apex. In the words of Professor Hawkes, 'The pride of the chieftain demands costly finery and weapons of war and ceremonial, which will be interchanged as 'presents' even over great distances: this feature of Mycenaean culture is constantly portrayed in the Homeric poems, and when the archæologist speaks of such interchange as 'trade', he does well to remember it as a social as much as an economic phenomenon.'

Our knowledge of the period immediately following the establishment of Beaker and Single/Grave dominance is derived almost exclusively from the contents of graves under round barrows. No hiatus in the archæological record can be discerned, merely an increase in material wealth occasioned by expanding commercial connexions and the gradual fusion by intermarriage and absorption of the various cultural traits we have already noted. Unfortunately we have absolutely no knowledge whatsoever of the existence of any contemporary habitation or occupation site in Wessex. This is all the more surprising in areas of such high barrow density as those of Dorset and Wiltshire, and to a very great extent limits our understanding of the people themselves. Where and how they lived we just do not know; but there can be no doubt about their intense desire to furnish their dead with suitable and costly trappings for the underworld.

Round barrows constitute by far the most numerous group of prehistoric earthworks on the chalk and surrounding downs; in Wessex alone some six thousand have been recorded, and without doubt many more have been destroyed by the plough. Many have suffered considerably in the past from ransacking by treasure seekers and from explorations by former antiquaries of an earlier school whose techniques of excavation were necessarily primitive. However, we should be grateful to a few of them for their records and for preserving some of the objects discovered. In two sumptuous volumes entitled *Ancient Wilt/ shire,* Sir Richard Colt Hoare described and illustrated the contents of the many barrows which he and William Cun/ nington dug on Salisbury Plain in the early years of the nineteenth century; and somewhat later, Charles Warne did a similar service for the barrows of Dorset, but less satisfactorily.

It was not until 1938, however, that Professor Piggott analysed the contents of a number of these explored barrows and was able to show that many of distinctive type contained grave/goods which represented a consistent culture sharply demarcated from their predecessors and which included ob/ jects indicating very widespread European trade contacts. His distribution maps demonstrated that the main nucleus of the culture was centred in Wiltshire with the Stonehenge district at its nodal point, though outlying extensions of the culture occurred also in Dorset, Devon and Cornwall, eastwards sporadically to Sussex, and northwards to the Upper Thames Valley with related but smaller centres in Norfolk and eastern Yorkshire. Appropriately enough, he termed the culture the 'Wessex Culture' of the British Bronze Age, whilst fully appreciating the one/sided nature of the evidence derived from graves only. Certain types of pottery vessels, metal and other substances are virtually unknown outside Wiltshire, whilst their distribution and that of other articles clearly mark Salis/ bury Plain as the core of this Early British Bronze Age which now grew with such vigour and flourished through direct contacts with Ireland, Central Europe and the Mediterranean World.

The barrows themselves are of very varied form, though few have been excavated by modern standards. The Bowl/shaped ones are by far the most numerous, whilst those that have been proved by their contents to belong specifically to the Wessex

Plate 37

Culture are very distinctive in shape and have been known since Thurnam's day as Bell, Disc, Saucer and Pond barrows, all of which frequently occur together in closely knit groups. All but the last are characterized by having an encircling, usually continuous, ditch carefully and often accurately dug with a wide flat base, and hence can be grouped together as Circle Barrows. The so-called Pond barrow, about which we shall say more later, does not contain an internal mound, but consists of a pond-like circular area up to 100 feet in diameter with an embanked rim.

The burial rite was either by inhumation or cremation, and the associated grave-goods suggest that the former was the earlier in the case of male burials but that this was later super-seded by the universal rite of cremation, a practice that we have seen was already in use in Late Neolithic times. This re-assertion of the rite, after the first impact of the Beaker-Folk habit of inhumation had receded, may conceivably have been due to female influence, since there is some reason for thinking that a preference for cremation may have persisted throughout in the female line. At all events, it would seem that the rite of Disc barrow burial was reserved very largely for women-folk.

Unfortunately we know very little about contemporary burial ritual. In a few instances some form of mortuary-house can be inferred within the mound, whilst in others, dug-out coffins—possible boats to the underworld—were used. But not until more careful barrow excavations on the lines of those recently carried out by N. and C. Thomas on Snail Down, and P. Ashbee near Bulford, can we expect any great advance in knowledge of structural features or other rites accompanying the actual inhumation or cremation of the body.

Fig. 9

Nowhere is the barrow concentration more marked than in the Stonehenge region. Here are to be seen cemeteries suggesting dynastic or tribal groupings of burials under barrows, with what we may call a 'Founder's Grave' containing a Beaker often associated and sometimes a long barrow as well. The impressive Winterbourne Stoke Cross-roads group is a particularly good instance of this and, although not so well documented, the Normanton group with the famous Bush Barrow as possibly its earliest member. Similar but smaller groups of Circle Barrows are to be seen in Dorset, especially on Oakley Down, in the Avebury district and elsewhere in Wiltshire. These barrow cemeteries with a 'Founder's Grave' attached are important as proving continuity of tradition from Beaker times well into those of the Wessex Culture, with cremation replacing inhumation as the sequence progresses. Primary burial in these cemeteries was probably accorded only to members of the ruling or wealthier classes; a considerable body of evidence exists for the presence of secondary interments of the less distinguished or poorer relations in these and earlier mounds, as for instance in the Stockbridge barrow already referred to with its small necklace of imported beads and bronze awl.

The contents of the graves are very varied, some being of indigenous origin, others clearly imports or close copies. Furthermore, it is now apparent that the culture can be divided into two phases, an earlier one centred round 1500 B.C. with its inhumation graves, grooved bronze daggers, probably amber space-plate necklaces and some of the cups of the Aldbourne Plates 38, 39, 55 and Manton types; and a later one around 1400 B.C. embracing cremations, sometimes in cinerary urns, incense or pygmy cups, Plates 58, 59 ogival bronze daggers and faience beads. However, in neither phase can any form of mass migration or invasion be inferred comparable with that of the earlier Beaker invasions. The obvious derivation of much from the parallel Bronze Age communities of Central Europe and especially of the Saale-Elbe region of Saxo-Thuringia, which was itself in close touch with the great Aunjetitz Culture of Bohemia, and the contemporary appearance of elements of a similar culture in

Brittany (the 'dagger graves') suggest westward movements of merchants or traders in quest of metals rather than of small bands of a conquering military aristocracy. For we must not forget that the Early Bronze Age of Saxo-Thuringia was also based on the same Single-Grave traditions as those of Wessex with similar richly furnished barrow burials and timber mortuary-houses, and that these regions must have remained closely linked both commercially and by kinship.

The native element is especially marked in the pottery forms and insignia of prestige. But here again we must never forget that we are dealing almost entirely with grave-goods. Vessels of beaker type suddenly cease to be deposited with the dead; but we do not know whether they continued in use for domestic purposes. Their place was taken initially by small cups of the Aldbourne and Manton types derived almost certainly from Rinyo-Clacton wares developed locally and in parallel from the same Chassey II source as the *vase-support* of Brittany and the Channel Islands; they were slightly later to emerge as the incense or pygmy cups accompanying cremations in the Middle Bronze Age. Some of the latter look remarkably like representations of Stonehenge itself. Larger vessels of tripartite collared form also begin to appear as food vessels with inhumations, and these again later develop into the normal and universal receptacles for cremations. We now know that these collared urns were also derived from local Secondary Neolithic wares, since early specimens have been found with other Late Neolithic pots in the West Kennet long barrow. Here they had been used in the first place for domestic purposes, an aspect we know so little about, and it was only later that they were deemed worthy to accompany the dead. We cannot disregard the fact that these substitutes for the sepulchral beaker may imply the rise to power of a new dominant caste having a considerable Secondary Neolithic background, the Beaker element meanwhile having become absorbed or submerged.

Plates 38, 39

Plate 40

However, two or three vessels suggest imports from farther afield. A small undecorated cup with handle from Colling/ bourne Ducis closely resembles the large series of handled vessels of the Central European Bronze Age, whilst a similar one with four small feet from Oakley Down represents a well/ known Aunjetitz type.

We have already noted the native burial from Upton Lovel with its bone/fringed garment, stone tools and battle/axes, and other objects that formally belong to the Wessex Culture. To a similar native origin we must also ascribe the ceremonial sceptres or maces of authority. The Bush Barrow mace, of attractive fossiliferous limestone probably from the Teign/ mouth district, with its zigzag bone inlays is a famous example and with it should be included the even more ornate gold/ studded shale specimen from the Clandon Barrow near Dorchester found with an amber cup, a lozenge/shaped gold plate and a bronze dagger. Well made and sometimes orna/ mented stone battle/axes with symmetrically expanded blade and butt fall into the same class of native object developed possibly to resemble the profile of the Minoan double/axe, four bronze examples of which have been found in the British Isles. Some of these stone battle/axes are now known to have emanated from picrite outcrops at Cwm Mawr near Corndon in Shropshire, others from the Whin Sill of the Teesdale area. Grooved arrow/straighteners, whetstones, bone tweezers and flint and pyrites for making fire often accompany the dead; whilst from one of the Normanton barrows a perforated swan's bone has been interpreted as a musical pipe.

But it is only when we examine the remarkable increase in armament that we begin to appreciate to the full the emergence of the true Bronze Age with its repertory of bronze daggers, spear/heads, knives, axes, awls and tracers. All have been found in Wessex Culture graves; spear/heads occur only in quantity in the two well/known trader's hoards from Arreton

Fig. 13

Plates 41, 42

Plates 43, 44

Plate 13

Plates 47–50
Plate 46

III

Down and Totland, both in the Isle of Wight. The bronzes themselves appeared initially through trade relations with Central Europe, but were soon copied and often improved by smiths in the British Isles, whose introduction of the bronze halberd was to be so eagerly accepted in return. Wessex itself, through lack of raw materials, never became an industrial centre for bronze manufacture; its unique position attracted products from elsewhere but it never seems to have acted other than as an *entrepôt* for their dissemination over wider fields. Nevertheless, the right situation had been created and the impetus given for the British Isles now to enter the forefront of the newly awakened bronze industry.

Plate 41

The daggers characteristic of the period are of two main types. The earlier forms, as those from Bush Barrow, are often large with grooves parallel to the blade and with six rivets for fixing to the haft; they are closely related to both Breton and Saxo-Thuringian types. The later forms are ogival in shape with grooves, a thickened midrib and normally three rivets at the heel. They also may be of Central European origin, or

Plates 47-50

represent parallel developments in the British Isles. But the hafts and pommels are on occasion characteristically British and were possibly developed from specimens of the Milston type. Some of these hafts are richly decorated with thousands of tiny gold pins arranged in zones and zigzags; whilst the pommels (of Central European types) may be of bone or

Plate 45

amber, again ornamented with gold pins or plating. This gold pin technique was, however, in current use by Mycenæan armourers, and for the original inspiration we may have perhaps to turn our eyes in that direction.

Plates 41, 46;
Fig. 16

Bronze axe-blades of hammer-flanged type are almost certainly of Irish origin, but cast-flanged axes of similar type were being imported into our eastern counties from Germany. Crutch-headed, ring-headed and globe-headed pins were now in normal use in Central Europe for fastening clothing, but not in this country where as we have seen, V-perforated buttons, now sometimes gold-plated, were in vogue; the occasional appearance of these pins in Wessex Culture contexts may be presumed to denote trade relations; but they do not seem to have found much favour.

Gold was certainly being imported from Ireland, but pro-bably in the raw state for working up into ornaments by local craftsmen, as the objects produced are not found in that country. Extensive use was made of the metal mainly in the form of decorated thin sheets for attachment to wood, leather or conical shale buttons, and also for beads and pendants. Two of the finest gold plates came from Bush Barrow and from Clandon Barrow in Dorset, the former also with a magnificent gold-plated belt-hook of Central European type. The truly astonishing ribbed gold cup from Rillaton in Cornwall, with its close Mycenæan parallels in gold-working technique, might almost represent a Mycenæan gift to some contemporary British chieftain.

Amber, that much prized golden fossil resin of the Ancient World, still deemed of value, looms large in the products of the North that found their way to the Mediterranean. As we might expect, the Wessex barrows contain numerous objects of the material mainly in the shape of beads and pendants. Small quantities may have been obtained from our eastern coasts but these could never have been adequate to meet all demands. A large piece of raw amber weighing 2¾ oz., found at Westbury in Wiltshire in 1956, may have been so derived but unfortunately it is now impossible to know whether it was lost accidentally at the time. No doubt much was obtained direct from the Baltic, the home of European amber; the neck-lace of amber, segmented tin and segmented faience beads from Odoorn, Holland, and the segmented faience bead from Fjallerslev in Jutland support a direct northern coastal route to the mouth of the Elbe, as do also a number of Danish amber

Plates 42, 43, 44, 45

Plates 56, 57

Plate 52

Plates 54, 55, 57, 60

H

beads which copy in detail some of imported faience found in Wessex Culture contexts.

But fabricated amber ornaments were also arriving from other sources. Three small pendants representing hafted halberds found at Hengistbury Head (the main port to Wessex), at Normanton and Manton must have been inspired by the parade weapons of Central Europe. Each of these miniature objects, perforated for suspension, has a small bronze blade held in a shaft in two instances, of amber, and in two instances bound with gold wire or plate; they must symbolize in trinket form the typical metalshafted halberds of SaxoThuringia. Also to be considered are necklaces of a distinctive type possessing complex transversely perforated spacingplates to separate multiple strings of beads. This particular form of spacingplate is not known in northern Europe but appears in southwestern Germany around the headwaters of the Rhine and the Danube, and even more significantly in early Mycenæan tombs, as at Kakovatos, *c.* 1450 B.C., clearly proving amongst other things that Mycenæan trade relations had been established along this European route to the British Isles and linked with the great amber route from the Baltic to Greece via the Brenner Pass and the Adriatic. Decorated goldmounted amber discs, possibly representing solar amulets, have been found at Normanton and Manton; these may well have been traded along the same route and, as pointed out by J. M. de Navarro, are more than likely to have emanated from the Ægean, since a similar one with plain gold band was found in the Tomb of the DoubleAxes at Knossos, and closely related but more elaborate ones of steatite are known from Enkomi in Cyprus.

However, without question, two of the finest objects found in the Wessex Culture are handled cups carved from single pieces of amber. One perfect specimen of red amber, which can hold nearly half a pint, was found in a barrow at Hove

Plates 54, 57

Plate 55

Plates 54, 57

Plate 51

with a battle-axe, of pronounced double-axe profile, and a bronze dagger; the other, now fragmentary, came from the famous Clandon Barrow in Dorset. Closely related cups of Plate 53 local shale are also known from Wiltshire and Farway Down, Devon.

But nothing can stir the imagination more than the evidence that exists for direct contacts with the literate civilizations of the Mediterranean world at this time. We have noted the appearance of a few exotic objects which may very likely be of Ægean if not Mycenæan derivation, and to these we may add a stone axe of emery or corundum from Calne, Wiltshire, which almost certainly originated from Naxos or a nearby island of the Greek archipelago. Such objects, however, are not very numerous and could well have arrived in Britain in the normal course of trade through passage from hand to hand.

When we come to examine the dissemination of numerous small articles of jewellery in the form of cheap brightly coloured beads, the matter assumes a very different light. Here we are almost certainly dealing with the by-products of trade expeditions or missions to far-off lands where a handful or so of attractively coloured trinkets had already been found to appeal to primitive minds, and which were valued in proportion to their relative scarcity. The remarkable synthetic material of which these beads were made is known as 'ancient faience' and appears to have been invented and later developed only by oriental communities that had reached a relatively high level of civilization. The industry, which involved a high degree of technological specialization and which was later to develop into the great glass industry of modern times, was in fact confined to the manufacture of such luxury articles and personal ornaments as beads, amulets, statuettes, seals and small vases that were required mainly to satisfy æsthetic needs, and could not be expected to enter into the economic life of more primitive peoples existing at lower levels of civilization. The evidence we possess at present suggests that faience was first invented in northern Mesopotamia during the fifth millennium B.C. and that it was only later introduced into Egypt in Predynastic times, where it found a congenial home and blossomed from then onwards into one of major importance for some three thousand years at least. Although in course of time the industry spread to the neighbouring civilizations of the Ægean and the Indus, it never appears to have attained in those regions the immense popularity that we find it did throughout all periods of Dynastic Egypt.

Faience is not a natural product but consists of a composite material formed by glazing a moulded core of finely powdered quartz grains already thermally fused together by the addition of small amounts of an alkali or lime, or both. The subsequent act of glazing involved the application of a pre-made soda-lime-quartz glass in powdered form as a slip to the pre-moulded core, the glass itself having usually been coloured bright turquoise blue or green by the addition during fusion of traces of copper compounds. An alternative and simpler process consisted in the use of powdered coloured glass alone to bind the quartz grains together; this process, after firing, resulted in a coloured matrix, the whole object being coloured uniformly throughout with the quartz grains appearing to float in a lake of glass. It will be appreciated that in both processes a preformed coloured glass had first to be made; nevertheless, this was not used as such for many centuries, the powdered material being used solely as a slip for the external glazing of moulded quartz cores.

It was not, however, until the second half of the second millennium B.C. that Egypt witnessed a sudden expansion of its glass and faience industries with a prodigious increase in the volume of goods turned out for both home consumption and foreign trade. During the XVIIIth Dynasty (1580-1314 B.C.) especially, factories such as those at Tell-el-Amarna were working at high pressure—they have been found littered with waste products and thousands of pottery moulds for making beads and pendants. Syria and Mycenæan Greece did not lag behind but their output never approached that of Egypt. Until the XVIIIth Dynasty the products of such factories had been confined to relatively restricted areas of the Middle East, to those areas in fact in which the four major literate civilizations had their being. But from 1500 B.C. onwards the new element of distant trade expeditions suddenly makes its appearance, and this almost certainly may be connected with the rise to power of the Greek Mainlanders with their wide sea-borne commercial interests and insatiable desire for precious and base metals, amber and other exotic substances.

We now encounter faience and glass beads of Eastern Mediterranean derivation scattered as trade beads along well defined routes and over vast distances; around the Black Sea to the Caucasus and the shores of the Caspian, and even up the Volga and Ural Rivers to Siberia; up the Nile to Central East Africa; up the Danube to Hungary, Poland and Moravia; and along the Mediterranean to the South of France and thence to the British Isles and the North. But these routes are almost precisely those hypothetically ascribed in ancient times to the legendary expeditions of Jason and the Argo in their quest for gold. Though it is highly speculative, the present writer feels that we can detect in the general scatter of these beads concrete echoes of these ancient Greek legends of commercial enterprise and exploratory voyages.

Certainly by 1450-1300 B.C. the Mycenæan commercial system embraced considerable areas of the Mediterranean, and faience beads appear in quantity in Malta, Sicily, the Lipari Islands and the South of France. From here they have been traced, together with small wire-wound glass beads, down the Garonne to the Atlantic coasts where they appear again in Brittany and in the British Isles.

Wessex

Fig. 19; Plate 60 Three distinct varieties amongst others are recognized in the British Isles: the segmented, the star and the quoit beads. The segmented variety is by far the most numerous, and the beads are concentrated mainly in the centre of the Wessex Culture where no less than thirty-three groups have been recorded from barrow burials. This particular form of bead was for long a favourite in Egypt, though beads of the exact shape and size of those found in Wessex appear only during a restricted period of the XVIIIth Dynasty. Identical beads have been found on a necklace from a grave at Abydos with a scarab of Amen-hotep III (1408-1372 B.C.), and on another from Lachish in Palestine associated with a plaque of Amenhotep II (1450-1425 B.C.). It is thus possible to date with a fair degree of accuracy the appearance of these beads in graves of the Wessex Culture to between 1400 and 1300 B.C.

Strangely enough the star and quoit beads, though in general contemporary with the segmented variety, lie peripherally to Wessex and are found mainly in graves nearer the coastline. This remarkable distribution could conceivably be due to a second expedition aimed not primarily at the heart of Wessex but largely coastally to spy out the lie of the land. It is remark-able, too, that the only analogues of these beads in Europe appear from a pile-dwelling on Lake Constance, from just that area from which our amber spacing beads with their Mycenæan connections were most probably derived. On the other hand, a small four-rayed faience star bead, typical of those found with segmented beads in Hungary and in Greece, has recently been discovered by G. V. Taylor in a cremation ceme-tery at Stainsby in Lincolnshire. This can only have arrived in the course of trade from the Middle Danube and very strongly supports the view that all British faience beads are of Eastern Mediterranean derivation.

Unfortunately it has so far proved impossible to deduce with accuracy the exact country of origin of many of these faience

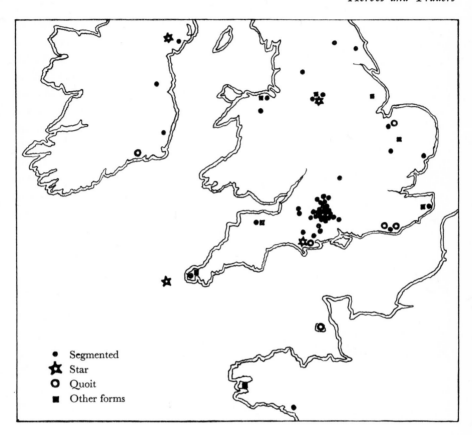

Fig. 19 Distribution of faience beads in part of the British Isles and France

beads. Spectrographic analysis has given equivocal results and we are, therefore, still forced to rely on morphological characters and archæological associations; but the present writer would nevertheless hazard the guess that great numbers of these trade beads will eventually be found to have emanated from Egyptian workshops even though disseminated by other seafaring people of Mediterranean origin.

If, then, we review in rapid summary the information we have been able to glean from the contents of the Wessex Cul/ ture tombs that surround Stonehenge, we find that we are presented with a consistent picture of dynastic or tribal groupings of burials of a rich aristocratic community that flourished between *c.* 1550 and 1300 B.C. The cause of its rise to power and wealth was due to its position on an exceedingly important trade route between the metalliferous regions of the West, and the Continent; but, as we shall see, when that trade stopped through the discovery and exploitation of metal deposits elsewhere, Wessex rapidly declined and entered a phase of almost complete stagnation. But during its *floruit*, it is by no means improbable that trading posts ultimately of Mycenæan origin may have been established possibly some/ where on the Wiltshire Avon near Amesbury; and we may even be rash enough to infer that their presence was the direct cause of the building of Stonehenge IIIA about 1500 B.C., at which time sufficient cultural cohesion had been secured to warrant such an outstanding achievement, never again to be repeated.

CHAPTER X

Aftermath

FROM ABOUT 1300 B.C. ONWARDS the rich Wessex
Culture ceases to be perceptible as an archæological entity.
Founded, as we have seen, exclusively on trade and on its fortunate position on a most important trade route, the culture
may be considered as almost a parasitic growth that was bound
to collapse when its life-blood was diverted to other quarters.
The culture appears as the expression of an heroic aristocracy
amassing unproductive weapons and luxury articles, and
doubtless supported by an agricultural society. Nevertheless,
under the favourable conditions created, the population may
well have increased and have moved to new regions beyond
Wessex. We have evidence of the widespread practice of
cremation, with the ashes frequently contained in a pottery jar
or cinerary urn, over the whole of the British Isles, to Caith-
ness and Ireland and even oversea to Holland; archæology only
gives us glimpses of a culture characterized by these cremated
burials in large cinerary urns of varied form and decoration
often accompanied by small pygmy vessels but usually, in the
South, without other grave-goods. These cinerary urns are
usually of the so-called 'collared' variety, but it is now recognized, as demonstrated by J. J. Butler and I. F. Smith, that
other forms, such as the biconical type with horseshoe, and
other finger-tipped, applied decoration, were also currently in
use. These, until recently, have been attributed to the Late
Bronze Age Deverel-Rimbury Culture, but it now seems
clear that they too were derived from native Secondary Neolithic wares. Wessex no longer affords us evidence of an heroic
warrior aristocracy, owing to the changing traditions of
funerary ritual, but we need not assume that the region necessarily became a cultural backwater, a dismal and dreary period

Plates 61–63

121

unlit by any spark of human endeavour. Developments in bronze technology at this time, for instance, are discussed below.

The collapse of the Wessex Culture might be correlated, as Professor Childe has suggested, with the large-scale exploita-tion by deep mining of the copper lodes of the Eastern Alps probably under Mycenæan influence. The Mycenæan World needed ever-increasing supplies of bronze, and no other rich civilization of the period could afford to subsidize the required specialist labour and at the same time consume the product. The resultant abundance and cheapness of bronze that now flooded the markets of Europe gradually diverted Ægean interest from the British Isles, and was the direct cause of the subsequent rise of the Late Bronze Age on the Continent which followed the slow decline and exhaustion of the brilliant Mycenæan Empire soon after 1250 B.C.

But the effect of these new sources of metal on the British Isles was not yet immediately apparent. The Irish-British bronze industries continued to expand locally and to maintain trade contacts with northern Europe. We now find as charac-teristic of the period, and largely as a result of contacts with northern Europe, the development and manufacture of bronze rapiers, palstaves (developed flanged axes with stop-ridges) and spearheads with sockets for firmer attachment to the shaft. Other bronze articles seem to have been confined mostly to metal-workers' tools and equipment; bronze was not yet abun-dant enough for ordinary daily use. The metal-workers them-selves apparently formed a class apart and, as Professor Childe has emphasized, could be regarded almost as a separate society liberated from the bonds of local custom and able to enjoy free-dom of movement and travel wherever they found markets for their products and skill. Their products are certainly very rarely found in graves; mostly they appear singly as lost objects or hidden in merchant's or trader's hoards, as did the twelve palstaves found in a gravel pit at Shappen near Burley in the New Forest. But such hoards and single bronzes are relatively rare in Wessex itself, though they become commoner as we penetrate westward into Somerset.

No Middle Bronze Age settlement sites have yet been iden/ tified; there may have been an increased element of pastoralism side-by-side with continued grain-growing and hunting. An oval enclosure 400 by 270 feet on Rams Hill in Berkshire (the only one of its kind) has been interpreted as a cattle enclosure of the period. Excavations proved the presence of one entrance with post-holes, the ditch being flat-bottomed and almost vertical-sided in the manner traditional since Neolithic times. Numerous sherds of a Middle Bronze Age collared urn, almost certainly domestic rather than sepulchral, were found scattered in a loamy layer in immediate contact with the primary silting at an early stage in the history of the ditch.

A possible pitfall trap for the capture of animals was dis/ covered in 1938 on Stockbridge Down in Hampshire. The oval-shaped pit was found on excavation to measure 14 by 6 feet at the surface and to be 8 feet 6 inches deep with almost vertical sides. So steep were they that a terrier fell in during operations and had to be rescued. The greater part of the pit was filled with dirty chalk dust and rubble; superimposed on this were 18 inches of a Middle Bronze Age refuse layer sealed in by a further 18 inches of top soil. This Bronze Age layer contained numerous fragments of collared urns ornamented with twisted cord, calcined flints, animal teeth and bones—some burnt and some split longitudinally for extraction of the marrow, frag/ ments of charcoal, a small bone awl and a fragment of a sand/ stone quern or rubber for grinding corn. Eleven flint scrapers, still formed by pressure flaking, were also recovered, which proved that flint was still in use for domestic purposes.

Two forms of contemporary native burial having certain ritual features in common, and rooted deeply in Secondary

Neolithic practices, have yet to be mentioned; the Pond barrows and the flat cremation cemeteries. The former were certainly in process of development during the period of the Wessex Culture, though their direct connection with that culture
may ultimately be proved to be illusory. On the other hand, we
have only two examples of recognized cremation cemeteries in
Wessex. Although, as we shall see, one contained some poor
Wessex Culture grave-goods, such cemeteries are a common
feature of the Middle Bronze Age in the Highland Zone of
Great Britain.

Pond barrows are circular depressions averaging 60 feet in
diameter and delimited by an accurately constructed embanked
rim. A few occur in the Avebury district but most of them are
concentrated around Stonehenge and in Dorset amongst the
extensive barrow-fields near Winterbourne Abbas. Their frequent association with Bell and Disc barrows has suggested that
they were in some way connected with the Wessex Culture,
but the few that were partly examined during the eighteenth
and nineteenth centuries yielded so little that their date and
purpose have remained open to question. Recently, however
Fig. 20 an example, on Sheep Down, Winterbourne Steepleton, in
Dorset, has been most carefully excavated with surprising and
interesting results. Here the whole of the inner area, about 2 feet
below the surrounding chalk, had been paved with tightly
packed flint nodules about 7 inches thick, below which, and
just outside the edge, were thirty-four pits cut into the natural
chalk. Of these, eight contained soil only, seven contained urnless cremations, whilst twenty contained pots mostly crushed,
three with cremations and two with dismembered inhumations.
Since only eleven of the pits had human remains in them, the
excavators concluded that this Pond barrow was not primarily
sepulchral but had been used as a place for offerings and other
ritual purposes comparable with those of some of the henge
monuments, and that its situation in close proximity to round

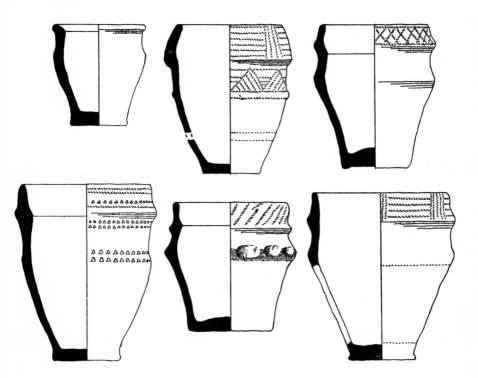

Fig. 20 Pots from pond-barrow on Sheep-Down, Winterbourne Steepleton, Dorset. Scale ¼

barrows suggested that the cult it served must have been that of the dead. The pots themselves are typically local native pro-ducts with no admixture of Wessex Culture grave-goods and clearly imply the existence or persistence of native traditions and practices behind the Wessex Culture façade.

As long ago as 1866, C. Warne perceived the close relation-ship that must have existed between these Pond barrows and flat cremation cemeteries, when describing one of the latter found by agricultural labourers on Launceston Down in Dorset.

At a depth of 6 inches below the surface the workmen here found a compact bed of flints under which was much dark mould with charcoal, ashes, pieces of bone and potsherds; and cut into the chalk were numerous cists filled with cremations and ashes. A similar cemetery was found very much later by the present writer close to the flint-mine shafts on Easton Down. An area 60 feet by 20 feet, rising about 3 inches above the surrounding ground and undisturbed by rabbits, was also found to consist of a 6-inch layer of flint nodules and flint-mine debris including roughed-out axes. This layer covered seven small cists cut in the chalk, four of which contained urns, two urnless cremations, and one filled with mould only. The largest of the urns contained the cremated bones of an eight-year-old girl together with a small necklace of lignite and amber beads with one faience segmented bead and a small bone awl. Although these beads suggest a Wessex Culture date, they could as easily represent an heirloom buried a hundred or so years after the cessation of that culture. In any event, the presence of this native cemetery in the flint-mine area in such close proximity to the shafts and workshop floors can only imply that flint was still a useful commodity and that the mines were still being worked at this late stage, as seems to have been the case in the mines at Blackpatch in Sussex.

The preservation of organic remains in the damp alkaline soils of the chalk-lands we should expect to be an exceedingly rare occurrence. For that very reason we cannot forbear from mentioning one very interesting secondary burial in an inverted urn of handled Cornish appearance found in 1814 in the famous 'Bell-Barrow of Chalk' at Winterslow near Salisbury. Here the conditions for preservation were favourable, the cremation within the urn appearing to have been wrapped in linen which had the appearance of fine lace and which blew away on exposure to the wind. Amongst the bones were a fluted bronze razor, now recognized as a Middle Bronze Age

Fig. 21

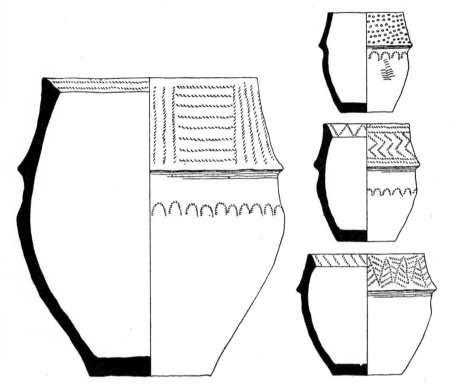

Fig. 21 Pots from the Easton Down cremation cemetery, Wilts. Scale ¼

type, a bronze awl, a necklace of amber beads, V-bored buttons and some human hair. Very fortunately this hair was
preserved and now lies in the Ashmolean Museum at Oxford.
Recent examination by J. L. Stoves has shown that it consists
of human eyebrows from a number of individuals, which is an
interesting sidelight on a contemporary mourning practice that
has persisted to the present day amongst certain peoples.

CHAPTER XI

New Farmers

THE HAZE AND MIST that surrounds the 'heroic' stage of the Bronze Age past, its immediate aftermath now clears a little and we find ourselves no longer compelled to construct our picture of later prehistoric events in Wessex solely from the evidence available from burials, with their implications of chieftains and their followers whose burial rites involved the building of complex barrows and the decking of the dead with objects of prestige and adornment for display in an underworld. From 1000 B.C. onwards, thanks to archæological evidence from settlements as well as graves, we enter a world of a familiar if primitive pattern, and one which we can perhaps more easily understand. Thanks to the more abundant evidence and its nature, we can for the first time visualize men and women pursuing their daily tasks in a manner not dissimilar from that perceptible for instance in early medieval societies. In central and northern Europe from the twelfth century B.C. onwards there was a period of unrest and of technological development, not unconnected, it seems, with the break-up of the political balance of power in the Near East to be followed shortly by the emergence of Celtic-speaking and iron-using peoples. The Late Bronze and Early Iron Ages being periods of some complexity in Wessex, we can attempt only a bare outline here.

The relative abundance of bronze tools and their availability was now to place these commodities within the reach of a larger section of the population than in earlier times, whilst the introduction of new agricultural techniques presumably resulted in an increase in the food supply, allowing for a concomitant growth of population.

A new series of migrations to our southern shores is now perceptible in the archæological record, and may be attributed to the disturbed conditions on the European continent already mentioned. There resulted a displacement of groups of people including those of the retarded Tumulus Bronze Culture of the Middle Rhine and northern France. Some apparently migrated or were pushed farther west; others crossed the Channel. Amongst the first refugees from Picardy, Professor Hawkes has recognized certain settlers at Ramsgate in Kent and the Thames estuary, whilst others from the Seine-Somme region crossed to Sussex, where at sites such as Plumpton Plain we encounter evidence for new methods of agriculture: enclosed farmsteads associated with cattle-ways separating small, squarish fields, presumably cultivated with a traction-plough rather than with a hoe. This type of agricultural economy was to form the foundation of that which persisted in southern England up to, and into, the Roman occupation.

In Wessex, as elsewhere, we meet with the sporadic begin-nings of a new and concurrent phenomenon, the appearance of hoards of bronze implements and ornaments buried or lost, perhaps an indication of a time of insecurity. These hoards, which appear in Britain in much greater numbers than those of earlier days, probably represent in some instances the stock-in-trade of itinerant smiths or tinkers, 'international' in all probability; and their contents throw a flood of light on the advances in metallurgical techniques that were now taking place on the Continent, and on the new types of tool and weapon that were now deemed common necessities. New types of tools and weapons of Continental origin, such as socketed axes, carpenter's tools including saws, gouges and chisels, and leaf-shaped swords capable of slashing as well as thrusting, were being peddled and copied, and the tinker was not averse to accepting in exchange broken and scrap metal for re-casting. Objects in beaten bronze, showing a knowledge of the tech-nique of annealing, also appear in Britain for the first time.

But, as we have seen, Wessex had never been a centre of

I

bronze-working, due to the absence of raw materials. It seems also to have had little to offer in trade exchange for imported metal goods. But bronze hoards and single objects are widely distributed, mostly peripherally to the chalk massif along the south coast and in Somerset, with relatively few inland; the majority can be ascribed to the period of the migrations to Wessex under discussion, beginning probably about 1000 B.C. But before we glance at the contents of these hoards and at the wealth of articles that were now becoming available we should first meet the new immigrants themselves, named (not very happily) after their two well-known cemeteries in the Deverel barrow and at Rimbury in Dorset.

We have seen that owing to a variety of causes the period from the twelfth century B.C. onwards was one of disruption and movement over much of Europe. The British Isles were not unaffected by these movements of conflict, migration and change, one of the results of which was the emergence of a cul-ture recognizably similar to those of the historical Celts in Central Europe east of the Rhine. The archæological evidence suggests that the immigrations affecting Wessex from *c.* 1000 B.C. onwards (and which we must now consider) had their origin along the Channel coasts westwards of the Seine, and from areas outside the early Celtic world.

Some of our knowledge of these intrusive Deverel-Rimbury people is derived from their burials; these are scattered thickly over Dorset and Hampshire (where they are centred on Christ-church), appearing as multiple cremations in flat cemeteries, in low scraped-up mounds or as secondary burials in older bar-rows. The cremations were sometimes placed in urns, at other times not, with practically no grave-goods; their numbers in any one cemetery sometimes exceeded a hundred, as in the Rimbury necropolis, an index of settled, peaceful conditions based on an economy no longer wholly dependent on pastora-lism or the chase. Three types of urn, when used for the ashes, have been distinguished; the globular, the barrel and the bucket-shaped. Although the details of their derivation are still matters of relative uncertainty and need much more study, the globular urn may well have been derived from the Neolithic and Bronze Age channelled ware of western France. The barrel-shaped urn, often ornamented with straight or horseshoe-shaped, finger-tipped applied bands may owe its origin in part to British Middle Bronze Age styles of pottery. On the other hand, the rough bucket urn is a generalized type of vessel with roots going back to Neolithic and Bronze Age traditions in north-western Europe.

Plate 66

The distribution of these urnfields containing ten or more burials thins out considerably northwards as we approach Salisbury, and on Salisbury Plain they are practically non-existent. Here we encounter instead an increasing number of contemporary urns inserted singly as secondary burials in pre-existing barrows, from which it would almost seem as if the inhabitants already in possession of this region had at first raised some sort of barrier against further northward encroachment. Yet this cannot have been entirely the case, since it is on the chalk downlands of Cranborne Chase and of southern and northern Wiltshire that we meet with the other and very much more important manifestation of the Deverel-Rimbury immigrants, their agricultural and stock-breeding activities. But even here it remains a moot point whether this new form of agricultural economy formed part of the originally introduced culture, or whether the ditched and embanked cattle-kraals we have yet to consider were not taken over from the indigenous enclosures of the natives, such as those of the Rams Hill type, and adapted by the immigrants as they slowly penetrated northwards. It is a noteworthy fact, as first pointed out by Mrs. C. M. Piggott, that a marked dichotomy exists when we plot the distribution of major urnfields and of enclosures known to have been constructed and used by these same people. This may, of course, merely mean that we have not as yet discovered traces of such earthworks in the areas of primary settlement. Yet major urnfields are conspicuously absent in the vicinity of many of the enclosures, especially of those on the Marl-borough Downs and of those running along the South Downs to Sussex where we first met with the phenomenon, and from which conceivably they could have emanated, to be incor-porated later into the Deverel-Rimbury complex.

The enclosures themselves conform to no standard pattern; some are squarish, others have curvilinear sides. They usually range from ¼ to 2 acres in extent and may have single or mul-tiple entrances. Martin Down Camp and South Lodge Camp in Cranborne Chase are the two classic examples; they were excavated by General Pitt-Rivers, who proved them to belong to the Late Bronze Age. A third was identified later on Bos-combe Down East closely associated with a complicated system of linear ditches, to be followed by five others on the Marlborough Downs where it was shown that one was earlier and another later than a small squarish field system. The egg-shaped enclosure close to Woodhenge excavated by Mrs. Cunnington probably belongs to the same class.

The area of most intensive Deverel-Rimbury activity so far studied is that of the Bourne Valley running north-eastwards from Salisbury. Both sides of this valley are scored with a com-plex system of univallate and bivallate V-shaped ditches running at more or less regular intervals down to the river and enclosing large tracts of land which have been interpreted as cattle ranches. These boundary ditches can be seen occasionally to separate areas of pasture; at other times, as on Milston Down, the ditch cuts ruthlessly through a system of fields showing that these must have reverted to pasture at an early date. In some in-stances it is evident that these ditches were used as cattle-ways separating areas of arable; one runs underneath an Early Iron Age hill-fort on Quarley Hill and so must have preceded it.

Intensification of the field system with attendant ditches in the later Early Iron Age naturally renders dating of certain of the systems hazardous, but there can be no doubt that cultivation by the plough was first introduced by the Deverel-Rimbury people. On Marleycombe Hill, for instance, three Late Bronze Age barrows were found to have been built on top of the edges of fields, whilst at Ebbesbourne Wake a hoard of six-teen contemporary bronze bangles and a bronze torque was discovered buried in a shallow hole in one of a system of small rectangular fields that had early been allowed to revert to grass.

But it was the discovery of the enclosure on Boscombe Down East, actually attached to one of these boundary ditches, that clinched the matter and suggested that these enclosures were kraals for impounding cattle from the ranches. Excavations did not disclose signs of human habitation within, though the en-circling ditch yielded much Deverel-Rimbury pottery and bones of horse, dog, pig, sheep and oxen. The appearance of a small breed of horse here and in the Martin Down enclosure shows that this animal was at last taking its place in rural economy.

The subsequent discovery of the remains of an actual farm-stead on Thorny Down, some 2½ miles to the south-west of the Boscombe Down enclosure, has added materially to our know-ledge of contemporary human settlement. Though situated on uncultivated downland, no surface indications of the remains of dwellings below were visible but for the presence of a few rabbit scrapes containing numerous identifiable potsherds. Almost total excavation of the area produced the outlines of a small compound enclosing discrete groups of post-holes in the chalk and representing some nine small dwellings of a farmer and his family. A number of the holes had been duplicated, suggesting that in process of time replacement of rotted posts had become necessary. The structures seem to have been grouped round a central rectangular-shaped house with porch, Plates 64, 65 and it was noted that the housewife had kept their interiors remarkably clean; most of the objects recovered occurred in the post-holes; probably, during periodical cleaning, rubbish had accumulated in the dark recesses and was subsequently over-looked. Cooking was carried out by roasting in holes with red-hot flints (pot-boilers), and grain, mostly wheat and barley, was ground to flour on saddle-querns. Flint scrapers and knives were still in use as in the Boscombe Down enclosure, the raw material having almost certainly been obtained from the old flint-mines on Easton Down, 2½ miles away, where a contem-porary broken pot had been found earlier. Perhaps to bring luck to the community, an old Cornish greenstone axe had been placed in one of the post-holes, whilst a somewhat similar one may have been used for the same purpose in the Boscombe Down kraal.

Spinning and weaving of wool occupied part of the atten-tion of the women of the house, who must have possessed an upright loom, as cylindrical clay loom weights were found in the principal house, similar to those found with spindle whorls in comparable sites in Sussex and in a strange pit at Swanwick in Hampshire which may have been a pitfall trap with a pointed stake at its base. The nearest source of water (apart from rain-water) was the river Bourne 2 miles away.

This picture of relatively primitive life must not, however, blind us to the fact that more developed and costly articles were now becoming available to the farmer and his wife. In this case, by some mishap the farmer's wife had broken her bronze ribbed bracelet in her inner room and left the pieces on the floor, whilst her husband had carelessly mislaid his double-looped bronze spearhead behind the house. He may even have been thoughtless enough to have laid aside and lost his valuable leaf-shaped bronze sword, for one such was subsequently found, two thousand years later, on the site of Figsbury Rings less than a mile away.

Bronze smiths and tinkers were now actively plying their wares and skill, and without doubt their visits were eagerly anticipated at these isolated farmsteads. Nevertheless, their trade seems to have been a somewhat hazardous one, otherwise we should not so frequently find their hoards buried to await their return from some extended journey. Actually few foun/ der's hoards have been recovered from the heart of Wessex; the few that have been found are confined mostly to areas of known Deverel/Rimbury occupation. Thus, one of nine socketed axes comes from Manton Down near Marlborough, and another containing six of Breton type from Nether Wallop in Hampshire. At the headwaters of the River Ebble, apparently on a trade route to Somerset and the West, three hoards of in/ terest have been found relatively close together. One large one at Donhead St. Mary contained eight winged axes of West Alpine type, three socketed axes and a bronze mould, a socketed hammer and gouge drill, a large bronze ring and bundles of wire. A small one at Ansty Hollow near Alve/ diston produced a socketed axe and some broken scraps, whilst the hoard of sixteen bronze bangles and a torque or neck ornament of northern European derivation, which we have already noted, was found along the same ancient trackway at Ebbesbourne Wake. Another hoard of a torque and bracelets was found at Lake in Wiltshire.

Plate 67

Two similar cast bronze twisted torques and a bronze looped pin found with a clay loom/weight and fragments of a globular urn from another Deverel/Rimbury settlement at Plaitford, Hampshire, have raised points of interest. It is now accepted that the production of such torques, pins and ribbed bracelets of the Thorny Down type, once they had been introduced into Britain, became a speciality of a Late Bronze Age indus/ try centred in Somerset, where they are well known in such remarkable hoards as those from Edington Burtle, Monkswood near Bath, and West Buckland amongst others. From this centre they were peddled to Dorset, Wiltshire, Hampshire and even to Sussex. Long looped pins imply adoption of the Continental method of fastening clothing; no longer were V-perforated buttons considered *de rigueur:* the 'waistcoat age', as it has been jocularly called, had ended.

The monopoly, too, of these skilled workers in bronze was now in sight, and much of their livelihood was very shortly to be snatched from them by the blacksmith. The outstanding properties of iron as a material for weapons and edge-tools, and its ready availability, had already effected a profound change in the economic life of the Continent; by 500 B.C. a slow trickle of iron objects from across the Channel presaged momentous events that were again to transform the face of Wessex and the southern counties. Technological progress had at last mastered this new and indispensable metal; the blacksmith entered the field, leaving the bronze worker's output restricted to objects other than edge-tools.

Far away in the Mediterranean, the Greeks of the Periclean Age concerned themselves with their own affairs, too remote, materially and intellectually, to cast an eye on barbarian Britain; Rome was engaged in dispute with the Sabines. Yet both these powers were, in the immediate sequel, to produce indirectly very marked changes in the economic and artistic life of Wessex, and to demonstrate once again the dependence of the north on the civilizing influences of the south. To their influence on Britain is to be added that of a third and more barbarous people, The Celts. With their arrival, at the beginning of what is archæologically the Early Iron Age, Wessex and the rest of the British Isles move into a new phase. But to round off the story of pre-Celtic Wessex, we must, in an epilogue, consider the outlines of this Celtic episode before the Roman Conquest.

CHAPTER XII

Epilogue: Celtic Wessex

ALTHOUGH SPORADIC MIGRATION to our eastern and southern shores continued throughout the Late Bronze Age, the first clear-cut evidence of intensification of folk-movements into Wessex does not become apparent until the fourth century B.C. when, perhaps as a result of population pressure and land hunger, groups of Celtic-speaking and farming communities from north-western France, their material culture a version of the Hallstatt Cultures of the Continent, settled on our coasts at such sites as Hengistbury Head at the mouth of the Hampshire Avon, and farther inland on the chalk downs. A climatic change (from the relatively dry Sub-Boreal, to the wetter Sub-Atlantic period) may have been broadly contemporary with such migration and may indeed have been a partial cause, as the chalk uplands might be regarded as now fit for more intense and concentrated tillage. In any event, we find from now onwards and until the Roman Conquest, rapid and widespread expansion of downland settlement to the point of almost complete saturation. The settlers themselves seem to have met with no obvious resistance from their Late Bronze Age relatives already in occupation and, at first, ample room must have been available for all to co-exist peacefully. No sites have yet been recognized on which continuity of occupation can be claimed, though it may be suspected in certain instances.

It would be wrong to minimize the complexity of the movements and interactions of the various groups of Early Iron Age peoples and their manifestations in the south of Britain; a whole book could well be devoted to this most fascinating and formative period of prehistory when, in the sequel, we shall meet for the first time with peoples and places whose names have actually survived historical record. No longer shall we have to rely wholly on cultural debris discarded by illiterate communities. But at first we have to depend solely on archæological evidence and to that we must revert, though only a very brief sketch can here be attempted, as epilogue to our main story.

The farmsteads of the earliest settlers have certain features in common that distinguish them sharply from those of the preceding Late Bronze Age; they are clearly dependent on radically new and more advanced forms of agricultural economy. Whilst stockbreeding and occasional hunting supplemented the fare, cereals grown on a new scale unquestionably formed the bulk of their produce. Stable conditions appear soon to have been established and, with capital invested wholly in land, much of the downland landscape must eventually have assumed the form of a patchwork of small squarish fields cultivated by the twoox plough, now mostly obliterated by later cultivation but still largely visible and traceable on aerial photographs.

The cereals grown included Emmer wheat, hulled barley, various forms of oats and chess and, amongst innovations, rye and a completely new form of wheat known as Spelt (*Triticum spelta*). The introduction of this new cereal is of considerable importance, as it goes far to explain hitherto puzzling features found in these farmsteads such as the not infrequent finds of carbonized grain associated with the remains of baking ovens and great heaps of ashes and burnt flints. Now, these deposits indicate some essential agricultural process which H. Helbaek has convincingly shown to have been connected with the threshing of Spelt. Grains of Spelt are clamped so tightly in their husks as to be impossible to thresh unless the spikelets have been first rendered fragile by baking. Occasional accidents would have caused some of the grain to become overheated and burnt.

The harvested grain had now to be stored. A selected portion for the coming year's seed was placed in reserve in ratproof granaries built on platforms held on four posts above ground, whilst the bulk for use was buried in containers below ground in deep, carefully dug storage-pits covered by some sort of lid. These storage-pits are very numerous on all farmsteads so far examined, though their contents and state of preservation do not suggest that many were in use at any one time. Not only did they attract vermin, but the damp climate and moist chalk walls favoured the growth of moulds and bacteria which soon caused them to become fouled. When this happened, clean fresh pits were immediately dug, and the old ones filled in with the freshly excavated chalk and any other domestic refuse found lying about on the farm. They were not, as was previously supposed, human dwelling-pits.

Life in these farms must have been active at all seasons of the year. The grain was ground on saddle-querns and the flour used for baking cakes and buns. Spindle-whorls, decorated bone combs and loom-weights prove that weaving of cloth had now become an essential occupation, though we know nothing of probable dyeing processes to render clothing more attractive. Besides the use of iron tools and implements, the farmer and his wife were now able to deck themselves with bronze brooches and bracelets, glass beads, and decorated armlets hand-cut from Kimmeridge shale. In the evenings they were able to amuse themselves with games employing decorated bone counters. Their furniture has not survived; but there is no reason to deny them stools, cupboards and tables, and basketry almost certainly entered into their home industries.

As at all times and in all places, pottery looms large as an index of changing peoples and traditions. And so it is that in these early farmsteads we find new wares: some of the coarser varieties have features based on Late Bronze Age traditions but include new shouldered forms derived from the Hallstatt bronze situla; others are of a very much finer kind, bowl-shaped, furrowed initially but in the later phases incised after firing, and covered with a bright red burnished hæmatite slip to imitate the colour of bronze. The inclusion of this attractive hæmatite ware, concentrated largely in Wessex northwards from the harbours of the Hampshire and Dorset coasts, must have glowed alluringly in the evening fire-light and added appreci-ably to the farm-wife's delight. Their uniformity of style and shape strongly suggests that many were made at one place and marketed over a wide area.

Our knowledge of the farm buildings in Wessex is confined to one almost completely excavated example, that of Little Woodbury about 1½ miles south of Salisbury. This farmstead with its associated storage-pits and other features was partly examined and most exhaustively interpreted by G. Bersu for the Prehistoric Society in 1938-39. Here the post-holes of a large circular wooden house, about 45 feet in diameter with entrance porch, were found towards the centre of a palisaded enclosure; but whether this was typical of contemporary buildings must for the present remain an open question. Little can be said of any form of internal partitioning; but the roof of the farmhouse was probably thatched.

Clusters of storage-pits suggestive of similar isolated farm-steads occur in great numbers especially in southern Wiltshire and over the border in Hampshire, but none has been so care-fully explored as that of Little Woodbury. All Cannings Cross near Devizes, the type-site of the culture, was the first to be recognized, and its large extent suggested the makings of a village rather than that of a single farm. The existence of larger agricultural units thus implied was confirmed in 1948-49 during levelling operations on Boscombe Down aerodrome when closely spaced pits, ditches and working hollows were found to cover an area of some 76 acres. Continuity of settle-ment was here remarkable in that it was proved to have covered some 800 years from the very beginning of the Early Iron Age right through to the end of the Romano-British

Plate 68

period. A conservative rural economy and an apparent freedom from political upheavals for the majority were here strikingly evident and indicate the underlying strength and tenacity of settlement in Wessex at the time, though no doubt inter-tribal skirmishes and cattle-raiding relieved monotony.

The conservatism of the peasants and their stubborn provincialism, with so much capital sunk in land, was in fact the keynote and strength of the Wessex Early Iron Age throughout the greater part of its history; it was almost certainly the direct cause of the diversion of aggressive raiders to other parts of Britain about 250 B.C. A war-scare from across the Channel suddenly threatened our southern coasts and, no doubt with a frenzy that all can understand, the farmsteads were strengthened by digging deep defensive ditches around them, as at Little Woodbury, whilst, by concerted action, massive earthen hill-forts were constructed on numerous commanding hill-tops. The great contour hill-forts of Wessex are indeed one of its grandest and most impressive features, and it is now generally agreed that the majority of the simpler univallate type, such as those of Quarley Hill, Figsbury Rings and the earlier phases of Maiden Castle and Yarnbury Castle, were built at this time as temporary camps of refuge rather than as permanent living quarters, though occupation has been attested in some. Resistance on such a scale proved effective and the scare seems to have rapidly subsided, as some of the forts were left unfinished as that on Ladle Hill in Hampshire; so was the defensive ditch surrounding Little Woodbury. Plates 69, 70

This attempted invasion of our southern coasts is likely to have been caused by an eruption of bands of warlike Celtic chieftains living in the Marne region. Their panoply of war, including war chariots, was now more elaborate and we know that they were also active patrons of new forms of Celtic art. The old Hallstatt Culture had gradually given place to that of La Tène, a brilliant Celtic culture that had arisen north of the Alps as a direct result of barbarian commercial contacts down the Rhône with the prosperous and well-established Greek colony at Massilia (Marseilles) and with the Etruscans of Italy, tempered perhaps with other contributions from such sources as the Scythians of eastern Europe. In return for nume-rous products from the North, including tin and slaves, these civilized Mediterranean centres were now flooding Gaul with a host of new articles; jars of wine, metal table services and other desirable objects appealing to barbarian fancy. And many of these were highly decorated in conventionalized classical style. Celtic artist-craftsmen, quick to appreciate the potentialities of new designs and styles, were not content to copy them slavishly. Their genius lay in other directions; artistry in their hands, especially in metal-work, became transformed and transmuted to heights that have rarely if ever been equalled and which was later to flower so conspicuously in other parts of the British Isles.

Thus well equipped and ripe for trouble, these chieftains from the Marne sought adventure across the Channel. Tem-porary lodgment was apparently effected on Hengistbury Head, but the main weight of invasion was concentrated in Sussex and in east Yorkshire. In the latter region the tribal name of the Parisi betokens their place of origin, and there they implanted the first seeds of Celtic art which inspired the exquisite metal-work with its abstract motifs that was to have so far-reaching an effect in these islands in subsequent years.

The Wessex peasantry for their part appear to have settled down to two further centuries of relative and uninspired peace, content to continue their humdrum farming activities and to absorb by slow infiltration minor cultural traits, mainly ceramic, from the surrounding districts but not, as pointed out by Sir Mortimer Wheeler, embracing tangible exports or im-ports. One might say that these dull, unenterprising peasant communities, in seeking security, and with a misplaced conception of freedom, unconsciously diverted the seeds of a higher culture from their doors: they made Wessex, however, the granary of Iron Age Britain and by so doing enabled the Roman Province to establish its civil settlement on a firm agricultural basis.

For, on both the western and eastern boundaries of Wessex, events were shaping that foreshadowed foreign domination. Certainly from the beginning of the second century B.C. and probably earlier, the tin trade between Cornwall and Brittany, for ultimate passage down the Loire or Garonne to the Massi-liot Greek merchants, was passing through the hands of the Veneti, a powerful seafaring Gaulish tribe occupying north-western France. The close relations thereby established, not unmixed with tribal skirmishes and successful endeavours on the part of the Veneti to gain a firmer foothold in Cornwall, inevitably resulted in cultural interchange. New methods of defence invariably accompany new weapons of offence, and the Veneti were noted and skilled users of the sling, a more deadly long-range weapon than the spear. Safety from its pene-trating power could be obtained only by increasing the distance between combatants, and this was accomplished by the deve-lopment in Brittany of new forms of fortification distinguished by the possession of multiple ramparts. Complex forts and cliff-castles based on these prototypes now appear in Cornwall and gradually spread, with probable Venetic settlement, in-land and up the coasts of the Severn where we find great stone-girt multivallate forts such as those of Worlebury above Weston-super-Mare enclosing 10½ acres, and Dolebury on the Mendips (22½ acres).

It is now generally agreed that the year 56 B.C. marks an important turning-point in the fortunes of Wessex. History records that it was during this year that Julius Cæsar inflicted his resounding defeat of the Veneti of Brittany both on sea and land and that, to teach the Gauls a lesson, all who had not perished were sold into slavery. Now this event has been very plausibly equated by Wheeler with the sudden appearance on our Dorset and Hampshire coasts of refugees and fugitive chieftains who had survived the disaster and who had, in their hour of need, appealed to their relatives in Britain for help. On Hengistbury Head we find the remains of their domestic ware; an iron anchor and chain probably of similar origin was found in Bulbury Camp near Poole Harbour. But these immigrants are best represented at Maiden Castle in Dorset, already in-habited by Wessex peasantry within a small univallate fortress, there to make it their tribal home and headquarters. Wheeler's extensive and illuminating excavations have shown that it was very probably at this time that the fortress assumed its present revolutionary shape in the hands of a master-mind, necessita-ting total remodelling on a colossal scale and embodying stupendous multiple ramparts and outworks designed to keep the defenders out of effective sling-range. Large hoards of up to 22,260 sling-stones were in fact found during excavations at strategic points within the defences.

The sudden introduction into Wessex of this new form of de-fensive military architecture, closely linked with the appearance of bead-rim pots, simulating metal prototypes, countersunk handles and rotary querns, may be taken to imply the intrusion of a military minority of Breton origin sufficiently strong to achieve effective political domination and to secure a major labour force for the construction of defensive works. Their dominion or overlordship seems finally to have embraced a very large part of Wessex, by which time the tribe had become known as the Durotriges; it had considerable political control and its own coinage based on that of Gaul.

Plate 71

We now find old forts being reconstructed and new ones being built on the multivallate principle. We have only to re-call such well-known forts as those of Badbury Rings, Hod Hill, Hambledon Hill, Yarnbury Castle, Battlesbury Camp,

Danebury and Sidbury Hill amongst others, to appreciate the Plate 70 insecurity and tenseness of these troublous times. Though few have been excavated, we may nevertheless be justified in ascribing all to this late period. Hambledon Hill is of special interest, as it is still possible to see the remains of house platforms within its inner ramparts.

The necessity for building so many forts on such a scale is now considered to have been connected with new dangers that threatened the eastern boundaries of Wessex. By 50 B.C. much more formidable invaders, the Belgæ, from northern Gaul, had conquered south-eastern Britain and their sway extended westwards through Hampshire practically to the River Test. The line of multivallate defence works, including Danebury and Bury Hill, up this valley and northwards, has been interpreted by Professor Hawkes as a barrier of frontier forts built by Wessex sub-tribes to keep at bay these invaders under Commius, a prince of the Atrebates. For a time they proved availing, but slowly the advance westwards continued until, by about A.D. 10-25, the greater part of Wiltshire, Hampshire and possibly parts of Dorset had been occupied by these new masters. Belgic wheel-turned pottery and imported Gallo-Belgic wares now become superimposed on the cruder wares of the natives who, at Boscombe Down, Rotherley and Wood-cuts, amongst other places, continued to pursue their old rural occupations and seem to have accepted the position in preference to eviction. But other farmsteads, as that of Little Woodbury, had already been abandoned.

We must not forget to notice, however, one small enclave of people of outstanding interest who had by 50 B.C. or a little earlier settled amongst the inhospitable marshes and lakes of Somerset on artificially made islands or crannogs, no doubt for security. The lake-dwellings at Glastonbury and Meare have been for more than 50 years systematically examined by A. Bulleid and H. St. G. Gray and have thereby become famous for the very complete picture of contemporary life thus obtained and so fortunately preserved in wet, peaty soil. That at Glaston-bury is the more complete. Within a palisaded enclosure of just over 2 acres the whole surface of the peat had been covered by a platform of logs and brushwood on which were built some eighty-nine circular buildings with artificially laid clay floors. As these floors sank, new layers of clay were added; in one dwelling ten superimposed floors with baked clay hearths were encountered. A specially made causeway led from the village to drier ground for wheeled traffic, while dug-out canoes were available for water transport and fowling. The finds in so favourable a situation were exceptionally rich and included numerous skilfully made and decorated tools, weapons, recep-tacles and ornaments of bronze, tin, lead, iron, wood, bone, glass, jet and Kimmeridge shale. Industries included weaving,

Fig. 22

potting and metal-working, and gambling with dice appears to have been a favourite pastime. Milling was carried out with rotary querns. The whole culture in fact represents a society of artist-craftsmen engaged in trade, including the use of Dobun-nic iron currency-bars, and living a very much more elevated and richer life than that of the downland farmers with whom there seems to have been little or no contact except possibly southwards to Dorset and Maiden Castle.

The clue to the origin of this small group of people, who also at times inhabited the Mendip caves and the hill-fort of Worle-bury, almost certainly lies in the great quantities of sling-stones at their disposal and their highly ornamented, attractively incised La Tène pottery which is paralleled in Brittany. It is reasonable to assume that we have here a small group of settlers founded on the old Cornish-Breton tin trade—possibly Strabo's Venetic emporium—and later augmented considerably by Venetic refugee families who had managed to escape the wrath of Cæsar. But their escape was short-lived. Being less acquies-cent towards new masters, their end came in massacre, as at

Worlebury, and this is more likely to have been due to conflict
with the Belgæ than with the Roman legionaries.

The Belgic state and its sphere of influence had long been a
thorn in the flesh of the Romans and so, with the death of King
Cunobelin, the chance was seized by the Emperor Claudius in
A.D. 43 to subdue for ever these unruly barbarians. Having con-

Fig. 22 Decorated pots from Glastonbury, Somerset. Height of smaller pot 4¼ in., larger pot 8¼ in.

quered and consolidated their position in the south-east, the
Second Augustan Legion under the future Emperor Vespa-
sian struck west demolishing in their advance, amongst other
pockets of resistance, the singly ditched Belgic enclosure at
Bury Hill and the doubly entrenched plateau-fort on Boscombe
Down West. The final active defence of the Durotrigian capital
and stronghold at Maiden Castle, with its hurriedly but carefully dug war cemetery at its gates, has been graphically described by Wheeler. This is no place to discuss subsequent

events, except to recall that the Romanization of the downland farmsteads and villages must have followed rapidly. Their gleaming fields of corn must soon have attracted the attention of the Roman invaders. As far as we can judge at present, Salisbury Plain and Cranborne Chase were turned, without interruption, into Imperial Estates with administrative head, quarters possibly at Sorviodunum (Old Sarum) and Badbury Rings for the main purpose of feeding the army of occupation.

Native deities would have continued to be worshipped, even if assimilated to Roman types, and on the hill,side at Cerne Abbas in Dorset there still survives one of the most remarkable representations of a pagan god north of the Alps—a huge figure
Plate 72 of a phallic, club,bearing giant, over 200 feet high and cut into the turf,covered chalk of the steeply,sloping hill. While the conventions of the figure suggest Roman provincial art, and an assimilation to the Hercules type, it must nevertheless represent a local cult,centre of native origin.

Here we must leave Wessex, brooding on its apparent mis, fortunes and stubbornly conserving its strength—a Wessex still unsuspecting a later act of Imperial administration that was to turn its rich farmlands into sheep,walks, unaware of the disastrous Saxon invasions in store, and of its final and glorious rebirth under Alfred the Great which was destined to turn Wessex pre,history into English history.

Bibliography

GENERAL WORKS

DOBSON, D. P. *The Archaeology of Somerset* (1931).
HELBAEK, H. Early Crops in Southern England. *Proc. Prehist. Soc.,*
XVIII (1952), 194.
PEAKE, H. J. E. *The Archaeology of Berkshire* (1931).
PIGGOTT, S. Archaeology in Wessex, I–III. *Arch. News Letter,* IV
(1951–2), 33, 65, 113.
PIGGOTT, S. AND HAWKES, C. F. C. *Victoria County History of Wilt-shire,* Vol. I, Part I (forthcoming).
TRATMAN, E. K. The Prehistoric Archaeology of the Bristol Region.
Chap. IX of *Bristol and its Adjoining Counties* (1955).

CHAPTER I

RANKINE, W. F. Stone 'Maceheads' with Mesolithic associations in S.E.
England. *Proc. Prehist. Soc.,* XV (1949), 70.
RANKINE, W. F. Mesolithic Research in Southern England. *Arch.
News Letter,* V (1954), 37.
RANKINE, W. F. Mesolithic Finds in Wiltshire. *Wilts. Arch. Mag.,*
LVI (1955), 149.
SUMMERS, P. G. A Mesolithic Site near Iwerne Minster, Dorset. *Proc.
Prehist. Soc.,* VII (1941), 145.

CHAPTERS II–V

PIGGOTT, S. *The Neolithic Cultures of the British Isles* (1954), with full
bibliography.
PIGGOTT, S. Windmill Hill—East or West? *Proc. Prehist. Soc.,* XXI
(1955), 96.
STONE, J. F. S. AND WALLIS, F. S. Third Report of the Sub-Committee . . . on the Petrological Examination of Stone Axes. *Proc.
Prehist. Soc.,* XVII (1951), 99.

149

CHAPTER VI

CALKIN, J. B. The Bournemouth Area in Neolithic and Early Bronze Age Times. *Proc. Dorset N.H. and Arch. Soc.,* LXXIII (1951), 32.

PIGGOTT, S. AND C. M. Excavation of Barrows on Crichel and Launceston Downs, Dorset. *Arch.,* XC (1944), 47.

PIGGOTT, S. A Trepanned Skull of the Beaker Period from Dorset . . . *Proc. Prehist Soc.,* VI (1940), 112.

PIGGOTT, S. AND C. M. The Excavation of a Barrow on Rockbourne Down, Hants. *Proc. Hants F.C. and Arch. Soc.,* XVI (1946), 156.

PIGGOTT, C. M. Excavation of Fifteen Barrows in the New Forest . . . *Proc. Prehist. Soc.,* IX (1943), 1.

STEVENS, F. AND STONE, J. F. S. The Barrows of Winterslow. *Wilts. Arch. Mag.,* XLVIII (1938), 174.

STONE, J. F. S. A Settlement Site of the Beaker Period on Easton Down . . . *Wilts. Arch. Mag.,* XLV (1931), 366.

STONE, J. F. S. A Case of Bronze Age Cephalotaphy on Easton Down. *Man,* 1934, No. 51.

STONE, J. F. S. An Early Bronze Age Grave in Fargo Plantation . . . *Wilts. Arch. Mag.,* XLVIII (1938), 357.

STONE, J. F. S., AND HILL, N. G. A Round Barrow on Stockbridge Down, Hampshire. *Ant. Journ.,* XX (1940), 39.

WILLIAMS, A. Bronze Age Barrows on Charmy Down and Lansdown. Somerset. *Ant. Journ.,* XXX (1950), 34.

CHAPTERS VII AND VIII

ATKINSON, R. J. C. *et al. Excavations at Dorchester, Oxon: First Report* (1951), Chap. VIII, with full bibliography.

ATKINSON, R. J. C. *Stonehenge* (1956).

CUNNINGTON, M. E. The 'Sanctuary' on Overton Hill, near Avebury. *Wilts. Arch. Mag.,* XLV (1931), 300.

CUNNINGTON, M. E. *Woodhenge* (1929).

STONE, J. F. S., PIGGOTT, S. AND BOOTH, A. ST. J. Durrington Walls, Wiltshire . . . *Ant. Journ.,* XXXIV (1954), 155.

TAYLOR, C., AND TRATMAN, E. K. The Priddy Circles. *Proc. Univ. Bristol Speaeo Soc.,* VII (1957), 7.

Bibliography

CHAPTERS IX AND X

APSIMON, A. M. Dagger Graves of the 'Wessex' Early Bronze Age. *Univ. Lond. Inst. Arch. Ann. Report*, X (1954), 37.
ATKINSON, R. J. C. *et al.* A Pond Barrow at Winterbourne Steepleton, Dorset. *Arch. Journ.*, XVIII (1952), 1.
DE NAVARRO, J. M. The British Isles and the Beginning of the Northern Bronze Age. *Early Cultures of N.W. Europe* (1950), Chap. V.
PIGGOTT, S. The Early Bronze Age in Wessex. *Proc. Prehist. Soc.*, IV (1938), 52.
PIGGOTT, S. AND C. M. Excavations on Ram's Hill, Berks. *Ant. Journ.*, XX (1940), 467.
STONE, J. F. S. AND THOMAS, L. C. The Use and Distribution of Faience in the Ancient East and Prehistoric Europe. *Proc. Prehist. Soc.*, XXII (1956), 37.
STONE, J. F. S. A Middle Bronze Age Urnfield on Easton Down, Winterslow. *Wilts. Arch. Mag.*, XLVI (1933), 218.

CHAPTER XI

HAWKES, C. F. C., AND PRESTON, J. P. Three Bronze Age Barrows on the Cloven Way. *Ant. Journ.*, XII (1933), 414.
HAWKES, C. F. C. The Deverel Urn and the Picardy Pin. *Proc. Prehist. Soc.*, VIII (1942), 26.
HAWKES, C. F. C. Excavations at Quarley Hill, 1938. *Proc. Hants F.C. and Arch. Soc.*, XIV (1939), 136.
PIGGOTT, C. M. A Middle Bronze Age Barrow and Deverel-Rimbury Urnfield at Latch Farm . . . *Proc. Prehist. Soc.*, IV (1938), 169.
PIGGOTT, C. M. Five Late Bronze Age Enclosures in North Wiltshire. *Proc. Prehist. Soc.*, VIII (1942), 48.
SHORTT, H. DE S. A Hoard of Bangles from Ebbesbourne Wake . . . *Wilts. Arch. Mag.*, LIII (1949), 104.

CHAPTER XII

BERSU, G. Excavations at Little Woodbury, Wiltshire (Part I). *Proc. Prehist. Soc.*, VI (1940), 30.
BRAILSFORD, J., Excavations at Little Woodbury, Wiltshire (Parts II–V). *Proc. Prehist. Soc.*, XIV (1948); *ibid* XV (1949), 156.

CHAPTER XII—*continued*

CUNNINGTON, M. E. *All Cannings Cross* (1923).
HAWKES, C. F. C. Hill-Forts. *Ant.*, V (1931), 60.
HAWKES, C. F. C. Britons, Romans and Saxons round Salisbury and in Cranborne Chase. *Arch. Journ.*, CIV (1947), 27.
WHEELER, R. E. M. *Maiden Castle, Dorset*, 1943.

SOURCES OF ILLUSTRATIONS

The line illustrations and maps are either original drawings, or re-drawn from published illustrations by the author, except for Figs. 10, 11, 12, 17, which are the work of Mrs. C. D. Fergusson of the School of Scottish Studies, University of Edinburgh.

The photographs for the plates are by Malcolm Murray, Department of Prehistoric Archæology, University of Edinburgh, except for the following: Aerofilms, Plate 32; British Museum, Plates 34, 52, 55, 56; Crown Copyright, Plates 26, 37, 69, 70, 72; E. Cecil Curwen, Plate 51; Dorchester Museum, Plates 43, 44, 45, 46; Alexander Keiller, Plates 1, 2, 3, 4; Newbury Museum, Plates 21, 22; Salisbury Museum, Plate 71; Edwin Smith, Plate 29; *Southern Journal*, Plate 30; J. F. S. Stone, Plates 5, 9, 12, 20, 23, 27, 28, 31, 33, 35, 36, 58, 59.

1

2

3

4

5

6

7

8

9

10

11

12

13

14

15

17

16

18

19

20

21

22

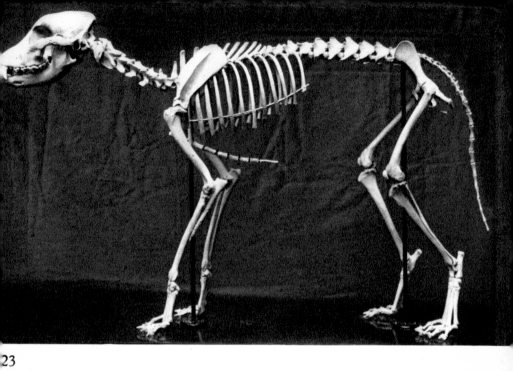

23

24

25

26

27

28

30

31

34

35

36

37

38

39

40

41

43

44

45

46

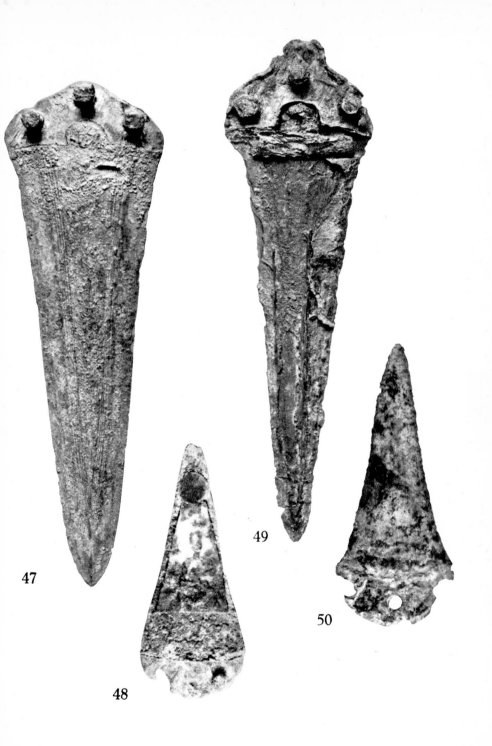

47

48

49

50

51

52

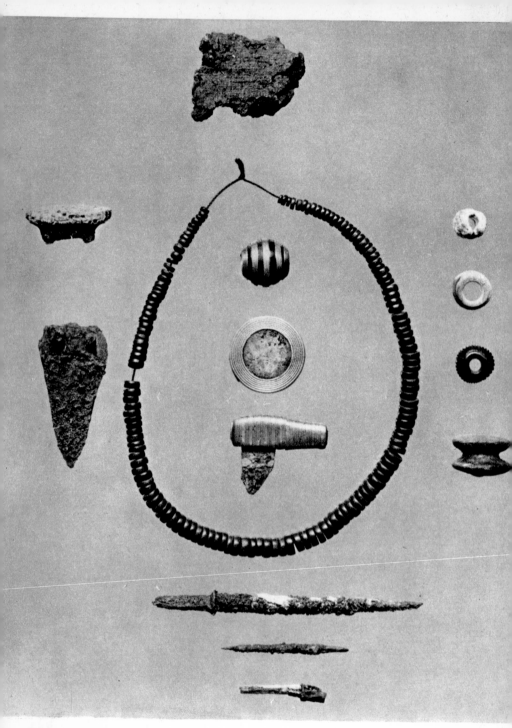

55

56

58

59

60

61

62

63

64

65

66

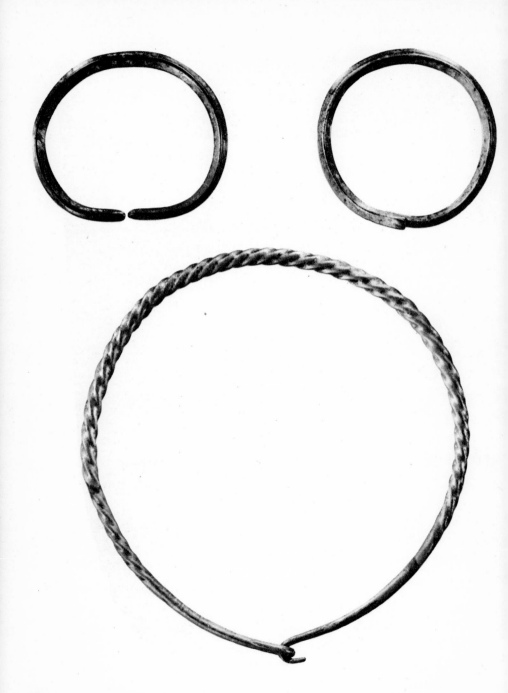

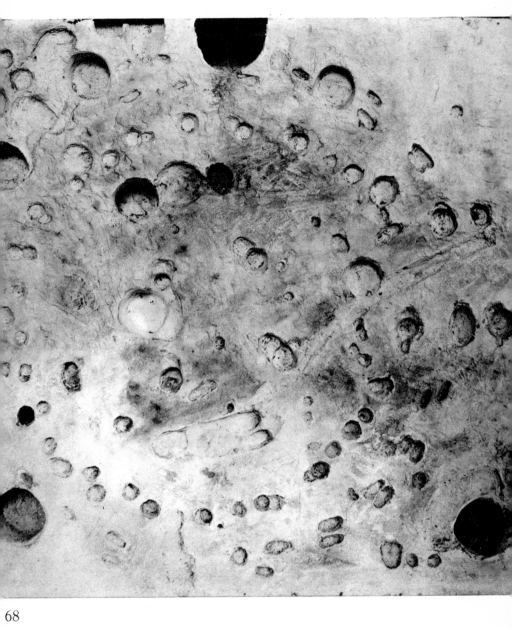

68

69

70

Notes on the Plates

1–4 Four bowls of Neolithic pottery from the lower levels of the ditches at Windmill Hill. No. 1 is 6 in. diameter at the mouth. Avebury Museum.

5 View of the East Kennet Long Barrow, from the north.

6 View of the frontal façade of the West Kennet Long Barrow after excavation and reconstruction, 1956, looking north towards Silbury Hill in the background.

7 View inside the passage of the West Kennet Long Barrow, after excavation, 1956, looking west into the terminal burial chamber.

8 Primary burials in the south-west chamber of the West Kennet Long Barrow, 1955.

9 View of the flint-mine shaft on Easton Down during excavation, 1930.

10 Axe-blade of polished jadeite from Breamore, Hants. 8 in. long. Devizes Museum.

11 Vessel of Rinyo-Clacton ware, from the settlement site adjacent to Durrington Walls, Wilts. Height $5\frac{1}{2}$ in. Salisbury Museum.

12 Axe-hammer or battle-axe with shaft-hole, made of stone from the Prescelly Mountains, Pembrokeshire, found at Fifield Bavant, Wilts. Length 9 in. Private collection (cast in Salisbury Museum).

13 Objects with burials under a round barrow at Upton Lovel, Wilts. Above are bone points and a graduated series of bone objects probably serving as a collar or fringe to a garment; below are stone objects including (centre) a grooved shaft-smoother and (right) a stone battle-axe. The largest bone object in the collar is $7\frac{1}{2}$ in. long. Devizes Museum.

K

14 Bell-beaker found inverted and almost intact in the uppermost layers of the filling of the north-west chamber in the West Kennet Long Barrow. Height 7½ in. Devizes Museum.

15 Bell-beaker from an inhumation grave at Normanton, Wilts. Height 7¼ in. Devizes Museum.

16 Necked Beaker from grave at Durrington, Wilts. Height 7½ in. Devizes Museum.

17 Gold disc from Early Bronze Age grave at Monkton Farleigh, Wilts. 1¾ in. diameter. Private collection (electrotype in Devizes Museum).

18 Gold disc from a Bell-Beaker grave at Mere, Wilts. 1½ in. diameter. Devizes Museum.

19 Early Bronze Age head-burial, with lower jaw detached and a flaked flint bar leaning against the skull, as reconstructed in Salisbury Museum, from Easton Down, Wilts.

20 Trepanned skull, with roundel removed from the skull, found in a Bell-beaker grave on Crichel Down, Dorset, photographed immediately after finding, 1938. Museum of the Royal College of Surgeons.

21 Four-footed pottery bowl found in a sand-pit together with the Bell-Beaker, no. 22, at Inkpen, Berks. Height 6¾ in. Newbury Museum.

22 Bell-beaker found with the four-footed bowl, no. 21, at Inkpen, Berks. Height 10¼ in. Newbury Museum.

23 Complete skeleton of dog, from the Early Bronze Age settlement-site on Easton Down, Wilts. Height at shoulder 15 in. Salisbury Museum.

24 Necked Beaker found with the food vessel no. 25 in a grave in Fargo Plantation, Wilts. Height 6 in. Salisbury Museum.

25 Food vessel found with the Necked Beaker no. 24 in the Fargo Plantation grave. Height 5 in. Salisbury Museum.

26 Oblique air view of Stonehenge from the south-west, showing the ditch and bank, the Aubrey Holes (white spots) and the central stone structures. The Heel Stone stands outside, by the road.

27 View looking southwards down the line of the West Kennet Avenue, Avebury, showing stones standing and re-erected, and sites of missing stones marked by concrete blocks.

28 The entrance stones of the Great Circle, Avebury, with the bank of the earthwork behind, looking south.

29 View of the stone structures of Stonehenge, looking south from the Outer Circle towards the bluestone Horseshoe and the Trilithons.

30 Dragging a replica bluestone on a sledge at Stonehenge, 1954.

31 Excavations on the line of the bluestone circle of Stonehenge, 1954, showing standing and fallen bluestones, and the stumps and sockets of others in the excavated area. The stone in the foreground is one of the two re-used bluestone lintels (no. 150).

32 Oblique air view of the Avebury circles from the north-west, showing the bank and ditch, the standing stones of the circles, and the modern village within the monument.

33 Carvings of a hafted dagger and two axe-blades (to right and bottom left) on Stone 53 of the sarsen trilithons at Stonehenge. The dagger is 12 in. in length.

34 Carvings of hafted daggers, flat axe-blades and cup-marks, on a sandstone slab from the Badbury Barrow, Dorset. The larger dagger is 12 in. in length. British Museum.

35 Underside of the bluestone lintel no. 36 at Stonehenge, showing mortise-holes visible during temporary excavation and lifting, 1954.

36 View in the inner area at Stonehenge, showing bluestone uprights of the Horseshoe setting, that on the left with a groove worked on its edge, and Trilithons in the background.

37 Oblique air view of a Disc Barrow completely excavated on Snail Down, Wilts., 1953. The regularly cut circular ditch is seen enclosing pits which held burials.

38 Wessex Culture cup of Manton type, with knobbed surface and perforations between the knobs, from a grave at Normanton, Wilts. $2\frac{1}{4}$ in. high. Devizes Museum.

39 Wessex Culture cup of Aldbourne type, with incised and punctuated ornament, from a grave on Oakley Down, Dorset. $1\frac{3}{4}$ in. high. Devizes Museum.

40 Wessex Culture cup with 'slashed' sides and cord-impressed decoration, from a grave at Normanton, Wilts. $1\frac{3}{4}$ in. high. Devizes Museum.

41 Equipment from a Wessex Culture warrior's grave, Bush Barrow, Normanton, Wilts., comprising two bronze dagger-blades, a bronze axe-head, and a mace or sceptre with polished stone head and shaft (reconstructed) inlaid with zigzag bone mounts. In the grave were also found the gold objects in Plate 42. Length of larger dagger, $14\frac{1}{2}$ in. Devizes Museum.

42 Gold objects from the same burial as the objects in Plate 41, from Bush Barrow, Normanton, Wilts. The upper object is the gold plating of a belt-hook, and the large gold plate, $8\frac{1}{2}$ in. across, lay on the man's chest, presumably sewn to a garment or corselet, and the smaller plate was probably similarly mounted. British Museum (electrotypes in Devizes Museum).

43 Head of mace or sceptre of polished jet or shale with inlaid gold studs, from a Wessex Culture grave in the Clandon Barrow, Dorset. Width 3 in. Also in the grave were other objects including an amber cup and the gold plate, Plate 44. Dorchester Museum.

44 Gold plate from the same Wessex Culture grave in the Clandon Barrow, Dorset, as the mace-head, Plate 43. The plate is 6 in. across, and like that from Bush Barrow (Plate 42) was probably sewn on a garment. Dorchester Museum.

45 Bronze axe-blade from a Wessex Culture burial in Barrow 7 on the Ridgeway, Dorset, with remains of finely woven woollen cloth on it, in which it had been wrapped. Length 3½ in. In the same grave were found bronze dagger-blades and the gold pommel-mount, Plate 46. Dorchester Museum.

46 Gold pommel-mount for a dagger, from a Wessex Culture burial in Barrow 7 on the Ridgeway, Dorset. Width 2 in. Found with bronze dagger-blades and the axe, Plate 45. Dorchester Museum.

47, 48 Bronze dagger-blade and knife-blade from a Wessex Culture burial at Winterbourne Stoke, Wilts. Length of dagger, 8½ in. Devizes Museum.

49, 50 Bronze dagger-blade and knife-blade from a Wessex Culture burial at Normanton, Wilts. Length of dagger, 8¾ in. Devizes Museum.

51 Amber cup from a Wessex Culture burial at Hove, Sussex. The cup is 3½ in. diameter, and was found in a hollowed tree-trunk coffin with a bronze dagger and stone battle-axe. Brighton Museum.

52 Gold cup from a Wessex Culture burial at Rillaton, Cornwall. The cup is 3½ in. high, and the handle fastened by rivets. British Museum.

53 Two cups of shale, from Wessex Culture burials probably in the Ames-bury region of Wiltshire, 3½ and 3¾ in. high. Salisbury Museum.

54 Objects from a woman's grave of the Wessex Culture at Manton, Wilts. Above is a fragment of textile, and below three bronze awls; on the left a bronze knife-blade with a bone pommel, on the right, shale and stone beads. A string of shale disc-beads encircles a shale bead with gold inlaid bands, an amber disc in a gold mounting, and a pendant in the

form of a miniature halberd with gold-plated shaft and bronze blade. The knife-blade on the left is 1¼ in. long. Devizes Museum.

55 Amber beads and spacing-plates of a crescentic necklace from a Wessex Culture grave at Lake, Wilts. The largest spacing-plate is 3 in. across. British Museum.

56 Gold plate from a Wessex Culture burial at Upton Lovel, Wilts., 6 in. wide. British Museum (electrotype in Devizes Museum).

57 Objects from a woman's grave of the Wessex Culture at Normanton, Wilts. Above are pendants of amber, and centrally a large conical shale button with its gold casing (in two parts), and a gold object with criss-cross decoration. Below are two amber discs mounted in gold, as in the Manton burial (Plate 54), and a pendant in the form of a miniature halberd, made of amber with gold mounts, and a bronze blade, again similar to that from Manton. At the bottom is a gold-plated bronze pendant representing a miniature neck-ornament. The gold-mounted shale button is 1½ in. diameter. Devizes Museum.

58, 59 A cremated burial of the Wessex Culture at Stockbridge, Hants., as excavated. The upper photograph shows the inverted cinerary urn, and below, the cremated bones immediately on lifting the urn, with (in circle) a blue segmented faience bead. British Museum.

60 Reconstructed necklace from a Wessex Culture grave at Upton Lovel, Wilts., with beads of amber, shale and blue faience, of segmented and quoit forms. The quoit beads are ¾ in. across. Devizes Museum.

61 Middle Bronze Age cinerary urn from Bulford, Wilts. Height 13 in. Salisbury Museum.

62 Middle Bronze Age cinerary urn from Amesbury, Wilts. Height 12 in. Salisbury Museum.

63 Wessex Culture urn from Normanton, Wilts., found with an inhumation burial and ornaments of gold and amber. Height 8 in. Devizes Museum.

64, 65 Domestic vessels of the Late Bronze Age, from the settlement on Thorny Down, Wilts., $5\frac{1}{4}$ and $8\frac{3}{4}$ in. high. Salisbury Museum.

66 Late Bronze Age cinerary urn from a barrow near Stonehenge, $22\frac{3}{4}$ in. high. Devizes Museum.

67 Bronze twisted torc or neck-ornament, and bronze armlets of the Late Bronze Age, from Lake, Wilts. The torc is $5\frac{1}{4}$ in. diameter inside. Salisbury Museum.

68 Vertical view of a scale model of the excavated site of an Early Iron Age circular house and storage-pits at Little Woodbury, Wilts. The larger holes are pits for corn-storage (about 6 feet across), the smaller represent post-holes for the structure of a circular house some 40 feet across. Salisbury Museum.

69 Vertical air-photograph of the Early Iron Age hill-fort of Figsbury Rings, Wilts. The inner enclosure is a quarry-ditch used to heighten the main rampart in a secondary phase. The fort is 1050 ft. over-all.

70 Vertical air-photograph of the Early Iron Age hill-fort of Yarnbury Castle, Wilts. The main earthworks consist of multiple ramparts, some 1500 ft. over-all, with elaborate entrance outworks at the top right-hand corner, and a later enclosure at the bottom left. Inside the main defences can be seen faint traces of an earlier Iron Age earthwork, about 750 ft. across, and the grid pattern of the comparatively recent pens for the sheep fair held on the site.

71 Iron Age coinage (staters) of the tribe of the Durotriges. The top coin (two sides) is of gold, from the Chute hoard; the centre coin is silver, from Hanging Langford Camp, Wilts., the lower a bronze coin from Teffont Evias Quarry, Wilts. All $1\frac{1}{2}$ times actual size.

72 Oblique air view of the turf-cut figure known as the Giant of Cerne, Dorset. The outline of this figure of a club-bearing giant is cut down to the solid chalk, and is probably a representation of a native god in the period of the Roman Occupation. Above the giant can be seen a small earthwork enclosure, of unknown date.

Index

Abercromby, Lord, 61

Ægean civilization, contacts with, 115

Agriculture: European and Near Eastern cultures (Neolithic), 18; advent in Britain, 19–20; Neolithic, 26; Late Bronze Age, 129; Deverel-Rimbury Culture, 132–3; Early Iron Age, 138–9; farm buildings of Early Iron Age, 140

Amber ware, Early Bronze Age, 113–14

Ansty Hollow, Deverel-Rimbury axe from, 135

Antler combs, Neolithic, 23

Armsley, Hants., Lower Halstow forest culture site, 16

Arreton Down, Isle of Wight, Early Bronze Age spear-heads from, 111–12

Atkinson, R. J. C., 35, 76, 77, 96, 98

Atrebates, the, 145

Aubrey, John, 78, 84

Avebury, Wilts., 36, 76, 83–90

Axe-blades, Early Bronze Age, 112–13

Axes: of igneous rocks (Neolithic), 27, 43, 46–50; distribution, 44–50; Cult of the Double Axe (Minoan), 49–50; Dorchester Culture, 58–9; Early Bronze Age, 111; flanged, 122; Deverel-Rimbury Culture, 135

Balstone Down, Cornwall, Neolithic axes from, 46

Barley cultivation, Neolithic, 26

Barrows. *See* Long barrow; Pond barrows; Round barrows

Bath, Lower Halstow forest culture site, 16

Battle-axes: of Beaker-Folk, 68, 69–70; Early Bronze Age, 111, 115

Beaker-Folk, 60–3; their Bell-Beakers, 63–7; practice of trepanning, 64–5; their Necked Beakers, 67–73

Beaulieu, Hants., Lower Halstow forest culture site, 16

Belgæ, conquer south-eastern Britain, 145–7

'Bell-Barrow of Chalk', Winterslow, 126

Bell-Beakers, 63–7

Bersu, G., 140

Blackdown Hills, Somerset, Lower Halstow forest culture site, 17

Bokerly Down, long barrow on, 37

Boscombe Down, Early Iron Age agriculture on, 140

Boscombe Down East, Hants.: Beaker-Folk dwelling-pit at, 66; Deverel-Rimbury enclosures at, 132

Bournemouth, Neolithic axes from, 46, 48

Bowl's Barrow, 31

Brean Down, Beaker ware from, 83

Bridlington, Yorks., Neolithic axes from, 47

Bulbury Camp, Dorset, Gaulish remains at, 144

Bulleid, A., 145

Bunter Pebble Beds, 17

Burials, of Beaker-Folk, 62–4

DATE DUE

CORRECTIONS:
PROBLEMS AND PROSPECTS

CORRECTIONS:
PROBLEMS AND PROSPECTS

Edited by

David M. Petersen
Georgia State University

Charles W. Thomas
College of William and Mary

PRENTICE-HALL, INC., ENGLEWOOD CLIFFS, NEW JERSEY

Library of Congress Cataloging in Publication Data

Petersen, David M   comp.
   Corrections: problems and prospects.

   (Prentice-Hall series in law enforcement)
   Includes bibliographical references.
   1. Corrections—United States—Addresses, essays,
lectures. 2. Prisons—United States—Addresses,
essays, lectures. I. Thomas, Charles W., 1940-
joint comp. II. Title.
HV9304.P4   365'.973   74-7369
ISBN 0-13-178293-2

© 1975 PRENTICE-HALL, INC., Englewood Cliffs, New Jersey

Prentice-Hall Series in Law Enforcement
James D. Stinchcomb, Editor

Printed in the United States of America

10 9 8 7 6 5 4 3 2 1

Prentice-Hall International, Inc., *London*
Prentice-Hall of Australia, Pty. Ltd., *Sydney*
Prentice-Hall of Canada, Ltd., *Toronto*
Prentice-Hall of India Private Limited, *New Delhi*
Prentice-Hall of Japan, Inc., *Tokyo*

CONTENTS

v

PART II

CONFINEMENT, INMATES

AND PRISON PROBLEMS

PART III

TREATMENT IN INSTITUTIONS

AND THE COMMUNITY 175 - 27.

PART IV

FUTURE DIRECTIONS

FOR CORRECTIONS

277

CORRECTIONS:
PROBLEMS AND PROSPECTS

Introduction

During the past several years we have witnessed a dramatic increase in the extent to which the American public has become concerned with the numerous facets of crime and its correction. The political dimensions of the emotionally charged "crime in the streets" issue notwithstanding, few would deny that criminality is now viewed as one of the most critical problems that confront our society. While much of the present polemic stems from factors far removed from any objective consideration of reliable information, the available data clearly point to the need for concern and action. Indeed, both the sheer volume of offenses and the proportion of scarce societal resources that must be diverted into the criminal justice and correctional systems have become staggering. During any one year we can certainly expect some five million major criminal offenses. More than twice that number of minor offenses seems equally probable. A considerable body of research has shown that the preponderance of these cases will never be brought to the attention of the criminal justice system, and only a relatively small fraction of those reported will ultimately result in the apprehension, prosecution, conviction, or confinement of an offender. Still, given the existing capabilities of both the criminal justice and correctional systems, the volume of offenders who are processed far exceeds the number that can be effectively and equitably handled. As an illustration of what the correctional system alone must do on a continuing basis—on any given day during the year almost one million offenders will be under the supervision of probation or parole agencies, some 250,000 will actually be confined in state or federal correctional institutions, roughly 200,000 will be confined in local jails, and something in excess of 50,000 juveniles will be held in detention or treatment centers. In terms of financial outlay, were we to calculate only the costs directly attributable to the offenses themselves and to the maintenance of a system that is even minimally capable of processing such a large number of offenders, the most conservative estimates would run into billions of dollars annually.

Apart from the heightened public concern, none of these facts are at all new to those who are professionally or academically interested in the field of corrections. The basic character of the problem, including both its magnitude and its complexity, has been with us for many decades. Recently, however, the entire country has been jolted by a series of events that include Attica and Watergate, and we can now observe a kind of sensitivity to criminality that can only be described as a paradoxical blend of concern, fear, disgust, anger, and a determination to resolve the problem in some as yet unspecified way. Whatever else it involves, the weight of public opinion seems to support a major reassessment of the procedures and purposes of the entire criminal justice system and correctional system. The alternative courses of action are no longer limited to whether we should pursue the traditional goals of the present correctional system in a way relatively similar to that which has been followed up to now. The long-standing defense that greater effectiveness will come with time, experience, more and better-qualified personnel, higher levels of funding, and more modern facilities has become patently unacceptable to a substantial number of citizens and professionals. Indeed, unilateral and forceful demands for significant changes are coming with increasing frequency from all levels of government, the courts, the mass media, the private foundations and pressure groups, the academicians, the correctional practitioners, and the offenders themselves. Thus, basic and far-reaching changes appear more likely today than at any other time in recent history, and those systems that hesitate too long may well find many of their traditional prerogatives and powers eliminated by both legislative enactments and judicial precedents.

Fortunately or unfortunately, experience has taught us that change *per se* does not necessarily lead to the resolution of any social condition. On the contrary, simply moving away from one approach without moving toward a well-defined alternative can often do little more than demonstrate that the cure can be worse than the disease. This is not to say that many important and needed changes have not been made in the field of corrections. We know that such changes have occurred. Significant strides have been made in the direction of eliminating many of the inhumane conditions that characterized many prisons in the not-so-distant past. Inmates are not nearly as subject to corporal punishment, grossly inadequate diets, unreasonably crowded and unsanitary conditions, excessive periods of solitary confinement, or economic exploitation as they once were. Living conditions have improved in most areas. Medical, psychiatric, and psychological treatment are far more readily available. Educational, vocational training, and recreational programs have improved and proliferated. Particularly in the last decade or so both the Federal Bureau of Prisons and the states of California, Texas, Florida, North Carolina, Massachusetts, and Ohio have shown a remarkable willingness to experiment with and honestly evaluate a variety of treatment modalities, educational and work release programs, updated technical and vocational training, basic revisions of probation and parole statutes, halfway house centers, indeterminant sentences, and so on. Thus, the point is certainly not that correctional systems have flatly refused to move away from the *status quo*. On the other hand, we do wish to emphasize that while the net effect of these changes has been a movement away from the traditional punitively oriented penitentiary toward a much more humanitarian stance, the changes have unfortunately not been very successful mechanisms of resocialization or rehabilitation. Inmates still return to prison at about the same rate as they did prior to the changes. Program evaluations continue to show that contemporary treatment modalities and rehabilitation programs have little, if any, significant impact on recidivism. Such findings can be interpreted in a number of ways. Certainly the movement toward a more humanitarian response to offenders strikes a responsive chord in the minds of most of us. Even the hard-line correctional employees whose "shotgun guard mentality" dominated the field for so many years have been forced to admit that the humanitarian changes have not made the situation any worse. On the other hand, even the most obstinate among the "bleeding heart liberals" must also admit that the best-designed and most heavily funded of their programs have fallen far short of minimum expectations.

In light of the foregoing comments, several points seem clear. American correctional systems have entered what many observers believe will be a decade of broad-sweeping and necessary change. Despite the arguments advanced in support of some existing policies and programs, the basic premise that large numbers of offenders can be isolated in correctional institutions that do, in fact, correct appears fallacious and misleading. Even with the hard work and dedication of many, and the good intentions of many more, what is now being done simply and flatly does not work. This is not offered as an indictment of the present system, nor is it an attack on those who continue to believe that effective programs of treatment, rehabilitation, and resocialization are possible. On the contrary, we share many of the same ideological convictions as well as the belief that such programs can and should be implemented. But to believe that such things are possible does not make them appear, and to assume that the present state of our knowledge is sufficiently sophisticated that we can effectively initiate attitudinal and behavioral changes at will seems overly pretentious. (Indeed, there is little basis at this time for specifying what it is that offenders should be changed into apart from the obvious desire to reduce their participation in illegal behavior.)

Why, then, have we bothered gathering together these materials on comments imply? The reasons are really quite simple. First, we feel that beginning students of corrections should be made aware of the major criticisms and problems that confront the field early in their training. Toward that end, we have tried to collect materials that are both appropriate for their level of training and relevant for their needs. More importantly, however, correctional institutions and programs are going to be with us in one form or another throughout the future. Changes will be made. Failures will almost certainly outnumber successes for quite some time. Those changes that are initiated can be based on a careful consideration of the existing knowledge or on far less systematic hunches and intuitions. We hope that collections of this type will complement the training of those oriented toward the former basis for significant change.

D.M.P.

C.W.T.

REFERENCES

Final report of joint commission on correctional manpower and training, *A Time to Act*. American Correctional Association, 1969.

President's commission on law enforcement and administration of justice, *Task Force Report: Corrections*. Washington, D.C.: Government Printing Office, 1967.

Part I

CHALLENGE, REFORM, AND AMERICAN PENOLOGY

Over half a million juveniles and adults are now confined in jails, detention centers, or prisons somewhere in the United States. At least half of this number are either awaiting trial or serving relatively short sentences for minor offenses. The remainder are scattered throughout the state or federal correctional systems. Regardless of what they experience during the course of their confinement or where they are confined, the vast majority will be returned to the larger society within the next few years. Almost all will ultimately be released.

On a coldly practical level, the massive costs of establishing and maintaining the type of system we have in this country can only be justified if an explicit, attainable purpose is involved. Moreover, particularly in a society that purports to highly value such abstract values as equality, justice, and individual freedom, the withdrawal of freedom and the disruption of any citizen's life would be expected only under the most extreme conditions. It is appropriate, therefore, that we start our examination of the current state of American corrections with a series of articles that provides a serious challenge to the viability of contemporary correctional practices and programs. Each of the four authors writes with an authority based on some combination of his recognized expertise, professional training, and personal experience. Each rather emphatically challenges the notion that corrections if the current state of the field is as dismal as many of our significant changes in the attitudes, values, and behavior of offenders can be initiated within the current structure of our correctional systems.

Certainly these authors have personal values and convictions that are offended by what they have seen and experienced. Each in his own way argues that the system is ineffective. More than one flatly states that the discrimination, violence, brutality, and degradation that many offenders necessarily confront is counterproductive to any rehabilitative goal. Their comments and criticisms cannot, however, be taken lightly, nor can they be written off as attacks based on nothing more than isolated and unusual cases. Certainly the reader should not passively accept each point as being equally applicable to every correctional institution in the country. Not every system has to overcome the stigma of allowing the mindless brutality that occurred at the Cummins and Tucker prison farms in Arkansas. Not every system has experienced an Attica. And though few can match the sophistication of such "model systems" as those supported by the Federal Bureau of Prisons or the state of California, even in these systems the criticisms made by these four authors are not inappropriate.

In brief, Bruce Jackson, Philip Zimbardo, Richard McGee, and Ramsey Clark have each provided us with thoughtful and reasoned challenges to the basic credibility of much that is now characteristic of American corrections. Even if these men challenge the system in part because of their own ideological convictions, the facts derived from public investigations, court proceedings, and hundreds of pieces of sound research attest that their comments are far from groundless.

1

Beyond Attica

Bruce Jackson

Prison is the only garbage dump we have that is so repulsive we encircle it with barbed wire and a stone wall.

You get there in a closed van and the doors of the van don't open until the big iron gates have clanged shut behind you. You aren't released until a group of old men like no old men you ever knew decide you are something like a nice tractable person now. For years you don't touch the hand of a woman or child, wear clothing of your own choice, go somewhere on the spur of the moment; you don't eat what you feel like eating, talk to whomever you'd like to talk to, read a magazine you happen to see on the stand and find interesting. That is because there are no women and children in prison (save those beyond the wire grills of visiting rooms), and all the clothing is the same in prison, and there are those walls and barbed wire and bars to keep you from going anywhere at all; it is because the only food you get is what the mess hall manages to set out that day or what you can hustle on the side; it is because conversations in prison are guarded or tight or secret and there are no telephones with which you may have casual chats with casual friends, and there are no magazine stands on which to find that potentially interesting magazine.

Prison is a place where all sorts of things are not there.

What is there hurts: sameness, bars, guards on towers with guns,

Published by permission of Transaction Inc. from *trans*action, Vol. 9 (November/December 1971). © 1971 by Transaction Inc.

guards walking the halls with clubs who find you strange and alien and perhaps even hateful and evil because you've been adjudged a criminal by a group the law insists represents your peers. They look at you with fear or hate or contempt, perhaps only because you're a nigger or a spic or perhaps just because they don't know what is going on in your head, and that alone is frightening enough to make them hate you or fear you. And you them—hate and fear are always bilateral affairs. In addition to the guards are the people you must live with—other convicts: suspicious, mean, guarded and as frightened as you are perhaps, surely as mistrusting as you.

The days are short, the nights interminable. In most prisons in this country there is little for inmates to do, so men spend up to 18 hours of each day locked in small cells, waiting to be tired enough to sleep, waiting for sleep to descend long enough to break up the boring run of days in which almost nothing happens save an occasional letter from home, a fight to watch, an argument to have, a hustle to make.

What work there is in prison is usually demeaning and boring: inmates are paid humiliating wages (New York 30 cents a day, California up to a dollar for a few, Texas nothing at all) for tedious and often exhausting and usually uninstructive work (picking cotton, stamping out license plates on an ancient machine in extreme heat, pushing a mop, and—yes—even breaking rocks).

A good inmate is one who makes no trouble for the institution. He may do whatever he wants—have homosexual affairs, run gambling concessions, deal dope, brutalize his fellows, peddle soft jobs—but so long as he is quiet about it and makes no trouble the administration cannot ignore, he will not be bothered by guards and he will be paroled out reasonably early in his sentence. A bad inmate is one who makes ripples, someone who complains about treatment or food or lack of educational opportunity or humiliation by guards; a very bad inmate is one who talks such things up among his fellows; an outrageously bad inmate is one who suggests to his fellows that they do not have to stand for such treatment, who tells them that the courts may have sentenced them to punishment by incarceration but that does not mean the prison authorities have any duty or right to punish them further. Such inmates do the maximum amount of time the law permits, for authorities— parole boards and such—feel they are not fit to be released in society for they have not learned how to "get along."

California for years has ridden along on the crest of a prison reputation that derived from some petty changes it made over 20 years ago. But California prisons are cesspools, where inmates with politically deviant ideas are locked away for years in euphemistically named "Adjustment Centers," prisons within prisons where men are locked in cells 23½ hours every day and given nothing to do, where guards and convicts engage in a spiraling game of mutual brutalization. There is no appeal from commitment to an

Adjustment Center, there is no right to know why one was placed there or who one's accusers are, there is no chance to present evidence on one's own behalf. California has the indeterminate sentence—a pretty idea that says fit the punishment to the criminal and not the crime—that results in longer sentences than most other states, for the time in prison is fixed by a board of ex-law enforcement officials all appointed by the governor, and their desiderata of good citizenship have little to do with anything but internal order of the prison.

Texas makes sure it has a good parole statistical show by paroling people only very late in their sentence—that means there are very few parole violators and officials can say their parole workers do good work. New York's parole system is capricious and arbitrary; people are returned to prison for the silliest of reasons and without the most basic legal rights. In much of the North, prison officials encourage racial disharmony among inmates because they know if the inmates are hating and fighting one another they will have little energy left to hate and fight the prison administrators. Occasionally that backfires and the inmates get together and say, "Hey, *we're* not our enemies." California solves that problem by locking everyone up (half the inmates at San Quentin are in 24-hour lockup; 280 have been moved to special lockup cells). New York solved the problem with high-powered rifles and shotguns so eagerly triggered they gunned down hostages and inmates alike in a greedy fusillade that articulated law enforcement anxieties we can be sure no state official will ever honestly admit.

"I know of no institution," says Texas Department of Corrections Director George Beto, "unless it be organized Christianity, which has shown a greater reluctance to measure the effectiveness of its varied programs than has corrections." But almost everyone—observers, prison administrators, convicts—feel American corrections are a dismal failure; I know of no public official other than Spiro Agnew who thinks they do any real good at all. We have the longest prison sentences in the West and the greatest problem in the West with our prisoners and our ex-prisoners. Something is surely screwed up.

The problem is a well-known one in public policy: the lawmakers say they want the institution to do one thing, the people who run the institutions know that isn't what the lawmakers mean at all. The lawmakers say they want reform, but there is money only for hardware and guards; the lawmakers say the prisons should make better people, but only take notice what goes on when someone escapes or goes berserk. No warden has ever been fired because no inmate was helped in any noticeable way while under his care, but quite a few have been fired because some inmates in their care found the prison so horrid they chose to go over the wall or burn down the buildings.

People are more educated about prisons than they were three months ago: they know something about San Quentin, something about Attica, they wonder about the secrecy, the brutality, the racism, the prices paid. There are noises for legislation: hardly anyone objected to the first 28 demands of the Attica convicts, demands that would move the prison toward a condition of minimal decency; they were the same demands made by Folsom inmates two years ago, *none* of which was granted. There will be committees, lots of committees, and they will make reports that will be distributed and filed.

But we've all read those reports before and know that one function of committees and reports is to make it unnecessary to engage in other action: the investigations and the writing-up of the investigations become ends in themselves, and we are all properly decathected by that time, for we've read the reports and shaken our heads and agreed with no mean passion with the conclusions.

Meanwhile, the same wardens are there, the same walls are there, the same old guards are there. Most of the wardens came up through the ranks in this business of no lateral entry, most of the walls are superfluous and expensive, most of the guards have no training whatsoever in anything but the use of their club or rifle.

Great wrongs have occurred, but who will be punished? The guard who killed three black convicts for fighting at Soledad was not indicted, nor was there even an official statement that fighting is not necessarily an offense punishable by death; none of the state police who went berserk in Attica will be indicted, just as the guardsmen at Kent State and the police at Jackson were not indicted. Some inmates will be indicted, and a lot of inmates will have no formal charges placed against them, but will spend years before a parole hearing again has any point for them.

I remember after the Democratic Convention in Chicago in 1968: the squares were informed and outraged, the cops really *do* beat people up indiscriminately; that's not just a bunch of stories made up by niggers, freaks and dope fiends. And I remember how it faded. And I see around me how the cops still freely do just what they did in Chicago, the only difference being they are a little more free with it now because they have learned that not even the once awesome power of the press (Cronkite was enraged, NBC was saddened) brings down any real heat. No police went to jail for Chicago. That's one reason they were so free to shoot at Jackson State, Kent State, at Fred Hampton's apartment, at all those other places. The squares just shook their heads and said, "See, more of the same."

No public official in California has raised a voice in outrage at the hundreds of men locked 24 hours a day in cramped and crowded cells for no prison crime other than that the warden of San Quentin thinks they *might* be harboring political thoughts about the death of George Jackson last August.

I worry that all the present concern will dissipate, will attenuate, will dribble away in trivial cocktail conversations about "How awful it is isn't it yes it is someone ought to do something really I wonder who it will be maybe tomorrow."

I worry that prisons will continue operating as they have because after the heat dies down and the various commissions self-destruct, we will once again leave the operation of prisons to those whose job it is, those who "know what they are doing." And we will help them do that job simply by not telling them they really do have to stop it now.

I think here of a priest I know in one prison who a few years ago was telling me his experiences on Death Row giving counsel and comfort to condemned men on their way out. Some of his stories were witty and entertaining and I chuckled and nodded along with everyone else. Some time later, it occurred to me that those executions probably could not have occurred without that priest's cooperation and tacit approval: his presence laid the sure hand of church and social righteousness on sending 12,000 volts of juice through some shaved and oiled poor bastard who was too dumb to cop out when he was first arrested or too poor to get a sharp lawyer. Not only did the priest literally help seat the man in the chair, but he lent the moral tone to the event that made it socially legitimate. I wonder what would have happened if the priest boycotted the execution, if he had screamed, "This is murder!" I suspect the warden would not have been so quick to push the button, the newsmen would have gone bananas. But the priest didn't do that, of course, and no one expected him to; he disapproved of executing people, but it wasn't his job to scream "This is murder!" His job was only to grease the condemned's way into the Promised Land.

Prison is perhaps necessary to protect society from the violent, but no more than 10 percent of any prison's population is really violent, and most of those people should be receiving psychiatric help (if that can be made to work) rather than simple lockup anyway. Prison is supposed to reform, but who—after all this evidence to the contrary—can suppose men are reformed by being locked for years on end in six-by-nine-foot cages in communities where homosexuality is a norm, mistrust a necessity, and hate a social commodity? What kind of foolishness informs a parole board which assumes a person who adjusts well to *that* sort of community is fit to come back outside and someone who challenges it should be welded away forever?

Confusion, violence and repression seem more and more common in prisons, and more and more inmates are responding with riots, strikes, assassinations and sabotage. The institutions are cracking at the seams and though one hopes they will crack enough to let in some light and decency, one fears they will again snap shut like a giant sea clam, suffocating in darkness everything and everyone within.

And they will blow up again. There will be more George Jacksons, men turned bitter as gall by years behind a welded door, there will be more Atticas, men spitting back in the face of almost certain death because they find that defiance preferable to the slow death of day-after-day living in brutality and squalor and lawlessness.

There is a simple economy to the social effects of the operation of public institutions: when public institutions make primary decisions on the basis of internal institutional priorities their ultimate social utility decreases accordingly. What makes for good management of prisons does not necessarily make for good treatment of offenders, what makes it possible to run a prison neatly does not necessarily make it possible to send once-convicted men back into society ready to be free men.

When public institutions make their decisions without reference to the needs of the public which they presumably serve, we get a range of disasters: the killing of Fred Hampton and other Black Panthers is within that range, the development of the war in Vietnam is within that range, the harassment of the poor by welfare workers is within that range. The police make decisions on the basis of what makes sense within the police perception of the world, the military set priorities on the basis of what makes sense within the military perception of the world, the welfare worker doles out money on the basis of what makes sense in the welfare worker's perception of the world. And time and again we find ourselves with the sour feeling that the police or the military or the welfare agents have sold us out: they've worked their own hustle, we haven't been protected or served, our money has been thrown away and our energies have been squandered.

The same thing has long gone on in prison; the only difference now is more people suddenly know about it because a lot of inmates recently refused to submit to the foolishness of their keepers. It was there all the time, that anger, that injustice, that perfectly absurd counter-productivity.

Our chickens have once again come home to roost, and once again we learn that the first thing the returning fowl does is shit all over the henhouse. Our decision is whether to get used to the stink and live with it or take on the unpleasant job of cleaning it up.

But Americans, sadly, seem able to become used to almost anything.

2

Pathology of Imprisonment

Philip G. Zimbardo

I was recently released from solitary confinement after being held therein for 37 months [months!]. A silent system was imposed upon me and to even whisper to the man in the next cell resulted in being beaten by guards, sprayed with chemical mace, blackjacked, stomped and thrown into a strip-cell naked to sleep on a concrete floor without bedding, covering, wash basin or even a toilet. The floor served as toilet and bed, and even there the silent system was enforced. To let a moan escape your lips because of the pain and discomfort . . . resulted in another beating. I spent not days, but months there during my 37 months in solitary. . . . I have filed every writ possible against the administrative acts of brutality. The state courts have all denied the petitions. Because of my refusal to let the things die down and forget all that happened during my 37 months in solitary . . . I am the most hated prisoner in [this] penitentiary, and called a "hard-core incorrigible."

Maybe I am an incorrigible, but if true, it's because I would rather die than to accept being treated as less than a human being. I have never complained of my prison sentence as being unjustified except through legal means of appeals. I have never put a knife on a guard's throat and demanded my release. I know that thieves must be punished and I don't justify stealing, even though I am a thief myself. But now I don't think I will be a thief when I am released. No, I'm not rehabilitated. It's just that I no longer think of be-

Published by permission of Transaction Inc. from *Society*, Vol. 9 (April 1972). © 1972 by Transaction Inc.

coming wealthy by stealing. I now only think of killing—killing those who have beaten me and treated me as if I were a dog. I hope and pray for the sake of my own soul and future life of freedom that I am able to overcome the bitterness and hatred which eats daily at my soul, but I know to overcome it will not be easy.

This eloquent plea for prison reform—for humane treatment of human beings, for the basic dignity that is the right of every American—came to me secretly in a letter from a prisoner who cannot be identified because he is still in a state correctional institution. He sent it to me because he read of an experiment I recently conducted at Stanford University. In an attempt to understand just what it means psychologically to be a prisoner or a prison guard, Craig Haney, Curt Banks, Dave Jaffe and I created our own prison. We carefully screened over 70 volunteers who answered an ad in a Palo Alto city newspaper and ended up with about two dozen young men who were selected to be part of this study. They were mature, emotionally stable, normal, intelligent college students from middle-class homes throughout the United States and Canada. They appeared to represent the cream of the crop of this generation. None had any criminal record and all were relatively homogeneous on many dimensions initially.

Half were arbitrarily designated as prisoners by a flip of a coin, the others as guards. These were the roles they were to play in our simulated prison. The guards were made aware of the potential seriousness and danger of the situation and their own vulnerability. They made up their own formal rules for maintaining law, order and respect, and were generally free to improvise new ones during their eight-hour, three-man shifts. The prisoners were unexpectedly picked up at their homes by a city policeman in a squad car, searched, handcuffed, fingerprinted, booked at the Palo Alto station house and taken blindfolded to our jail. There they were stripped, deloused, put into a uniform, given a number and put into a cell with two other prisoners where they expected to live for the next two weeks. The pay was good ($15 a day) and their motivation was to make money.

We observed and recorded on videotape the events that occurred in the prison, and we interviewed and tested the prisoners and guards at various points throughout the study. Some of the videotapes of the actual encounters between the prisoners and guards were seen on the NBC News feature "Chronolog" on November 26, 1971.

At the end of only six days we had to close down our mock prison because what we saw was frightening. It was no longer apparent to most of the subjects (or to us) where reality ended and their roles began. The majority had indeed become prisoners or guards, no longer able to clearly differentiate between role playing and self. There were dramatic changes in virtually every aspect of their behavior, thinking and feeling. In less than a week the experience of imprisonment undid (temporarily) a lifetime of learning; human values were suspended, self-concepts were challenged and the ugliest, most base, pathological side of human nature surfaced. We were horrified because we saw some boys (guards) treat others as if they were despicable animals, taking pleasure in cruelty, while other boys (prisoners) became servile, dehumanized robots who thought only of escape, of their own individual survival and of their mounting hatred for the guards.

We had to release three prisoners in the first four days because they had such acute situational traumatic reactions as hysterical crying, confusion in thinking and severe depression. Others begged to be paroled, and all but three were willing to forfeit all the money they had earned if they could be paroled. By then (the fifth day) they had been so programmed to think of themselves as prisoners that when their request for parole was denied, they returned docilely to their cells. Now, had they been thinking as college students acting in an oppressive experiment, they would have quit once they no longer wanted the $15 a day we used as our only incentive. However, the reality was not quitting an experiment but "being paroled by the parole board from the Stanford County Jail." By the last days, the earlier solidarity among the prisoners (systematically broken by the guards) dissolved into "each man for himself." Finally, when one of their fellows was put in solitary confinement (a small closet) for refusing to eat, the prisoners were given a choice by one of the guards: give up their blankets and the incorrigible prisoner would be let out, or keep their blankets and he would be kept in all night. They voted to keep their blankets and to abandon their brother.

About a third of the guards became tyrannical in their arbitrary use of power, in enjoying their control over other people. They were corrupted by the power of their roles and became quite inventive in their techniques of breaking the spirit of the prisoners and making them feel they were worthless. Some of the guards merely did their jobs as tough but fair correctional officers, and several were good guards from the prisoners' point of view since they did them small favors and were friendly. However, no good guard ever interfered with a command by any of the bad guards; they never intervened on the side of the prisoners, they never told the others to ease off because it was only an experiment, and they never even came to me as prison superintendent or experimenter in charge to complain. In part, they were good because the others were bad; they needed the others to help establish their own egos in a positive light. In a sense, the good guards perpetuated the prison more than the other guards because their own needs to be liked prevented them from disobeying or violating the implicit guards' code. At the same time, the act of befriending the prisoners created a social reality which made the prisoners less likely to rebel.

By the end of the week the experiment had become a reality, as if it were a Pirandello play directed by Kafka that just keeps going after the audience has left. The consultant for our prison, Carlo Prescott, an ex-convict with 16 years of imprisonment in California's jails, would get so depressed and furious each time he visited our prison, because of its psychological similarity to his experiences, that he would have to leave. A Catholic priest who was a former prison chaplain in Washington, D.C. talked to our prisoners after four days and said they were just like the other first-timers he had seen.

But in the end, I called off the experiment not because of the horror I saw out there in the prison yard, but because of the horror of realizing that *I* could have easily traded places with the most brutal guard or become the weakest prisoner full of hatred at being so powerless that I could not eat, sleep or go to the toilet without permission of the authorities. *I* could have become Calley at My Lai, George Jackson at San Quentin, one of the men at Attica or the prisoner quoted at the beginning of this article.

Individual behavior is largely under the control of social forces and environmental contingencies rather than personality traits, character, will power or other empirically unvalidated constructs. Thus we create an illusion of freedom by attributing more internal control to ourselves, to the individual, than actually exists. We thus underestimate the power and pervasiveness of situational controls over behavior because: a) they are often non-obvious and subtle, b) we can often avoid entering situations where we might be so controlled, c) we label as "weak" or "deviant" people in those situations who do behave differently from how we believe we would.

Each of us carries around in our heads a favorable self-image in which we are essentially just, fair, humane and understanding. For example, we could not imagine inflicting pain on others without much provocation or hurting people who had done nothing to us, who in fact were even liked by us. However, there is a growing body of social psychological research which underscores the conclusion derived from this prison study. Many people, perhaps the majority, can be made to do almost anything when put into psychologically compelling situations—regardless of their morals, ethics, values, attitudes, beliefs or personal convictions. My colleague, Stanley Milgram, has shown that more than 60 percent of the population will deliver what they think is a series of painful electric shocks to another person even after the victim cries for mercy, begs them to stop and then apparently passes out. The subjects complained that they did not want to inflict more pain but blindly obeyed the command of the authority figure (the experimenter) who said that they must go on. In my own research on violence, I have seen mild-mannered co-eds repeatedly give shocks (which they thought were causing pain) to another girl, a stranger whom they had rated very favorably, simply by being made to feel anonymous and put in a situation where they were expected to engage in this activity.

Observers of these and similar experimental situations never predict their outcomes and estimate that it is unlikely that they themselves would behave similarly. They can be so confident only when they were outside the situation. However, since the majority of people in these studies do act in non-rational, non-obvious ways, it follows that the majority of observers would also succumb to the social psychological forces in the situation.

With regard to prisons, we can state that the mere act of assigning labels to people and putting them into a situation where those labels acquire validity and meaning is sufficient to elicit pathological behavior. This pathology is not predictable from any available diagnostic indicators we have in the social sciences, and is extreme enough to modify in very significant ways fundamental attitudes and behavior. The prison situation, as presently arranged, is guaranteed to generate severe enough pathological reactions in both guards and prisoners as to debase their humanity, lower their feelings of self-worth and make it difficult for them to be part of a society outside of their prison.

For years our national leaders have been pointing to the enemies of freedom, to the fascist or communist threat to the American way of life. In so doing they have overlooked the threat of social anarchy that is building within our own country without any outside agitation. As soon as a person comes to the realization that he is being imprisoned by his society or individuals in it, then, in the best American tradition, he demands liberty and rebels, accepting death as an alternative. The third alternative, however, is to allow oneself to become a good prisoner—docile, cooperative, uncomplaining, conforming in thought and complying in deed.

Our prison authorities now point to the militant agitators who are still vaguely referred to as part of some communist plot, as the irresponsible, incorrigible troublemakers. They imply that there would be no trouble, riots, hostages or deaths if it weren't for this small band of bad prisoners. In other words, then, everything would return to "normal" again in the life of our nation's prisons if they could break these men.

The riots in prison are coming from within—from within every man and woman who refuses to let the system turn them into an object, a number, a thing or a no-thing. It is not communist inspired, but inspired by the spirit of American freedom. No man wants to be enslaved. To be powerless, to be subject to the arbitrary exercise of power, to not be recognized as a human being is to be a slave.

To be a militant prisoner is to become aware that the physical jails are but more blatant extensions of the forms of social and psychological oppression experienced daily in the nation's ghettos. They are trying to awaken the conscience of the nation to the ways in which the American ideals are being perverted, apparently in the name of justice but actually under the banner of apathy, fear and hatred. If we do not listen to the pleas of the prisoners at Attica to be treated like human beings, then we have all become brutalized by our priorities for property rights over human rights. The consequence will not only be more prison riots but a loss of all those ideals on which this country was founded.

The public should be aware that they own the prisons and that their business is failing. The 70 percent recidivism rate and the escalation in severity of crimes committed by graduates of our prisons are evidence that current prisons fail to rehabilitate the inmates in any positive way. Rather, they are breeding grounds for hatred of the establishment, a hatred that makes every citizen a target of violent assault. Prisons are a bad investment for us taxpayers. Until now we have not cared, we have turned over to wardens and prison authorities the unpleasant job of keeping people who threaten us out of our sight. Now we are shocked to learn that their management practices have failed to improve the product and instead turn petty thieves into murderers. We must insist upon new management or improved operating procedures.

The cloak of secrecy should be removed from the prisons. Prisoners claim they are brutalized by the guards, guards say it is a lie. Where is the impartial test of the truth in such a situation? Prison officials have forgotten that they work for us, that they are only public servants whose salaries are paid by our taxes. They act as if it is their prison, like a child with a toy he won't share. Neither lawyers, judges, the legislature nor the public is allowed into prisons to ascertain the truth unless the visit is sanctioned by authorities and until all is prepared for their visit. I was shocked to learn that my request to join a congressional investigating committee's tour of San Quentin and Soledad was refused, as was that of the news media.

There should be an ombudsman in every prison, not under the pay or control of the prison authority, and responsible only to the courts, state legislature and the public. Such a person could report on violations of constitutional and human rights.

Guards must be given better training than they now receive for the difficult job society imposes upon them. To be a prison guard as now constituted is to be put in a situation of constant threat from within the prison, with no social recognition from the society at large. As was shown graphically at Attica, prison guards are also prisoners of the system who can be sacrificed to the demands of the public to be punitive and the needs of politicians to preserve an image. Social scientists and business administrators should be called upon to design and help carry out this training.

The relationship between the individual (who is sentenced by the courts to a prison term) and his community must be maintained. How can a prisoner return to a dynamically changing society that most of us cannot cope with after being out of it for a number of years? There should be more community involvement in these rehabilitation centers, more ties encouraged and promoted between the trainees and family and friends, more educational opportunities to prepare them for returning to their communities as more valuable members of it than they were before they left.

Finally, the main ingredient necessary to effect any change at all in prison reform, in the rehabilitation of a single prisoner or even in the optimal development of a child is caring. Reform must start with people—especially people with power—caring about the well-being of others. Underneath the toughest, society-hating convict, rebel or anarchist is a human being who wants his existence to be recognized by his fellows and who wants someone else to care about whether he lives or dies and to grieve if he lives imprisoned rather than lives free.

3

Our Sick Jails

Richard A. McGee

Thoughtful practitioners and scholars alike have condemned this old derelict of local government for decades on end, but the common jail lives on with pathetically little change. Even when a new one comes into being, smelling of fresh paint and civic righteousness, it usually gets worse and worse until it also joins the ranks of what President Nixon's Task Force on Prisoner Rehabilitation calls "the most glaringly inadequate institution on the American correctional scene."[1]

Nearly 50 years ago, Fishman called these institutions "Crucibles of Crime."[2]

President Johnson's Commission on Law Enforcement and Criminal Justice, in its report on *Corrections*,[3] points out with commendable diligence a bare handful of "Programs of Promise" out of 3,473 local jails in the country.

Richard W. Velde, associate administrator of the Law Enforcement

From "Our Sick Jails," *Federal Probation*, 35 (March 1971), 3–8. Reprinted by permission.

---

[1]"The Criminal Offender—What Should be Done?" Report of the President's Task Force on Prisoner Rehabilitation, April 1970.

[2]*Crucibles of Crime: A Shocking Story of American Jails.* By Joseph F. Fishman. New York: Cosmopolis Press, 1923. Reprinted 1969 in "Series on Criminology, Law Enforcement and Social Problems," No. 35, *Jails*, Patterson-Smith, Publishers.

[3]*Task Force Report: Corrections*, The President's Commission on Law Enforcement and Administration of Justice, 1967, p. 53.

Assistance Administration of the U.S. Department of Justice, made this statement recently:

> Jails are festering sores in the criminal justice system. There are no model jails anywhere; we know, we tried to find them. Almost nowhere are there rehabilitative programs operated in conjunction with jails. It's harsh to say, but the truth is that jail personnel are the most uneducated, untrained and poorly paid of all personnel in the criminal justice system—and furthermore, there aren't enough of them.
>
> The result is what you would expect, only worse. Jails are, without question, brutal, filthy, cesspools of crime—institutions which serve to brutalize and embitter men to prevent them from returning to a useful role in society.[4]

Sheriff Michael H. Canlis, president of the National Sheriffs' Association, said as recently as October 1970:

> It has been said that most (jails) are only human warehouses. We must ask ourselves, is merely keeping our prisoners secure, enough?
>
> If we content ourselves with maintaining nothing more than a human warehouse, we are not only perpetutating the so-called failure of an element in the system of criminal justice, but we might, to some degree, be responsible for a contribution for some of the increases in crime.[5]

I personally opened the Rikers Island Penitentiary in New York City as its first warden, and later, as deputy commissioner and for a time acting commissioner of the New York City Department of Correction, was responsible for the administration of all of New York City's local lockups, detention prisons, and misdemeanant institutions. Since then I have inspected scores of local jails.

Only a few months ago, at the request of the San Francisco Crime Committee, I visited the jails of that proud city. The committee has made its report and I shall not add to it here, except to say that some of the conditions observed in San Francisco's new Hall of Justice Jail were shocking even to so jaded an eye as mine.

In fairness, however, it must be added that in San Francisco, as in numerous other jurisdictions, it is virtually impossible to fix responsibility for the glaring and obvious inadequacies because control of the resources of the local government are so fragmented that when the chips are down the

---

[4]From *The Correctional Trainer*, Newsletter for Illinois Correctional Staff Training, Fall 1970, p. 109.

[5]*The National Sheriff*, publication of the National Sheriffs' Association, October-November 1970.

"buck" is usually on someone else's desk. Then when the heat is off, the "buck" gets lost and nothing much happens until the next scandal hits the headlines.

But let us set aside the scandals, the instances of mis-management and local political Indian-wrestling. Surely we don't need another century of indictments to convince us that the local city and county jails as now organized and managed simply must be replaced by a more rational system.

So, what can be done?

MANAGEMENT OF LAW OFFENDERS
AFTER ARREST

First, let us discuss the larger problem, of which the jail is only the most visible part—visible because it is a physical place peopled by public offenders and public employees. The total problem is not the jail alone, but the whole agglomeration of public services involved in the *management* of *law offenders* after *arrest*.

The management problem involves all the parts of the criminal justice system—police, courts, prosecutors, defense attorneys, detention jails, probation services, and parole at the local level. Then there is the state government's correctional system; and overlapping these the federal system. The total so-called "system" must deal with the whole gamut of illegal acts, from minor traffic infractions to the most heinous of felonious crimes. The persons who commit the offenses include every imaginable kind of human being in the society—murderers, drunk drivers, prostitutes, thieves, forgers, mental cases, alcoholics, drug addicts, muggers, juveniles out of control, rioters, beggars—everybody is eligible if he gives cause to be arrested.

As a practical matter, however, we find the local jail being occupied principally by drunks, addicts, and petty thieves. And as for the women, if the prostitutes were eliminated from the jail populations, most of the women's quarters would be virtually empty most of the time.

Based on a very rough estimate, about 7 percent of the 3 million persons, more or less, who pass through these jails each year are charged with or convicted of felonies, and 93 percent are misdemeanants. It can be seen readily enough that the problem of jail administration, aside from holding a few felons awaiting disposition by the courts, is that of managing a miscellaneous array of persons charged with or convicted of offenses of a relatively minor nature. Only a very few of these are incarcerated for periods of 6 months to 1 year. A study of two large counties in California revealed that about one-third of the sentenced prisoners on a given day were serving terms of 30 days or less, one-third 1 month to 3 months, and one-third over 90 days up to and including 1 year.[6]

The question is often posed, what can be accomplished toward treating, managing, or rehabilitating persons who receive sentences of 30 days or less. As has been pointed out, this only accounts for about one-third of misdemeanants who are sentenced. The same question might be asked about those who receive sentences of 30 to 90 days, who constitute another one-third. The group that we might well be most concerned about is the third that receives sentences of 3 months to 1 year. What, also, of the substantial number of untried defendants presumed innocent under our law who may wait in jail for periods of 3 months to a year or more while the judicial machinery unwinds, leading to the day when the judge can finally render his decision? In some metropolitan jurisdictions 60 percent or more of the daily jail population is made up of persons who are unsentenced. The warehousing practice is bad enough for the unsentenced, but it has no validity whatsoever for those serving sentences. One month in jail may not seem long either to the judge or the sheriff, but to the prisoner it may be the longest 720 hours in his life, and just one of those hours could include the most damaging experience in his lifetime. Contrariwise, short stays in jail are a way of life for thousands of deteriorated middle-aged alcoholics and petty offenders. A 1963 study of some 7,000 inmates in five New York county penitentiaries showed that over 20 percent were serving a term which was their tenth or more.

SOME REMEDIES

The remedies for the deficiencies and abuses of the common jail are many. Some are relatively easy to find and can be applied by simple shifts in procedures. Others will require substantial changes in law and in administrative organization.

Among the procedural changes which are available, some of which are already in use in many jurisdictions, include:

1. The use of citations instead of jail booking for selected cases at the time of apprehension.

2. Release on "own recognizance" by the court at the time of arraignment by many of those unable to post money bail as a guaranty of appearance in court when ordered to do so.

[6]*Task Force Report: Corrections.* The President's Commission on Law Enforcement and Administration of Justice, chapter 7, pp. 77–81.

3. Adoption of a policy by the courts of giving priority in court disposition to those in jail as opposed to those awaiting trial while out on bail.

4. The use of short form or "quicky" presentence probation reports in misdemeanor cases, so that the judge may have information about each defendant which might have relevance to his decision to choose among such alternative dispositions as suspended sentence, supervised probation, fine, and length and type of jail sentence.

5. Provision for payment of fines on the installment plan in cases wherein the defendant is employed but does not have enough ready cash on the day when sentence is pronounced.

6. The use of work-furlough releases for employable and reasonably reliable jail inmates.

7. The use of parole and postinstitutional supervision for most jail inmates and especially for men with families who receive jail sentences of more than 60 days.

8. Development of detoxification and rehabilitation programs outside the jail system for chronic alcoholics.

There is nothing either startling or new or illegal in the above list of procedural practices. What is really startling to any taxpayer who is concerned about the effectiveness of his dollar is that the number of jurisdictions which exploit *all* of these practices to the fullest are almost nonexistent.

Assuming the same number of officers and the same degree of police vigilance and efficiency now existing, and assuming that the above practices were fully utilized, it is probable that the *daily populations of the Nation's local jails could be cut by as much as 50 percent without risk to the public safety*. Then, it is fair to ask, why isn't it being done?

The reasons are not difficult to find. Some are so obvious they need only to be mentioned without elaboration. Others are more elusive.

ADMINISTRATIVE PROBLEMS

The most apparent reason for inefficiency and ineptitude in jail management lies in the governmental organizational structure in which the jails are embedded. According to the President's Commission on Law Enforcement and Administration of Justice, there were at the last count (1965), 3,473 local jails in this country. These were projected to have by 1975 an average daily population of 178,000. If this population were evenly distributed, each jail would have each day only 51 inmates. The fact, of course, is that hundreds of jails are mere lockups for a dozen or so and many of these are completely empty part of the time. In addition to the city and county jails there are thousands of police lockups in our towns and hamlets which are little more than cages. On the opposite end of the size distribution, we see great metropolitan facilities like those in Chicago, Los Angeles, and New York City, which number their inmates in the thousands. They are uniformly overcrowded, impersonal, undermanned, and under-programmed.

Seven hundred sixty-two, or 22 percent of all local jails, are a part of city government, and with rare exceptions these are operated by the municipal police. Except for inertia and vested interest, there is no logical reason for the municipal police to run any jail where offenders are confined for more than 48 or 72 hours to permit delivery in court and transfer to a county or regional jail. This is especially obvious in a place like Sacramento, California, where the county detention jail and the police jail are located on the same city block, or in San Francisco, where the sheriff's jail and the city police jail are on the sixth and fifth floors respectively of the Hall of Justice.

The most common practice is for local jails to be a part of county government and to be operated by the county sheriff. Twenty-five hundred and forty-seven, or 73.3 percent of all local jails, are so managed. A few jurisdictions, like New York City and Denver, Colorado, have city-county governments, with the jails operated by an administrator appointed by the mayor or the board of supervisors. At the 1965 count, there were 149 such jails or city prisons and only 15 were operated by state governments.

A revealing survey of the jails of Illinois was made recently by the Center for Studies in Criminal Justice, the Law School, University of Chicago.[7] Of the 160 jails studied, 101 were county-operated and 59 were city jails. Even worse, of the 13 very large jails, four were city and nine county. In California, as of September 26, 1968, there were 27,325 prisoners in local jails and camps. Of these, 2,151, or about $8\frac{1}{2}$ percent, were in city-operated facilities. This percentage had dropped from about 22 percent in 1960.

Municipal police forces have trouble enough enforcing the law and keeping the peace in the cities without expecting them also to be either expert or very much interested in managing local jails with all the challenges presented by their diverse inhabitants and the ever present potentialities for crisis and scandal inherent even in the best of them.

---

[7]*Illinois Jails, Challenge and Opportunity for the 1970's.* A Summary of a 400-page Report by Hans W. Mattick and Ronald P. Sweet, based on *The Illinois Jails Survey* of 1967–68, conducted by the Center for Studies in Criminal Justice, the Law School, University of Chicago.

It appears, then, that there is substantial movement away from the practice of placing the jail management function under the city police. This begins to tidy up the administrative picture somewhat, but moves only a short step toward more rational and efficient systems of preadjudication, detention, and correctional programs provided by local government.

There is no real agreement in concept or practice at this time as to how services for corrections at the local levels of government are best organized and managed. In Vermont and Connecticut the jails are under state jurisdiction. In New York City, with its "Home Rule" Charter, there is no county sheriff and the city's detention jails and institutions for sentenced misdemeanants are administered by a Department of Correction headed by a Commissioner appointed by the Mayor. In San Diego County, California, the sheriff runs the jail for pretrial detention and a separate Department of County Camps, headed by an administrator appointed by the County Board of Supervisors, operates the facilities for most of the sentenced misdemeanants.

Other patterns involve regional jail districts comprised of two or more counties, or contractual relations between adjoining jurisdictions, in which one county serves another for some kinds of prisoners on a cost reimbursement basis.

Most of these joint operations are fraught with very real problems of transportation, funding for building construction, and petty political friction.

In the preceding discussion of local jails, we have been speaking exclusively about such institutions for the care and confinement of adult men and women. These appear to have developed historically largely as unwanted appendages of agencies charged with the jurisdiction's police power. However, with the movement of population to the cities, county sheriffs have been losing more and more of their direct enforcement functions to the city police. As a result, the county jails have tended to become a larger share of each sheriff's patronage empire, and hence a function he is less willing to relinquish. The prison systems of the state governments have been used traditionally mostly for the more serious and more persistent convicted felons. In some states they may also accept sentenced misdemeanants of certain classes, especially women. But even with nearly 200,000 prisoners in state prisons, the lion's share of the day-to-day prisoner traffic is still in the local jails.

A DIFFERENT PATTERN FOR JUVENILES

Parallel with this development in the adult offender field, we have seen different patterns in the delivery systems of services for juvenile offenders. Just as confinement and treatment programs for adults have tended to grow out of the police function, the juvenile services have emerged from the judicial function. This is because probation services originated in the courts. Detention halls and probation supervision for wards of the juvenile courts are more often than not adjuncts of the judicial rather than the executive branch of local government.

In spite of the division of the management of detention facilities for adults and juveniles between the sheriffs and the probation departments in most counties, probation services for both adult and juvenile offenders are combined in the local probation department in most jurisdictions. Here, again, we find every conceivable kind of variation of organization, of policy development, of control over employees, and of financial support.

A few examples support this point. In California, each county has a probation department within the court system, serving both juveniles and adults, except in two counties. In Los Angeles County, the head of this largest county probation department in the State is appointed by and reports to the board of supervisors, not to the courts. Stranger still, in some counties he is appointed by the judge of the juvenile court, even though there are usually more adults than juveniles in the total caseload. In Wisconsin, probation and parole services are in the State Division of Corrections except in Milwaukee. In Washington State, adult probation is combined with the state parole system and is under the State Division of Institutions, but juvenile probation is under the juvenile courts, with some state financial aid provided. New York State has just created a unified state department of probation, but with typical illogic, has separated it from the State Department of Correction.

Viewed by anyone outside the correctional field who is possessed of the most elementary sense of administrative order and common logic, the ways in which we in this country organize our resources to deal with millions of law breakers, from the point of arrest on, must look as if it were designed by a madman with the advice of Public Enemy No. 1.

WHAT NEEDS TO BE DONE

The time must come soon for concerned and responsible public officials to review this organizational "weed patch" with a view of making some sense out of it—sense to the taxpayer, even if not to all the vested interests, ideological hangups, traditions, and political bickering over power and sources of money.

That so little movement has taken place in the last century might make the problem seem hopeless if it were not for some contemporary developments. Without elaboration out of scale with the scope of this article, some of these are worth mentioning.

The first is a growing concern about the Nation's unbalanced tax structure. We argue that crime and the treatment of offenders are essentially a local problem, but the tax bases of the cities and counties grow weaker and weaker in comparison with those of state governments and the Federal Government. We must either find ways to feed state and federal moneys back to the local units of government or the higher levels of government must assume more of the burden for rendering direct services. "Correctional" services have always been at the end of the parade—behind health, hospitals, welfare, transportation, and education in these fiscal adjustments. Weak though recent efforts toward state subsidies and federal aid in this field have been, there are encouraging signs that our political leaders are beginning to recognize the problem.

Another hopeful sign is the increasing number of states which are developing stronger state departments of corrections, headed by competent administrators. This, coupled with stronger career services and better educated professionals at the journeyman and middle-management levels, cannot help but bring more pressure from within toward sounder organization and better performance.

It is also encouraging to note the interest shown last year by President Nixon in the appointment of a White House Task Force on Prisoner Rehabilitation, the statements of concern by Chief Justice Warren E. Burger, and the American Bar Association's recent establishment of a Commission on Correctional Facilities and Services.

The anxiety of the average citizen about the crime and delinquency problem generally must inevitably put the whole system on its mettle. All the participants in the administration of criminal justice are creatures of government. They must begin to produce, or perish.

If we would attempt to think logically about some portion of the "Justice System," such as the jails, we ought to come to some conclusions as to how to divide the total task among mutually supportive entities in the system without doing violence to our constitutional law and our established form of government.

We must start out, then, by calling to mind our doctrine of the separation of powers among the judicial, executive, and legislative branches. First, let us consider the role of the judiciary with particular reference to developments in the supervision of convicted persons placed on probation. It seemed sensible enough for the trial court judge in a one-man court with one or two probation officers, to appoint these persons as functionaries of his office to make presentence investigations and to report to him from time to time on how a handful of probationers were doing. But now, with most of our population concentrated in great metropolitan complexes, this arrangement is as archaic as a one-cow dairy. In Los Angeles County, for example, the Probation Department has some 4,000 employees, administers an annual budget of $53 million, runs 30 detention facilities for juveniles, and supervises a caseload of adults and juveniles of 41,000 persons. The decision to grant or revoke probation is and should no doubt continue to be a judicial function, but the operation of the probation department is as clearly an executive function as is the city police department or the operation of the state prison system. Accordingly, except in those rural counties with one-man courts, we must conclude that the administration of probation should be an executive function and a unit of state or county government. Except for the historical development of the services, there is no more logic in having the judge administer the probation service than there is for him to run the jails and prisons to which he commits defendants. If it is logical for the courts to administer large correctional (probation) programs, why then should we not suggest that the jails for adult offenders are as rational a component of court administration as detention halls for juveniles?

Looking at the question in another way, one might inquire why the sheriff or other police official should not administer the probation services with just as much logic as supports the notion that he is best fitted to manage the jails. If we persist in mixing the judicial roles of the courts with functions which are clearly executive, we may be running the risk of raising constitutional questions of jurisdiction.

The President's Commission on Law Enforcement and Administration of Justice, commenting on this issue, says:

> Most jails continue to be operated by law enforcement officials. The basic police mission of apprehending offenders usually leaves little time, commitment, or expertise for the development of rehabilitative programs, although notable exceptions demonstrate that jails can indeed be settings for correctional treatment. Many law enforcement officials, particularly those administering large and professionalized forces, have advocated transfer of jails to correctional control.
>
> The most compelling reason for making this change is the opportunity it offers to integrate the jails with the total corrections network, to upgrade them, and to use them in close coordination with both institution and community-based correctional services. As long as jails are operated by law enforcement officials, no matter how enlightened, it will be more difficult to transform them into correctional centers. As a major step toward reform, jails should be placed under the control of correctional authorities who are able to develop the needed program services. The trend should be away from the isolated jail and toward an integrated but diversified system of correctional facilities.[8]

---

[8]*Task Force Report: Corrections*, President's Commission on Law Enforcement and Administration of Justice, 1967, p. 79.

A dispassionate view of the best possible way to organize the criminal justice system cannot but lead to the conclusion that there are three major groups of functions, each requiring different emphasis, different attitudes, and different professional training and occupational skills. In skeletal outline, they are as follows:

/ *The Police*
>   Direct prevention and peace keeping
>   Detection and apprehension
2   *The Courts,* including prosecution and defense
>   Application of the law
>   Judgmental disposition
3   *The Correctional Agencies*
>   Presentence investigation and community supervision of probationers and parolees
>   Management and control of defendants awaiting adjudication (jails and juvenile halls)
>   Management of residential facilities and programs for all committed offenders (jails, prisons, correctional schools, and halfway houses)

If the above is a rational division of functions, it is clear that each political jurisdiction, be it a state or a county or a regional district within a state, should establish the equivalent of a department of corrections, which would be responsible for the management of all offenders under its jurisdiction, whether accused or convicted, and whether incarcerated or under community supervision.

This would mean: First, that the courts should relinquish administrative direction of probation services.

Second, that jails and camps for adult offenders must be removed from the administrative direction of police agencies.

Third, that in jurisdictions (usually counties) with too small a population to operate efficiently, they must either combine into regional districts or turn the functions over to state government.

Fourth, that the unrealistic administrative dichotomy between youth and adult correctional programs existing in many local jurisdictions be discontinued.

Fifth, that to encourage these changes and to ensure equality of treatment throughout the system, both the state governments and the Federal Government must provide financial assistance based upon adherence to decent standards.

"Equal Justice Under Law" are noble words engraved in marble over the entrance to the Supreme Court of the United States in the Nation's Capitol. If we really believe in this great democratic concept, we can hardly continue to tolerate the spectacle of a mental case charged with disorderly conduct sitting naked on the concrete floor of a bare isolation cell in a local jail while in another jurisdiction he would be in a hospital.

It is equally incongruous for a minion of organized crime charged with felonious assault to be walking the streets free on bail while scores of minor but indigent offenders sit idly in overcrowded jails awaiting court disposition.

Finally, it is not enough to say that the local jail as we know it is a failure—it is a scandal! All the palliatives and all the uncoordinated efforts at patching up the present system will continue to fail. Basic reorganization of the whole structure for managing offenders at the local levels of government is required. Nothing less will do!

4

Prisons: Factories of Crime

Ramsey Clark

No activity of a people so exposes their humanity or inhumanity, their character, their capacity for charity in its most generous dimension, as the treatment they accord persons convicted of crime. Here are individuals who have offended, who have done those things society holds to be most abhorrent. Are not criminals the least deserving and the most dangerous of people? We owe them nothing. They owe us their liberty, perhaps their lives.

The history of penology is the saddest chapter in the history of civilization. It portrays man at his worst. His cruelty, brutality and inhumanity are unrestrained through most times in most places. Virtually absolute power over nearly helpless people has often wholly corrupted.

When Dostoevsky wrote of his years in prison in Siberia, he called it *The House of the Dead*. The title told the story. Living there was like death. Of the bathhouse—filthy, stinking, hot, filled with dense steam and hundreds of naked bodies—he wrote that if he died and awoke in hell, he would expect it to be no worse. On his last night in prison, while walking the fence that had confined him for four years, he concluded that, on the whole, the men there were no better and no worse than people generally. Among them were exceptionally strong and gifted people; the waste of their lives was an intolerable cruelty. From this experience he defined man as "a creature that can become accustomed to anything."

From *Crime in America*. New York: Simon & Schuster, Inc., © 1970, 1971. Reprinted by permission of Simon and Schuster.

It sometimes seems that prisons try to disprove Dostoevsky's definition by brutalizing beyond the ability of man to bear. Jails and prisons in the United States today are more often than not manufacturers of crime. Of those who come to jail undecided, capable either of criminal conduct or of lives free of crime, most are turned to crime. Prisons are usually little more than places to keep people—warehouses of human degradation. Ninety-five percent of all expenditure in the entire corrections effort of the nation is for custody—iron bars, stone walls, guards. Five percent is for hope—health services, education, developing employment skills.

A glimpse of prison custody at its worst is afforded by investigations begun in 1966 of the Cummins and Tucker prison farms in Arkansas, where discipline was basically maintained by prisoners themselves—trustees with shotguns—with only a handful of paid employees supervising. Allegations, at least partially verified and largely credible, included the murder of inmates, brutal beatings and shootings. Shallow graves with broken bodies were uncovered. Food unfit to eat was regularly served. Forced homosexuality was openly tolerated. Extortion of money by wardens and sexual favors from families of inmates to protect their helpless prisoner relatives from physical injury or death were alleged. Torture devices included such bizarre items as the "Tucker telephone," components of which were an old telephone, wiring and a heavy duty battery. After an inmate was stripped, one wire was fastened to his penis, the other to a wrist or ankle, and electric shocks were sent through his body until he was unconscious.

Many American prisons include large dormitory rooms with a hundred beds or more where guards do not venture at night. There is no way of controlling violence in such an area. Beatings, deaths and suicides are frequent. Rape and homosexual cultures involve most of the inmates by choice or force. When riots and fires do not occur in these prisons, it is only because no one feels like starting them. They are breeding places of crime, violence and despair.

It would be difficult to devise a better method of draining the last drop of compassion from a human being than confinement in most prisons as they exist today. In a climate of fear and violence many wardens work only to avoid the general disorder that can wreck their prisons. They hope only to release the most violent inmates before they cause trouble inside and are so relieved to see the dangerous ones go that they disregard the public safety—and the fact that most will be back before long.

Meaningless or obsolete work is the best that prisons generally offer. More often no work is available. There is no chance for most young dropouts to continue school while they are in prison. Nearly all of the prisoners in federal youth centers are school dropouts. The offense for which they were convicted nearly always occurred after they dropped out. Youth corrections often deprive young offenders of their last chance for an education

—and today that may mean their last chance for fulfillment. When that chance is lost, the probability is great that they will turn to lives of crime.

The opportunity for treatment of the mentally ill in prison is virtually nonexistent. Most prisoners suffered from some mental disturbance at the time they committed crime. More have mental health problems on leaving prison than on entering. Psychotics are frequently left for the inmates to control. Sometimes it is the psychotics who control.

Simple physical illnesses generally are poorly treated in prison, if treated at all. Most prisoners, for example, need dental care. Because they are poor, they have never had any dental work, but few get adequate attention in prison. Personalities are shaped by such factors as the loss of teeth. When that loss is but one of many disadvantages and part of a dehumanizing existence, it adds its measure of brutalization. Human dignity is lost.

Drug addiction is common in prison. Many become addicted there. Even with close surveillance it is nearly impossible to keep drugs out of prisons. Guards are bribed. Some visitors with the slightest opportunity for physical contact attempt deliveries. Packages contain hidden drugs. Prisoners who get outside on work release programs, to attend funerals, visit sick relatives, or for court hearings smuggle dope in even where body searches are routine. Many have swallowed rubber or plastic packages before entering the institution and retrieved them inside.

In the light of existing conditions, knowledgeable observers find it incredible to hear those less knowing say that we coddle prisoners—that penitentiary life should be harsher. Such people do not know the facts. Much of our crime is caused by the inhumanity of our prisons and by our failure to rehabilitate those we send to them.

It is one of the larger ironies of our time that, concerned as we are about crime, the one area within the whole system of criminal justice that offers the best opportunity to prevent crime is the most neglected. In fact, neglect in the criminal justice system reaches its zenith in the neglect of corrections. There may be no comparable neglect within the whole range of government service. Yet, until the underlying causes of crime are relieved, corrections is by far the best chance we have to significantly and permanently reduce crime in America.

The most important statistic on crime is the one which tells us that 80 percent of all felonies are committed by repeaters. Four-fifths of our major crimes are committed by people already known to the criminal justice system.

We know further, indeed we have demonstrated, that recidivism—the repetition of crime by individuals—can be cut in half. It can be cut far more than that. But if only one-half of the repeated crime we now suffer could be eliminated, society would be free of 40 percent of all serious crime. If we are really concerned about crime, if we really care about our own character, how can we fail to make a massive effort?

Corrections in its entire range of services includes pretrial and post-conviction detention in jails and prisons as well as a variety of community-based activities, among them probation, parole, work release, halfway houses and prerelease guidance centers. Neglect debilitates corrections efforts across this whole spectrum of activity. Probation and parole are rarely what they profess to be—few if any prison systems have adequate manpower to give meaningful supervision. The personnel available rarely have the training or professional competence to provide the service needed.

Jails, generally located in cities and towns, house prisoners awaiting trial and persons convicted of minor offenses and sentenced to short periods of confinement. They are manned by untrained people with no professional skills. Prisons, where serious offenders serve penitentiary sentences, are usually located in remote areas where it is difficult to obtain personnel with professional skills or to retain those that do have them. Salaries are so low, working conditions so unpleasant and opportunity for advancement so limited that few want to work in prisons. Many who might help, affected by our general fear of prisons and prisoners, would not work there whatever the conditions, while others seek the power and authority over people offered by guard duty. Many prison guards are slowly brought to brutality by the environment of the prison itself. It can happen to anyone.

We spend less than 1.5 billion on all corrections—federal, state and local—although the process offers us the chance to save many billions of dollars through reduced crime and more in terms of human suffering. As public concern over crime rises, prison budgets are cut while police budgets swell. Governor Ronald Reagan caused the best leadership in the California prison system to resign by cutting already inadequate budgets while he simultaneously sought increases for the state police.

The Federal Bureau of Prisons is probably the most effective corrections system in the nation. Its directors, Sanford Bates, James V. Bennett, Myrl E. Alexander and now thirty-seven-year-old Norman A. Carlson, are among the most sensitive professionals in the history of penology. It is responsible for 20,000 federal civilian prisoners, yet its budget for 1968, including the cost of owning, maintaining and operating expensive prison facilities, was $77 million. By contrast, the FBI, one of the more than twenty substantial federal investigative and enforcement agencies, has a budget of nearly $200 million. Every year the prison budget is the first of those in the Department of Justice to be cut by the Congress. The FBI budget is often increased above its own request. The Bureau of Prisons struggles to keep old facilities operational. Only two federal prisons, one at Marion, Illinois, the other at Morgantown, West Virginia, have been built since World War II. As recently as 1965 the only all-female federal prison had no toilets in many units—the inmates used jars.

Fewer than twenty psychiatrists are available for the entire federal corrections system, though most prisoners need mental health services that the Bureau is unable to provide. When Congress reviewed the Manpower Development Training Act program for budget savings in 1968, the first cut—and the only 100 percent cut—was for prisoner training. That training might have kept hundreds or thousands of young men from further crime.

During Congressional consideration of the Omnibus Crime Control Act of 1968 designed to provide federal funding for state and local criminal justice needs, the issue of corrections caused a major battle. Nationwide, corrections receives about 25 percent of all funds provided for the criminal justice process. Self-styled tough crime fighters like Senators John McClellan of Arkansas and Strom Thurmond of South Carolina wanted to limit funds available for corrections under the bill to 5 percent. They joked in public hearings about raising it to $7\frac{1}{2}$ percent. Could the reason have been that they knew the jails and prisons of their states and many others are full of Negroes? Fortunately, such a tragic limitation was avoided. Instead, up to 20 percent of the grant funds were expendable for corrections. This compared with a 30 percent allocation for police to combat organized crime and an additional 30 percent for police to control riots. Corrections remains the stepchild of the criminal justice process. The hard-liners have no interest in corrections. They want punishment.

Philosophers have debated the purpose of penology since organized societies first began killing, maiming and confining individuals for conduct or expression they did not like. In early and simple times, vengeance was the major motivation for such responses to criminal acts. Among small closely knit groups, always threatened by nature and warring tribes, vengeance may have been thought to balance accounts. From today's perspective, such acts seem cruel, as they were. But life was cruel, a bare existence often, scratched from the earth with crude tools and fiercely protected with feeble weapons. In a way, too, vengeance shows how much, how emotionally, a people care—no nonsense here, an eye for an eye. Vengeance evokes a violent response. Vengeance as a motive for punishment evidences outrage, hatred, fear and self-righteousness.

The day—if there ever was one—when vengeance could have any moral justification passed centuries ago. Vengeance, at most, can be only a private balancing, not an atonement between the individual and the state. Sheer multitudes of people in a modern society make balancing between one and so many a meaningless form of retribution. Slowly civilization came to see that action by the state could not be compared with action by individuals. The state must act justly, coolly, rationally, deliberately and systematically. No human emotion or disability, no intoxicant can overwhelm it.

Centuries before vengeance as an admitted motive passed from general practice in the most advanced nations, it was recognized as an aggravant of crime. It caused crime. Society, in its quest for justice, sought vengeance through the action of a major social institution to which the people could look for leadership—government. At a time when civilized men could hope to create a gentle, nonviolent, humane society, vengeance served as a brutalizing throwback to the full horror of man's inhumanity in an earlier time when he contended unequally against nature for survival.

The modern penitentiary grew from another theory of penology. The very name is rooted in the Latin word that gives us "penitence." To seek divine forgiveness, to repent, to be sorry for one's sins, to be alone to contemplate the pity of one's own wrongdoing—this was the theory, if not the practice, of the early penitentiary.

For the Puritan conscience, penitence may have been a powerful regimen. In our mass culture it is rarely relevant. Some who commit crime are stricken with overpowering remorse. They are tortured by their own acts. These few pose little threat to society. Remorse comes from within. No prison will create it. But for those who pose America's crime problem penitence has little meaning. By and large, their lives are so empty, they are so full of frustration and despair, they are so sick in mind and body, and their entire life experience providing them grist for thought is so totally lacking in charity that contemplation is more likely to cause anger at society's sins than remorse for their own.

Punishment as an end in itself is itself a crime in our times. The crime of punishment, as Karl Menninger has shown through his works, is suffered by all society because punishment has regularly given rise to subsequent criminal acts inflicted on the public. The use of prisons to punish only causes crime.

We cannot say we practice any theory of penology in America today. We do what we do. And what we do has practically no relationship to what we say we do. Essentially, we use penology, without saying so, to confine— as inexpensively as possible—and thus separate for a time people who have committed crime. Simultaneously, if incidentally, we punish by providing an unpleasant experience. The combination tends to turn the prisoner from any sense of compassion that he may have and from concern for anyone but himself. Where he has lived, abuse of the individual's integrity and personality has been almost total. When he comes out of prison, no other individual seems very important to him. He will try to take care of himself. He will take what he wants or needs. He will be a threat to society.

Rehabilitation must be the goal of modern corrections. Every other consideration should be subordinated to it. To rehabilitate is to give health, freedom from drugs and alcohol, to provide education, vocational training, understanding and the ability to contribute to society.

Rehabilitation means the purpose of law is justice—and that as a generous people we wish to give every individual his chance for fulfillment. The theory of rehabilitation is based on the belief that healthy, rational people will not injure others, that they will understand that the individual and his society are best served by conduct that does not inflict injury, and that a just society has the ability to provide health and purpose and opportunity for all its citizens. Rehabilitated, an individual will not have the capacity—cannot bring himself—to injure another or take or destroy property.

Rehabilitation is individual salvation. What achievement can give society greater satisfaction than to afford the offender the chance, once lost, to live at peace, to fulfill himself and to help others? Rehabilitation is also the one clear way that criminal justice processes can significantly reduce crime. Those who are sent to jail and prison commit most of our crime. We know who they are. There is no surprise when they strike again. Unlike some crimes, theirs were predictable. All we had to do was act. Our failure to act demeans our character and tortures our lives.

The end sought by rehabilitation is a stable individual returned to community life, capable of constructive participation and incapable of crime. From the very beginning, the direction of the correctional process must be back toward the community. It is in the community that crime will be committed or a useful life lived.

Prisons create the starkest possible segregation from the community—distant, isolated and full of subcultures strange to urban life. Months or years in a prison environment followed by sudden release and full responsibility for one's self—for food, clothing, shelter, associations, employment, handicapped by a criminal record and in a new, strange and emotional environment—is enough to unsettle the most stable individual. We could not devise a more traumatic social experience. Hanging over most who are released is a deep self-doubt and a long-pent-up desire for the old ways—whisky, women, cars, money. There lingers a personal disorganization, an emotional instability and the threat—almost the expectation—of returning to prison. So most return. We almost seem to want it to happen this way.

From the moment a person is charged with crime, corrections personnel should work toward the day he will return to unrestrained community life. Accused people should be released pending trial; we say they are presumed innocent, and that presumption should be respected. They may need help and can be given it, including supervision that will protect the public and that is not inconsistent with their presumed innocence. Many of the personal problems tending them toward crime were visible long before a first arrest. They were having trouble in school—and dropped out—or were unemployed, running with a gang, drinking too much, taking dope, or obviously mentally unstable. Counseling, guidance and treatment can be offered to them immediately. If the suspect is on parole from an earlier sentence when arrested, there is a high risk that earlier correctional effort has failed. Parole supervision should be so effective that a quick estimate is possible. A hearing can be held to determine whether the conditions under which he was placed on parole have been violated. If they have been, the parolee should be fitted back into his program or into a revised program more carefully tailored in the light of his apparent failure.

Following a conviction, an analysis of the individual, his background, his history and his personal physical, mental, emotional, family and social condition must be made. Its accuracy should be tested by the prisoner's review of its content. This study, with continuing observation and treatment, will be the basis for designing his individual program. It should be available to the judge and carefully analyzed by him before sentencing.

If rehabilitation is the goal, only the indeterminate sentence will be used. Such a sentence sets an outer limit beyond which the state may no longer restrain the liberty of the individual. Depending on the offense and the condition of the prisoner, the sentence may be for a period not to exceed ten years, or six months, or thirty days. The prisoner may be unconditionally released or gradually released under restrictive conditions designed to assure rehabilitation at any time within the period of the sentence. The sentence contemplates a rehabilitation program specially designed for each individual convicted. Professionally trained correctional authorities can then carefully observe a prisoner and release him at the earliest time within the limits fixed which his personal situation indicates, and under conditions reasonably calculated to protect the public. Techniques of release may begin with family visits of a few hours' duration. Later, part-time or full-time employment may be possible or public or private schools attended from a community correction center. Overnight visits with the family may follow and finally a release, requiring continued schooling with good performance, employment at a productive level, or a stable family situation. Close communication, personal counseling and assistance, and regular phone calls or appearances will help the individual and improve chances for the program to succeed. Excessive drinking, associations with an old gang, staying out late in the evening without explanation may justify changes in supervision. An intensive supervisory effort for a period of months will get prisoners through their most difficult times and achieve a high level of rehabilitation.

The indeterminate sentence is premised on the fact that a judge has no way of predicting how an individual will develop or what he will be like in one year, or five, or ten. Fixing a period of years in advance during which a convict must be confined in jail cannot be rationally explained if rehabilitation, not punishment, is our goal. An immutable sentence for years is largely arbitrary—a guess or reflex—reflecting a judge's habit or frame of mind. The sentence to a fixed term of years injures beyond its irrationality. What motivation does a prisoner condemned to prison for seven certain years have in the first, the second or the fifth year? He is waiting. A program designed to rehabilitate him is waiting, too. There is no incentive. The cost and waste and harm are immense. If even in the early months of an indeterminate sentence for a maximum period of ten years the prisoner can see the chance to work days, to attend school, to learn a trade, to visit home, to move to a community correction location, he has the strongest motivation to try, to work with his supervisors and to prepare for the future. For many prisoners such efforts may be sheer cunning—an effort to appear to be what they are not. But the light at the end of the tunnel is visible, and it always looks good. It can be a goal—perhaps the first goal of a lifetime. Sometimes cunning may fool even professional correctional personnel. We can afford that risk. We are not fooled now. We know most prisoners who are released will commit more crimes. Sometimes the cunning will be entrapped by their own cleverness and the game they played will become their way of life.

Judges dislike sentencing intensely. It is the most difficult part of their whole job. No sensitive person can easily make a critically important decision for society and, without rational guidance, the most important decision in the life of another human being. Many judges dread the day they must impose sentence. It may look easy for them in the courtroom. They may seem stern, even indifferent, but some judges will tell you they sleep little the night before they impose sentences. They are, after all, exerting a greater influence on the life of another man in a single moment than most men do in a lifetime. Asked to do the impossible—to foresee the effect of a sentence on the life of a person for years into the future—how can they be just? They must try to guess what period of confinement will rehabilitate someone they will never know, under unknown future conditions they cannot control or even affect.

Some judges sentence long, some short. Illustrations of the inequality in sentencing occur every day, often in different courtrooms in the same courthouse. Two boys fail to report for military induction—one is sentenced to five years in prison, the other gets probation and never enters a prison. One judge sentences a robber convicted for the third time to one year in prison, while another judge on the same bench gives a first offender ten years. One man far more capable of serious crime than another and convicted of the same offense may get a fine, while the less fortunate and less dangerous person is sentenced to five years in the state penitentiary. One judge, because of his personal values, thinks homosexuality the most heinous of crimes and gives long sentences. Another hates prostitution. A third judge would never jail juveniles for either offense. Some judges regularly give juvenile offenders prison terms for first-offense car theft, while others turn them over to the custody of their parents.

Indeterminate sentencing affords the public the protection of potentially long confinement without the necessity that long sentences be served. It gives the best of both worlds—long protection for the public yet a fully flexible opportunity for the convict's rehabilitation. It provides the chance constantly to adapt correctional programs to personal needs even as individuals develop.

The day of the indeterminate sentence is coming. Less than fifteen years old in the federal system, indeterminate sentences are given in more than 20 percent of all convictions in which imprisonment is ordered. The number of indeterminate sentences given in the federal system doubled between 1964 and 1969. Still, many federal judges have never given an indeterminate sentence, while others give little else. There remain whole federal judicial districts where an indeterminate sentence has never been given. The greatest deterrent to the use of the indeterminate sentence is the slowness with which the judicial system adapts to obvious and urgently needed changes.

No correctional system in the United States is yet staffed to make effective use of the indeterminate sentence. In some prison systems benefits would be immediate because professional skills are available. In all, however, even those with no skills, the change to indeterminate sentencing would be for the better. The judges would at least be relieved of committing acts that inherently cause unequal justice. The prisoner would have the chance, however remote, of release at any time. The correctional system would have its opportunity to rehabilitate.

There are risks, of course, in the use of the indeterminate sentence, as there are in any technique. The method does not, obviously, guarantee rehabilitation; it is only the beginning—only an opportunity. Parole authorities and prison personnel can abuse this additional power, use it arbitrarily or fail to use it through timidity. But we must reform personnel standards and techniques in the system, anyway, and there is the opportunity for judicial review. Due process in the administration of indeterminate sentences can be assured. If there is arbitrary administration of indeterminate sentences, appeals can be taken through the correctional system and subjected to judicial scrutiny.

Under any system most prisoners will be released someday. Very few will be held until maturation, senility or death itself has stilled criminal instincts. If we release persons who have the capacity for further crime, only temporary safety has been afforded. In the meanwhile, imprisonment has often increased the individual's capacity for crime. If nothing but selfish interest impelled us, then rehabilitation is worth the effort, for when it works, it reduces crime, reduces the cost of handling prisoners, reduces the cost of the criminal justice system and even relieves pressure to provide the basic and massive reforms that are necessary to affect the underlying causes of crime.

One billion dollars would nearly double our entire expenditure for corrections. Spent for the right purposes, a billion dollars could show immediate results. Correctional expenditures protect the public and should therefore be more readily acceptable to the public. They lack the charitable qualities of the purely preventive expenditure. They are direct, practical and effective.

No set program of corrections can fit the needs of more than a small number of the prisoners in any system. The backgrounds, experience, deficiencies and needs of inmates are as diverse as our total society. For many offenders a program of rehabilitation should be only the effort of society to communicate clearly the reasons for its rule of law and the purposes of its penalties.

Young men who refuse induction into the military service because they oppose war often believe they adhere to a higher moral standard. Many do. Certainly from the standpoint of their potential for violence or property crime, there is no quality in their character requiring rehabilitation. But they should understand that the rule of law is not mindless, that it has a purpose, and that if the system is to have integrity, the purpose must be fulfilled. The question is not who has the higher morality, but shall the system of law do what it says. For society to consume years, or even days, of the lives of these young men in prison idleness and brutality or blight their personal potential through social stigma is tragically wasteful and desperately wrong. Until laws can be reformed, sensitive corrections systems must afford the hundreds of young men serving sentences for violations of the Selective Service Act the chance to make constructive contributions outside the prison environment. We should not make criminals of those who oppose war.

The young boy convicted of smoking a marijuana cigarette and the young girl in prison for having an abortion present difficult challenges, as does the drunken driver who has caused a fatal accident. The latter may never drink again and, sober, be incapable of antisocial conduct. Merely to confine such people in prison or place them in an irrelevant program designed to rehabilitate persons who have deliberately committed serious crimes against others is senseless. Special programs for such offenders can protect the public without the waste and injury risked by imprisonment.

Some crimes are acts of momentary irrationality by people who will never commit another serious crime. Murder—a crime of passion—is often such an act. Occurring most often within families, and between friends and neighbors, it is sometimes the result of an uncontrollable impulse, of sudden overwhelming anger or hatred, spontaneous, unpredictable and nonrecurrent. To place the tormented people who have committed such a crime among hardened criminals who lead lives of crime can be cruel and senseless.

The preponderance of all efforts by correctional agencies must be directed at the youngest offenders, those from backgrounds and with personal histories and conditions that indicate emotional instability and the probability of continuing and increasing antisocial activities. Numbering in the tens of thousands, they commit most common crimes of violence and most burglaries, larcenies and thefts.

Many coming to prison are so disorganized, so confused and so lacking in self-control that they cannot focus on any subject more than a few moments. Their span of any intellectual effort is too short to permit training. Before they can begin their rehabilitation, they must live in a calm, orderly, organized atmosphere in which they can learn to concentrate. For many this is the highest hurdle. It is something they have never known. Born in bedlam, physically abused in infancy and childhood, they have lived amid chronic violence, fear and confusion. Their physical and mental illnesses— alcoholism and drug addiction among their most common manifestations— must be professionally treated and dealt with as the medical problems they are. Major portions of the population in every prison have such needs.

At the earliest possible time schooling should be resumed for those capable of it. In federal youth centers, probably 90 percent of the inmates are high school and junior high school dropouts, the great majority years behind their appropriate grade level. Special tutoring is essential if they are to advance. If they do not advance, if they do not get back in school, with their history and handicaps their chances for a life free of crime are slight.

Meaningful vocational training in high-employment fields will be the best program for many. Learning a skill is more than a possibility for most prisoners. It is what has been missing in their lives. Often they absorb skills quickly and take pride in their workmanship. From there the opportunity for rehabilitation is great.

Throughout the history of federal corrections most prisoners have been faced with two alternatives—the total custody of a prison or release to the community with insignificant parole supervision. For decades dormant skills were largely undeveloped. While Federal Prison Industries trained and meaningfully employed some, its programs were located in a prison environment. The skills learned were minimal and often in trades in which employment is hard to find. In the early days it was agriculture, still a dominant occupation in some state prison systems. Later textile work, bricklaying, tire recapping, auto repair and metal work were offered some. Now automatic data processing and white-collar training are afforded a few.

In 1965, in what seemed a bold step at the time, supervision of prisoners in normal community employment situations was first attempted. A work release program authorized by Congress permitted prisoners to leave prison in the morning for a place of employment, work there during the day, and return to prison when the work day ended. The potential was immediately apparent. Jobs were found. Prisoners were cautiously selected and assigned to the program, nearly always during the last months of their incarceration. Other prisoners often made it clear to those chosen that they had better not abuse the opportunity, for nearly every prisoner wanted work release. If those who were released failed, others would never have the chance, and they all knew it. Bricklayer, carpenter, automobile mechanic, tire recapper, bookkeeper, college student: these were among the first jobs offered prisoners in the program. One young man traveled sixty miles a day by commercial bus from the federal institution at Seagoville, Texas, worked a half day in the dean's office in a state college, took three courses and made three A's.

The strain was great on these prisoners. The meaning of imprisonment had never been so clear. Freedom had new meaning to them. Some admitted the great difficulty of returning to prison at night, and the contrast between liberty and detention seemed much sharper. But by the end of 1968, thousands had been in the program, and more than 500 of the 20,000 federal prisoners were always on work release.

Fewer than one in twenty failed to comply with all the conditions of work release. Alcohol was the cause of failure in nearly two-thirds of the cases. In most of these the tavern looked too inviting after work and the prospect of the prison too dismal. We should not be surprised that 5 percent failed. After all, before the program was launched, 50 percent were failing when finally released. The real surprise was that there were so few failures. The policy was far too cautious and the supervision inadequate, but a good beginning was made.

Since we know that better than one-half of all the people who leave prisons return convicted of a subsequent crime, it is clearly worth risking six months on work release after a convict has spent many months or years in prison. Among the 95 percent who did not fail in the work release program, perhaps only a third will return to prison. As to the 5 percent who failed to meet the conditions of release and sought to escape, all were caught and returned to prison, where they served more time. People do not really escape from prison successfully. In the history of the Federal Bureau hundreds of thousands have been imprisoned and thousands have escaped, but fewer than twenty have not been recaptured or otherwise accounted for. It is only a matter of time—usually not very long.

Perhaps the most discouraging thing about work release is the timidity of the program and the opposition it arouses. It is a small, late and uncertain step in a direction in which we must move forcefully. Even so, the hard-liners—those who would control crime by long brutalizing penitentiary sentences and the fear of eternal damnation—have attacked work release as if it caused crime. Blind to the fact that prisoners will soon be released anyway, they prefer six more months of incarceration to a chance to test the personal stability of the individual in community life. What perversity so deprives such critics of compassion that they will not give a prisoner any chance, as a job will do, or see that by failing to give that chance, they assure more crime? The worst that can happen when work release begins only six months before a prison term ends is that the length of the term is shortened six months if the prisoner flees and is never caught. Perhaps some crimes may therefore be committed six months earlier, but if we are not willing to take that small gamble, what do we expect will happen six months later when the inmate will not return to prison at night and authorities will not know what he is doing? We are admitting the total failure of the rehabilitative power of penology.

From work release men can move back into society with a job and a history of work at it. Many have said they feel human again—for the first time in years. Of all the loneliness of our mass society that of the former convict is greatest.

A typical releasee in the very first group that began in the late fall of 1965 worked on a construction crew in Texarkana, Texas. He liked the men he worked with and they liked him. A camaraderie developed between him and his co-workers. They became buddies. He was kidded: "How about going fishing with us Saturday?" and he said, "Wait until spring." They slapped him on the back—it had been a long time since anyone had done that. He said he felt like a man again. Before, he had been alone against the world. His family, on relief for five years, was off relief and moving to Texarkana. He was supporting them. He could send them money. He was going to live and work in Texarkana. He would be the best carpenter there, he said. He would work hard and raise his family. He may.

Work release, halfway houses, prerelease guidance centers—these are only the beginning. Community supervision is the future of corrections. Work release affords a good test of the ability of a prisoner to relate to other people in an unrestrained environment. It is in society that the individual must master his frustrations, temptations and weaknesses. When a young offender who can continue schooling is placed in a regular public school, he often need not be identified to his fellow students as a prisoner. The greatest difficulty that the former prisoner confronts in establishing relationships with people is they tend to think of him first, last and always as a convict—not as a person. We tend to be what people expect us to be. Few things are more important to us than the regard of others. Identified as a troublemaker or a criminal, we tend to be troublemakers and criminals. We want to live up to our reputations.

As soon as their condition indicates that it is consistent with safety and rehabilitation, prisoners should be moved from conventional prisons to community facilities such as a floor of a YMCA, a wing in an apartment building, or a house. Special plans for security and supervision will permit easy control. In such settings they can learn to live in an environment approaching the kind they must adjust to before they will be released. They can attend school and return after school, take the vocational training their aptitudes and experience indicate, or work at jobs that test their ability to make it on their own. Their freedom, their associations, their schedules can be controlled as needed to help achieve rehabilitation. Family visits can begin, followed by church attendance if desired, perhaps a movie or a date, and later a whole weekend. This is what they must learn or relearn. Who will say they cannot? And if they cannot, what then? We should stop deceiving ourselves with sentences for a term of years; we might as well lock up offenders and throw away the keys.

Like all pioneer endeavors, our experience with community corrections is hardly definitive. There have been successes and failures. Those close to the experience know it will work if sufficient effort is made. It will work because it has to work. We can neither abandon these people nor permit them to injure society.

The California Youth Authority experimented with young offenders chosen at random—pure chance determined the selection—from all except those convicted of the most serious crimes. One group was confined in conventional prison facilities. A second was sent to the celebrated California Forest Camps, initiated in the 1930s. Somehow, perhaps because of the dignity and solemnity of the forests, the fresh air and nature, it was thought that the big trees would make decent citizens of kids from the slums of Oakland. A third group was treated in small community centers near areas they would live in when released. From there they were slowly worked back into the communities.

The test began in 1960 in three counties. Hundreds of youngsters were involved. By 1967 recidivism among conventional facilities and forest camp inmates ran about 54 percent. For the community correctional program the recidivism rate was 29 percent.

In the years to come millions of boys and hundreds of thousands of girls throughout the United States will be confined in prisons. They will be the youngest offenders, representative of the American child in trouble. They will come, in the main, from poor families and broken homes. They will be school dropouts. So little loved are they that in the federal system, 70 percent will never have a visitor—relative or friend—while they wait in prison. No one cares. Most will be afflicted with mental and physical illnesses, and many will be addicted to drugs.

How many crimes are committed by persons with congenital brain damage and chemical imbalances in body processes? How many slum children with brain injuries will get the medical and psychiatric help they need? How many crimes are caused by the neglect of mentally retarded children of the poor? When mental retardation afflicts wealthy families, for all the sadness it may cause, the children at least are well cared for. But when this tragic handicap strikes the poor, it can overpower their remaining will to cope with life. Families and individuals disintegrate. When we know that mental retardation may be five times more common in the ghetto and that 25 percent of the prisoners in state penitentiary systems such as Texas' are mentally retarded, we may know more than we care to know about the causes of crime. Had we known and cared, the physically or mentally deficient youngster could have been helped. Instead, because he was different, a handicap that did not of itself make him antisocial alienated him from all love, and he became antisocial. In time, he committed criminal acts. Should we treat him, then, like a worthless life, penning him up and dismissing his case as hopeless? We do not need to go on like this.

If we permit history to repeat itself, most such youngsters will commit crimes after they are released. Nearly all who live lives of crime, who repeat and repeat, began with insignificant crimes when they were kids. Here then is our major opportunity and high duty.

We know that corrections can rehabilitate. We know that the younger the offender the better his and society's chance. We know that when we fail it is all of us who suffer. America is a nation with the skills and resources to provide the necessary elements of rehabilitation: physical and mental health, all the education a youngster can absorb, vocational skills for the highest trade he can master, a calm and orderly environment away from anxiety and violence, living among people who care, who love—with these a boy can begin again. With these we can restore a reverence for life, a sense of security and a self-assurance amid all the pressures of modern community life. These attitudes will not be developed in a laboratory. They must be developed in the community itself: first, sometimes, in the prison community but finally in the open society in which the individual must make his way by himself.

To youth corrections we must bring the most advanced research and best techniques. We must provide ample resources to implement both. We must assure funds and professional skills to guide a boy when he may need it most—on the hard return home. Every prison can be just another manufacturer of crime—just another place to hold bad boys out of sight, out of mind. Better that we tear them down now than that we let that happen. What nobler work could involve us than to save one boy from the horror, for himself and for all who sense his empty heart, of a life of crime?

One of the unanswered questions in modern mass society is whether institutions, organizations and associations can meet the challenge of change effectively and efficiently. Can they adapt to new conditions with reasonable speed? Can they serve present needs rather than old habits? There is substantial evidence that most such institutions do not have the inner force or motivation for the task.

Prisons are a classic illustration. Some 125,000 full-time employees are scattered through an impossible maze of jurisdictions throughout the country. Jails across the street from each other—one run by the county, the other by the city—are still commonplace. The time spent moving prisoners from one facility to the other and the risk involved each time are reasons enough to abolish one. But the waste in manpower and resources available for rehabilitation effort is outrageous. Resources for corrections are so grossly inadequate to begin with that continued waste and inefficiency are intolerable.

Even in the biggest city there should be but one jail system. It will need many facilities and varied programs, but it should manage all correctional activities in the area. Persons in pretrial detention, whether charged with federal, state or local crime, can be boarded in the facility best suited to their need and most convenient to the courts and other agencies that may require frequent contact with them. By such methods reasonably efficient use can be made of facilities and manpower.

A single agency serving all jurisdictions—federal, state, and local—will have greater resources and be subject to the scrutiny of several masters. Different courts can insist on good performance, as federal courts have often demanded that a county jail provide regular and decent meals, beds for every inmate, and separation of youngsters and first offenders from hardened criminals. The manager of the overall agency will be involved with other agencies, which will be more likely to complain about his performance than they would of their own.

Federal jail standards assuring adequate care and custody by local jails holding federal prisoners have done much to raise the overall conditions for other prisoners in the same jails. Federal inspectors make sure the standards are enforced. Other political jurisdictions can do the same. Excellence can be attained with one comprehensive service, if properly funded. Now there are usually several bad ones, none with enough qualified personnel or proper rehabilitation programs. Someone mugged by a teenager just released from county jail can derive little comfort from the news that the federal youth center is doing a marvelous job. Unified service can bring quality to all.

Prison administration is an extremely complex business. It includes most of the problems known to guard agencies, hotels, restaurants, schools, hospitals, infirmaries, mental institutions, psychologists' clinics, small businesses, vocational and athletic training departments, employment bureaus, libraries and law offices. To provide all the services needed, and the size necessary to attract, train and retain professional excellence, a statewide system is required. City and county prisons or jails rarely look beyond mere confinement as their purpose. They are restricted by geography and finances to large old brick buildings downtown. An occasional county prison farm will teach slum boys how to cultivate crops that their families left the South ten years ago to get away from growing. Local prisons do not, and in the nature of things cannot, have the staff, the range of skills, or the numbers of prisoners necessary to provide all of the services required. They are even less able to provide the special services needed by female and juvenile offenders. A basic reorganization of corrections is necessary in nearly every state if we are to have any hopes of achieving rehabilitation.

The federal system has too few women prisoners to offer needed services to them. Coming from all over the United States, federal female prisoners number fewer than eight hundred. How far from their homes are the women's reformatories at Alderson, West Virginia, and Terminal Island, California? How many will have visitors while in prison? What will happen to their children, whom they will not see during the entire time they are in prison? What does this deprivation mean to the child and the family—and to the crime rate? It is doubtful that confinement is meaningful for 10 percent of the women prisoners, but there they are, in penitentiaries in the hills of Appalachia and on the harbor at Long Beach.

The whole system of corrections for women needs analysis. Prisons for women began by analogy to male prisons after the penitentiary system developed in the nineteenth century. Techniques have been refashioned only slightly to reflect the very great differences in the conduct of male and female prisoners. Women are rarely violent in prison. They are not a threat to the public. Confinement will not break a drug habit or train a girl for employment or make less likely her return to prostitution. Mental health services are a need of most women inmates, but prisons rarely provide them, nor are penal institutions the best environment for treatment. The only benefit possible for many is the calming influence of what can be, but in most women's prisons is not, a quiet, orderly, attractive environment. Regular meals, never experienced before, and a clean private room can be shown as life possibilities. Such amenities—and the habits they imply—can soon become desirable, but iron bars will not speed the process. The community is where life will be lived out.

There is a need to reallocate manpower between prison and community services. Eighty percent of all corrections manpower guards jails and prisons. The larger number of criminals on probation—800,000 out of 1,200,000 serving sentence on the average in the late 1960s—is serviced, theoretically, by one-fifth the total national correctional personnel. The community-based officers have additional duties that add to the impossibility of meaningful supervision. Surveys have revealed federal judicial districts where probation service officers carry four to five times the case load of forty persons that the National Council on Crime and Delinquency considers desirable. Some such officers devote up to 85 percent of their time preparing presentence reports for judges and are therefore left with only minutes a day to supervise hundreds of persons recently released from prison. In those districts, as is the case nearly everywhere, probation and parole supervision is negligible if not meaningless.

When a prisoner is released on parole after prison confinement of perhaps many years' duration, he needs help desperately. He may not know it, and he may not want it, but he needs help, careful supervision, a steady hand, a voice with his employer and fellow workers, a friend to eat dinner with once in a while, a visit with a family. The early months are the hardest; once he gets through them, his chances for making it all the way are much higher. But instead of help most of his supervision now takes the form of routine office visits, spot phone checks, pointless report writing, all of it often surrounded with an aura of mistrust.

The allocation of manpower between custodial care in prisons and supervision in community settings must be reversed. Only when we devote 20 percent and less for institutional care and 80 percent and more for community supervision can we begin to rehabilitate. Only a dedicated community supervision staff properly trained with high skills can cut recidivism substantially.

There is no effort within the criminal justice system that holds a fraction of the potential to reduce crime offered by a vigorous, thoughtful corrections program. Not even efforts directed at the underlying causes of crime, such as health services, education, employment or decent housing, offer the same immediate potential at near the cost. Corrections focuses directly on the highly distilled mainstream of criminal conduct. Three of every four persons that it deals with have a potential for antisocial conduct. Here are identified offenders. The risks are clear and substantiated by statistical evidence from over the entire country. If all of our research and learning about human behavior, if all the teaching in our great universities about medical science, mental health, psychiatry, psychology, sociology, hereditary and environmental influences has any applicability to real life, here in corrections it has an immense and critically important role. Yet, divorcement of all those lessons and skills from the people who need them is almost total.

If America cares for its character, it must revolutionize its approach to corrections.

Part II

CONFINEMENT, INMATES, AND PRISON PROBLEMS

Any discussion of the present state of the field of corrections must necessarily include a careful consideration of some of the more salient problems that both correctional practitioners and offenders must deal with on a daily basis. The public has become aware of at least some of these problems because of their extensive, though often distorted, coverage in the mass media. Perhaps the most significant and enduring problem for everyone concerned is represented by the broad-spectrum of deprivations and degradations that come with confinement. The discussion provided by Gresham Sykes is instructive in this regard. Several of the more specific issues, including the problems of consensual and coercive involvement in homosexual relationships, interpersonal violence, and full-scale prison riots, are more fully developed in the selections by David Ward and Gene Kassebaum, John Gagnon and William Simon, Alan Davis, and Vernon Fox.

A number of other less well understood problems are also relevant to our discussion, and the remaining readings in this section focus on two general issues that have not been given adequate attention. The articles by Michael Miller and by Richard Schwartz and Jerome Skolnick make important and related points. Miller's work illustrates that the implementation of treatment and training programs that are not coordinated with the needs and requirements of the larger society are, at best, poor risks. This is amplified in the selection by Schwartz and Skolnick in the sense that they demonstrate that biases and stereotypes over which the correctional system has little if any control can render the reintegration of the offender into the free society exceedingly difficult even if the programs themselves are sound. The remaining selections by Daniel Glaser and Richard McCleery speak on a somewhat different issue, but one that is of crucial importance today. Specifically, both articles focus on important aspects of change—Glaser on the changing character of the offender population; McCleery on the impact of organizational change on the correctional process.

5

The Pains of Imprisonment

Gresham M. Sykes

THE DEPRIVATION OF LIBERTY

Of all the painful conditions imposed on the inmates of the New Jersey State Prison, none is more immediately obvious than the loss of liberty. The prisoner must live in a world shrunk to thirteen and a half acres and within this restricted area his freedom of movement is further confined by a strict system of passes, the military formations in moving from one point within the institution to another, and the demand that he remain in his cell until given permission to do otherwise. In short, the prisoner's loss of liberty is a double one—first, by confinement to the institution and second, by confinement within the institution.

The mere fact that the individual's movements are restricted, however, is far less serious than the fact that imprisonment means that the inmate is cut off from family, relatives, and friends, not in the self-isolation of the hermit or the misanthrope, but in the involuntary seclusion of the outlaw. It is true that visiting and mailing privileges partially relieve the prisoner's isolation—if he can find someone to visit him or write to him and who will be approved as a visitor or correspondent by the prison officials. Many inmates, however, have found their links with persons in the free community weakening as the months and years pass by. This may explain in part the fact that an examination of the visiting records of a random sample of the inmate population, covering approximately a one-year period, indicated that 41 percent of the prisoners in the New Jersey State Prison had received no visits from the outside world.

It is not difficult to see this isolation as painfully depriving or frustrating in terms of lost emotional relationships, of loneliness and boredom. But what makes this pain of imprisonment bite most deeply is the fact that the confinement of the criminal represents a deliberate, moral rejection of the criminal by the free community. Indeed, as Reckless has pointed out, it is the moral condemnation of the criminal—however it may be symbolized—that converts hurt into punishment, i.e., the just consequence of committing an offense, and it is this condemnation that confronts the inmate by the fact of his seclusion.

Now it is sometimes claimed that many criminals are so alienated from conforming society and so identified with a criminal subculture that the moral condemnation, rejection, or disapproval of legitimate society does not touch them; they are, it is said, indifferent to the penal sanctions of the free community, at least as far as the moral stigma of being defined as a criminal is concerned. Possibly this is true for a small number of offenders such as the professional thief described by Sutherland[1] or the psychopathic personality delineated by William and Joan McCord.[2] For the great majority of criminals in prison, however, the evidence suggests that neither alienation from the ranks of the law-abiding nor involvement in a system of criminal value is sufficient to eliminate the threat to the prisoner's ego posed by society's rejection.[3] The signs pointing to the prisoner's degradation are many—the anonymity of a uniform and a number rather than a name, the shaven head,[4] the insistence on gestures of respect and subordination when addressing officials, and so on. The prisoner is never allowed to forget that, by committing a crime, he has foregone his claim to the status of a full-fledged, *trusted* member of society. The status lost by the

---

[1]Cf. Edwin H. Sutherland, *The Professional Thief*, Chicago: The University of Chicago Press, 1937.

[2]Cf. William and Joan McCord, *Psychopathy and Delinquency*, New York: Grune and Stratton, 1956.

[3]For an excellent discussion of the symbolic overtones of imprisonment, see Walter C. Reckless, *The Crime Problem*, New York: Appleton-Century-Crofts, Inc., 1955, pp. 428–429.

[4]Western culture has long placed a peculiar emphasis on shaving the head as a symbol of degradation, ranging from the enraged treatment of collaborators in occupied Europe to the more measured barbering of recruits in the Armed Forces. In the latter case, as in the prison, the nominal purpose has been cleanliness and neatness, but for the person who is shaved the meaning is somewhat different. In the New Jersey State Prison, the prisoner is clipped to the skull on arrival but not thereafter.

prisoner is, in fact, similar to what Marshall has called the status of citizenship—that basic acceptance of the individual as a functioning member of the society in which he lives.[5] It is true that in the past the imprisoned criminal literally suffered civil death and that although the doctrines of attainder and corruption of blood were largely abandoned in the 18th and 19th Centuries, the inmate is still stripped of many of his civil rights such as the right to vote, to hold office, to sue in court, and so on.[6] But as important as the loss of these civil rights may be, the loss of that more diffuse status which defines the individual as someone to be trusted or as morally acceptable is the loss which hurts most.

In short, the wall which seals off the criminal, the contaminated man, is a constant threat to the prisoner's self-conception and the threat is continually repeated in the many daily reminders that he must be kept apart from "decent" men. Somehow this rejection or degradation by the free community must be warded off, turned aside, rendered harmless. Somehow the imprisoned criminal must find a device for rejecting his rejectors, if he is to endure psychologically.[7]

THE DEPRIVATION OF GOODS AND SERVICES

There are admittedly many problems in attempting to compare the standard of living existing in the free community and the standard of living which is supposed to be the lot of the inmate in prison. How, for example, do we interpret the fact that a covering for the floor of a cell usually consists of a scrap from a discarded blanket and that even this possession is forbidden by the prison authorities? What meaning do we attach to the fact that no inmate owns a common piece of furniture, such as a chair, but only a homemade stool? What is the value of a suit of clothing which is also a convict's uniform with a stripe and a stencilled number? The answers are far from simple although there are a number of prison officials who will argue that some inmates are better off in prison, in strictly material terms, than they could ever hope to be in the rough-and-tumble economic life of the free community. Possibly this is so, but at least it has never been claimed by the inmates that the goods and services provided the prisoner are equal to or better than the goods and services which the prisoner could obtain if he were left to his own devices outside the walls. The average

---

[5]See T. H. Marshall, *Citizenship and Social Class*, Cambridge, England: The Cambridge University Press, 1950.

[6]Paul W. Tappan, "The Legal Rights of Prisoners," *The Annals of the American Academy of Political and Social Science*, Vol. 293, May 1954, pp. 99–111.

[7]See Lloyd W. McCorkle and Richard R. Korn, "Resocialization Within Walls." *Ibid.*, pp. 88–98.

inmate finds himself in a harshly Spartan environment which he defines as painfully depriving.

Now it is true that the prisoner's basic material needs are met—in the sense that he does not go hungry, cold, or wet. He receives adequate medical care and he has the opportunity for exercise. But a standard of living constructed in terms of so many calories per day, so many hours of recreation, so many cubic yards of space per individual, and so on, misses the central point when we are discussing the individual's feeling of deprivation, however useful it may be in setting minimum levels of consumption for the maintenance of health. A standard of living can be hopelessly inadequate, from the individual's viewpoint, because it bores him to death or fails to provide those subtle symbolic overtones which we invest in the world of possessions. And this is the core of the prisoner's problem in the area of goods and services. He wants—or needs, if you will—not just the so-called necessities of life but also the amenities: cigarettes and liquor as well as calories, interesting foods as well as sheer bulk, individual clothing as well as adequate clothing, individual furnishings for his living quarters as well as shelter, privacy as well as space. The "rightfulness" of the prisoner's feeling of deprivation can be questioned. And the objective reality of the prisoner's deprivation—in the sense that he has actually suffered a fall from his economic position in the free community—can be viewed with skepticism, as we have indicated above. But these criticisms are irrelevant to the significant issue, namely that legitimately or illegitimately, rationally or irrationally, the inmate population defines its present material impoverishment as a painful loss.

Now in modern Western culture, material possessions are so large a part of the individual's conception of himself that to be stripped of them is to be attacked at the deepest layers of personality. This is particularly true when poverty cannot be excused as a blind stroke of fate or a universal calamity. Poverty due to one's own mistakes or misdeeds represents an indictment against one's basic value or personal worth and there are few men who can philosophically bear the want caused by their own actions. It is true some prisoners in the New Jersey State Prison attempt to interpret their low position in the scale of goods and services as an effort by the State to exploit them economically. Thus, in the eyes of some inmates, the prisoner is poor not because of an offense which he has committed in the past but because the State is a tyrant which uses its captive criminals as slave labor under the hypocritical guise of reformation. Penology, it is said, is a racket. Their poverty, then, is not punishment as we have used the word before, i.e. the just consequence of criminal behavior; rather, it is an unjust hurt or pain inflicted without legitimate cause. This attitude, however, does not appear to be particularly widespread in the inmate population and the great majority of prisoners must face their privation without the aid of the wronged man's sense of injustice. Furthermore, most prisoners are unable to fortify themselves in their low level of material existence by seeing it as a means to some high or worthy end. They are unable to attach any significant meaning to their need to make it more bearable, such as present pleasures foregone for pleasures in the future, self-sacrifice in the interests of the community, or material asceticism for the purpose of spiritual salvation.

The inmate, then, sees himself as having been made poor by reason of his own acts and without the rationale of compensating benefits. The failure is *his* failure in a world where control and possession of the material environment are commonly taken as sure indicators of a man's worth. It is true that our society, as materialistic as it may be, does not rely exclusively on goods and services as a criterion of an individual's value; and, as we shall see shortly, the inmate population defends itself by stressing alternative or supplementary measures of merit. But impoverishment remains as one of the most bitter attacks on the individual's self-image that our society has to offer and the prisoner cannot ignore the implications of his straitened circumstances.[8] Whatever the discomforts and irritations of the prisoner's Spartan existence may be, he must carry the additional burden of social definitions which equate his material deprivation with personal inadequacy.

THE DEPRIVATION OF HETEROSEXUAL RELATIONSHIPS

Unlike the prisoner in many Latin-American countries, the inmate of the maximum security prison in New Jersey does not enjoy the privilege of so-called conjugal visits. And in those brief times when the prisoner is allowed to see his wife, mistress, or "female friend," the woman must sit on one side of a plate glass window and the prisoner on the other, communicating by means of a phone under the scrutiny of a guard. If the inmate, then, is rejected and impoverished by the facts of his imprisonment, he is also figuratively castrated by his involuntary celibacy.

Now a number of writers have suggested that men in prison undergo a reduction of the sexual drive and that the sexual frustrations of prisoners are therefore less than they might appear to be at first glance. The reports of reduced sexual interest have, however, been largely confined to accounts of

---

[8]Komarovsky's discussion of the psychological implications of unemployment is particularly apposite here, despite the markedly different context, for she notes that economic failure provokes acute anxiety as humiliation cuts away at the individual's conception of his manhood. He feels useless, undeserving of respect, disorganized, adrift in a society where economic status is a major anchoring point. Cf. Mirra Komarovsky, *The Unemployed Man and His Family*, New York: The Dryden Press, 1940, pp. 74–77.

men imprisoned in concentration camps or similar extreme situations where starvation, torture, and physical exhaustion have reduced life to a simple struggle for survival or left the captive sunk in apathy. But in the American prison these factors are not at work to any significant extent and Lindner has noted that the prisoner's access to mass media, pornography circulated among inmates, and similar stimuli serve to keep alive the prisoner's sexual impulses.[9] The same thought is expressed more crudely by the inmates of the New Jersey State Prison in a variety of obscene expressions and it is clear that the lack of heterosexual intercourse is a frustrating experience for the imprisoned criminal and that it is a frustration which weighs heavily and painfully on his mind during his prolonged confinement. There are, of course, some "habitual" homosexuals in the prison—men who were homosexuals before their arrival and who continue their particular form of deviant behavior within the all-male society of the custodial institution. For these inmates, perhaps, the deprivation of heterosexual intercourse cannot be counted as one of the pains of imprisonment. They are few in number, however, and are only too apt to be victimized or raped by aggressive prisoners who have turned to homosexuality as a temporary means of relieving their frustration.

Yet as important as frustration in the sexual sphere may be in physiological terms, the psychological problems created by the lack of heterosexual relationships can be even more serious. A society composed exclusively of men tends to generate anxieties in its members concerning their masculinity regardless of whether or not they are coerced, bribed, or seduced into an overt homosexual liaison. Latent homosexual tendencies may be activated in the individual without being translated into open behavior and yet still arouse strong guilt feelings at either the conscious or unconscious level. In the tense atmosphere of the prison with its known perversions, its importunities of admitted homosexuals, and its constant references to the problems of sexual frustration by guards and inmates alike, there are few prisoners who can escape the fact that an essential component of a man's self conception—his status of male—is called into question. And if an inmate has in fact engaged in homosexual behavior within the walls, not as a continuation of an habitual pattern but as a rare act of sexual deviance under the intolerable pressure of mounting physical desire, the psychological onslaughts on his ego image will be particularly acute.[10]

---

[9]See Robert M. Lindner, "Sex in Prison," *Complex*, Vol. 6, Fall 1951, pp. 5–20

[10]Estimates of the proportion of inmates who engage in homosexuality during their confinement in the prison are apt to vary. In the New Jersey State Prison, however, Wing Guards and Shop Guards examined a random sample of inmates who were well known to them from prolonged observation and identified 35 percent of the men as individuals believed to have engaged in homosexual acts. The judgments of these officials were substantially in agreement with the judgments of a prisoner who possessed an apparently well-founded reputation as an aggressive homosexual deeply

In addition to these problems stemming from sexual frustration per se, the deprivation of heterosexual relationships carries with it another threat to the prisoner's image of himself—more diffuse, perhaps, and more difficult to state precisely and yet no less disturbing. The inmate is shut off from the world of women which by its very polarity gives the male world much of its meaning. Like most men, the inmate must search for his identity not simply within himself but also in the picture of himself which he finds reflected in the eyes of others; and since a significant half of his audience is denied him, the inmate's self image is in danger of becoming half complete, fractured, a monochrome without the hues of reality. The prisoner's looking-glass self, in short—to use Cooley's fine phrase—is only that portion of the prisoner's personality which is recognized or appreciated by men and this partial identity is made hazy by the lack of contrast.

THE DEPRIVATION OF AUTONOMY

We have noted before that the inmate suffers from what we have called a loss of autonomy in that he is subjected to a vast body of rules and commands which are designed to control his behavior in minute detail. To the casual observer, however, it might seem that the many areas of life in which self-determination is withheld, such as the language used in a letter, the hours of sleeping and eating, or the route to work, are relatively unimportant. Perhaps it might be argued, as in the case of material deprivation, that the inmate in prison is not much worse off than the individual in the free community who is regulated in a great many aspects of his life by the iron fist of custom. It could even be argued, as some writers have done, that for a number of imprisoned criminals the extensive control of the custodians provides a welcome escape from freedom and that the prison officials thus supply an external Super-Ego which serves to reduce the anxieties arising from an awareness of deviant impulses. But from the viewpoint of the inmate population, it is precisely the triviality of much of the officials' control which often proves to be most galling. Regulation by a bureaucratic staff is felt far differently than regulation by custom. And even though a

---

involved in patterns of sexual deviance within the institution and who had been convicted of sodomy. But the validity of these judgments remains largely unknown and we present the following conclusions, based on a variety of sources, as provisional at best: First, a fairly large proportion of prisoners engage in homosexual behavior during their period of confinement. Second, for many of those prisoners who do engage in homosexual behavior, their sexual deviance is rare or sporadic rather than chronic. And third, as we have indicated before, much of the homosexuality which does occur in prison is not part of a life pattern existing before and after confinement; rather, it is a response to the peculiar rigors of imprisonment.

few prisoners do welcome the strict regime of the custodians as a means of checking their own aberrant behavior which they would like to curb but cannot, most prisoners look on the matter in a different light. Most prisoners, in fact, express an intense hostility against their far-reaching dependence on the decisions of their captors and the restricted ability to make choices must be included among the pains of imprisonment along with restrictions of physical liberty, the possession of goods and services, and heterosexual relationships.

Now the loss of autonomy experienced by the inmates of the prison does not represent a grant of power freely given by the ruled to the rulers for a limited and specific end. Rather, it is total and it is imposed—and for these reasons it is less endurable. The nominal objectives of the custodians are not, in general, the objectives of the prisoners.[11] Yet regardless of whether or not the inmate population shares some aims with the custodial bureaucracy, the many regulations and orders of the New Jersey State Prison's official regime often arouse the prisoner's hostility because they don't "make sense" from the prisoner's point of view. Indeed, the incomprehensible order or rule is a basic feature of life in prison. Inmates, for example, are forbidden to take food from the messhall to their cells. Some prisoners see this as a move designed to promote cleanliness; others are convinced that the regulation is for the purpose of preventing inmates from obtaining anything that might be used in the *sub rosa* system of barter. Most, however, simply see the measure as another irritating, pointless gesture of authoritarianism. Similarly, prisoners are denied parole but are left in ignorance of the reasons for the decision. Prisoners are informed that the delivery of mail will be delayed—but they are not told why.

Now some of the inmate population's ignorance might be described as "accidental"; it arises from what we can call the principle of bureaucratic indifference, i.e., events which seem important or vital to those at the bottom of the heap are viewed with an increasing lack of concern with each step upward. The rules, the commands, the decisions which flow down to those who are controlled are not accompanied by explanations on the grounds that it is "impractical" or "too much trouble." Some of the inmate

---

[11]We have suggested earlier, in our discussion of the defects of prison as a system of power, that the nominal objectives of the officials tend to be compromised as they are translated into the actual routines of day-to-day life. The modus vivendi reached by guards and their prisoners is oriented toward certain goals which are in fact shared by captors and captives. In this limited sense, the control of the prison officials is partly concurred in by the inmates as well as imposed on them from above. We will explore this issue at greater length in the analysis of crisis and equilibrium in the society of captives, but in discussing the pains of imprisonment our attention is focused on the frustrations or threats posed by confinement rather than the devices which meet these frustrations or threats and render them tolerable. Our interest here is in the vectors of the prison's social system—if we may use an analogy from the physical sciences—rather than the resultant.

population's ignorance, however, is deliberately fostered by the prison officials in that explanations are often withheld as a matter of calculated policy. Providing explanations carries an implication that those who are ruled have a right to know—and this in turn suggests that if the explanations are not satisfactory, the rule or order will be changed. But this is in direct contradiction to the theoretical power relationship of the inmates and the prison officials. Imprisoned criminals are individuals who are being punished by society and they must be brought to their knees. If the inmate population maintains the right to argue with its captors, it takes on the appearance of an enemy nation with its own sovereignty; and in so doing it raises disturbing questions about the nature of the offender's deviance. The criminal is no longer simply a man who has broken the law; he has become a part of a group with an alternative viewpoint and thus attacks the validity of the law itself. The custodians' refusal to give reasons for many aspects of their regime can be seen in part as an attempt to avoid such an intolerable situation.

The indignation aroused by the "bargaining inmate" or the necessity of justifying the custodial regime is particularly evident during a riot when prisoners have the "impudence" to present a list of demands. In discussing the disturbances at the New Jersey State Prison in the Spring of 1952, for example, a newspaper editorial angrily noted that "the storm, like a nightmarish April Fool's dream, has passed, leaving in its wake a partially wrecked State Prison as a debasing monument to the ignominious rage of desperate men."

The important point, however, is that the frustration of the prisoner's ability to make choices and the frequent refusals to provide an explanation for the regulations and commands descending from the bureaucratic staff involve a profound threat to the prisoner's self image because they reduce the prisoner to the weak, helpless, dependent status of childhood. As Bettelheim has tellingly noted in his comments on the concentration camp, men under guard stand in constant danger of losing their identification with the normal definition of an adult and the imprisoned criminal finds his picture of himself as a self-determining individual being destroyed by the regime of the custodians.[12] It is possible that this psychological attack is particularly painful in American culture because of the deep-lying insecurities produced by the delays, the conditionality and the uneven progress so often observed in the granting of adulthood. It is also possible that the criminal is frequently an individual who has experienced great difficulty in adjusting himself to figures of authority and who finds the many restraints of prison life particularly threatening in so far as earlier struggles over the

---

[12]Cf. Bruno Bettelheim, "Individual and Mass Behavior in Extreme Situations," in *Readings in Social Psychology*, edited by T. M. Newcomb and E. L. Hartley, New York: Henry Holt and Company, 1947.

establishment of self are reactivated in a more virulent form. But without asserting that Americans in general or criminals in particular are notably ill-equipped to deal with the problems posed by the deprivation of autonomy, the helpless or dependent status of the prisoner clearly represents a serious threat to the prisoner's self image as a fully accredited member of adult society. And of the many threats which may confront the individual, either in or out of prison, there are few better calculated to arouse acute anxieties than the attempt to reimpose the subservience of youth. Public humiliation, enforced respect and deference, the finality of authoritarian decisions, the demands for a specified course of conduct because, in the judgment of another, it is in the individual's best interest—all are features of childhood's helplessness in the face of a superior adult world. Such things may be both irksome and disturbing for a child, especially if the child envisions himself as having outgrown such servitude. But for the adult who has escaped such helplessness with the passage of years, to be thrust back into childhood's helplessness is even more painful, and the inmate of the prison must somehow find a means of coping with the issue.

THE DEPRIVATION OF SECURITY

However strange it may appear that society has chosen to reduce the criminality of the offender by forcing him to associate with more than a thousand other criminals for years on end, there is one meaning of this involuntary union which is obvious—the individual prisoner is thrown into prolonged intimacy with other men who in many cases have a long history of violent, aggressive behavior. It is a situation which can prove to be anxiety-provoking even for the hardened recidivist and it is in this light that we can understand the comment of an inmate of the New Jersey State Prison who said, "The worst thing about prison is you have to live with other prisoners."

The fact that the imprisoned criminal sometimes views his fellow prisoners as "vicious" or "dangerous" may seem a trifle unreasonable. Other inmates, after all, are men like himself, bearing the legal stigma of conviction. But even if the individual prisoner believes that he himself is not the sort of person who is likely to attack or exploit weaker and less resourceful fellow captives, he is apt to view others with more suspicion. And if he himself is prepared to commit crimes while in prison, he is likely to feel that many others will be at least equally ready. . . . For the moment it is enough to point out that regardless of the patterns of mutual aid and support which may flourish in the inmate population, there are a sufficient number of outlaws within this group of outlaws to deprive the average prisoner of that sense of security which comes from living among men who can be reasonably expected to abide by the rules of society. While it is true that every prisoner does not live in the constant fear of being robbed or beaten, the constant companionship of thieves, rapists, murderers, and aggressive homosexuals is far from reassuring.

An important aspect of this disturbingly problematical world is the fact that the inmate is acutely aware that sooner or later he will be "tested" —that someone will "push" him to see how far they can go and that he must be prepared to fight for the safety of his person and his possessions. If he should fail, he will thereafter be an object of contempt, constantly in danger of being attacked by other inmates who view him as an obvious victim, as a man who cannot or will not defend his rights. And yet if he succeeds, he may well become a target for the prisoner who wishes to prove himself, who seeks to enhance his own prestige by defeating the man with a reputation for toughness. Thus both success and failure in defending one's self against the aggressions of fellow captives may serve to provoke fresh attacks and no man stands assured of the future.

The prisoner's loss of security arouses acute anxiety, in short, not just because violent acts of aggression and exploitation occur but also because such behavior constantly calls into question the individual's ability to cope with it, in terms of his own inner resources, his courage, his "nerve." Can he stand up and take it? Will he prove to be tough enough? These uncertainties constitute an ego threat for the individual forced to live in prolonged intimacy with criminals, regardless of the nature or extent of his own criminality; and we can catch a glimpse of this tense and fearful existence in the comment of one prisoner who said, "It takes a pretty good man to be able to stand on an equal plane with a guy that's in for rape, with a guy that's in for murder, with a man who's well respected in the institution because he's a real tough cookie. . . ." His expectations concerning the conforming behavior of others destroyed, unable and unwilling to rely on the officials for protection, uncertain of whether or not today's joke will be tomorrow's bitter insult, the prison inmate can never feel safe. And at a deeper level lies the anxiety about his reactions to this unstable world, for then his manhood will be evaluated in the public view.

6

Sexual Assaults in the Philadelphia Prison System

Alan J. Davis

In the summer of 1968, Joseph F. Mitchell, a slightly-built 19-year-old, was brought to trial before Alexander F. Barbieri, judge of the Court of Common Pleas No. 8 in Philadelphia County. Mitchell's lawyer, Joseph E. Alessandroni, told Judge Barbieri that his client, while being transported in a sheriff's van, had been repeatedly raped by a gang of criminals. A few weeks later, Alessandroni informed the judge that George DiAngelo, a slender 21-year-old whom Barbieri had committed to the Philadelphia Detention Center merely for pre-sentence evaluation, had been sexually assaulted within minutes of his admission.

Judge Barbieri thereupon appointed me, then Chief Assistant District Attorney of Philadelphia, to investigate these allegations. Police Commissioner Frank L. Rizzo started a parallel investigation; then these two investigations were merged.

In the Philadelphia prison system there are three facilities: the Detention Center, Holmesburg Prison, and the House of Correction. The period we chose to study was from June 1966 to July 31, 1968—a little over two years. Out of the 60,000 inmates who passed through the prison system in those 26 months, we interviewed 3,304—virtually all of them

Published by permission of Transaction Inc. from *trans*action, Vol. 6 (December 1968). © 1968 by Transaction Inc.

inmates during the period of our investigation. We also interviewed 561 out of the 570 custodial employees. We took 130 written statements from those who had given us important information, and gave polygraph ("lie-detector") examinations to 45 of them. We asked 26 employees to take polygraph tests: 25 refused, and the one employee who took the test "passed." We asked 48 inmates: seven refused, and of the 41 remaining, 10 failed the test and 31 passed. (We ignored the statements of those prisoners and employees who either would not take the test or who failed it.) In addition, we interviewed several people whom we believed had special information, and we reviewed all of the reports dealing with homosexuality issued by the prison system since June 1966. Finally, we made a number of detailed personal inspections of the prison facilities and of the sheriff's vans.

In brief, we found that sexual assaults in the Philadelphia prison system are epidemic. As Superintendent Hendrick and three of the wardens admitted, virtually every slightly-built young man committed by the courts is sexually approached within a day or two after his admission to prison. Many of these young men are repeatedly raped by gangs of inmates. Others, because of the threat of gang rape, seek protection by entering into a homosexual relationship with an individual tormentor. Only the tougher and more hardened young men, and those few so obviously frail that they are immediately locked up for their own protection, escape homosexual rape.

After a young man has been raped, he is marked as a sexual victim for the duration of his confinement. This mark follows him from institution to institution. Many of these young men return to their communities ashamed, and full of hatred.

This, then, is the sexual system that exists in the Philadelphia prisons. It is a system that imposes a punishment that is not, and could not be, included in the sentence of the court. Indeed, it is a system under which the least hardened criminals, and many men later found to be innocent, suffer the most.

A few typical examples of such sexual assaults may convey the enormity of the problem. In an early draft of our report, an attempt was made to couch this illustrative material in sociological, medical, and legal terminology less offensive than the raw, ugly language used by the witnesses and victims. This approach was abandoned. The incidents are raw and ugly. Any attempt to prettify them would be hypocrisy.

A witness describes the ordeal of *William McNichol*, 24 years old and mentally disturbed:

"That was June 11th, I was assigned to E Dorm. Right after the light went out I saw this colored male, Cheyenne—I think his last name is Boone. He went over and was talking to this kid and slapped him in the face with a belt. He was saying come on back with us and the kid kept saying I don't want to. After being slapped with the belt he walked back with Cheyenne and another colored fellow named Horse. They were walking him back into E Dorm. They were telling him to put his hand down and stop crying so the guard will not know what is going on. I looked up a couple of times. They had the kid on the floor. About 12 fellows took turns with him. This went on for about two hours.

"After this he came back to his bed and he was crying and he stated that 'They all took turns on me.' He laid there for about 20 minutes and Cheyenne came over to the kid's bed and pulled his pants down and got on top of him and raped him again. When he got done Horse did it again and then about four or five others got on him. While one of the guys was on him, raping him, Horse came over and said, 'Open your mouth and suck on this and don't bite it." He then put his penis in his mouth and made him suck on it. The kid was hollering that he was gagging and Horse stated, 'you better not bite it or I will kick your teeth out.'

"While they had this kid they also had a kid named William in another section in E Dorm. He had his pants off and he was bent over and they were taking turns on him. This was Horse, Cheyenne, and about seven other colored fellows. Two of the seven were brothers.

"Horse came back and stated, 'Boy, I got two virgins in one night. Maybe I should make it three.' At this time he was standing over me. I stated, 'What are you looking at?' and he said 'We'll save him for tomorrow night.' "

Julius Brown, 18 years old:

"Brown stated that he has been in Holmesburg since March 29, 1968, and that about a week and a half ago, on Thursday, he was in I block; his cell was number 926. On this date, in the morning after breakfast, James Williams called him into his cell; he went into Williams's cell. Donald Reese was in there also. Further that he had owed Williams four cartons of cigarettes. Williams said to him that he would have to give the cigarettes back right now or he would have to give them something else. He [Brown] then started to walk out of the cell and Williams pushed him down. Williams picked up the window pole, Reese picked up a bench and stood blocking the door. Reese told him that if he goes to the guard they are going to get him anyway; there were other men outside the cell.

"Further that he walked out of the cell, they were all around him and walked to cell 971, and they pushed him inside. He went over and sat on the toilet seat. Twin [Roger Jones] came into the cell, they made him lay down on the floor, and Twin pulled his [Brown's] pants down and made him lay face down. Twin pushed his [Brown's] legs apart and Twin put his penis into his [Brown's] rectum. He was on him until he discharged. When he got through, Brown saw that he was bleeding from the rectum. Then Twin, Williams, Reese, and McDuffy told him that if he went to the guard their boys would get him to D block, and he was scared then to tell the guard. Further that he did cry out when Twin did this to him, but the guard wouldn't be able to hear him because the block is long.

"Brown went on to say that the next day after chow [breakfast] James Williams, McDuffy, Ike (Isaiah Franklin), and Leftenant got him in cell 972 [Roger Jones's cell]. They told him that everything is cool now as long as he doesn't tell. Further that he had never been in jail before and he was too scared to tell anybody. Then four of them did it to him—they put their penises into his rectum, James first, Ike second, Leftenant third, McDuffy fourth. Twin did not bother him that time. That after they did this he was bleeding and got sick.

"That night, Roach [Thomas Roach] came into his cell and changed with his partner. Roach told him that he would have to do it. When the guard came to check the cells, Roach turned over so he wouldn't be recognized. After the guard counted and left, Roach got on top of him, put his penis into his [Brown's] rectum, and discharged."

NINETEEN-YEAR-OLD IS BEATEN

Charles Williams, 19 years old:
"On Tuesday morning, the first week of June at about 9:30 A.M., I was in my cell 412 on D block and I had started to clean up. A tall, heavy-set fella came into the cell and asked for a mirror and shaving brush and a comb, and that my cell partner said he could borrow.

"He then said that he heard something about me concerning homosexual acts. I told him what he had heard was not true. He then started to threaten me and if I didn't submit to him. Then I hit him with my fist in his face before he could hit me. Then about three more men came into the cell, and they started to beat me up, too. I fought back the best I could and then I fell on the floor and I got kicked in the ribs. Three guys were holding me while the other one tore my pants off; I continued to fight until one of the guys knocked me out. One of the guys was holding me on the floor and had my arm pinned to the floor. And about seven or eight guys came into the cell and they took turns sticking their penis up my ass. When they finished they left my cell, and I was still laying on the floor."

Clarence Garlick, 26 years old:
"Back in April this year, about 10:30 A.M. I was in my cell 455 on block D when Joe Lovett came into my cell. I was laying on my bed. When he came in I jumped up. He told me to get greased up. I told him I wasn't going to do nothing. He told me, 'You're going to do something.' He started punching me. I had backed up into a corner of the cell. He seen some

mineral-oil grease I had on the table and he reached over and handed it to me saying, 'Put this on.' I put some on and layed down on the bed. He took out his penis and got on top of me. After he did what he wanted to do he got up and got some toilet paper and wiped himself off and went out of the cell.

"This is the second incident. He came to me on July 18, 1968, in the morning about 10 o'clock. I was standing up in the doorway of my cell, 455. He told me to 'Get it fixed.' I told him I wasn't going to do nothing, that today was my birthday. He walked on away.

"The next day, on the 19th, he came to me again. I was in my cell, this was about the same time. He stated, 'Today isn't your birthday, you're going to do something.' I told him I wasn't going to do anything. He started punching me again. I told him I was going to call the guard. He stated, 'Go ahead and call, you'll only call him one time and I'll knock you out.' He got the grease from off the table and handed it to me, told me to put some on, which I did. I laid down on the bed, he took out his penis and got on top. A friend he walks with, Kincaid, was standing out by the door, he was laughing. Joe got up after he got through, got toilet paper and wiped himself off. He then walked out of the cell."

During the 26-month period, we found, there had been 156 sexual assaults that could be documented and substantiated—through institutional records, polygraph examinations, or other corroboration. Seven of the assaults took place in the sheriff's vans, 149 in the prisons. Of the sexual assaults, 82 consisted of buggery; 19 of fellatio; and 55 of attempts and coercive solicitations to commit sexual acts. There were assaults on at least 97 different victims by at least 176 different aggressors. With unidentified victims and aggressors, there were 109 different victims and 276 different aggressors.

For various reasons, these figures represent only the top of the iceberg.

1. Our investigators, as mentioned, interviewed only a twentieth of the inmates who passed through the prison system. We discovered 94 assaults—excluding those reported in institutional records. This suggests that if all 60,000 inmates had been interviewed, 20 times 94—or 1880—additional assaults would have come to light.

2. Almost all of the victims still in prison were so terrified of retaliation by other prisoners that they were very reluctant to cooperate with us.

3. Many guards discouraged complaints by indicating that they did not want to be bothered. One victim screamed for over an hour while he was being gang-raped in his cell; the block guard ignored the screams and laughed at the victim when the rape was over. The inmates who reported this passed a polygraph examination. The guard who had been named refused to take the test.

Then too, some guards put pressure on victims not to complain—such complaints, after all, would indicate that the guards were failing in their duty. We found many cases where victims, after filing complaints, had "voluntarily" refused to prosecute, and a number of them told us that guards urged them to rely on prison discipline rather than to bring the facts out into the open. Very often, these guards asked the victim if he wanted his parents and friends to find out about his humiliation.

1. Without prompting from the prison guards, many victims and their families wanted to avoid the shame and dishonor they believed would follow such a complaint.

2. Inmates have little faith in the ability of a guard to protect them from retaliation should they complain. Their fears are justified by the lack of supervision by guards, and the inadequate facilities to provide security for complainants.

3. Inmates who complain are themselves punished by the prison system. It is usual procedure to place a victim of a sexual assault on "lock-in feed-in," obstensibly for his own protection. This means that after a complaint is made, and especially if it is pressed, the complainant is locked in his cell all day, fed in his cell, and not permitted recreation, television, or exercise until it is determined that he is safe from retaliation. Many victims consider this "solitary confinement" worse than a homosexual relationship with one aggressor.

4. Sometimes very little comes of a complaint. Some complaints are just not acted upon; action, when taken, usually consists of putting the aggressor in the "hole" for 30 days or less. Meanwhile, the victim also is usually locked in, and looks forward—when released —to terror from the aggressor's friends, and from the aggressor himself when he is let out of the "hole." Finally,

5. Many of the victims themselves distrust and are hostile to constituted authority, and could not bring themselves to cooperate by filing a complaint.

Taking all of these facts into consideration, we conservatively estimate that the true number of assaults in the 26-month period was about 2000. Indeed, one guard put the number at 250 a year in the Detention Center alone.

Of the estimated 2000 assaults that occurred, 156 of which were documented, the inmates reported only 96 to prison authorities. Of this 96, only 64 were mentioned in the prison records. Of these 64, only 40 resulted in internal discipline against the aggressors; and only 26 incidents were reported to the police for prosecution.

CONSENSUAL HOMOSEXUALITY EXCLUDED

Now, in our study of sexual assaults we excluded any that were cases of truly "consensual" homosexuality. Nonetheless, it was hard to separate consensual homosexuality from rape, since many continuing and isolated homosexual liaisons originated from a gang rape, or from the ever-present threat of gang rape. Similarly, many individual homosexual acts were possible only because of the fear-charged atmosphere. Thus, a threat of rape, expressed or implied, would prompt an already fearful young man to submit. Prison officials are too quick to label such activities "consensual."

At the opposite end of the spectrum from innocent victims of homosexual rape are the male prostitutes. These homosexuals—referred to as "sissys," "freaks," or "girls"—were supposed to be segregated from the general prison population, yet they were readily available. We learned of repeated instances where homosexual "security" cells were left unguarded by a staff that was too small or too indifferent, or who turned their backs so that certain favored inmates could have sexual relations.

Many of these male prostitutes were created not only by force and the threat of force, but by bribery. The fact is that a person with economic advantage in prison often uses it to gain sexual advantage. Typically, an experienced inmate will give cigarettes, candy, sedatives, stainless-steel blades, or extra food pilfered from the kitchen to an inexperienced inmate, and after a few days the veteran will demand sexual repayment. It is also typical for a veteran to entice a young man into gambling, have him roll up large debts, and then tell the youth to "pay or fuck." An initial sexual act stamps the victim as a "punk boy," and he is pressed into prostitution for the remainder of his imprisonment.

Despite the important role that economic advantage plays in the creation of homosexuality, it is virtually impossible to obliterate economic distinctions between inmates. Even a small accumulation of money or luxuries gives an inmate substantial economic advantage: In the prison economy, a shopworker earns 15 to 25 cents a day; half of the inmates have no prison jobs at all, and most inmates get little or no material help from friends or relatives outside the prison.

It is the duty of prison officials to reduce the economic power that any inmate might exercise over another inmate. Yet we discovered one area in which Philadelphia prison officials, either through neglect or indifference, disregarded this duty. As a result, at least one inmate became so powerful economically that he was able to choose, as cellmates, a series of young men he found attractive, and then use bribery to sexually subvert each one.

The University of Pennsylvania and a private concern operate a large laboratory on H block of Holmesburg Prison, where they test inmates' reactions to new medicines and to experimental commercial products like soaps, shaving creams, suntan lotions, and toilet tissue. The prisoners are excellent "human guinea pigs" (1) because they live under controlled conditions, and (2) because they will submit to tests for a fraction of the fee that a free individual would demand. Prison officials—because there is very little other activity for the prisoners, and because the laboratory pays 20 percent of the inmates' wages to the prison system—have allowed the project to expand to the extent that it constitutes a separate government within the prison system.

All the inmates at Holmesburg wanted to "get on the tests" because, by prison standards, they can earn a fortune. Just by wearing a chemical patch on his back, for example, a prisoner can earn $10 to $15 a week. By participating in some tests that last longer, a prisoner—for doing almost nothing—will receive over $100. Altogether, the Holmesburg inmates earn more than $250,000 a year from the project. A few prisoners end up with bodies crazyquilted with motley scars and skin patches, but to these men, in the context of a prison economy, it seems well worth it.

To save money another way, the operators of the project also use inmates as laboratory assistants. An experienced assistant, working an eight-hour day, will get $100 a month—in the prison economy, the equivalent of a millionaire's income. Even a few prison guards are employed in the project, after their regular hours, and they work side by side with the prisoners.

UNIVERSITY OF PENNSYLVANIA PROJECT DISASTROUS

Generally, the "U. of P." project has had a disastrous effect upon the operations of Holmesburg Prison; it is one of the reasons why morale of the employees is at the lowest in that institution. The disproportionate wealth and power in the hands of a few inmates leads to favoritism, bribery and jealousy among the guards, resulting in disrespect for supervisory authority and prison regulations. What is more, the project contributed to homosexuality in the prison.

Stanley Randall, a 38-year-old con man serving a four- to eleven-year sentence, was employed in laboratory cell 806, H block, as an assistant. Although prison and laboratory officials at first denied it, Randall had the power to decide which inmates would serve as subjects on various tests. Since the 806 cell disbursed $10,000 to $20,000 a year, Randall's power was considerable.

Randall's special taste was newly admitted young inmates. Through his influence with the guard staff he had his pick of these young men assigned to him as cellmates—and for as long as he wished. When his victims moved in, Randall solicited them to engage in sexual acts in return for his giving them a steady stream of luxuries and for "getting them on the tests." At least half a dozen of these inmates submitted, and went on to profit handsomely from the University of Pennsylvania project.

Although top prison officials assured us that no inmate was permitted to earn more than $1200 a year, and that $400 was unusually high, in six months Randall's present cellmate had earned over $800. The record was held by a prior cellmate of Randall's, who had earned $1740 in just 11 months. When we asked university project managers about these high incomes, they told us they had never heard of any $1200-a-year limit. The prison's accounting office had apparently never heard of this $1200-a-year limit either, because that office had credited these high amounts to the accounts of Randall's cellmates.

How had Randall managed to get his choice of cellmates? One guard told us that H-block guards had been instructed by "higher ups" not to interfere in the affairs of inmates working for the U. of P. Another guard reported he had received such instructions, and said they had come from the guard lieutenant. The lieutenant denied this, and agreed to take a lie-detector test. Later he reversed his position and refused. Randall admitted he had often given cigars to this lieutenant.

Other inmates besides Randall exploited their powerful positions. One inmate worker, for example, forged test results and fee vouchers, and got fees for inmates who had not actually been test subjects. It also seems that at least a few guards were also corrupted.

As a result of our investigation, prison officials have relieved the powerful inmate workers of their positions with the U. of P. project. They are also considering phasing out the project entirely.

How did sexual aggressors in the prisons differ from their victims? On the average, aggressors tended to be older, heavier, taller, and more serious offenders. Data on hundreds of victims and aggressors yielded the following comparisons:

	Victims	*Aggressors*
Average Age	20.75	23.67
Average Height	5'8¼"	5'9"
Average Weight	140.9	157.2

Both victims and aggressors tended to be younger than the average inmate, as comparison with the following table shows:

Average Age of Prisoners
(July 31, 1968)

Detention Center	27.9
Holmesburg	29.3
House of Correction	28.9
All Prisons	28.8

Yet although aggressors on the average are older and larger than victims, these differences are rather slight. In many cases, there may be no differences, and in others they are reversed. Still, after having observed hundreds of victims and aggressors we believe that there are other, more subjective, physical criteria which can be used to differentiate between aggressors and victims:

1. Victims tend to look young for their age.
2. Victims tend to look less athletic, and less physically coordinated.
3. Victims tend to be better-looking.

A comparison of 164 aggressors and 103 victims showed that 68 percent of the former and only 38 percent of the latter had been charged with serious felonies. Among aggressors, violent assaultive felonies were particularly common. Thus, 14 aggressors had been charged with rape, but only three victims; six aggressors had been charged with weapons offenses, and no victims; 34 aggressors with robbery and aggravated robbery, but only eight victims; and seven aggressors with assault with intent to kill, but only one victim. As many victims as aggressors, however, had been charged with homicide. On the other hand, many more victims than aggressors were charged with relatively less serious offenses, such as the larceny of a car, going AWOL from the armed forces, violating parole, and delinquency.

We also made a study of the 129 documented assaults in which the races of both aggressors and victims had been ascertained, and found that a disproportionate number involved Negro aggressors and white victims:

Type of Incident	Number of Incidents	Percentage
White Aggressors & White Victims	20	15%
Negro Aggressors & Negro Victims	37	29%
White Aggressors & Negro Victims	0	0%
Negro Aggressors & White Victims	72	56%
Total	129	100%

These statistics in part reflect the fact that 80 percent of the inmates are Negro—it is safer for a member of a majority group to single out for attack a member of a minority group. Then too, Negro victims seemed more reluctant than white victims to disclose assaults by Negro aggressors. But it also seems true that current racial tensions and hostilities in the outside community are aggravated in a criminal population.

Now, we are not professionally qualified to offer a scientific theory to explain the sexual aggression in the Philadelphia prison system. We have, however, reached certain conclusions that should be recorded for possible use by psychiatrists, psychologists, and social scientists. The conclusions and the analysis set forth are based upon our observations, upon pertinent literature, and upon discussions with a psychiatrist and a psychologist who are experts in forensic psychology.

1. We were struck by the fact that the typical sexual aggressor does not consider himself to be a homosexual, or even to have engaged in homosexual acts. This seems to be based upon his startlingly primitive view of sexual relationships, one that defines as male whichever partner is aggressive and as homosexual whichever partner is passive.

2. It appears that need for sexual release is not the primary motive of a sexual aggressor. After all, in a sexually segregated population, autoeroticism would seem a much easier and more "normal" method of release than homosexual rape. As recent studies have shown (Masters and Johnson, *Human Sexual Response*, 1966), autoerotic stimulation yields a measure of physical release and pleasure similar to that yielded by sexual intercourse.

3. A primary goal of the sexual aggressor, it is clear, is the conquest and degradation of his victim. We repeatedly found that aggressors used such language as "Fight or fuck," "We're going to take your manhood," "You'll have to give up some face," and "We're gonna make a girl out of you." Some of the assaults were reminiscent of the custom in some ancient societies of castrating or buggering a defeated enemy.

4. Another primary goal of many of the aggressors, it appears, is to retain membership in the groups led by militant sexual aggressors. This is particularly true of some of the participants in gang rapes. Lacking identification with such groups, as many of the aggressors know, they themselves would become victims. And finally,

5. Most of the aggressors seem to be members of a subculture that has found most nonsexual avenues of asserting their masculinity closed to them. To them, job success, raising a family, and achieving the respect of other men socially have been largely beyond

reach. Only sexual and physical prowess stands between them and a feeling of emasculation. When the fact of imprisonment, and the emptiness of prison life, knock from under them whatever props to their masculinity they may have had, they became almost totally dependent for self-esteem upon an assertion of their sexual and physical potency.

In sum, sexual assaults, as opposed to consensual homosexuality, are not primarily caused by sexual deprivation. They are expressions of anger and aggression prompted by the same basic frustrations that exist in the community, and which very probably were significant factors in producing the rapes, robberies, and other violent offenses for which the bulk of the aggressors were convicted. These frustrations can be summarized as an inability to achieve masculine identification and pride through avenues other than sex. When these frustrations are intensified by imprisonment, and superimposed upon hostility between the races and a simplistic view of all sex as an act of aggression and subjugation, then the result is assaults on members of the same sex.

Assuming that this analysis is valid, then the principal psychological causes of sexual assaults in the Philadelphia prison system are deeply rooted in the community—in that millions of American men, throughout their lives, are deprived of any effective way of achieving masculine self-identification through avenues other than physical aggression and sex. They belong to a class of men who rarely have meaningful work, successful families, or opportunities for constructive emotional expression and individual creativity. Therefore, although sexual assaults within a prison system may be controlled by intensive supervision and effective programing, the pathology at the root of sexual assaults will not be eliminated until fundamental changes are made in the outside community.

7

Homosexuality: A Mode of Adaptation in a Prison for Women

David A. Ward

Gene G. Kassebaum

THE PROBLEM

Compared to the sociological literature on men's prisons, little is known about the women's prison, and virtually no systematically collected empirical data have been published. Sociological investigations of prisons for men have in recent years been conducted from a theoretical perspective which views the behavior of inmates as a response to the material, social and psychological pains of imprisonment.[1] It has been consistently reported that one response of male prisoners to these deprivations is the establishment of a social system militating against the process of degrada-

From "Homosexuality: A Mode of Adaptation in a Prison for Women," *Social Problems*, 12, No. 2 (Fall 1964), 159–77. Reprinted by permission.

[1]See Gresham M. Sykes and Sheldon L. Messinger, "The Inmate Social System" in *Theoretical Studies in Social Organization of the Prison*, New York: Social Science Research Council, Pamphlet 15 (March 1960), pp. 5–19; Erving Goffman, "On the Characteristics of Total Institutions," in Donald R. Cressey, editor, *The Prison*, New York: Holt, Rinehart and Winston, Inc., 1961, Chapters 1 and 2; and Richard A. Cloward, "Social Control in the Prison," *Theoretical Studies in Social Organization of the Prison, op. cit.*, pp. 20–48.

tion, mortification of the self, depersonalization and anomie. In response to these deprivations and pains inmates come to play certain roles, and these roles come to constitute the inmate social system to which the new prisoner adapts. The rules and maxims covering these adaptations constitute the so-called inmate code. New inmates find information available from inmate *politicians* and scarce goods are available from *merchants*. Rationalizations are provided for criminal behavior; solutions for getting scarce goods and services are made known; and methods of dealing with the staff and for interacting with fellow inmates are detailed. The code provides a philosophy for doing time and the inmate social organization provides the mechanism for implementing the maxims of the code. It has, however, become increasingly apparent that prisoner behavior is rooted in more than just the conditions of confinement. In a number of studies the impact of the inmate culture and degree of support of the inmate code have been shown to vary over time and according to type of prisoner.[2]

These studies have prompted consideration of other factors in accounting for prisoner behavior. One theory which has been advanced to explain discrepancies in support of the inmate code and internalization of inmate culture focuses on the pre-prison characteristics and experiences of inmates.[3] Irwin and Cressey have recently argued that there are a number of subcultures in the prison community, reflecting the presence of different types of prisoners.[4] Salient factors related to past experience seem to be the history of involvement in criminal activity, the extent of experience in "doing time" and the influence of latent culture and latent identities which inmates bring to prison with them.[5]

The bases for prisoner behavior are now seen to be the kinds of deprivations, limitations and hardships posed by confinement, coupled with

[2]See Stanton Wheeler, "Socialization in Correctional Communities," *American Sociological Review*, 26 (October, 1961), pp. 706–711; Daniel Glaser and John R. Stratton, "Measuring Inmate Change in Prison," in Donald R. Cressey, editor, *The Prison, op. cit.*, pp. 388–390; Peter G. Garabedian, "Social Roles and Processes of Socialization in the Prison Community," *Social Problems*, 11 (Fall, 1963), pp. 139–152; and Gresham M. Sykes, "Men, Merchants, and Toughs," *Social Problems*, 4 (October, 1956), p. 134.

[3]This emphasis may be found in the work of Clarence Schrag, "Some Foundations for a Theory of Correction," in Donald R. Cressey, editor, *The Prison, op. cit.*, pp. 346–357; and Donald L. Garrity, "The Prison as a Rehabilitation Agency," in Donald R. Cressey, editor, *The Prison, op. cit.*, pp. 358–380.

[4]Donald R. Cressey and John Irwin, "Thieves, Convicts, and Inmate Culture," *Social Problems*, 10 (Fall, 1962), pp. 142–155; see also Lloyd W. McCorkle and Richard R. Korn, "Resocialization Within Walls," *The Annals*, 293 (May, 1954), pp. 88–89.

[5]The concept of latent culture is described by Howard S. Becker and Blanche Geer, "Latent Culture: A Note on the Theory of Latent Social Roles," *Administrative Science Quarterly*, 5 (September, 1960), pp. 304–313; see also Alvin W. Gouldner "Cosmopolitans and Locals: Toward an Analysis of Latent Social Roles I," *Administrative Science Quarterly*, 2 (December, 1957), pp. 281–306.

the pre-prison backgrounds of the inmates. For any prison the content and degree of support given to an inmate code (or the number of inmates making adaptations of various kinds) should provide clues as to the kinds of needs which are being denied to that population.

From this perspective we shall describe a mode of adaptation to the pains of confinement utilized by many of the inmates in the largest prison for women in the United States. Specifically, we shall direct attention to the question of whether the behavior of female prisoners is similar to, or different from, that of male prisoners. If differences are found, to what extent are they due to differential sex roles in the free society or to dissimilarities in the physical, legal and social deprivations of prison experienced by women when compared with prisons for men?

During the study various sources of information were utilized. Demographic and background data were obtained through analysis of the record files of 832 inmates, not all of whom were confined at the same time. Over a period of sixteen months repeated interviews were conducted with 45 inmates. These individual interviews provided basic information necessary to conceptualize the process and varieties of adaptive behavior. An anonymous 69-item questionnaire was administered to 293 inmates (a 45 percent random sample of the population).

Toward the end of the study an anonymous questionnaire was administered to all staff members who had sustained and direct contact with inmates. Throughout this period we also attended meetings of the disciplinary committee and held private discussions with staff members.

IMPACT OF THE TOTAL INSTITUTION

It is a trait of Western culture to be more protective toward females and consequently to manifest a general reluctance to submit them to measures deemed appropriate for their allegedly more aggressive and dangerous male counterparts. Women are far less often arrested, tried, convicted and sentenced to prison than are men.[6] The impact of imprisonment is, we believe, more severe for females than for males because it is more unusual. Female inmates generally have not come up through the "sandlots of crime," in that they are not as likely as men to have had experience in training schools or reformatories. Statistics on the prior commitment records of male and female prisoners in the state in 1963 indicate that 31 percent of the females had had no prior commitments compared to 11 per-

---

[6]Women account for only 3.6 percent of imprisoned adult felons in state institutions and 3.8 percent of federal prisioners. "Prisoners in State and Federal Institutions 1961," *National Prisoner Statistics*, No. 30 (August, 1962).

cent for males. In our own data we found that of the 293 inmates who filled out our questionnaire, only 15 percent had been committed to a juvenile training school and 65 percent had never had a prior adult commitment to prison. While jail terms, especially for prostitution and petty theft, are fairly frequent, there are many for whom long-term confinement in an institution for felons represents a completely new experience.

During their first weeks in the institution most inmates report two major emotions: surprise and fear. Most of the women are pleasantly surprised at the physical appearance of the institution and the demeanor of the staff and other inmates:

> It's less difficult than I assumed, it's not like home but it's going to be easy compared to how I thought it would be. It's neater, cleaner, you got combs, towels, etc. If you just have patience. I got time. The girls as a whole are not rough or tough, they've got more heart than the people I associated with on the outside. We can talk to each other, knowing it will only go that far. I'll tell you what scared me—that rolled wire. I said, "Take one last look" [at the outside], but the inside looked better than the parks in the city.

Being frightened is also characteristic of most new arrivals: they fear being mistreated by staff or other inmates, the rigors of prison life, and suffer from uncertain expectations, including not knowing how long they will be locked up and how their families and friends will react to their imprisonment. In addition, there is another concern that becomes particularly serious for a woman in prison—the severing of ties with her children.[7] The male prisoner can serve time with the knowledge that, although the family may experience great difficulty while he is not the breadwinner, the wife can care for the children. The confined mother, however, loses her ability to fill what is, in our society, her most important role. Her concern is not only with separation from her children but also with how they will be cared for while the husband works; moreover, she fears that the children may be taken under official care or the husband may look for another female to take over the maternal role. The impact of separation from family is evident in response to a question asking about the aspects of prison life to which the women found it most difficult to adjust.[8] The frustration does not appreciably lessen over time, as may be seen in Table 1. It is in regard to coping with these fears and deprivations that women are especially ill-

---

[7]Sixty-eight percent of the inmates are mothers; more than half have minor children. *Women Prisoners and Their Families*, Serapio R. Zalba, Department of Welfare and of Corrections, State of California (in press), pp. 27–32.

[8]Some respondents could not be coded because they marked more than one answer. Of the 44 who did this, 27 selected "absence of home and family," among their other choices.

prepared. Many of them have played the generally dependent role characteristic of women in our society and the removal of emotional support which has been provided by parents, husbands or lovers is a shattering experience. Upon arrival at the prison many inmates immediately turn to the staff for information as well as material goods.[9]

The reception program offered by the institution has, however, been unable to meet the needs of new commitments. The social distance between staff and inmate and the severe limitations on the number of professional clinical personnel make it difficult for inmates to get from the staff the kinds of information, support and guidance they especially need during the initial confinement period. These inadequacies coupled with the need to deal with the pains of separation from family, the limitations on freedom of choice and activity, the stigma resulting from the process of status degrada-

TABLE 1

Inmate Responses to the Question, "What is the Most Difficult Aspect of Adjustment," Correlated with Time at the Institution (percent)

Most Difficult Aspect of Adjustment	Less than 6 months	6 months to 1 year	1 year or more	Total
Rules and regulations	5	6	6	5
Other inmates	9	10	19	13
Lack of privacy	6	8	9	8
Custodial officials	2	3	4	3
Absence of home & family	43	42	38	42
Absence of social life and friends on the outside	11	7	6	8
Nothing, adjustment is easy	5	3	4	4
Other	4	3	6	4
More than one answer	16	17	8	13
Total	100 29(82)	100 31(88)	100 40(108)	100(282)*

*No answer to one or the other question = 14 cases.
Chi-square = 61.9, significant at more than 99.95.

[9]The women can bring in with them or have sent in: coats, jackets, raincoats (all with "no quilting, padding or fur"), sweaters ("no turtle neck, V-neck or tight slipover"), gowns or pajamas, bathrobes ("no quilting or padding"), shoes ("low heels, bedroom, thongs, tennis"), "simple costume jewelry—earrings, necklaces, scatter pins, bracelets," non-electric clocks, dark glasses, unopened packages of cigarettes, suitcases (no larger than 18″ × 26″), unfinished knitting and light hand sewing material, tooth brush, hair rollers, etc. Thus the complete stripping of all personal possessions that occurs in prisons for men does not take place. The pains of the admission experience are perhaps mitigated slightly by permitting girls to have these items. Since all inmates can have these belongings, and because so many articles are permitted, there is no evidence that we know of which suggests any organized merchandising of these goods by inmates.

tion, the apprehension about length of confinement due to indeterminate sentencing laws, and the lack of experience in doing "big time," are the pains of imprisonment to which the inmate must adjust. Male prisoners have adjusted in characteristic ways, and in the next section we shall discuss their adaptations and those of female prisoners.

INMATE SOLIDARITY

In the institution we studied there is little evidence of the differentiated inmate types and degree of social solidarity reported in studies of prisons for men. In all interviews inmates reported that informing on other inmates was characteristic of almost the entire inmate population.[10]

TABLE 2

Proportion of 293 Female Prisoners Approving Inmate Loyalty Items

Item	%	N
1. Two inmates, who are planning an escape, ask one of their close inmate friends, Brown, to distract the supervisor's attention so that they will have a chance to get out of her sight. Brown refuses, stating that she doesn't want to get involved. Agree with Brown	88	258
2. Inmates Brown and Henry are planning an escape. They threaten inmate Smith with a beating unless she steals some rope for them from the maintenance shop where she works. She thinks they mean business. While she is trying to smuggle the rope out, she is caught by a supervisor and is accused of trying to escape. She may have her parole date changed unless she describes the whole situation. Smith can avoid this by blaming Brown and Henry, but she keeps quiet and takes the punishment herself. Agree with Smith	39	116

[10]The prison "rat" has always been present in prisons for men, but efforts have been made by inmates to levy punitive sanctions against informers. In the women's prison the label of "snitch" was applied to almost the entire inmate population at one time or another. For some discussions of the "rat" role in prisons for men, see Elmer H. Johnson, "Sociology of Confinement: Assimilation and the Prison 'Rat,'" *Journal of Criminal Law, Criminology and Police Science*, 51 (January–February, 1961), pp. 528–533; S. Kirson Weinberg, "Aspects of the Prison's Social Structure," in *American Journal of Sociology*, 47 (March, 1942), pp. 217–226; and Gresham M. Sykes, *Society of Captives*, Princeton, New Jersey: Princeton University Press, 1958, pp. 87–90.

In the questionnaire survey, descriptions of problematic situations, in which one alternative was an affirmation of inmate solidarity,[11] were endorsed in this manner by only 41 and 12 percent respectively.

Of six items measuring elements of the "inmate code,"[12] only two were strongly endorsed, three were endorsed by about half of the inmates and one was agreed to by only a fifth of the sample. These six items formed a Guttman Scale indicating that the items were perceived as a dimension of response in a meaningful manner. The scale is shown in Table 3.

When the scale scores were cross-tabulated with time in prison, time before release and number of prior commitments and offense, no significant correlations were obtained. In studies of prisons for men, Wheeler and Glaser and Stratton found that orientation to conventional norms was highest for those who had been in prison only a short time and for those near the end of their terms. We found no evidence of either a U-shaped curve of normative orientation or a linear progression of increasing support of criminal norms as length of time served increases.[13] The most important factor related to degree of support of the code was, in fact, a variable which took into account experience outside of prison—age at first arrest. As can be seen in Table 4, women first arrested after the age of twenty-five less often endorsed the code than women whose first officially recorded contact with the police came earlier in life.

Length of involvement in criminal activity, as measured by age at first arrest, seems to be more important in accounting for the attitudes of these female prisoners than the experience of serving time in prison—what Clemmer has referred to as *prisonization*. The importance of pre-prison experiences evident here will also be noted in the sections dealing with inmate roles to follow. To complete this brief discussion of the contrast between male and female prison communities, it should be noted that,

---

[11]These items were developed by Peter Garabedian in his study, *Western Penitentiary: A Study in Social Organization*, unpublished doctoral dissertation, University of Washington, 1959, pp. 51–52, and by Stanton Wheeler, "Role Conflict in Correctional Communities," in Donald R. Cressey, editor, *The Prison, op. cit.*, p. 232. Wheeler found that 70 percent of the male inmates in his sample approved of the inmate keeping quiet.

[12]The six items were based on descriptions of the inmate code by Gresham M. Sykes and Sheldon L. Messinger, "The Inmate Social System," *op. cit.*, pp. 5–19; Lloyd E. Ohlin, "The Theory of Individualization in Treatment and Institutional Practice" (mimeo) paper presented at the 11th Annual Institute of the Illinois Academy of Criminology, Chicago, Illinois (April, 1959); Peter Garabedian, *op. cit.*; and Richard R. Korn and Lloyd W. McCorkle, *Criminology and Penology*, New York: Henry Holt and Co., Inc., 1959, pp. 512–530.

[13]For a discussion of the view that internalization of criminal norms is related to length of time served, see Donald Clemmer, "Imprisonment as a Source of Criminality," *Journal of Criminal Law, Criminology and Police Science*, 41 (September–October, 1950), pp. 311–319. For an opposing view see Garrity, *op. cit.*, pp. 358–380.

TABLE 3

Proportion of 293 Female Prisoners Endorsing Inmate Code

Item	%	N
1. In her dealings with the staff the inmate should stick up for what she feels is right and not let the staff set her standards or morals for her. (Positive)	92	264
2. When the inmates stick together it is a lot easier to do time. (Positive)	77	213
3. The best way to do time is to grin and bear it and not let the staff know that anything is getting you down. (Positive)	61	173
4. In some situations, it is all right to inform on another inmate. (Negative endorsement)	57	163
5. In prison, a good rule to follow is to share any extra goods with your friends. (Positive)	56	157
6. There are basically just two kinds of people in the world, those in the know and those who are suckers. (Positive)	22	63

These items constitute a Guttman Scale with a coefficient of reproducibility of .88 and a marginal reproducibility of .68. The cutting points were established as follows:

	%	N
Strong rejection	16	(44)
Moderate rejection	32	(93)
Strong endorsement	16	(48)
Moderate endorsement	37	(108)
	100	(293)

consistent with the lack of support for the inmate code, few inmates were found to play the roles of *merchants* or *politicians* characteristic of prisons for men. In addition, there were virtually no women who played the role of the *tough* or *gorilla*.

That female prisoners do not endorse more strongly norms which characterize the male prison community and, in particular, that they do not feel bound to maintain group solidarity by rules prohibiting informing, may, however, indicate more than just a low degree of cohesion in the female prison community and absence of resulting role types. Lack of support of these norms does not preclude the possibility of consensus on different norms. There may be little support of this code because such maxims are not as relevant for women. The components of the code may more accurately reflect male needs for status, independence, autonomy, and masculine self-image. (It should be noted that a number of sociologists, including

TABLE 4

Degree of Endorsement of Inmate Code and Age at First Arrest
(percent)

	Age at First Arrest		
	17 or younger	*18 to 25*	*26 or older*
Strong rejection	11	6	31
Moderate rejection	29	31	33
Moderate endorsement	39	46	24
Strong endorsement	21	17	12
	100	100	100
	(72)	(125)	(91)

Chi square = 30.25, significant at more than 99.95.

the authors, are now questioning the assumption that most male prison communities are characterized by even a moderate degree of group solidarity.) The culture and social structure of prisons for men seems to reflect a wider variety of pains of imprisonment than is the case in the women's prison. There are homosexuals in male prisons and norms surrounding homosexuality, but there are other important concerns and these are articulated in the roles of *merchant, politician, tough, right guy,* and *square john.* Emotional deprivation and lack of experience in fending for oneself combine in the women's prison to promote one predominant compensatory response, that of homosexual involvement. Inmate roles in the female prison community are thus differentiated primarily along sexual lines. In the sections to follow we shall describe the process of *turning out,* the dynamics of prison love affairs, the principal homosexual roles and the extent to which this type of adaptation has been made.

THE PREVALENCE OF HOMOSEXUAL BEHAVIOR

Estimates of the prevalence of homosexuality in the prison vary widely. Official records identify 19 percent of the population as homosexual. In the survey of staff members, more than half of the respondents estimated between 30 and 70 percent of the inmates "have sexual affairs while in prison." Estimates were higher on the inmate questionnaire, with 69 percent of the respondents estimating that between 30 and 70 percent of the girls were having homosexual affairs and an additional 7 percent estimating as high as 90 percent or more. These data, with comparative estimates made by prisoners in a medium security prison for men located in the same state, can be seen in Table 5.[14]

In the interviews with female inmates, guesses of the extent of homosexuality were never less than 50 percent, with most estimating 60 to 75 percent. Individual conversations with staff members yielded similar estimates. Overall, it can be conservatively estimated that at least 50 percent of the inmates are sexually involved at least once during their prison terms. By sexually involved we mean kissing and fondling of the breasts, manual and oral stimulation of the clitoris and simulation of intercourse. Our definition of homosexuality does not include mere emotional arousal, or kissing, hand holding and embracing, when these activities are not followed by overt sexual behavior and are not seen as being sexual in intent by the participants.[15]

TABLE 5

Estimates of Prevalence of Institutional Homosexuality (percent)

Replies of women's prison staff and female and male inmates to the statement:

"A rough estimate of the number of women (men) who have sexual affairs at one time or another with other women (men) while in prison would be:"

Estimate of Homosexuality	Women's Prison Staff	Female Inmates	Male Inmates
5 percent or less	12	12	29
15 percent	31	12	25
30 percent	29	25	25
50 percent	14	22	12
70 percent	9	22	6
90 percent or more	5	7	3
	100(58)	100(263)	100(744)

Note: 6 staff members, 30 female inmates, and 127 male inmates refused or were unable to make an estimate.

---

[14]In addition to our own data estimating the incidence of homosexuality among male prisoners, Donald Clemmer's study of an institution for adult male felons indicated that ". . . 16 percent of the sampling admitted to homosexual activity during their present incarceration. Of these 38 men, only two were partners with each other in the abnormal acts, so it is suggested that since homosexuality cannot occur singly, that the actual percentage of men engaging in this practice is 32 percent." Donald Clemmer, "Some Aspects of Sexual Behavior in the Prison Community," *Proceedings of the Eighty-Eight Annual Congress of Correction of The American Correctional Association*, Detroit, Michigan, 1958, p. 383.

[15]These figures may be compared with other data that have been gathered on homosexuality among girls in youth institutions. A study by Selling, published in

Reliable estimates of the extent of homosexual involvement of women in other institutional settings—the military, mental hospital, schools—are non-existent. However, in the outside community, data from the Kinsey Report indicate that, of their national sample, 13 percent experienced orgasm in homosexual relations, an additional 6 percent had had homosexual experience, and another 9 percent had experienced "psychological arousal" for a total of 28 percent of the population.[16] Comparatively, the incidence of overt homosexual behavior in this prison is high.

HOMOSEXUAL ROLES

In the prison setting the total number of women involved sexually with other inmates is less interesting sociologically than the sharp distinction between those referred to by the inmates as "true" homosexuals and those identified as "jailhouse turnouts."

The _jailhouse turnout_ or _J.T.O._, in contrast to the true homosexual, has her introduction to homosexuality in jail or prison. All inmates interviewed and 80 percent of the staff who filled out the questionnaire asserted that 90 percent or more of the homosexually involved women had their first affair in jail or prison. In addition, 84 percent of the inmates and 85 percent of the staff agreed on the questionnaires that most of the homosexually involved women return to heterosexual relationships when they leave prison.

The _true homosexual_ is, as defined by the inmates, a woman who was homosexual before she arrived at the institution and will be after she leaves. Incidentally, a few of the true homosexuals remain faithful to lovers on the outside and do not become involved with other inmates. Such persons would not, therefore, be included in our estimate of institutional homosexuality.

Those true homosexuals who are active in prison come to the rela-

---

1931, estimated that two percent of the population of a girl's institution were involved in an overt homosexual existence and another 40 percent engaged in behavior which involved embracing, kissing and fondling of another inmate. Lowell S. Selling, "The Pseudo Family," _The American Journal of Sociology_, 37 (September, 1931), pp. 247–253. A more recent study by Halleck and Hersko indicates that 69 percent of the girls in a training school were homosexually involved. The majority of these cases did not, however, involve breast fondling, or direct genital contact. Seymour L. Halleck and Marvin Hersko, "Homosexual Behavior in a Correctional Institution for Adolescent Girls," _American Journal of Orthopsychiatry_, XXXII (October, 1962), pp. 911–917.

16Alfred C. Kinsey, Wardell B. Pomeroy, Clyde E. Martin, Paul H. Gebhard, _Sexual Behavior in the Human Female_, Philadelphia, Pa.: W. B. Saunders Co., 1953, pp. 452–454.

tionship with a perspective based on experience. They believe the impact of a homosexual affair is never forgotten, and they feel that they enter such relationships more for the positive features they perceive than in reaction to the negative features of confinement. It is also likely that the labels of "criminal" and "prisoner" are less traumatic for people who already have a self-conception of being stigmatized by most of the general community. As a result of homosexual affairs many of these women appear to have made adjustments in their self-conceptions which make adjustment to the pains of imprisonment less difficult. Our data indicate that among those few inmates who can be classified as prison politicians and merchants, there are a large number of true homosexuals. Like the experienced male con, they are more concerned with alleviating the material deprivations of confinement, getting a good prison job and living quarters, and doing time without attracting attention. In the following remarks a young woman who is a true homosexual playing the masculine or *butch* role, speaks with disdain of the blatant and opportunistic behavior of the jailhouse turnouts:

> . . . They want companionship, they just want to play a little game with you, you know, and they LOVE you, oh, everybody loves you, God, they're in love with you. They've seen you once, but they're in love with you. They turn out right away because they need somebody to care, someone to look up to. They're afraid, and somehow a butch is sort of a protective symbol—"She'll take care of me so nobody will hurt me." They need somebody to talk to, they're lonesome. And they've been taken away from everything they love, and they sort of project all of this love into the butch. . . . But mostly, it's just a big game with them. They're lonesome, there's nothing else to do, and I'm the closest thing they can get to a man. . . . These other ones [butch turnouts] I can't see at all—the ones that come in here with long hair and all of a sudden they're big romp-stomping butches. . . . I can respect a person that's been that way all their life and knows what's happening, but these kids that just cut their hair and think they're really hitting on something, and then they can't wait to get out on the streets to get with a dude again—they make me sick. While they're in here you'd swear to God they'd been gay their whole life. There's nothing but women in this world for them—while they're in here. They have their hair short one week and then, God, they're just too lovely the next—I mean it. One week they're my brother and the next week they're hitting on me. They swagger and drop their belt and all of a sudden they're big stuff. When really they're not. They don't feel any of this inside, they don't go through any of the emotions that a butch [true homosexual] goes through, they're not involved in this and they're gonna forget it as soon as they're out of the institution.

Whether homosexuality is learned prior to imprisonment or is restricted to the prison experience, another distinction involves the roles played by homosexuals in their affairs. These roles are represented by a combination of appearance, behavior and personality characteristics, and are found among both true homosexuals and jailhouse turnouts. The most obvious is the *butch, stud broad,* or *drag butch*,[17] the aggressive, active sexual partner. Her hair is close-cropped or worn in pixie or "D.A." style; she wears no makeup; her legs are unshaven; she usually wears pedal pushers or, if a dress, the belt is worn low on the hips. Masculine gait, manner of smoking and other gestures are adopted. A variation of this is the woman who dresses femininely, but acts aggressively and plays the dominant role in her homosexual relationship. The transition to the role of butch is a dramatic manifestation of inversion of sexual role, representing such a change that a disproportionately small number of women in prison actually make it. Our personal observation is that many of the jailhouse turnouts who are butches are singularly unattractive, according to some of the criteria used to judge feminine attractiveness in our society. Many of these women are overweight or underweight, have skin disorders or appear unusually wiry or muscular.[18] Some of the severely unattractive women and the women possessing aggressive personality traits and inclined toward masculine habits and demeanor express themselves in the butch role when these predisposing factors are combined with the experience of imprisonment. In prison they have found that by emphasizing dissimilarity to the female role and appearance, they can attract attention from some members of their own sex. Here they can take the initiative in both social and sexual interaction and these women find in prison a functional role they did not find outside.[19] The role of the butch in the prison community seems to be an effort to solve a variety of problems and conflicts of which adjustment to imprisonment is one.

---

[17]Neither staff nor inmates use the term *lesbian*. Staff members use the term homosexual because it is consistent with departmental directives, rule books and references to male prisoners. Inmates use more colloquial terms such as *playing, being together, making it,* and *turning out*. The term lesbian apparently suggests what staff and inmates agree is usually not the case —a long-term definite commitment to homosexuality.

[18]There is, however, no evidence of any unusual physiological or anatomical features which characterize these masculine-appearing women. Physicians at the prison reported that they had observed no constitutional differences in terms of distribution and abundance of body hair, size of the clitoris, muscle distribution or any other factor.

[19]For a description of the butch role among female homosexuals living in the free world, see Jane McKinnon, "I am a Homosexual Woman," in A. M. Krich, editor, *The Homosexuals*, New York: The Citadel Press, 1954, pp. 4–5. The butch role played by call girls is described by Harold Greenwald in *The Call Girl*, New York: Ballantine Books, 1958, pp. 119–122. See also Frank S. Caprio, *Female Homosexuality*, New York: Grove Press, Inc., 1954, pp. 16–18. While the author has a more general point to make, an excellent discussion of the "masculine protest" can be found in Simone De Beauvoir, *The Second Sex*, New York: Bantam Books, 1961, pp. 379–399.

The complementary role of the butch is the *femme*, who maintains a feminine appearance and ideally plays a more submissive, passive role. Of the two, the butch appears to have a greater commitment to homosexuality. The butch changes the love object and her behavior, thereby substituting a role. The femme changes only the love object. It is less difficult to describe and to understand the role of the femme because she often does in the homosexual affair what she did in heterosexual relationships. She continues to play the role often expected of women—to be relatively more submissive and passive in sexual relations, to be dependent, and to provide housekeeping services. The role of the femme provides relief from the need to fend for oneself in a strange and threatening environment. This role provides for the establishment of supportive relationships similar to those which characterized relationships with fathers, husbands or lovers. The femme does not have to make the radical transition to a new role that the butch has made. She often comes to view herself as bisexual and she expects to resume heterosexual relations upon release—both of which militate against homosexual self-definition.

While the butch can display her role in terms of dress, mannerisms and appearance, the femme emphasizes her role largely in behavior. She walks with her arms around the butch, embraces and kisses her in public, and allows the butch to speak in her behalf.[20] Recently the staff has attempted to reduce these public demonstrations of affection by making inmates liable for disciplinary action. Couples flaunting their relationship are often housed in separate cottages in an effort to prevent them from seeing one another. The staff has also required 48 butches to change their hair style to a less masculine coiffure and more effort has been devoted to preventing personal (bodily) contact on the institution grounds. While there has been less visible evidence of homosexuality, these efforts, to date, have not reduced the number of homosexual involvements.

THE DYNAMICS OF PRISON LOVE AFFAIRS

For many girls the pressure to *turn out* begins when they enter the receiving unit. Two types of women in particular are the object of concerted attention by the general population. The arrival of a *butch broad* causes a stir on the campus as the femmes vie for her affection. The rush is intense, and the femme makes it clear that she is available:

---

[20]For descriptions of the butch role in a girl's school, see Halleck and Hersko, *op. cit.*, p. 912, and for the femme role see the description of the *soft mama* by Romolo Toigo, "Illegitimate and Legitimate Cultures in a Training School for Girls," *Proceedings of the Rip Van Winkle Clinic*, Vol. 13, No. 3 (Summer, 1962), pp. 9–11.

It's just like the outside. I flirted, I got things for her, I did her clothes, I woke her in the morning, we went to dances—the same things you do for a man on the outside. Girls are approached in the same way a man approaches a woman. He . . . she . . . looks at her and the way she looks back gives him the clue as to further action. He . . . she . . . looks at you like she wants you, a look of desire.

The rushing process includes plying the butch with love notes, candy, coffee, cigarettes and other articles, referred to as *commissary*.

This adaptation by femmes of the usual tactics employed by males in heterosexual affairs was explained by our respondents as a matter of supply and demand because there are fewer butches then femmes in the population. (Our interviews and analysis of inmate file data indicate that about one-third of the jailhouse turnout population are butch, with a somewhat higher proportion of butches among the true homosexuals.) In addition, broken love affairs sustain a supply of femmes who express great interest in the relatively small number of new butches. A twenty-year-old true homosexual butch described her reception at the institution:

When I came into the institution I didn't go after anybody. I had a bad experience on the street that was part of what got me here, and I didn't want anything to do with any more women. So I was very bitter. But I got here and all of a sudden I was getting all these kites [notes] and I had all these girls come to me—I never went to them. They're real aggressive with a new butch, everybody wants to snatch her up before somebody else gets her. And so I looked around at some of the people I was getting messages from —I checked them out and there wasn't too much there that I wanted. But I played the field for about six weeks, and like I said, I'd get a message from a girl to please come over and see her and she'd give me cigarettes and, you know, give me everything I needed. So I'd walk her out to the field, or to the canteen, and then I dated a few girls, I took some of them to the show, but I never saw anybody that I wanted.

In other instances butches approach new arrivals, exert special attention on young, homosexually uninitiated and attractive girls, win them over and then exploit them for contraband, commissary items, and other services.

Once the butch has secured the affection of the femme, she may then exact tribute in the form of goods and services in exchange for her assurance that she will not play around with anyone else (as one woman paraphrased the song: "I love you for commissary reasons"). In each of these cases the butch role has the advantage of material gains in addition to sexual recompense. However, many of the homosexual pairs do not involve exploitation of one lover by the other and are not dissimilar to love affairs between males and females on the outside. Exploitation, when it does occur in these relationships, comes when one of the parties is tiring of the other.

There was only one report that butch broads had stables (more than one femme of her own). This case, it is our impression, involved a transitional stage at which time a butch was getting over her affair with one femme and beginning another. There were no indications of homosexual families or clans.[21] Finally, in contrast to prisons for men, no inmate reported, nor was there any evidence of, any inmate using force to exact sexual favors from another.

The behavior of one partner often appears to be exploitative of the other in the actual sexual relationship. Interviews conducted with both homosexual and non-homosexual inmates indicated that in about one-third of the homosexual relationships at the institution the butch refuses to let the femme touch her or reciprocate sexually. Some butches remain completely clothed during sexual activity. This seems in part to facilitate maintaining the illusion of masculinity which would be exposed by the removal of her clothing. The role of the femme, in these cases, is one of complete passivity in which the butch *gives work* (also referred to as *giving some head*), i.e., engages in cunnilingus, manual manipulation of the clitoris, and breast fondling. While the butch gives work, the denial of sexual gratification for herself is called *giving up the work*. Such self-denial militates against becoming obligated to the femme and from developing emotional ties that would be painful to disturb or break. Participation in a relationship where only the butch gives work is functional for some femmes as well. They can receive sexual satisfaction and at the same time avoid viewing themselves as homosexual. For a number of women, homosexual self-definition only follows active participation in sexual activity.[22]

The following statement from a tape recorded interview describes the practice of giving up the work as seen by a femme jailhouse turnout:

---

[21] The building of family constellations has been reported in studies of youth institutions for females by Sheriff in Michela Robbins, "The Inside Story of a Girl's Reformatory," *Colliers*, 132 (October 30, 1953), p. 76; Sidney Kosofsky and Albert Ellis, "Illegal Communication Among Institutionalized Female Delinquents," *The Journal of Social Psychology*, 48 (August, 1958), pp. 155–160; see also Charles A. Ford, "Homosexual Practices of Institutionalized Females," *The Journal of Abnormal and Social Psychology*, XXIII (January–March, 1929), p. 446; by Selling, *op. cit.*, pp. 248–253 and by Toigo, *op. cit.*, pp. 3–29. It is not surprising to find young girls who are still oriented toward the consangual family establishing substitute *daddies, brothers* and *cousins*. The separation from parents, siblings and other relatives seems to be less a source of real stress for older women. Most of them have established their own families and the pain of separation comes from being away from conjugal rather than the consangual family.

[22] The attitude of the femme here is similar to that of the young male delinquents who permit male adults to perform fellatio on them but who do not think of themselves as homosexuals. The boys define themselves and each other not on the basis of homosexual behavior *per se*, but on the basis of non-participation in the role which is perceived as the homosexual role, that of the fellator. Albert J. Reiss, Jr., "The Social Integration of Queers and Peers," *Social Problems*, 9 (Fall, 1961), pp. 118–119.

Giving up the work means who's gonna do who. I mean, which one of you is going to commit the sexual act on the other one. Usually the one that's the aggressor and doing the lovemaking is the one that's giving up the work. [Note the butch is *giving* work at the same time she is giving *up* reciprocal sexual interaction.] The other one isn't giving up anything, she's receiving. It usually refers to the stud broad and usually the stud broad will be very modest and strict about who knows if she's been receiving any work or not.

I think it's that butches realize a woman is satisfied by a man, as a rule, this is the natural role, and that they want to satisfy you as much as a man would, if not more. They want to get this certain edge over you, this certain control over you. But being aware in the back of their minds that they're a woman too, they know that it's just as possible for you to get control over them, and I think that they fight this because in their minds their main goal is to satisfy and control you, and keep you.

The butch partner of the respondent quoted above reported her reason for wishing to have a relationship where only she gave work:

In myself—the only desire I have is to make love and not have love made to me. I don't feel the need for it or the desire for it. The desire for it can be aroused and has been—I'm not saying that a girl hasn't made love to me—but it's very few and far between that I want somebody to make love to me. I want to do the work, and that's the way I get my pleasure, by making love to her, a woman. When I make love to a woman I like the power of being able to satisfy her. It gives me a good feeling to know that she responds to me and that I can satisfy her desires. And this is where I get my enjoyment.

Q. When you talk about satisfaction for yourself, is this satisfaction in terms of orgasm, or is satisfaction in other terms?

It's a satisfaction more or less mentally, and not really—it's a physical satisfaction but merely because I know I've done a good job, or I hope I have, and I'm satisfied with knowing that I've pleased her and I'm just relaxed through the whole act. Otherwise, no, I don't reach a climax. I have, but it's very seldom that I do. I don't lose myself that much, and I don't like to lose that much control. I like to keep my mind as clear as I can so I'm aware of exactly what I'm doing, and I'm aware of my timing, and I'm aware of the girl—if she's responsive at a certain time then I know that's what she likes, and then if she's not responding then I can do something else. Where, if I was just lost in passion I don't recognize any of these things, and I don't feel that I would satisfy her as fully as if I didn't lose myself all that much and kept concentrating on her, watching her—that's what I do. And when the act is over I'm tired and that tiredness brings on a satisfaction in itself. And it gives me a form of release, the tension sort of release, after I've made love to somebody. But I don't reach a climax—not generally.

In practice, however, giving up the work seems to characterize the early stage of a homosexual relationship. Presuming that there is some mutual attraction to begin with, it seems to be difficult to have such intimate contact without, over time, developing more intense affectional ties. It often happens that the butch comes to ask for sexual reciprocity and that the femme is then ready to reciprocate. Hence, this behavior can, in some cases, be an effective means of total seduction in which the femme who is resistant or feeling guilty is brought along slowly. Stresses accompanying attempted transitions from giving up the work to reciprocal sexuality result in the failure of some sexual affairs that are carried on satisfactorily until the femme finally refuses to reciprocate. Such refusal is interpreted by the butch as lack of affection and low degree of commitment to the homosexual role.

There is an apparent parallel between a prostitute receiving the attentions of a customer and the femme receiving a butch who gives up the work, but there is a major difference implicit in the rationale for the latter. The male customer, while an active sex partner and to some degree the aggressor, is not viewed as being in danger of becoming emotionally involved with the prostitute. The action of the active and aggressive butch is specifically directed toward preventing herself from becoming more deeply attached to her partner. For many women who have assumed the butch role because they were unsuccessful in heterosexual affectional relationships, there is still the danger of being rejected again. For the butch then, the initial period during which the femme remains passive serves the important function of screening out femmes who are "chippying" (promiscuous). As one respondent said, "You check them out, to see if she's gonna stay." In addition, the period of giving up the work serves to more deeply involve the femme, as she may experience satisfaction with the relationship. Thus, after this trial period, the butch may ask for reciprocity if the femme has not indicated that she wants to play a more active sexual role. It is beyond this point that some femmes refuse to go, and this usually terminates the affair. Enough women stop here to confirm the fears of butches so that they must continue the same testing process.

The term jailhouse turnout indicates, and inmates confirm, that most prison love affairs are temporary and situational.[23] The insecurity and anxiety which is promoted by the movement of the population out of the institution results in the use of certain defense mechanisms to protect one-

---

[23]In the male homosexual community, Hooker reports that there is a constant searching for sexual partners, and that long-enduring relationships are rare, with change not stability the rule. Evelyn Hooker, "A Preliminary Analysis of Group Behavior of Homosexuals," *The Journal of Psychology*, 42 (October, 1956), pp. 223–224. Halleck and Hersko report that homosexual relationships among the girls in the youth institution they studied were usually short-lived and characterized by jealousy and unfaithfulness. Halleck and Hersko, *op. cit.*, p. 913. The shifting of homosexual roles among girls in the youth institution is also reported by Toigo, *op. cit.*, p. 10. The ability to play both roles—active and passive—is reported by Helene Deutsch, "On Female Homosexuality," in Robert Fliess, editor, *The Psychoanalytic Reader*, New York: International Universities Press, Inc., 1948, p. 243.

self from being hurt too badly. This is especially the case for butches who
have made a more definite and dramatic commitment to homosexuality.
They cannot count on holding the affection of the femme, not only because
of separation by staff or parole, but also because femme jailhouse turnouts
do not have a long-term commitment to the *gay life*. This is apparent in the
high percentage of women whom the inmates believe will return to heterosexual affairs once they leave prison. The prison homosexuals who are expected to revert to heterosexuality are the femmes and not the butches.

In summary, the process of turning out seems to represent socialization of the new inmates into practices which provide support, guidance and
emotional satisfactions during a period when these are lacking. This mechanism for coping with the stress of imprisonment is presented to the new
inmate at a time when she is likely to be most responsive and when she is
least aware of alternative courses of action. Turning out often involves a
series of steps through which both partners initially seek to insulate themselves from strong involvement. Reciprocity of sexual behavior is often
delayed until confidence in the stability of the union is felt. This is particularly true for those butches who have made more definite commitments
to homosexuality. However, instability is not unknown for other butches
who change from homosexual involvements to heterosexual involvements
and back again as they are paroled, violate parole and are returned to
prison. (This role alteration prompted one inmate to remark, "There's
something hypocritical about a pregnant butch.")

Inmates believe that most homosexual involvement occurs early in imprisonment, that most affairs are situational with heterosexual relationships
to be resumed upon release, and that many are "once-only" affairs.[24] The
folklore of the female prison community provides rationalizations for homosexuality by emphasizing that women involved in prison affairs are not
homosexual but bisexual, by referring to those who do not play as "prudes,"
by emphasizing the alleviation of loneliness that such involvements can
bring, by alleging greater satisfactions than can be found in heterosexual
affairs and by repeating stories about the women who return to men upon
release. While the intrinsic satisfactions are described it is made clear that

---

[24]In view of these characteristics of institutional homosexuality, Ford questions
whether such involvements represent true sexual inversion. See Ford, *op. cit.*, p. 448.
Deviant behavior in prison may be temporary because ties to significant others in the
free world are not voluntarily severed. Their absence is forced and they remain
significant others. Thus while escape into institutional deviance can be rationalized
on the basis of "they aren't around" or "they won't know," long-term commitment is
unlikely because it is to these others and not to those in prison that long-run loyalty
is given. Loyalty to a homosexual partner in prison is fortuitous. For a discussion of
deviant careers and of the important implications of membership in an organized
deviant group see Howard S. Becker, *Outsiders*, New York: The Free Press of
Glencoe, pp. 25–39.

one may return to heterosexual relationships without any damaging effects. Such a rationale helps make homosexual involvement a more likely adaptation than other mechanisms of adjustment. There can be a number of reactions to stress and each of these may assume a variety of forms. For some of the inmates psychological withdrawal and fantasy is one adaptation.[25] Other inmates actively rebel and become chronic rule violators (so-called troublemakers and malcontents) who fight with staff and fellow inmates. Our analysis of the files of 832 inmates, however, indicates that this is not a frequent reaction. Eighty-two percent (668) of the sample had never violated rules pertaining to staff authority.[26] Sixty-two percent had never been reported for any violation of prison rules and an additional 22 percent had received only one or two such reports.

There are some inmates who are continually in trouble, but it is our impression that they fall into two principal categories—severely emotionally disturbed individuals and young homosexuals who use the violation of institutional rules and abuse of authority to demonstrate their love for partners or to react to staff interventions in their affairs.

Another adaptation is what Goffman has called "colonization," the acceptance of institutional life as a satisfactory existence. These are inmates who are commonly referred to as "having found a home."[27] Generally, they do not want to bother or be bothered by staff or inmates or by institutional programs as they perform the ritual of doing time. A small number of women, in most cases older and serving long sentences for serious offenses such as homicide, used this mode of adjustment. Their age, a number of inmates reported, precluded these women from being sought as desirable homosexual partners. Not all inmates use one or more of these adaptations. Some women play a role referred to in prisons for men as "square johns"—persons who maintain a view toward criminality consistent with that of the larger community and who tend to be more receptive to staff efforts at rehabilitation. The worst feature of confinement for these inmates is the forced association with other inmates. These women tend to accept the pains of imprisonment as justified penalties for their behavior.

For the majority of women in the prison, however, we did not observe such accommodations to deprivations and limitations of confinement. The lack of experience in doing time, the lack of criminal sophistication and

---

[25]This reaction is described by Gresham M. Sykes, *The Society of Captives, op. cit.,* p. 80. See also Erving Goffman, *Asylums,* Garden City, New York: Anchor Books, 1961, pp. 61–62; and Terence and Pauline Morris, "The Experience of Imprisonment," *The British Journal of Criminology,* 2 (April, 1962), pp. 351–352.

[26]Included as rule violations were refusal to work, destruction of state property as a protest gesture, insolence, disrespect, disobedience to staff, assault (or attempted) on staff, escape (or attempted escape), and rioting.

[27]Goffman, *op. cit.,* pp. 62–63, and Terence and Pauline Morris, *op. cit.,* pp. 350–351.

the absence of conventional sources of emotional support by husbands, lovers, or families combine to make many inmates receptive to homosexuality as a mode of adjustment when it is offered to them upon arrival at the prison. Our data clearly indicate that more inmates resort to homosexuality than to psychological withdrawal, rebellion, colonization or any other type of adaptation.

CONCLUSIONS

Homosexuality exists because it serves a variety of functions for a large number of women, not because prison inmates are callous, unprincipled or basically amoral or because the institution staff is lax or "soft" on inmates. In fact, it has been suggested that the maladjustment of prison inmates may reflect demands on the behavior of the individual made by the special environment of the prison. These modes of behaving may be viewed as maladaptive outside of prison, but they are adaptive in the prison setting.[28]

Initially, this study considered sex-role differences in the free community, and features of male prisons, as a way of understanding the female prison. From a knowledge of differences in the backgrounds, experiences and identities of males and females in the outside world, we surmised that women prisoners would be less likely to actively rebel in prison. We did not expect and did not find elaborate operations for obtaining and distributing contraband or for conducting gambling operations. We expected and found that women require more emotional support than do male prisoners. This need, and others, are reflected in the culture of the female prison community which contains maxims dealing with the experiences and problems of women in prison and in the inmate social system composed of roles which are responses to the pains of imprisonment as women experience them. It is on these bases that male and female prison communities can be distinguished.

Finally, a conjecture about the post-prison effects of institutional involvements. Prison homosexuality is viewed, even by many of those involved, as temporary, with heterosexual relations to be resumed upon release. We cannot answer definitely whether this actually happens. Some information was gleaned from conversations with all women parole officers in the state. While the parole agents had little knowledge of the patterns of homosexual behavior at the institution, they agreed that most of the women

---

[28]Patrick J. Driscoll, "Factors Related to the Institutional Adjustment of Prison Inmates," *The Journal of Abnormal and Social Psychology*, 47 (July, 1952), pp. 593–596.

they knew who had had homosexual experiences in prison returned to men upon release. The parole agents noted that the women who tended to continue playing a homosexual role were those who had made a greater commitment to homosexuality—the butches. However, the majority of the homosexual population are femme jailhouse turnouts who maintain a conception of themselves as bisexual. If we are correct that homosexual involvements begun in prison do not, in fact, usually persist on release, it is reasonable to raise the question of how problematic prison homosexuality is in terms of long-run rehabilitation goals of the institution.

Our study has focused attention on deviance in an institutional setting but our findings, however tentative, raise questions for research in the society at large. Unanswered questions involve delineation of the principal homosexual roles in the free community and the procedures by which women are induced to indulge in deviant sexual behavior outside the prison.

For example, it would be important to know whether initial deviant involvement leads to membership in an organized deviant group. Any follow-up study of parolees would require knowledge of the gay life in the larger community, since it is not known whether there are short-lived homosexual periods in civilian life as there are in prison and whether or not true homosexuals in the community need to utilize protective mechanisms such as giving up the work. Adequate description of the sexual deviance of the female prisoner awaits further inquiry into deviant behavior of women in the world outside the prison.

8

The Social Meaning
of Prison Homosexuality

John Gagnon
William Simon

The last half century has seen marked, if uneven, progress in most areas of prison management and perhaps even more marked progress in the creation of a new ideology of prison management. However, despite evidence of progress, there still remains a major area of behavior with which prison systems have been unable to cope. This is the problem of sexual adjustment that occurs in all institutions where one sex is deprived of social or sexual access to the other. It is in the area of sexuality that the prison is perhaps more limited than it is in other areas of activity, partially because of its very single-sex nature and partially because the society rarely provides clear guidelines for sexual behavior even outside the penal institution.

In the midst of the confusion about sexual standards and sexual behavior, the prison exists as the major single-sex institution in the society that has (unlike the mental hospital and other closed institutions) within its walls a population that is physically and, for the most part, psychologically, intact and is, at the same time, sexually experienced. The prison administrator is faced with a fundamental dilemma: He is aware of the sexual needs

From "The Social Meaning of Prison Homosexuality," *Federal Probation,* 32 (March 1968), 23–29. Reprinted by permission.

of the population that he is charged with holding and retraining, but he is also aware that he is not going to get much support or even a sympathetic hearing from the larger society if he focuses upon the problem of the sexual adjustment of his population.

SOME MAJOR CONSIDERATIONS

There are two major areas that require clarification before one can proceed to discuss the actual patterns of sexual adjustment among prison populations. The first is an unfortunate tendency to view the sexual adjustment of prisoners as arising exclusively from the contexts of prison life. It is frequently assumed that any group of people who were incarcerated for any period of time would react sexually in the same way as those who are presently in prison. This is a major oversimplification brought about primarily because of a lack of information about the prior sexual and nonsexual lives of those who are imprisoned and the way in which this prior experience conditions persons' responses not only to sexual deprivation, but also to a general loss of liberty.

The second element that is important to specify is the range of sexual responses that are available to those imprisoned. With the exception of the small number of prisons that allow conjugal visits, there are only three forms of sexual behavior that are generally available to a prison population (except for animal contact for those males on prison farms). These are nocturnal sex dreams, self-masturbation, and sexual contact with other inmates of the same sex. The meaning, amount, and the character of these adjustments will be strongly dependent on the meaning that these same behaviors had for the inmate before he or she was incarcerated. Thus, the problem for the inmate is not merely the release of sexual tension, but the social and psychological meaning that such release has and the motives and beliefs that it expresses for him. The source of this set of values does not reside in the prison experience, but outside the prison in the community at large. Thus, the prison provides a situation to which prior sexual and social styles and motives must be adapted and shaped.

There are two major dimensions on which most sexual activity is based. One is that of age, with the primary break occurring between adolescence and adulthood. The other, perhaps of greater significance, is the differential meaning of sexuality to the two sexes. Thus, the striking differences between the sexual orientations of men and women noted in the Kinsey volumes offer the best starting point for a discussion of sex in prison.[1] The discussion that follows focuses on the responses of adult male

[1] Alfred C. Kinsey, *et al., Sexual Behavior in the Human Female.* Philadelphia: W. B. Saunders Company, 1953, pp. 642–689.

and female inmates to the prison experience, with only passing reference to institutions for adolescents as they represent continuities to the adult institutions.

MALE RESPONSES TO IMPRISONMENT

Male prison populations are not random selections from the larger society and do not reflect the usual distributions of the population in terms of education, income, ethnicity, occupation, social class, and general life style. The men who make up the bulk of the imprisoned populations tend to be drawn from deprived sections of the society or from families imbedded in what we have now come to call the culture of poverty. As a consequence, the sexual experiences of these men and the meaning that sex has for them differs in significant ways from other portions of the population that are less likely to be imprisoned.

A number of dimensions of these differences may be found in the work of Kinsey and his colleagues in which they report the substantial differences to be found in the sexual activity and attitudes of men who have differing amounts of education.[2] These findings are further amplified in the volume, *Sex Offenders*, where a comparison of imprisoned men and men of the same social origins without delinquent histories showed that the men with prison histories generally have wider sexual experience of all kinds than do men leading conventional and nondelinquent lives.[3] These variables suggest that at least the modal male prison population enters institutions with differing commitments to sexuality than would a middle-class or working-class population. We can therefore suggest that the response of these latter groups to institutionalization will differ as well.

Prior Sexual Adjustment a Factor

Drawing on what we know about the dimensions of the prior sexual adjustments of men who go to prison, our first major sense of the experience is actually how little sexual activity of any sort occurs within the prison.[4] Thus, even after the shock of imprisonment has worn off (and often

---

[2]*Ibid., Sexual Behavior in the Human Male.* Philadelphia: W. B. Saunders Company, 1948, pp. 327–393.

[3]Paul H. Gebhard, *et al., Sex Offenders.* New York: Harper & Row, 1965.

[4]From a preliminary analysis of the differences between the preinstitutional and the institutional sexual oulet of adult male prisoners interviewed by the Institute for

for the recidivist this occurs quickly), there is no sudden burst of sexual activity of any type. Confirming these impressions is the low order of complaint one hears about sexual deprivation, even when prisoners are presenting a list of grievances after a riot or outbreak of some sort. Part of this is surely due to the closeness of custody in the institution and the fact that men move and live in close proximity, and, except for certain moments of the day, there is very little privacy—not so much from the custodial staff as from the inmates.

However, another cause of this reduction is that sexual activity is potentiated by or channeled through an existing set of social frameworks that do not exist in prison. The man in prison finds himself without the appropriate stimuli which suggest opportunities for sexual activity or situations that are appropriate for such activity. Without the existence of these social cues, the biological imperative of sexual arousal is never even elicited.[5] The absence of females, the sheer sensory monotony of the prison environment, the absence of those social situations that call for sexual responses (being out on the town, going drinking, etc.) serve as effective inhibitors of sexual responsiveness. The most successful aphrodisiacs seem to be an absence of anxiety, the presence of available sexual cues, an adequate diet, and plenty of rest. Of these, only the latter two are commonly in the prison environment and in some cases only the last is.

The other source of sexual cues is fantasy, those remembered or desired sexual experiences that commonly serve as the basis for masturbation. However, as a result of the social origins of the bulk of the prison population, there is a major taboo against masturbation and a paucity of complex fantasies that would sustain a commitment to sexual experience.[6] Thus, unlike the middle-class male who learns and rehearses sexual styles in the context of masturbation, the usual prisoner is drawn from a population in which sexual experience is concrete and not symbolic; in which there is a taboo on masturbation; and, finally, in which much of heterosexual experience is structured around the need to have sexual encounters that validate his masculinity among other men. In this environment it might be said that men have sex in order to be able to talk about it.

Sex Research, the institutional rates are only one-tenth to one-fifth of noninstitutional rates. For some males the institutional rates are nearly zero.

[5]For a discussion of the necessity of socially facilitating cues for sexual arousal and performance, see John H. Gagnon and William Simon, "Pornography: Raging Menace or Paper Tiger," *trans*action (Vol. 4, No. 8, July–August 1967), pp. 41–48; and William Simon and John H. Gagnon, "Pornography: The Social Sources of Sexual Scripts," a paper presented at the 17th Annual Meeting of the Society for the Study of Social Problems (San Francisco, August 1967).

[6]Alfred C. Kinsey, *et al., Sexual Behavior in the Human Male*. Philadelphia: W. B. Saunders Company, 1948, pp. 497–509.

The Kinsey evidence is that even among lower-class men who do masturbate there is often no conscious fantasy accompanying the behavior, and it serves primarily as a mechanical release of felt physical tension. This is quite unlike the middle-class situation in which masturbation occurs at relatively high rates accompanied by fantasies of sexual experience. These fantasies then begin to facilitate further masturbation and a continuing commitment to this sexual outlet. This adjustment rarely happens in the lower-class environment and, along with the sensory poverty of the prison environment, accounts for the ease with which strong commitments to sexuality are abandoned. Thus, prisoners may complain about sexual deprivation in terms such as "I would really like to have a piece," but often this is a continuation of lower-class male talk about sex, not a passionately felt drive that will eventuate in sexual activity.

Male Homosexuality More than Outcome of Sexual Desire or Need for Physical Release

Since most prisoners do not seem to feel an overwhelming sexual need, male homosexuality in this context must be seen as something more complex than merely the outcome of sexual desire or the need for physical release. There are varying estimates of the number of males who have homosexual contact during their periods of imprisonment, but the range is probably somewhere between 30 and 45 percent, depending upon the intensity of custody in the institution, the social origins of the population, and the duration of the individual sentence.[7] It seems quite clear that the frequency of homosexual contact is usually quite low, even among cellmates; and in no sense does it approach the rates of heterosexual or homosexual behavior of these same prisoners on the outside, except possibly for those prisoners who come into the institutions with well-developed homosexual commitments and who become the "passive" partners in homosexual liaisons. In some prisons, usually those with a very low order of custody inside the walls, high rates of homosexual behavior may be achieved; however, these are not the prevalent conditions in most prison systems.

It must be pointed out that homosexuality in prison is quite a different phenomenon than homosexual experience in the outside community. Thus,

---

[7]Estimates may be found in the following sources: Joseph Fishman, *Sex In Prison* (New York: National Library Press, 1934), 30–40 percent; Gresham Sykes, *Society of Captives* (Princeton: Princeton University Press, 1957), 35 percent; Donald Clemmer, "Some Aspects of Sexual Behavior in the Prison Community," Proceedings of the American Correctional Association (1958), 40 percent. Preliminary estimates from the Institute for Sex Research data are 35–45 percent.

the image of homosexuality as consisting of masculine-seeming men who are always "active" and feminine men who are always "passive" in the sexual performance derives primarily from both journalists and scientists observing homosexuality in prisons and then extending their observations unchecked to the outside world.[8]

Homosexuality in the prison context is partly a parody of heterosexuality, with the very sexual activity suggesting masculine and feminine role components. We now know that this is a basic oversimplification not only of homosexuality in general, but heterosexuality as well. It is, however, in the prison environment where this parody is most likely to occur, for the crucial variable is that many of the men who take part in the homosexual performances conceive of themselves, and wish others to conceive of them, as purely heterosexual.

Thus those prisoners known in prison parlance as "jockers" or "wolves" think of themselves as heterosexual; and, as long as there is no reciprocity in the sexual performance (aiding in the ejaculation of the other male) or the penis is not inserted in their mouth or anus, other inmates will continue to conceive of them in the same way. Thus the homosexual world of the prison is roughly divisible into aggressive "active" males (jockers, wolves) and "passive" males. The latter group commonly includes males who are heterosexual on the outside but who are coerced, either by fear or debt, to be homosexual (usually labeled "punks") and males who have already well-developed preferences for males from their outside experience and who enter prison as homosexuals.[9] The relationships of these males is usually highly stylized both socially and sexually, the aggressor providing protection, a measure of affection and perhaps gifts (in the case of older inmates), and the passive inmate providing sexual access, affection, and other pseudo-feminine services. In the cases of long-term inmates these relationships may be conceived of as pseudo-marriages, resulting sometimes in a greater degree of sexual reciprocity; however, such reciprocity results in a decline in other inmates' estimates of the aggressive male's masculinity.

---

[8]The notions of "active" and "passive" in homosexual relationships are more obscuring of the actual conditions of the behavior than they are enlightening. The psychiatrist Irving Bieber has suggested the words "insertor" and "insertee" be substituted for active and passive, since these latter words assume that role behavior in sexual act has major meaning in psychological personality terms. (*Homosexuality* New York: Basic Books, 1962, pp. 238–254.) For an attempt at clarification of this confusion, see William Simon and John H. Gagnon, "Homosexuality: The Formulation of a Sociological Perspective," *The Journal of Health and Social Behavior*, Vol. 8, No. 3, September 1967, pp. 177–185.

[9]Robert Lindner, "Sexual Behavior in Penal Institutions," in Albert Deutsch, *Sex Habits of American Men.* New York: Prentice Hall, 1948, pp. 201–215; Arthur Huffman, "Sex Deviation in a Prison Community," *Journal of Social Therapy*, Vol. 6, No. 3, 1955, pp. 170–181; George Devereaux and M. C. Moss, "The Social Structure of Prisons and the Organic Tensions, *Journal of Criminal Psychopathology*, Vol. 4, No. 2, October 1942, pp. 306–324.

Search for Meaningful Relationships

The sources of this homosexual activity for the predominantly hetero-sexual and aggressive male seem to be twofold. One element is certainly a search for meaningful emotional relationships that have some durability and which serve as a minimal substitute for affective relationships that they normally have on the outside. This is not unlike the chance homosexual contact between men during combat or in other situations of all-male com-munities under circumstances of fear and crisis. It represents an attempt to counter the effort of the prison to atomize the inmate community in order to reduce the potential for collusion, which could result either in conniving for goods and services or in attempting escape.

One of the collective responses to this attempt is the development of a resistant inmate community, and at the individual level one of the responses is the establishment of homosexual liaisons.

A second motivation underlying many of these relationships tran-scends the level of affectional need and essentially becomes a source for the continued validation of masculinity needs and a symbol of resistance to the prison environment. The male whose primary source of masculine valida-tion in the outside community has been his sexual success (rather than work, family, etc.) and who has conceived of himself as aggressive and controlling in his responses to his world finds himself in prison deprived of these central supports for his own masculinity. In reaction to this he enters into homosexual relationships in which he can be conceived as the mascu-line, controlling partner and which for him and for other males in the sys-tem validate continued claims to masculine status. A complicating factor here is that some men suffer a profound psychological crisis when the sup-ports for their masculine identity are removed. In these cases both severe homosexual panics or falling into "passive" homosexual roles are likely to result.

In general, these homosexual relationships are developed not through force, though there is evidence of homosexual rape, especially in poorly controlled detention institutions where the powerful threat of imprisonment to masculinity is first felt, in penal institutions that are inadequately con-trolled, and in juvenile institutions where the sexual impulse is less well-ordered and tends to be confused with aggression by the adolescent male. In most cases the "passive" partner drifts into the relationship through fall-ing into debt, being afraid of the environment, and feeling that he requires protection, or because he already has a well-developed commitment to homosexuality that he cannot or does not want to conceal. Once an inmate has fallen into this role it is extremely difficult to shift out of it, and, if a current relationship breaks up, there will be pressure to form a new one. Even in a reincarceration there will be a memory of his role from prior institutionalization and there will be pressure to continue. It is as if the prison required as one of its role types the "passive" homosexual, and, if a number of them are removed, there is pressure to restore to equilibrium the relationship between those playing aggressive-masculine roles and those playing passive-feminine roles.

Problems Facing the Prison Administrator

This conceptualization of the pattern of homosexuality in the prison for men suggests a number of problems that face the prison administrator in dealing with sexuality. It means that as long as the prison is an environment which is largely devoid of situations where legitimate affectional ties can be established there will be a tendency for the formation of homosexual relationships, especially among those men serving long sentences who have concomitantly lost contact with meaningful persons in the free community. If in addition the prison does not allow legitimate attempts of the inmates to control their own lives and does not give an opportunity for expressions of masculinity and self-assertion that are meaningful among men at this social level, there will be homosexual relationships created to fulfill this need. The proposal for conjugal visits does not meet this problem, in part because it is available for only the very small number of inmates who have intact families. There is little evidence that the society will tolerate sexual relationships for prisoners when these relationships are not sheltered under the umbrella of a marriage.

What is clear is that the prison is not a seething volcano of sexual passions, and that as a matter of fact most males survive the deprivation of the sexual outlet and usually even survive transitory homosexual commitments to return to relatively conventional heterosexual lives on the outside.

What the sexual problem in the male prison does represent is a series of land mines, some for the administration, more for the inmates. In the case of the inmates, men get into relationships which have some potential for shaping their future commitments to sexuality; relationships which leave them open to exploitation; and, especially for those who take the passive role, the possibility of distortion of their self-conceptions. Further, there is some tendency for these relationships to create problems of sexual jealousy. When a relationship deteriorates or when a transfer of affection takes place, there is a distinct possibility of violence. The violence that does occur often is extreme, and at this point becomes a serious matter for prison management.

The dilemma for the prison manager is that often he is not aware of the relationships until they erupt into violence. Attempts at intervention in this process through getting inmates to aid in the identification of those involved may result in serious scapegoating of these persons out of the sexual anxieties of the other prisoners. The segregation of these prisoners has also been attempted. However, one major difficulty with this measure seems to be that when the most obvious homosexuals are removed from the situation there is a tendency to co-opt other persons to take their place. This tendency is also noted when the aggressive male is removed, though the policy has usually been to remove only those men who are conventionally obvious, that is, who are excessively effeminate.

Probably the only long-term solution is to adopt the policy of home visits at intervals during incarceration and to provide alternative modes of self-expression for those social and psychological needs which, because of the current structure of the male prison, result in homosexuality.

FEMALE RESPONSES TO IMPRISONMENT

As we have noted before, the major dimension which differentiates between the sexual adjustment of persons in the larger society is gender; that is, men and women differ fundamentally in their sexual commitments. While this is obvious, the consequences for the differential sexual adaptation of the males and females in prison are not.

By and large, there is in society a bias against committing females to prison, especially when any alternative is available. Thus the women's prison often has within it women who have either committed major crimes (most commonly homicide) or had long careers in crime and who have been strongly recidivistic. Thus in a certain sense the female institution is composed of some women who have had no prior link to delinquent life-styles and a larger number who had long-term ties with such a life.

Women Have Fewer Problems than Men in Managing Sexual Deprivation

However, the sexual adjustment of these women to imprisonment is strongly linked to the general goals to which most women are socialized in the larger society. Probably the most significant difference between men and women in this regard is that women are socialized in the language of love before they learn about sex, while men are socialized in the language of sex before they learn about love. The consequence of this is that women commonly show considerably fewer problems managing sexual deprivation than do men, and while there is little evidence, one might expect that the frequencies of any sexually ameliorative behaviors, such as masturbation and homosexuality, are considerably less frequent for women than for men in prison. There is considerable evidence that such behaviors are less frequent among women in the free society than among men, and one should not be surprised that such continuity would be found inside the prison. In addition, women seem to tolerate the absence of overt sexual activity far better than do men, and thus the rates of overt sexual behavior in the female institutions should be considerably lower than those found in male institutions.

Women Tend to Establish Family Systems

The typical response of women to the depersonalizing and alienating environment of the penal institution differs substantially from that of males. Nearly universally in juvenile institutions, and in some observed cases in institutions for adult females, female prisoners appear to form into pseudo-families with articulated roles of husband and wife, and then, especially in juvenile institutions, extend the family to include father, mother, and children, and aunts, uncles, and cousins.[10] These family systems seem to arise from three sources. One source is a process of compensation; the majority of females in these institutions are from severely disordered homes, and the creation of the pseudofamily often compensates for this lack. A second source results from the socialization of women who, unlike males who form gangs in self-defense, tend to form families, the basic institution in the society in which they have stable and legitimate roles. Finally there is the fact that the pseudofamily operates to stabilize relationships in the institution and to establish orders of dominance and submission, the primary model for which women have in family relationships with fathers, husbands, and children. Since all social systems require some form of articulation which is hierarchical in nature, it is not odd that women model their experience on the institution that they know best in the outside community. There is some evidence that the pseudofamily is not as prevalent in institutions with older females, and it is possible to speculate that in these institutions dyadic friendship patterns are more frequent and may be more similar to those in male institutions.

---

[10]See Seymour L. Halleck and Marvin Hersko, "Homosexual Behavior in a Correctional School for Adolescent Girls," *American Journal of Orthopsychiatry*, Vol. 32, No. 5, 1962, pp. 911–917; Rose Giallombardo, *Society of Women: A Study of a Women's Prison*, New York: John Wiley & Sons, 1966; David Ward and Gene Kassebaum, *Women's Prison: Sex and Social Structure*, Chicago: Aldine, 1965; Sidney Kosofsky and Albert Ellis, "Illegal Communication Among Institutionalized Female Delinquents," *The Journal of Social Psychology*, Vol. 48, August 1958, pp. 155–160.

Inside the context of these familial structures there is the potential for and the acting out of overt homosexual contacts. In the two most recent studies of female prisons there are varying estimates of the number of women who are involved in homosexual practices, but this variation is probably a function of differing definitions, with one limiting the estimate to overt physical contact (yielding a rate of about one-half) and the other probably referring to the proportion of the population who are currently involved in roles in pseudofamily structures (yielding a rate of about 85 percent).[11]

Deprivation of Emotionally Satisfying, Stable, Predictable Relationships with Males

A minor part of the overt female homosexual contacts may arise from deprivation of sexuality, but the primary source is the deprivation of the emotionally satisfying relationships with members of the opposite sex and the desire to create the basis for a community of relationships that are stable and predictable. The overt homosexuality derives somewhat from the conventional sexual content role definitions of husband and wife, but also partially from the fact that a certain proportion of females who come into these institutions may well have experience with lesbian relationships through experience with prostitution in the free community. This is not to say that female homosexuals become prostitutes, but rather that among prostitutes homosexual relationships are sought because of the degraded conditions of contacts with men. The processes of induction into homosexual activity in the women's prison is often based on the same principles that one observes in male institutions as part of a search for affection and stability in personal relationships. The homosexual relationship offers protection from the exigencies of the environment and the physical homosexual contacts are less sought for the physical release that they afford than for the validation of emotionally binding and significant relationships.

CONCLUSION

From the arguments posed above it is suggested that what is occurring in the prison situation for both males and females is not a problem of

---

[11]The two volumes are Ward and Kassebaum, *op. cit.*, and Giallombardo, *op. cit.* For an excellent comparative discussion, see the joint review of these volumes by Sheldon Messinger, *The American Sociological Review*, Vol. 32, No. 1, February 1967, pp. 143–146.

sexual release, but rather the use of sexual relationships in the service of creating a community of relationships for satisfying needs for which the prison fails to provide in any other form. For the male prisoner homosexuality serves as a source of affection, a source of the validation of masculinity, or a source of protection from the problems of institutional life.

In a like manner, the females tend to create family structures in an attempt to ward off the alienating and disorganizing experience of imprisonment; the homosexual relationships are merely part of the binding forces of these relationships.

The problem for the prison administrator then becomes considerably more complex than merely the suppression of sexual activity—it becomes a problem of providing those activities for which the homosexual contacts are serving as substitutes. The inmates are acting out their needs for self-expression, control over their own behavior, affection, and stability of human relationships. The homosexual relationship provides one of the few powerful ways of expressing and gratifying these needs. Unless these needs are met in some other way, there is little opportunity for adequate control of homosexual activity in the prison environment. It might be hypothesized that any attempt to become more coercive and controlling of inmate behavior in order to reduce homosexual contacts may result not in a decrease in activity, but perhaps in an increase. By increasing coercion one increases the pressure to divide inmates from one another, and one decreases their capacity for self-expression and self-control. As the pressure builds there may well be a tendency for homosexual relationships to increase in importance to the inmate population as a reaction to the intensity of the pressure.

Imprisonment and the concomitant sexual deprivation of inmates obviously has some serious consequences, at least during imprisonment, and has a minor potential for complicating postinstitutional life. Little systematic research exists that links the prior nonprison experience of the prisoner, both sexual and nonsexual; methods of institutional management; and the consequences of the interaction of these two elements for the inmate's future functioning. The fact that many inmates adjust easily to the climate of deprivation in the prison may be a measure of their pathology and inability to get along in the outside community rather than a measure of healthy functioning. Just because we manage to make people conform to a climate of deprivation, both sexual and nonsexual, is no reason that we should.

9

Why Prisoners Riot

Vernon Fox

Finding valid, consistent, and reliable information as to why prisoners riot defies most standard methods of gathering data on human behavior. Official reports and most articles on the subject focus on overcrowding, poor administration, insufficient financial support, political interference, lack of professional leadership, ineffective or nonexistent treatment programs, disparities in sentencing, poor and unjust parole policies, enforced idleness of prisoners, obsolete physical plant, and a small group of hardcore and intractable prisoners.[1] Psychological viewpoints focus on aggression and acting-out personalities in the prison population.[2] Yet, while all the conditions mentioned in the sociological approaches exist in most prisons, the majority have not experienced riot. Further, all major prisons hold aggressive, hostile, and acting-out people. This leads to concern as to why these factors have been identified as causes of riot when riots have occurred in a small minority of prisons.

An examination of official reports following riots discloses a similar

From "Why Prisoners Riot," *Federal Probation*, 35 (March 1971), 9–14. Reprinted by permission.

[1]A succinct and comprehensive review of the literature is found in Clarence Schrag, "The Sociology of Prison Riots," *Proceedings of the American Correctional Association, 1960*, New York, 1961, pp. 136–146.

[2]For example, see the late Dr. Ralph Banay's excellent articles on causes of riots in *The New York Times*, July 26, 1959, sec. VI, p. 8; August 9, 1959, sec. VI, p. 2; August 16, 1959, sec. VI, p. 72.

propensity for generalities and platitudes regarding causes of riots. These same conditions are consistently identified as causes of riots almost everywhere. The purpose of official reports, of course, is political in the sense that they give assurance to the general public after a riot that the remaining power structure in the prison has analyzed the causes, taken corrective measures, and merits the confidence of the public in that their interests will be protected. Investigating committees from governors' offices, legislatures, or other political directions seek simplistic answers that seem to structure their interpretations in accordance with the best interests of their own identifications. Reinterpretation of the situation has to occur frequently. Sometimes, the focus is on the predisposing causes, such as poor morale among inmates fostered by poor food or injudicious or misunderstood paroling policies. Sometimes, it is more aimed at the precipitating causes, such as a confrontation between an officer and some inmates. Sometimes, it has been explained as an attempted mass escape that the administration successfully contained.

Many consultants who are invited from outside the jurisdiction as impartial experts tend to protect the person or group who invited them, which is ethical and logical. Diplomatic writing is a consultant's art. Other consultants invited from outside generally are not sufficiently well acquainted with the nuances and underlying intricacies of the power structure to understand as well as they might all the factors entering into a local situation. Whether the governor or the legislative committee chairman of an opposite political party was the source of the invitation seems to make a difference in the tone of the report. An impartial investigator must be aware of the political climate and what will and what will not be accepted in some political settings. Some reports have been rejected by political leaders, others have been used for political purposes, while many have just been shelved. In any case, the use of these reports for finding the real causes of riots must be tempered pending corroboration from other sources. Frequently, though, these reports may set the tone for further interpretation by the news media, political leaders, and writers of documentaries.

Identifying the causes of riot, then, is tenuous when official reports or statements *after* the riot are considered alone. Clearer vision can be obtained from news reports written *during* the riot. In decreasing order of validity and reliability, the materials that comprise this presentation are from (1) news stories during 20 serious riots since 1940 as reported in *The New York Times* during the action, (2) this writer's experience during the Michigan prison riot in 1952, (3) lengthy discussions with inmates involved in four prison riots, (4) conversations with prison personnel involved in seven prison riots, (5) literature concerning prison riots, (6) official reports and official statements *after* the riot, and (7) general literature on aggression, civil disturbances, and violence.

Causes must be divided into *predisposing* causes and *precipitating* causes. Just as in civil disobedience, there has to be a "readiness" to riot. Then, there has to be a "trigger." Too frequently, the predisposing causes have been used as causes for prison riots and the precipitating causes have been identified as causes for civil disorder. Neither is a cause, in itself. The total social situation, with emphasis on the interaction or lack of it between dominant people and subjugated people, either in the prison or in the ghetto, must be evaluated to determine why people riot. It cannot be based simplistically in overcrowding, political interference, lack of treatment programs, or any other simple answer.

PATTERNS OF RIOT

The way to make a bomb is to build a strong perimeter and generate pressure inside. Similarly, riots occur in prisons where oppressive pressures and demands are generated in the presence of strong custodial containment. Riots are reported more frequently from custodially oriented prisons. Even the riot in 1962 in the progressive and relatively relaxed District of Columbia Youth Center at Lorton, Virginia, involved suppression, real or imagined, of the Black Muslims.

Riots are spontaneous—not planned—detonated by a spontaneous event. The inmates know who has the weapons and who has the force. The inmates know that no administration ever has to negotiate with them. Planned disturbances end in sitdown strikes, slowdowns, hunger strikes, and self-inflicted injury. Escapes do not begin with disturbances unless they are planned as a distraction, though the disturbance may end in escape attempts. The spontaneous event that detonates the riot may be almost anything from a fight in the yard that expands, someone heaving a tray in the dining hall, to a homosexual tricking a new officer to open his cell, as happened in the Michigan riot in 1952. Violent riots must happen spontaneously. Otherwise, they would not happen. There has to be pressure, though, that builds up the predisposition or readiness to riot and a spontaneous precipitating event to trigger or detonate the riot.

Riots tend to pattern in five stages, four during the riot and one afterward. First, there is a period of undirected violence like the exploding bomb. Secondly, inmate leaders tend to emerge and organize around them a group of ringleaders who determine inmate policy during the riot. Thirdly, a period of interaction with prison authority, whether by negotiation or by force, assists in identifying the alternatives available for the resolution of the riot. Fourthly, the surrender of the inmates, whether by negotiation or by force, phases out the violent event. Fifthly, and most important from the political viewpoint, the investigations and administrative changes restore order and confidence in the remaining power structure by making "constructive changes" to regain administrative control and to rectify the undesirable situation that produced the riot.

The first stage of the riot is characterized by an event that triggered the unbridled violence. The first stage is disorganized among the prisoners and, too frequently, among the prison staff as well. It is at this point that custodial force could alter the course of the riot but, in most instances, custody is caught by surprise and without adequate preparation so that there is little or no custodial reaction other than containment. As a result, the riot pattern is permitted by default to move to the second stage.

The second stage is when inmate leaders emerge and the administrative forces become organized. Inmate leaders who emerge from this violence are people who remain emotionally detached sufficiently so that they lend stability to the inmate group. They "don't panic." They "keep their cool." As a result, they attract around them lesser inmate leaders or "ringleaders" who, similarly, do not panic but need to be dependent upon "the boss." In this manner, an inmate leader can gather around him probably two to six "lieutenants," each with some delegated authority, such as watching hostages, preparing demands, and maintaining discipline in the rest of the inmate group. Further, the inmate leader, like most political leaders, takes a "middle-of-the-road" position where he can moderate the extremes and maintain communication. In a prison riot, some inmates want to kill the hostages. Other inmates want to give up and surrender to the administration. The inmate leader controls these two extremes in a variety of ways and stabilizes the group into a position in the center.

The third stage is a period of interaction between inmates and prison officials. It has taken several forms, though they can be classified generally into (1) negotiation and (2) force or threat of force. No administration has to negotiate with prisoners, but the chances for negotiation are greater when the prisoners hold hostages. The chances for force or threat of force are greater when the prisoners do not have hostages. In either case, the decision on the part of the inmates to surrender is subject to the general principles of group dynamics. When the inmate group is cohesive and their morale is good, the prisoners will maintain the riot situation, whether faced with force or negotiation. When the group cohesion begins to disintegrate by some inmates wanting to surrender, others wanting to retaliate, and the leadership wanting to maintain the status quo, the administration may manipulate it for an early surrender. This disintegration of group cohesion may be promoted by negotiation or by force or threat of force, depending upon the situation. In case of negotiation, the group cohesion is diminished by the administration's demonstrated willingness to negotiate and by the personality of the official negotiators who convey a feeling of trust and confidence. The group can be disintegrated, also, by gas, rifle fire, and artillery shelling, all of which have been used recently in American prison riots. The less destructive approach, of course, is to await disintegration of cohesion by periods of inaction that places strain to hold the group together on the leadership by fatigue and impatience. Faced with this situation, the leadership frequently has to look for an honorable way out of a disintegrating situation.

The fourth stage, or surrender, may be the inmates' giving up after being gassed and shot at or they may surrender in an orderly way either after force or threat of force or by negotiation. Political interference at the wrong time in the prison riot can affect the total situation in terms of negotiation, surrender, and subsequent investigations and administrative decisions.

The fifth stage, that of investigations, consolidation of the remaining power structure, personnel and policy changes followed by political fallout, is really the most important stage, since it sets policy for the prison and the system for years to come. Editorials and news commentators suggest solutions and interpretations. Administrators have to respond satisfactorily to pressures from interest groups. This is why "get tough" policies become important after riots, even though they tend to intensify the problems.

Riots do not occur in prisons or correctional institutions with exceedingly high morale. Neither do they occur in prisons where the morale is so low that the prisoners endure penal oppression in a docile manner or break their own legs and cut their own heel tendons. Riots occur in prisons where inmates have medium to high morale and where some conflict appears in the staff, probably between treatment and custodial philosophies, and probably when the program is in a state of transition from one type of procedures and objectives to another.

Riots occur in prisons where there is a tenuous balance between controlling behavior and changing behavior. If there is a full commitment to either, riots do not occur. The riot itself, however, results in a political decision to *control* behavior. Consequently, the behavior changing in treatment forces always loses in a riot, at least in the immediate future.

There is also a direct relationship between news coverage by the mass media and the incidence of demonstrations, riots, and civil disturbances.[3] This is one reason why riots tend to cluster in terms of time.

One of the factors that contributed to the prison insurrections of 1952 was the decision of the administration to reverse the drift toward greater inmate control.[4] Abuses of official rules were curbed, preferential treatment for favored prisoners was eliminated, and the social system of the prison

---

[3]David L. Lange, Robert K. Baker, and Sandra J. Ball, *Violence and the Media*. Washington, D.C.: United States Government Printing Office, November 1969, p. 614.

[4]Gresham M. Sykes, *The Society of Captives*. Princeton, N.J.: Princeton University Press, 1958, p. 144.

was "reformed" in the direction of the image of what the free community thought a maximum-security institution should be.

DURING THE RIOT

Guidelines for action during the riot are important. The custodial staff is frequently untrained and the administration is just as frequently caught by surprise. Action during the riot has to be planned ahead of time and modified according to the situation.

During the first stage of a riot, the disorganized inmates could well be effectively faced with force. As a matter of fact, most riots appear to have been vulnerable to custodial force in the early stages because of the disorganization on the side of the inmates. If disorganization occurs on both sides, however, then the riot cannot be contained early. Immediate custodial action could have altered the course of several riots. The lack of training, preparation, or even expectation of riot has resulted in disorganization on both sides for hours.

During the second stage, after the inmates have organized and their leadership begins to emerge, there is the question as to whether force should be used. No prison administration ever needs to negotiate with rioting prisoners. The prisoners know this. If hostages are held, then negotiation becomes a real possibility, depending upon other factors. If the inmates holding the hostages are young, reformatory-type people with short sentences and have not already demonstrated their capability to kill, if they are psychiatric patients who cannot organize into a team, or if their majority can see parole sometime in the future, then negotiation is not necessary. In the Michigan riot of 1952, the decision to negotiate was not made until after the files of the inmates holding the hostages in 15-block had been reviewed. In that situation, negotiation was apparently the only way to save the lives of the hostages. This was supported by subsequent reports by inmates, nationally known clinical psychologists, and consultants brought in for impartial investigation.

The third stage of the riot is determined by the nature of the situation. If no hostages are held or if the prisoners holding hostages are not hardcore intractables with nothing to lose, then force or threat of force is appropriate. If the hostages are considered to be in serious danger, the administration is placed in a real dilemma in determining action because lives have to be considered in relation to public and internal reaction and consequences. If waiting for fatigue to reduce the cohesion of the rebellious inmate group will accomplish the objective, then force is not necessary.

The fourth stage of the riot is the surrender. The regaining of custodial control is all that is needed. Any further action beyond the basic need has to be for public consumption or for the satisfaction of the prison administration.

The fifth stage of the riot is the aftermath where investigations, reinterpretations, and scapegoats are involved. There is not much the prison administration can do about this because the real power lies in the political structure. Free movement of newsmen and free access to information, both inmates and staff, is the only logical approach to take during this period. In this way, the administration can demonstrate that it is attempting to hide nothing, that it recognizes it has problems, and is openly and honestly seeking the best solutions.

In summary, official reaction to riot is dependent upon the situation. As in judo, the reaction is determined by the action of the adversary. No negotiation is needed where no hostages are held or where they might be held by short-term prisoners not considered to be dangerous. Out-waiting might be an approach in doubtful situations. An overshow of force is becoming decreasingly effective in American society and it invites unnecessary derision from some segments of the public.

ADMINISTRATIVE DO'S AND DON'TS

Discretion, rather than negotiation or force, is at issue while handling a riot. A basic principle of police work or any other type of social control in a democratic society is to use the minimum amount of force and destruction needed to accomplish the objectives.[5]

Discretion is based on knowledge. Consequently, the first approach for a correctional administrator to improve his program is to increase the educational level of his staff by more selective recruitment and by inservice training. In modern democratic society, inservice training should be directed toward the social and behavioral sciences. This can be achieved by bringing neighboring junior colleges and universities into the educational program of the prison.[6] An understanding and knowledgeable prison staff from the custodial employee to the warden is important in the discretionary or decision-making process. It is this staff that determines whether a confrontation occurs or is avoided and, if it occurs, how it will be handled or

---

[5]See George E. Berkley, *The Democratic Policeman*. Boston: Beacon Press, 1969.

[6]For suggested curricula, see Vernon Fox, *Guidelines for Correctional Programs in Community and Junior Colleges*, American Association of Junior Colleges, Washington, D.C., 1969, and "The University Curriculum in Corrections," *Federal Probation*, September 1959. Also see *Criminology and Corrections Programs*, Joint Commission on Correctional Manpower and Training, Washington, D.C., 1968.

accommodated. This is why they need to know social problems, personality development and problems, criminology and correctional procedures, as well as the law, particularly as it relates to civil rights.

The correctional officer is the key to riot prevention, although a rough and harsh custodial lieutenant, captain, or deputy warden can use policies and behavior to neutralize the good work of a hundred officers. The entire custodial force has to be treatment-oriented, just as the entire treatment staff has to be aware of custodial problems, in order to emerge with an effective correctional program.

Readiness to riot results from the predisposing causes, such as bad food, oppressive custodial discipline, sadistic staff quick to write disciplinary charges against inmates, and general punitive attitude by administration and line personnel. The precipitating cause that "triggers" the riot is very seldom the real cause. As previously mentioned, a bomb is made by constructing a strong perimeter or casing and generating pressure inside. It blows at its weakest point, but it has to be detonated. The detonation is not the "cause" of the explosion, although it "triggered" it.

During the riot, the inmates want to smash the system that keeps them hopeless, anonymous, and in despair, and they will destroy at random.[7] They become so alienated from society that they regard violence as right and proper. Good treatment programs and an accepting custodial staff tend to reduce this problem. A relaxed atmosphere in a prison that avoids this alienation is most important for the eventual correctional objective and to avoid riots.

How to achieve a relaxed atmosphere is sometimes difficult for the administrator because it appears that he is "taking sides." Custodial personnel are generally concerned with good discipline, which is sometimes interpreted as "nipping problems in the bud" and is translated into overreaction to minor offenses and oppressive custodial control. Many treatment personnel, on the other hand, are in a relaxed atmosphere because it tends to lower the inmates' defenses and permit casework and psychotherapy to be better achieved. The inmates, of course, find the relaxed atmosphere more comfortable, so they favor it. This places the treatment staff "on the side of the inmates," although for different reasons. It is sometimes difficult for an administrator to interpret to the custodial staff the reasons for promoting a relaxed atmosphere in the prison. This is another reason for providing education and inservice training in behavior and social problems to all staff.

Good food, plentiful and well prepared, is important to maintaining a prison. Napoleon's famous remark that an army marches on its stomach

---

[7]"Violence and Corrections," *The Correctional Trainer*, Southern Illinois University, Carbondale, Vol. I, No. 4, Spring 1970, pp. 56–91.

could be applied to any group of men. Food becomes a primary source of pleasure to men deprived of many of the comforts of normal life. Consequently, the prison administration cannot realistically compute food costs on the basis of nutritional needs alone. The emotional needs are important. An institutional program can make a lot of mistakes if it has a good kitchen that provides plenty of food. Conversely, food is a tangible item on which can be focused all the discontents and deprivations of the prison. Many riots have begun in or near the dining room. Food simply becomes a tangible substitute target for other complaints. Consequently, an administrator should spend a little extra time and effort to find a good steward to handle food services and pay special attention to the food budget.

Despite the other abuses, riots do not occur in prisons that are essentially run by inmates. There are some Southern prisons where selected inmates carry guns and guard other inmates. All the generalities attributed to riot causation exist, but no riots have occurred in these prisons. This is because the inmate leaders have a vested interest in the status quo and will protect it.

Inmate leadership is present in all prisons, as leadership is present in all groups of people. The constructive use of inmate leadership is an obvious way to avoid riots. Some type of inmate self-government that involves honest and well supervised elections of inmate representatives to discuss problems, make recommendations and, perhaps, even take some responsibilities from the administration could be helpful. Possibilities might be some control of those activities related to formalized inmate activities like manuscripts sent to potential publishers, pricing hobbycraft items for sale, or processing inmate activities like Alcoholics Anonymous or chess clubs. In an era when movements to unionize prisoners appear, such as in West Germany and Sweden, and when litigation initiated by inmates result in court rulings that change conditions and procedures within the prisons, it is in the interest of the administration to know the inmates' thinking and their action. In any case, downward communication is not enough.

The pattern could be taken from student government functioning under a university administration. It could be taken from a civilian government operating under military occupation by the victors after a war, such as those civilian governments in Germany and Japan after World War II. The pattern in the Federal Bureau of Prisons and some other systems has been the inmate council, where elected inmates discuss problems and appropriate policies with the prison administration, making recommendations and suggestions. A suggestion box system for inmates might be instituted if other approaches appear to be too innovative. Regardless of how it is organized, it should promote upward and downward communication between inmates and prison administration and it should provide the inmate leadership with a vested interest in the status quo.

In summary, good communication can avoid the predisposing causes of riot. Whether by inmate council, inmate self-government programs, suggestion boxes, or free up-and-down communication of any type, knowledge by the inmate leadership of situations and their reasons can eliminate most predisposing causes. Establishment of the therapeutic community where inmates take responsibility for the improvement of other inmates, such as in the Provo Experiment in Utah in 1958–1964, the Minnesota State Training School at Red Wing, and some other places, would also provide a vested interest for the inmates in the institution and its program, as well as a constructive attitude. Raising the educational level of the prison staff, especially the correctional officers, would reduce the predisposing causes. Their better understanding of personality development and social problems would provide them with the capacity for discretion that would, in turn, reduce the precipitating causes. Prison riots can be eliminated when upward and downward communication, combined with discretionary use of authority, reduces the probability of serious confrontation that should not have to occur in a democratic society.

10

Vocational Training in Prisons: Some Social Policy Implications

Michael J. Miller

According to recent Department of Labor statistics, more than 100,000 persons leave Federal and state prisons each year, and from one-third to two-thirds of all of those released will eventually return to a penal institution. There is certainly no single reason for such high rates of recidivism, but among the more important factors noted in the literature are a variety of common problems that ex-prisoners face in trying to support themselves through steady, financially rewarding and intrinsically meaningful employment. The purpose of this article is to take a critical look at the nature of vocational training programs in prisons, paying particular attention to training as it is related to the probability of increasing the released inmate's life chances for stable employment and successful reintegration into society.

WORK AND PAROLE SUCCESS

Most offenders entering penal institutions have little if any training or occupational skills. Their prior work careers are typically characterized by sporadic work experiences, usually at unskilled labor levels, and they lack

From "Vocational Training in Prisons: Some Social Policy Implications," *Federal Probation*, 36 (September 1972), 19–21. Reprinted by permission.

standard middle-class conceptions of what constitutes proper work habits and attitudes. Unfortunately, far too many inmates leave prisons with little improvement in any of these areas.

Parole success is certainly not completely predictable, but studies have indicated that both the number and intensity of problems faced on the outside do relate to successful parole and reintegration into society. In one national study, for example, Glaser found that only about 20 percent of the released inmates in the sample utilized prison work experiences in post-release jobs, and that about half of these persons *already had* preprison jobs related to subsequent prison training. The net effect, then, is that about one inmate in 10 actually receives new formal or on-the-job training in prisons that he is able to use on the outside. Nevertheless, such training is clearly important. When comparing the parole success of those using the skills that were learned or developed in prisons with all other released inmates, it was found that those using the skills were *twice* as likely to become parole successes.

The causal reason behind this relationship between useful vocational training and parole success is not altogether clear, but there are numerous hypotheses in the sociological and criminological literature. On one hand, success may be viewed as a result of increased legitimate opportunities. On the other hand, as Sutherland and Cressey suggest, meaningful work contributes to greater upward mobility and contact with noncriminal populations. This, in turn, is related to the increased morale and psychological adjustment of those released.[1] Regardless of any theoretical reasons, the fact that prison training may be useful for parole success is quite important for practitioners. If, in fact, job-related experiences in prisons are important, it is crucial that job training, whether through formal instruction or on-the-job training, be associated with labor needs in the free society.

In the research literature, support for the common assumption that steady work experience in prisons instills "appropriate" work habits and attitudes that are applicable to all postprison job situations appears largely unfounded. Glaser, for example, found no differences between parole success and prison work experience except for those persons utilizing this experience in postprison jobs. This clearly indicates that job training programs are needed which have the greatest probability of utilization on the outside and which are matched with both the capabilities and interests of inmates and coordinated with various institutional financial constraints. It simply makes no sense to carry on vocational training programs for occupations with little current or future demand. As will be seen later in the article, however, this is precisely what happens in typical prison training programs.

---

[1]That is, differential association "in reverse." Note that the two positions are really not conflicting: that the opportunity structure may precede attitude change.

OCCUPATIONS AND EMPLOYMENT POTENTIALS

In discussing future occupational needs and social policy planning, several important distinctions need to be made. First, the number of people employed in occupational groups is not necessarily a good indicator of future demands, as a number of occupations are experiencing either no growth or a decline in demand (e.g., agricultural industries). Second, the growth rate of an occupation is important but may be somewhat misleading, for some very high growth rate occupations employ relatively few people (e.g., computer systems analysts). Projected average annual openings in specific occupations, however, provide perhaps the best basis for planning vocational training in correctional institutions. Projected job openings involve a composite index made up of three factors: (1) increases or decreases in occupational size determined by employment demands; (2) job turnover (caused by such things as upward mobility or women leaving to get married); and (3) the death or retirement of occupational members.

Some areas of high demand, such as for physicians or accountants, are inappropriate for the bulk of released inmates. The typical inmate, according to the 1960 Census, is a male, under 35 years of age, a person who has not completed high school, and who has worked as either a laborer or lower level operative. Clearly, we must be aware of the personal characteristics of inmates and their educational[2] and work backgrounds when discussing training programs. In conjunction with occupational demand and personal characteristics, we need to consider the social desirability of jobs in terms of relative prestige and income levels.[3] Such very high demand jobs as domestic service, for example, have neither high prestige nor much income potential. In addition, jobs which involve largely independent work, are low in competitiveness, and nonunionized appear to be both the easiest to secure and to hold for those persons who for some reason or another are discriminated against.

AREAS OF OPPORTUNITY

Recent Department of Labor statistics indicate a greatly increasing demand for personnel in the service occupations with a definite leveling off

---

[2]The often discussed "technological revolution" may be a misnomer, for even by 1980 the Department of Labor predicts that more than 80 percent of the available jobs will still require less than a college education.

[3]The Department of Labor reports a nearly consistent positive linear relationship between average annual income and parole success.

of demand for people involved in industrial production. The occupational projections indicate some fairly consistent trends, which may be essentially summarized as follows:

Farmworkers and Miners

The proportion of people employed in farming, including managers and foremen as well as laborers, has steadily declined since around 1900. This is clearly a depressed occupation with little future hope for improvement. Similarly, mining has suffered a decline in demand coupled with increased mechanization.

White-Collar Workers

Occupations in this category include not only professionals, but also sales, managerial, and office personnel. White-collar work has consistently increased since 1900, and is clearly expected to rise in demand through the 1970s.[4]

Blue-Collar Workers

The tremendous demand for blue-collar workers, as is characteristic of developing industrialization, has clearly leveled off. Current high demands are almost exclusively for foremen and highly skilled craftsmen to the exclusion of unskilled or semiskilled labor.

Service Workers

A number of service occupations are enjoying both high growth rates and considerable numbers of job openings. Particularly promising are such specific occupations as hospital attendants, nurses, and cosmetologists.

In sum, semiskilled and unskilled labor is not in great demand today and will continue to decline in relative importance in the future. Some skilled labor in industry, the services, and white-collar workers will continue

---

[4]Since the mid-1950s, white-collar workers have outnumbered blue-collar workers and the relative difference continues to increase.

to be in relatively great demand. Farming, mining and related occupations will continue to need fewer and fewer people.

VOCATIONAL TRAINING IN PRISONS TODAY

If meaningful job training is a desired goal, it seems obvious that one should stress training for jobs that will be less competitive and more in demand in the future. A cursory examination of the work assignments and vocational training programs typical of most prisons would appear to indicate training in areas of *low* rather than high demand.[5] Based on a national survey of released prisoners, a reexamination of a recent study supported by the Department of Labor indicates that the occupational categories involving the *greatest* number of inmates in training were generally those that were the *least* successful in terms of providing full-time employment. In other words, the greatest effort was being directed to areas without much payoff in terms of permanent employment potential. The data further indicate that over two-thirds (68.7 percent) of the work assignments in prisons are in occupational categories of the least demand (i.e., unskilled and semi-skilled maintenance and prison industries). The often cited notion that vocational training is not enough and that aggressive job searching and careful placement is crucial, neglects the obvious influence of a poor fit between the type of job training and current job demands.

CONCLUSION

Thus, the implications appear clear. Providing meaningful job training, particularly in view of anticipated future employment needs in society, should reduce recidivism. Job training in conjunction with the development of related "social" skills should have an even greater payoff (although I feel that the attitudinal dimension can be greatly overemphasized). Correctional personnel (as well as politicians) need to realize the dysfunctional effects of using inmates for meeting institutional maintenance goals under the guise of on-the-job training (simply because it is convenient and inexpensive on a short-term basis). They also need to realize that work for the sake of work has virtually no payoff except for the institution. The available statistical data would indicate that "good" work habits developed in

---

[5]Prior research has noted the considerable difficulty in placing skilled and semiskilled inmates upon release. Aggressive placement is often stressed, but the problem might also be that many inmates were trained in relatively low demand occupations.

one area (e.g., farming or kitchen services) simply do not translate to a greater degree of successful employment and reintegration into society. Vocational training for jobs meeting stiff competition on the outside because of their low demand appears useless. Quite accurate Department of Labor data are readily available on projected occupational demands for the future, and these data should comprise an integral part of the development and continuation of vocational training programs on both a national and local level. While no one would claim that this approach is a panacea, one can certainly visualize the potential for considerable benefit. While freeing inmates from the mundane and largely meaningless routine tasks necessary for institutional maintenance would be initially expensive, the current data support the contention that this expense would be offset in the long run by substantially reducing recidivism.

11

The Stigma of "Ex-Con"
and the Problem of Reintegration

Richard D. Schwartz
Jerome H. Skolnick

Legal thinking has moved increasingly toward a sociologically meaningful view of the legal system. Sanctions, in particular, have come to be
regarded in functional terms.[1] In criminal law, for instance, sanctions are
said to be designed to prevent recidivism by rehabilitating, restraining, or
executing the offender. They are also said to be intended to deter others
from the performance of similar acts and, sometimes, to provide a channel
for the expression of retaliatory motives. In such civil actions as tort or
contract, monetary awards may be intended as retributive and deterrent,
as in the use of punitive damages, or may be regarded as a *quid pro quo* to
compensate the plaintiff for his wrongful loss.

While these goals comprise an integral part of the rationale of law, little is known about the extent to which they are fulfilled in practice. Lawmen
do not as a rule make such studies, because their traditions and techniques
are not designed for a systematic examination of the operation of the legal

From "Two Studies of Legal Stigma," *Social Problems*, 10, No. 2, (Fall
1962), 133–42. Reprinted by permission.

---

[1] Legal sanctions are defined as changes in life conditions imposed through
court action.

system in action, especially outside the courtroom. Thus, when extra-legal consequences—e.g., the social stigma of a prison sentence—are taken into account at all, it is through the discretionary actions of police, prosecutor, judge, and jury. Systematic information on a variety of unanticipated outcomes, those which benefit the accused as well as those which hurt him, might help to inform these decision makers and perhaps lead to changes in substantive law as well. The present paper is an attempt to study the consequences of stigma associated with legal accusation.

From a sociological viewpoint, there are several types of indirect consequences of legal sanctions which can be distinguished. These include differential deterrence, effects on the sanctionee's associates, and variations in the degree of deprivation which sanction imposes on the recipient himself.

First, the imposition of sanction, while intended as a matter of overt policy to deter the public at large, probably will vary in its effectiveness as a deterrent, depending upon the extent to which potential offenders perceive themselves as similar to the sanctionee. Such "differential deterrence" would occur if white-collar anti-trust violators were restrained by the conviction of General Electric executives, but not by invocation of the Sherman Act against union leaders.

The imposition of a sanction may even provide an unintended incentive to violate the law. A study of factors affecting compliance with federal income tax laws provides some evidence of this effect.[2] Some respondents reported that they began to cheat on their tax returns only *after* convictions for tax evasion had been obtained against others in their jurisdiction. They explained this surprising behavior by noting that the prosecutions had always been conducted against blatant violators and not against the kind of moderate offenders which they then became. These respondents were, therefore, unintentionally educated to the possibility of supposedly "safe" violations.

Second, deprivations or benefits may accrue to non-sanctioned individuals by virtue of the web of affiliations that join them to the defendant. The wife and family of a convicted man may, for instance, suffer from his arrest as much as the man himself. On the other hand, they may be relieved by his absence if the family relationship has been an unhappy one. Similarly, whole groups of persons may be affected by sanctions to an individual, as when discriminatory practices increase because of a highly publicized crime attributed to a member of a given minority group.

Finally, the social position of the defendant himself will serve to aggravate or alleviate the effects of any given sanction. Although all three

[2]Richard D. Schwartz, "The Effectiveness of Legal Controls: Factors in the Reporting of Minor Items of Income on Federal Income Tax Returns." Paper presented at the annual meeting of the American Sociological Association, Chicago, 1959.

indirect consequences may be interrelated, it is the third with which this paper will be primarily concerned.

FINDINGS

The subjects studied to examine the effects of legal accusation on occupational positions represented two extremes: lower-class unskilled workers charged with assault, and medical doctors accused of malpractice. The first project lent itself to a field experiment, while the second required a survey design. Because of differences in method and substance, the studies cannot be used as formal controls for each other. Taken together, however, they do suggest that the indirect effects of sanctions can be powerful, that they can produce unintended harm or unexpected benefit, and that the results are related to officially unemphasized aspects of the social context in which the sanctions are administered. Accordingly, the two studies will be discussed together, as bearing on one another. Strictly speaking, however, each can, and properly should, stand alone as a separate examination of the unanticipated consequences of legal sanctions.

Study I. The Effects of a Criminal Court Record on the Employment Opportunities of Unskilled Workers

In the field experiment, four employment folders were prepared, the same in all respects except for the criminal court record of the applicant. In all of the folders he was described as a thirty-two year old single male of unspecified race, with a high school training in mechanical trades, and a record of successive short term jobs as a kitchen helper, maintenance worker, and handyman. These characteristics are roughly typical of applicants for unskilled hotel jobs in the Catskill resort area of New York State where employment opportunities were tested.[3]

The four folders differed only in the applicant's reported record of criminal court involvement. The first folder indicated that the applicant had been convicted and sentenced for assault; the second, that he had been tried for assault and acquitted; the third, also tried for assault and acquitted, but

---

[3]The generality of these results remains to be determined. The effects of criminal involvement in the Catskill area are probably diminished, however, by the temporary nature of employment, the generally poor qualifications of the work force, and the excess of demand over supply of unskilled labor there. Accordingly, the employment differences among the four treatment groups found in this study are likely, if anything to be *smaller* than would be expected in industries and areas where workers are more carefully selected.

with a letter from the judge certifying the finding of not guilty and reaffirming the legal presumption of innocence. The fourth folder made no mention of any criminal record.

A sample of one hundred employers was utilized. Each employer was assigned to one of four "treatment" groups.[4] To each employer only one folder was shown; this folder was one of the four kinds mentioned above, the selection of the folder being determined by the treatment group to which the potential employer was assigned. The employer was asked whether he could "use" the man described in the folder. To preserve the reality of the situation and make it a true field experiment, employers were never given any indication that they were participating in an experiment. So far as they knew, a legitimate offer to work was being made in each showing of the folder by the "employment agent."

The experiment was designed to determine what employers would do in fact if confronted with an employment applicant with a criminal record. The questionnaire approach used in earlier studies[5] seemed ill-adapted to the problem, since respondents confronted with hypothetical situations might be particularly prone to answer in what they considered a socially acceptable manner. The second alternative—studying job opportunities of individuals who had been involved with the law—would have made it very difficult to find comparable groups of applicants and potential employers. For these reasons, the field experiment reported here was utilized.

Some deception was involved in the study. The "employment agent" —the same individual in all hundred cases— was in fact a law student who was working in the Catskills during the summer of 1959 as an insurance adjuster. In representing himself as being both an adjuster and an employment agent, he was assuming a combination of roles which is not uncommon there. The adjuster role gave him an opportunity to introduce a single application for employment casually and naturally. To the extent that the experiment worked, however, it was inevitable that some employers should be led to believe that they had immediate prospects of filling a job opening. In those instances where an offer to hire was made, the "agent" called a few hours later to say that the applicant had taken another job. The field experimenter attempted in such instances to locate a satisfactory replacement by contacting an employment agency in the area. Because this procedure was used and since the jobs involved were of relatively minor consequence, we believe that the deception caused little economic harm.

---

[4]Employers were not approached in preselected random order, due to a misunderstanding of instructions on the part of the law student who carried out the experiment during a three and one-half week period. Because of this flaw in the experimental procedure, the results should be treated with appropriate caution. Thus, chi-squared analysis may not properly be utilized. (For those used to this measure, $P < .05$ for table 1.)

[5]Sol Rubin, *Crime and Juvenile Delinquency*, New York: Oceana, 1958, pp. 151–56.

As mentioned, each treatment group of twenty-five employers was approached with one type of folder. Responses were dichotomized: those who expressed a willingness to consider the applicant in any way were termed positive; those who made no response or who explicitly refused to consider the candidate were termed negative. Our results consist of comparisons between positive and negative responses, thus defined, for the treatment groups.

Of the twenty-five employers shown the "no record" folder, nine gave positive responses. Subject to reservations arising from chance variations in sampling, we take this as indicative of the "ceiling" of jobs available for this kind of applicant under the given field conditions. Positive responses by these employers may be compared with those in the other treatment groups to obtain an indication of job opportunities lost because of the various legal records.

Of the twenty-five employers approached with the "convict" folder, only one expressed interest in the applicant. This is a rather graphic indication of the effect which a criminal record may have on job opportunities. Care must be exercised, of course, in generalizing the conclusions to other settings. In this context, however, the criminal record made a major difference.

From a theoretical point of view, the finding leads toward the conclusion that conviction constitutes a powerful form of "status degradation"[6] which continues to operate after the time when, according to the generalized theory of justice underlying punishment in our society, the individual's "debt" has been paid. A record of conviction produces a durable if not permanent loss of status. For purposes of effective social control, this state of affairs may heighten the deterrent effect of conviction—though that remains to be established. Any such contribution to social control, however, must be balanced against the barriers imposed upon rehabilitation of the convict. If the ex-prisoner finds difficulty in securing menial kinds of legitimate work, further crime may become an increasingly attractive alternative.[7]

---

[6]Harold Garfinkel, "Conditions of Successful Degradation Ceremonies," *American Journal of Sociology*, 61 (March, 1956), pp. 420–24.

[7]Severe negative effects of conviction on employment opportunities have been noted by Sol Rubin, *Crime and Juvenile Delinquency*, New York: Oceana, 1958. A further source of employment difficulty is inherent in licensing statutes and security regulations which sometimes preclude convicts from being employed in their pre-conviction occupation or even in the trades which they may have acquired during imprisonment. These effects may, however, be counteracted by bonding arrangements, prison associations, and publicity programs aimed at increasing confidence in, and sympathy for, exconvicts. See also, B. F. McSally, "Finding Jobs for Released Offenders," *Federal Probation*, 24 (June, 1960), pp. 12–17; Harold D. Lasswell and Richard C. Donnelly, "The Continuing Debate over Responsibility: An Introduction

Another important finding of this study concerns the small number of positive responses elicited by the "accused but acquitted" applicant. Of the twenty-five employers approached with this folder, three offered jobs. Thus, the individual accused but acquitted of assault has almost as much trouble finding even an unskilled job as the one who was not only accused of the same offense, but also convicted.

From a theoretical point of view, this result indicates that permanent lowering of status is not limited to those explicitly singled out by being convicted of a crime. As an ideal outcome of American justice, criminal procedure is supposed to distinguish between the "guilty" and those who have been acquitted. Legally controlled consequences which follow the judgment are consistent with this purpose. Thus, the "guilty" are subject to fine and imprisonment, while those who are acquitted are immune from these sanctions. But deprivations may be imposed on the acquitted, both before and after victory in court. Before trial, legal rules either permit or require arrest and detention. The suspect may be faced with the expense of an attorney and a bail bond if he is to mitigate these limitations on his privacy and freedom. In addition, some pre-trial deprivations are imposed without formal legal permission. These may include coercive questioning, use of violence, and stigmatization. And, as this study indicates, some deprivations not under the direct control of the legal process may develop or persist after an official decision of acquittal has been made.

Thus two legal principles conflict in practice. On the one hand, "a man is innocent until proven guilty." On the other, the accused is systematically treated as guilty under the administration of criminal law until a functionary or official body—police, magistrate, prosecuting attorney, or trial judge or jury—decides that he is entitled to be free. Even then, the results of treating him as guilty persist and may lead to serious consequences.

The conflict could be eased by measures aimed at reducing the deprivations imposed on the accused, before and after acquittal. Some legal attention has been focused on pre-trial deprivations. The provision of bail and counsel, the availability of habeas corpus, limitations on the admissibility of coerced confessions, and civil actions for false arrest are examples of measures aimed at protecting the rights of the accused before trial. Although these are often limited in effectiveness, especially for individuals of lower socioeconomic status, they at least represent some concern with implementing the presumption of innocence at the pre-trial stage.

By contrast, the courts have done little toward alleviating the post-

---

to Isolating the Condemnation Sanction," *Yale Law Journal*, 68 (April, 1959), pp. 869–99; Johs Andenaes, "General Prevention—Illusion or Reality?," *J. Criminal Law*, 43 (July-August, 1952), pp. 176–98.

acquittal consequences of legal accusation. One effort along these lines has been employed in the federal courts, however. Where an individual has been accused and exonerated of a crime, he may petition the federal courts for a "Certificate of Innocence" certifying this fact.[8] Possession of such a document might be expected to alleviate post-acquittal deprivations.

Some indication of the effectiveness of such a measure is found in the responses of the final treatment group. Their folder, it will be recalled, contained information on the accusation and acquittal of the applicant, but also included a letter from a judge addressed "To whom it may concern" certifying the applicant's acquittal and reminding the reader of the presumption of innocence. Such a letter might have had a boomerang effect, by reemphasizing the legal involvement of the applicant. It was important, therefore, to determine empirically whether such a communication would improve or harm the chances of employment. Our findings indicate that it increased employment opportunities, since the letter folder elicited six positive responses. Even though this fell short of the nine responses to the "no record" folder, it doubled the number for the "accused but acquitted" and created a significantly greater number of job offers than those elicited by the convicted record. This suggests that the procedure merits consideration as a means of offsetting the occupational loss resulting from accusation. It should be noted, however, that repeated use of this device might reduce its effectiveness.

The results of the experiment are summarized in Table 1. The differences in outcome found there indicate that various types of legal records are systematically related to job opportunities. It seems fair to infer also that the trend of job losses corresponds with the apparent punitive intent of the authorities. Where the man is convicted, that intent is presumably greatest. It is less where he is accused but acquitted and still less where the court makes an effort to emphasize the absence of a finding of guilt. Never-

TABLE 1

Effect of Four Types of Legal Folder on Job Opportunities (in percent)

	No record	Acquitted with letter	Acquitted without letter	Con- victed	Total
	(N=25)	(N=25)	(N=25)	(N=25)	(N=100)
Positive response	36	24	12	4	19
Negative response	64	76	88	96	81
Total	100	100	100	100	100

[8] 28 United States Code, Secs. 1495, 2513.

theless, where the difference in punitive intent is ideally greatest, between conviction and acquittal, the difference in occupational harm is very slight. A similar blurring of this distinction shows up in a different way in the next study.

Study II: The Effects on Defendants of Suits for Medical Malpractice

As indicated earlier, the second study differed from the first in a number of ways: method of research, social class of accused, relationship between the accused and his "employer," social support available to accused, type of offense and its possible relevance to occupational adequacy. Because the two studies differ in so many ways, the reader is again cautioned to avoid thinking of them as providing a rigorous comparative examination. They are presented together only to demonstrate that legal accusation can produce unanticipated deprivations, as in the case of Study I, or unanticipated benefits, as in the research now to be presented. In the discussion to follow, some of the possible reasons for the different outcomes will be suggested.

The extra-legal effects of a malpractice suit were studied by obtaining the records of Connecticut's leading carrier of malpractice insurance. According to these records, a total of 69 doctors in the State had been sued in 64 suits during the post World War II period covered by the study, September, 1945, to September, 1959.[9] Some suits were instituted against more than one doctor, and four physicians had been sued twice. Of the total of 69 physicians, 58 were questioned. Interviews were conducted with the approval of the Connecticut Medical Association by Robert Wyckoff, whose extraordinary qualifications for the work included possession of both the M.D. and LL.B. degrees. Dr. Wyckoff was able to secure detailed response to his inquiries from all doctors contacted.

Twenty of the respondents were questioned by personal interview, 28 by telephone, and the remainder by mail. Forty-three of those reached practiced principally in cities, eleven in suburbs, and four in rural areas. Seventeen were engaged in general practice and forty-one were specialists. The sample proved comparable to the doctors in the State as a whole in age, experience, and professional qualifications.[10] The range was from the lowest professional stratum to chiefs of staff and services in the State's most highly regarded hospitals.

---

[9]A spot check of one county revealed that the Company's records covered every malpractice suit tried in the courts of that county during this period.

[10]No relationship was found between any of these characteristics and the legal or extra-legal consequences of the lawsuit.

Of the 57 malpractice cases reported, doctors clearly won 38; nineteen of these were dropped by the plaintiff and an equal number were won in court by the defendant doctor. Of the remaining nineteen suits, eleven were settled out of court for a nominal amount, four for approximately the amount the plaintiff claimed and four resulted in judgment for the plaintiff in court.

The malpractice survey did not reveal widespread occupational harm to the physicians involved. Of the 58 respondents, 52 reported no negative effects of the suit on their practice, and five of the remaining six, all specialists, reported that their practice *improved* after the suit. The heaviest loser in court (a radiologist), reported the largest gain. He commented, "I guess all the doctors in town felt sorry for me because new patients started coming in from doctors who had not sent me patients previously." Only one doctor reported adverse consequences to his practice. A winner in court, this man suffered physical and emotional stress symptoms which hampered his later effectiveness in surgical work. The temporary drop in his practice appears to have been produced by neurotic symptoms and is therefore only indirectly traceable to the malpractice suit. Seventeen other doctors reported varying degrees of personal dissatisfaction and anxiety during and after the suit, but none of them reported impairment of practice. No significant relationship was found between outcome of the suit and expressed dissatisfaction.

A protective institutional environment helps to explain these results. No cases were found in which a doctor's hospital privileges were reduced following the suit. Neither was any physician unable later to obtain malpractice insurance, although a handful found it necessary to pay higher rates. The State Licensing Commission, which is headed by a doctor, did not intervene in any instance. Local medical societies generally investigated charges through their ethics and grievance committees, but where they took any action, it was almost always to recommend or assist in legal defense against the suit.

DISCUSSION

Accusation has different outcomes for unskilled workers and doctors in the two studies. How may these be explained? First, they might be nothing more than artifacts of research method. In the field experiment, it was possible to see behavior directly, i.e., to determine how employers act when confronted with what appears to them to be a realistic opportunity to hire. Responses are therefore not distorted by the memory of the respondent. By contrast, the memory of the doctors might have been consciously or unconsciously shaped by the wish to create the impression that the public had not taken seriously the accusation leveled against them. The motive for such a distortion might be either to protect the respondent's self-esteem or to preserve an image of public acceptance in the eyes of the interviewer, the profession, and the public. Efforts of the interviewer to assure his subjects of anonymity—intended to offset these effects—may have succeeded or may, on the contrary, have accentuated an awareness of the danger. A related type of distortion might have stemmed from a desire by doctors to affect public attitudes toward malpractice. Two conflicting motives might have been expected to enter here. The doctor might have tended to exaggerate the harm caused by an accusation, especially if followed by acquittal, in order to turn public opinion toward legal policies which would limit malpractice liability. On the other hand, he might tend to underplay extralegal harm caused by a legally insufficient accusation in order to discourage potential plaintiffs from instituting suits aimed at securing remunerative settlements and/or revenge for grievances. Whether these diverse motives operated to distort doctors' reports and, if so, which of them produced the greater degree of distortion is a matter for speculation. It is only suggested here that the interview method is more subject to certain types of distortion than the direct behavioral observations of the field experiment.

Even if such distortion did not occur, the results may be attributable to differences in research design. In the field experiment, a direct comparison is made between the occupational position of an accused and an identical individual not accused at a single point in time. In the medical study, effects were inferred through retrospective judgment, although checks on actual income would have no doubt confirmed these judgments. Granted that income had increased, many other explanations are available to account for it. An improvement in practice after a malpractice suit may have resulted from factors extraneous to the suit. The passage of time in the community and increased experience may have led to a larger practice and may even have masked negative effects of the suit. There may have been a general increase in practice for the kinds of doctors involved in these suits, even greater for doctors not sued than for doctors in the sample. Whether interviews with a control sample could have yielded sufficiently precise data to rule out these possibilities is problematic. Unfortunately, the resources available for the study did not enable such data to be obtained.

A third difference in the two designs may affect the results. In the field experiment, full information concerning the legal record is provided to all of the relevant decision makers, i.e., the employers. In the medical study, by contrast, the results depend on decisions of actual patients to consult a given doctor. It may be assumed that such decisions are often based on imperfect information, some patients knowing little or nothing about the malpractice suit. To ascertain how much information employers usually have concerning the legal record of the employee and then supply that amount would have been a desirable refinement, but a difficult one. The alternative approach would involve turning the medical study into an experiment in which full information concerning malpractice (e.g., liable, accused but acquitted, no record of accusation) was supplied to potential patients. This would have permitted a comparison of the effects of legal accusation in two instances where information concerning the accusation is constant. To carry out such an experiment in a field situation would require an unlikely degree of cooperation, for instance by a medical clinic which might ask patients to choose their doctor on the basis of information given them. It is difficult to conceive of an experiment along these lines which would be both realistic enough to be valid and harmless enough to be ethical.

If we assume, however, that these methodological problems do not invalidate the basic finding, how may it be explained? Why would unskilled workers accused but acquitted of assault have great difficulty getting jobs, while doctors accused of malpractice—whether acquitted or not—are left unharmed or more sought after than before?

First, the charge of criminal assault carries with it the legal allegation and the popular connotation of intent to harm. Malpractice, on the other hand, implies negligence or failure to exercise reasonable care. Even though actual physical harm may be greater in malpractice, the element of intent suggests that the man accused of assault would be more likely to repeat his attempt and to find the mark. However, it is dubious that this fine distinction could be drawn by the lay public.

Perhaps more important, all doctors and particularly specialists may be immune from the effects of a malpractice suit because their services are in short supply.[11] By contrast, the unskilled worker is one of many and therefore likely to be passed over in favor of someone with a "cleaner" record.

Moreover, high occupational status, such as is demonstrably enjoyed by doctors,[12] probably tends to insulate the doctor from imputations of incompetence. In general, professionals are assumed to possess uniformly high ability, to be oriented toward community service, and to enforce ade-

---

[11]See Eliot Freidson, "Client Control and Medical Practice," *American Journal of Sociology*, 65 (January, 1960), pp. 374–82. Freidson's point is that general practitioners are more subject to client-control than specialists are. Our findings emphasize the importance of professional as compared to client control, and professional protection against a particular form of client control, extending through both branches of the medical profession. However, what holds for malpractice situations may not be true of routine medical practice.

[12]National Opinion Research Center, "Jobs and Occupations: A Popular Evaluation," *Opinion News*, 9 (Sept., 1947), pp. 3–13. More recent studies in several countries tend to confirm the high status of the physician. See Alex Inkeles, "Industrial Man: The Relation of Status to Experience, Perception and Value," *American Journal of Sociology*, 66 (July, 1960), pp. 1–31.

quate standards within their own organization.[13] Doctors in particular receive deference, just because they are doctors, not only from the population as a whole but even from fellow professionals.[14]

Finally, individual doctors appear to be protected from the effects of accusation by the sympathetic and powerful support they receive from fellow members of the occupation, a factor absent in the case of unskilled, unorganized laborers.[15] The medical society provides advice on handling malpractice actions, for instance, and referrals by other doctors sometimes increase as a consequence of the sympathy felt for the malpractice suit victim. Such assistance is further evidence that the professional operates as "a community within a community,"[16] shielding its members from controls exercised by formal authorities in the larger society.

In order to isolate these factors, additional studies are needed. It would be interesting to know, for instance, whether high occupational status would protect a doctor acquitted of a charge of assault. Information on this question is sparse. Actual instances of assaults by doctors are probably very rare. When and if they do occur, it seems unlikely that they would lead to publicity and prosecution, since police and prosecutor discretion might usually be employed to squash charges before they are publicized. In the rare instances in which they come to public attention, such accusations appear to produce a marked effect because of the assumption that the pressing of charges, despite the status of the defendant, indicates probable guilt. Nevertheless, instances may be found in which even the accusation of first degree murder followed by acquittal appears to have left the doctor professionally unscathed.[17] Similarly, as a test of the group protection hypothesis, one might investigate the effect of an acquittal for assault on working men who are union members. The analogy would be particularly instructive where the union plays an important part in employment decisions, for instance in industries which make use of a union hiring hall.

In the absence of studies which isolate the effect of such factors, our findings cannot readily be generalized. It is tempting to suggest after an initial look at the results that social class differences provide the explana-

[13]Talcott Parsons, *The Social System,* Glencoe: The Free Press, 1951, pp. 454–73; and Everett C. Hughes, *Men and their Work,* Glencoe: The Free Press, 1958.

[14]Alvin Zander, Arthur R. Cohen, and Ezra Stotland, *Role Relations in the Mental Health Professions,* Ann Arbor: Institute for Social Research, 1957.

[15]Unions sometimes act to protect the seniority rights of members who, discharged from their jobs upon arrest, seek re-employment following their acquittal.

[16]See William J. Goode, "Community Within A Community: The Professions," *American Sociological Review,* 22 (April, 1957), pp. 194–200.

[17]For instance, the acquittal of Dr. John Bodkin Adams after a sensational murder trial, in which he was accused of deliberately killing several elderly women patients to inherit their estates, was followed by his quiet return to medical practice. *New York Times,* Nov. 24, 1961, p. 28, col. 7. Whether the British regard acquittals as more exonerative than Americans is uncertain.

tion. But subsequent analysis and research might well reveal significant intra-class variations, depending on the distribution of other operative factors. A lower class person with a scarce specialty and a protective occupational group who is acquitted of a lightly regarded offense might benefit from the accusation. Nevertheless, class in general seems to correlate with the relevant factors to such an extent that in reality the law regularly works to the disadvantage of the already more disadvantaged classes.

CONCLUSION

Legal accusation imposes a variety of consequences, depending on the nature of the accusation and the characteristics of the accused. Deprivations occur, even though not officially intended, in the case of unskilled workers who have been acquitted of assault charges. On the other hand, malpractice actions—even when resulting in a judgment against the doctor—are not usually followed by negative consequences and sometimes have a favorable effect on the professional position of the defendant. These differences in outcome suggest two conclusions: one, the need for more explicit clarification of legal goals; two, the importance of examining the attitudes and social structure of the community outside the courtroom if the legal process is to hit intended targets, while avoiding innocent bystanders. Greater precision in communicating goals and in appraising consequences of present practices should help to make the legal process an increasingly equitable and effective instrument of social control.

12

Politicalization of Prisoners:
A New Challenge to American Penology

Daniel Glaser

American prison riots come in waves. The last crest, in 1952, included two dozen major disturbances. Among them were a dramatic revolt at Jackson, Michigan, in America's largest prison, the riot at Menard, Illinois, for which Governor Adlai Stevenson interrupted his presidential campaign, and others in New Jersey, Massachusetts, Ohio and elsewhere.

How big a prison riot era are we entering? Will it be limited to September's tragedy at Attica, August's shootout at San Quentin, the earlier upheavals in New York city jails, and in Idaho, Florida and California state institutions?

Answers to these questions must certainly reflect the fact that prison rebels of the 1970's differ from those of past decades. While inmate leaders of the 1950's sought mainly to publicize their complaints about correctional administrators, many now address themselves primarily to the so-called "Third World" of oppressed peoples everywhere. They dream of joining forces in a global revolt against alleged "imperialist domination."

From "Politicalization of Prisoners: A New Challenge to American Penology," *American Journal of Correction*, 33 (November-December 1971), 6–9. Reprinted with the permission of The American Correctional Association.

EXCLUSION AND REVOLUTION

Marxists, from Karl on for more than a century, have repeatedly predicted imminent intensification of discontent in capitalist nations and consequent Communist revolutions. They have always been wrong, at least in the countries with firmly established elective governments.

Their predictions err mainly because in these countries, before any issues unify those desiring specific changes into groups large enough to be a revolutionary threat, some leaders of dominant political parties recruit the votes available on any features of radical programs which gain wide appeal. Thus government-supplied unemployment insurance and old-age pensions, which in the United States in the 1920's were only Socialist and Communist party demands, were enacted by the Democratic Party in the 1930's and extended in the 1950's by Republicans. Communist revolutionary movements have succeeded only in countries like Russia, China and Cuba where the men in power excluded any effective representation of those with opposing interests and thus unified their opposition.

This lesson from world history is relevant to American prisons, and to our country as a whole, because prisons concentrate those who are most excluded from policy making—ethnic minorities and youth. More than half the persons arrested in recent years for the FBI's seven Index Crimes (Burglary, Grand Theft, Auto Theft, Robbery, Rape, Aggravated Assault and Murder) are less than 19 years of age at arrest. Three-eighths are black and the remainder are disproportionately of Mexican, Puerto Rican or Indian descent.

Narcotic offenses are the most frequent other basis for felony arrests. In drug crimes more than half the arrestees today are under 20, but only about a fifth are black. These statistics contrast with those of 20 years ago when most narcotics arrestees were over 25 and a majority was black. This trend reflects growth of drug use among white youth in the 1960's.

Increased separation of youth from adults is the pattern of all advanced industrialized countries. Due to technological changes, such as household appliances and preprocessed foods, adolescents are less needed than ever before for chores at home. There are also fewer family farms or shops where they can share their parents' tasks and concerns, and both parents work away from home more often than formerly. Furthermore, today's younger generation is expected to attend school in an age homogeneous social world for more years than prior generations and while students they are not regarded as fully adult, regardless of their ages. Even their recreation is largely separate, in establishments catering to the youth market.

SEPARATION MEANS DIFFERENCES

A fundamental law of sociology and anthropology is that social separation of groups produces differences in customs. That is how variation has developed in the world's languages and beliefs. The separation of youth promotes differentiation of their speech, fashions and moral standards. This creates a vicious circle: the more their behavior differs from that of adults, the more they must hide it from adults to avoid criticism and hence the more separate their social life becomes.

Exclusion of youth from older age society is not through anyone's intent but from automatic consequences of historical trends that can only be reversed if clearly recognized and deliberately offset.

Narcotic offenses dramatically illustrate how social separation of the generations creates contrasts in customs and tastes. Surveys repeatedly show that a majority of those 18 to 20 years of age have tried marijuana, as have large proportions in their early twenties, but this is an experience of less than five percent of the population over forty, which includes most public policy makers.

While we of the older generation eschew marijuana, we long ago abandoned efforts to prohibit use of a clearly more disabling drug—alcohol. This dangerous chemical is consumed fearlessly and millions suffer from its overuse, yet there is no longer any serious movement to declare it illegal. No wonder so many in their twenties or younger regard those over thirty as hypocrites and are reluctant to trust them!

The drug crimes which highlight age cleavage in our society cut across class and ethnic lines, but four out of five Index Crime arrests are for taking someone else's money or property. Property offense arrestees are predominantly poor, out of school and out of work, or at low-paying, unskilled and insecure jobs.

They are disproportionately of minority groups, due to generations of poverty and under-education, plus prejudice in hiring even those who are educated. This is nothing new in our history; it was also true in the 1920's, when the children of the poor and uneducated minority groups who were arrested for property crimes were predominantly the offspring of Polish and Italian peasant immigrants. What is new in today's criminal population is the ethnic and educational diversity of the youth who are unified by being excluded from "respectable" circles and declared outlaws. This gives them common interests and a shared outlook on political issues that have polarized our society.

"POLITICAL PRISONERS"

The concept "political crime," as giving a special status to certain prisoners, is alien to American legal philosophy. It is well established on the European continent, where criminal codes long specified that those imprisoned for a political offense are to be less harshly treated than those incarcerated for ordinary crimes. Thus when Hitler was sentenced to Landsberg Prison after his abortive *putsch* in 1923, he was given a comfortable apartment rather than a typical cell and it was here that he was able to write *Mein Kampf*.

American prisoners are sentenced for violations of criminal codes which make no references to political motivation, and all are sent to the same jails and prisons. Traditionally most offenders approve laws against the kinds of acts—such as burglary, theft or robbery—for which they are convicted, although many claim they are innocent or were victim of extenuating circumstances. This viewpoint has changed, however, as Americans increasingly are incarcerated not for victimizing others but for acts which they consider morally justifiable. These acts include use of narcotics and resistance to government policies they regard as illegal.

Large-scale overt resistance to government policies began in the 1950's, with massive demonstrations in behalf of minority groups. Where legitimate political procedures were blocked, as in Southern suppression of voting rights, civil disobedience of the law was espoused.

The targets of youthful rebels shifted in the 1960's from southern politics to the Indochinese war, many identified with guerilla leaders abroad and they found mass-media resources by creating theaters out of courtrooms and by growth of the so-called "underground" press. Youth of all backgrounds thereby became increasingly united in support of flouting the law. Their identification with the poor and with minority groups is evident in their styles of dress and in their music preferences. Most of this history unfolded outside the prisons but its meaning in prison may become understandable if we imaginatively view the outside world from the perspective of a typical prisoner.

HARD CORE DELINQUENTS

Most "hard core" inmates today were seriously delinquent as children. This gained them much attention from their youthful peers, which was especially attractive to those handicapped by ethnicity and poverty. When one outgrows being a juvenile "big shot," is without a diploma or job experience, and has a police record, the kinds of job opportunity available have small appeal.

Those who are repeatedly incarcerated, starting at an early age, have little successful experience at professional crime or at legitimate employment but dream of quick paths to success. That is why so many strive in prison to become professional athletes or popular musicians, two fields in which a few persons of their background have had highly publicized careers.

Indeed, every period of our history has seen the ethnic groups predominant in prisons also prominent in boxing and popular music.

The recent rise of militant group leaders with prison records, such as Malcolm X and Eldridge Cleaver, gave new career dreams to some young inmates but there were additional reasons for their attraction to militant movements.

Almost everyone who is degraded by others strives to interpret his experience so as to view himself favorably. It is normal to excuse oneself by blaming others or by complaining about conditions. Minority group membership in our society creates justifiable grounds for complaint but these are grasped with special eagerness by those most in need of excuses for their circumstances. This fact, of course, gives a minority movement distinctive appeal to prisoners; it reduces their isolation and sense of degradation. Indeed, some militant organizations actively recruit prisoners and provide a ready welcome for them on release. Furthermore, tactics which violate the law are less repugnant to convicts than to working people with a stake in conformity.

The revolutionary ethnic movements permit a prisoner to see himself as a patriot instead of a pariah, and the division of the prison community into predominantly white Anglo staff and minority group inmates provides a stage for playing heroic leadership roles. When parole is denied and solitary confinement is imposed because of such leadership, the idea that he is being punished as a political prisoner rather than as an ordinary criminal may often have some justification in fact; in any case, it has an understandable appeal to the prisoner. For this reason a diminution of the organized guerilla-type riots is not likely until the conditions which foster them diminish.

REMEDIES

It should be remembered that even the largest prison riots recruit only a minority of prisoners. This minority will shrink when it is less unified, not just with other inmates, but with supporters among youth and minority group members outside of prison.

This will only occur when the appeal of legitimate alternatives to rioting, in prison and out, can compete successfully with the appeal of rebelliousness. The easiest way to intensify inmate militancy is to coop all known or alleged militants in one structure. This is what happened at Attica, at San Quentin's "Adjustment Center," at Jackson's Cell Block 15 and at numerous other large penal tinder boxes. Agitators are more readily controlled or even changed, by other inmates and by staff, when more scattered in a penal system.

Research has repeatedly demonstrated that social separation of staff and inmates increases prisoner acceptance of anti-staff values. Federal prisons have dispersed youthful "trouble makers" in diverse programs of work and education, the activities in which personal relations between staff and inmate are closest, and have provided immediate and meaningful rewards for inmate achievements. There are many aspects of prison management—including food service planning, recreation program planning, safety programs, building maintenance, landscaping and numerous other activities —where elected inmate representatives can participate as individuals on committees with staff. There need be no risks in this, only benefits for rehabilitation and for morale.

Today's major advance, pioneered by the federal prisons, is transfer of inmates during their last several months before parole to small community correctional centers at their release destination, to permit employment or education outside of prison and thus to conquer post-prison problems gradually. This can be a major incentive to conformity in prison as well as a rehabilitation aid.

California and several other states have duplicated this pattern, after at first erroneously equating it with parole halfway houses and with work release from rural prisons. By charging employed prisoners about four dollars per day for room and board it can even be economical. This may make if feasible even in systems heavily burdened by maximum security monstrosities which provide most of their prison housing.

Most state prisoners today are young adults from urban minority groups, confined in rural locations, under non-minority staff recruited from the surrounding countryside. The prison is the major industry of the area and citizens there concentrate their political power in state legislatures to maximize autonomy of local staff. This has been the burden of Russell Oswald in his brief career as Commissioner of Corrections for New York, where prison programs are more impeded than enhanced by the overly rigid civil service tenure of guards.

It contrasts most markedly with the District of Columbia, where the racial composition of correctional staff not only approximates that of the prisoners but even includes some clearly rehabilitated exconvicts. California comes closer to this D.C. pattern than most states but still is far from it.

Prisons are also affected by the outside society. If youth and minority groups participate in government, they are not readily recruited by advocates of violent revolution. Extending the franchise to the 18- to 21-year-old population, and redistricting to promote rather than impede minority group representation, should indirectly promote prison progress. Indeed, providing absentee ballots to non-felon jail inmates and making restoration of voting rights automatic with discharge from a felony sentence might politicize prisoners legitimately.

Polarizing powerholders against the powerless, in prison and out, has brought us to acute conflict, which will only intensify if continued. Complete resolution of penal and societal problems cannot be immediate, but progress will replace retrogression only as we maximize the legitimate opportunities of rejected and alienated people for gratifying participation in our society.

13

Correctional Administration and Political Change

Richard McCleery

This paper will examine a series of events in the administrative history of a correctional agency, and the impact of constitutional change on that agency, as a basis for speaking to the general question posed to participants in this program—"The intellectual significance of administrative experience." In order to avoid the patent impossibility of that charge in its totality, it is necessary to reduce that task by definition and elimination. Risking the loss of implications that might seem vital from another point of view, the definitional fiat of the present paper is this: significance does not lie in the raw material of experience in any case, it lies in the processes of analysis which relate events to some more general, intellectual construct. That is to say, in criticism of a considerable amount of descriptive research, that one does not know what the significance of a case *is* until he knows what it is a case *of*.

Some may properly question the accuracy and completeness of the present paper, for it involves inherently personal elements of selection, but the events themselves are largely matters of public record. The significance of the events turns on the legitimately controversial question of whether

Paper presented at the Annual Meeting of the American Political Science Association, Washington, D.C., September 5–8, 1962. Reprinted by permission.

certain conflicts reported below should be interpreted as a case of official incompetence, personality conflict, administrative reorganization, or the politics of statehood. In brief, the present analysis rests on an assumption that significance lies in the richness of hypotheses rather than in the wealth of experience.

A second approach to narrowing the present task is to examine and eliminate alternative lines of analysis which might be pursued under the present general assignment. In the course of this examination, fundamental differences among alternative lines of analysis may be clarified. The line of reasoning employed in analysis of a given situation may be extended logically in either of two directions: toward practical administrative recommendations or toward general intellectual significance. Our assignment is the latter, but, by noting the bitterness and conflict so often generated by "practical" recommendations, we may be warned of potential controversies inherent in extending analysis to high levels of abstraction. Perhaps this effort to find significance in our assumptions, rather than in experience, may generate an electric but cleansing academic storm.

A possible approach to the assigned task might be to take the type of analysis implied by the title, "What I have learned about human nature in twenty years of prison work." The potentially rich option of that approach is rejected here because it is not yet supported by an adequate foundation of reflective thought, not because of the contempt it would generate in this company. Certain things should be noted in this connection, however. First, that is the type of analysis often advanced by men with a wealth of administrative experience. Second, such analyses are often treated by the company of scholars with summary contempt—a contempt matched only by the practitioner's response to research of a type implied by such titles as "The relationship of certain personnel techniques to administrative efficiency." There are crucial differences and, perhaps, different values in the two lines of approach.

It is of interest that the reflections of an administrative graybeard on "human nature" are closer to the abandoned, classical heritage of political theory than the calculations of his academic counterpart. Much of classical political thought addressed itself to a search for axiomatic propositions about human behavior. The obvious futility of that search appears only in the effort to cast such propositions in unconditional, universal terms. An essential characteristic of scientific, as opposed to metaphysical, propositions is that they are conditional. Thus Galileo's proposition about falling objects holds only in the unfamiliar condition of a perfect vacuum, and Hobbes' assertions about human nature specify the unfamiliar conditions of that "state of nature" to which they are limited in his analysis. There are times when the patterns of prison life occur in a near vacuum of civilizing traditions and internalized social controls. As the conditions of life approach those prescribed for Hobbes' state of nature, research evidence and the common-sense wisdom of administrative experience combine to support a number of Hobbesian observations about the behavior of men so situated.

We cannot anticipate what condition of human behavior may eventually be taken by political theory as the intellectual equivalent of Galileo's condition of a perfect vacuum for the statement of uniformities. Behavior under conditions of "perfect" panic, perfect rationality, perfect custody, or perfect love might serve equally well as an axiomatic base for analysis of behavior in experienced situations. We may suggest, however, that a final breakthrough to a science of politics awaits some such conditional propositions. Therein lies a potential significance for what is learned about human nature from twenty years of work under prison conditions, or, for that matter, of work in any standardized, institutional setting. Seen in the light of Rousseau's political theory, significant meaning may be found in the common-sense saying of the traditional prison yard, "You don't have to be a son-of-a-bitch to take a job here; you will make it in six months anyway." Is there as much general significance in typical pieces of contemporary technical research? Is there any answer to the charge of the experienced official against the academic consultant that, for all his degrees, titles, and statistics, he knows nothing about the prison, the state of the prison, or the prison state?

The conflict between practitioners and academics on concrete practice, so vividly expressed in regard to prison management, exposes the fundamental difference between alternative lines of analysis. The academic consultant sees significance in and bases recommendations on the functional interrelationship of positions at a given point of time. This is the only type of significance developed in most analyses and, indeed, the only type possible in most consulting practices or single-shot research studies. Stripped of their protective jargon, the concrete implications of such an analysis are similar to and little better than the suppressed criticisms of raw recruits. They identify internal contradictions in the logic of events at a moment in time or dysfunctions with regard to the agency's purpose as legally defined. But the operating values in the logic of agency action are never precisely those that are legally defined. Except where senior officials are suitably mystified by the cult of science or coerced by the sanctions of superior authority, they resist the recommendations of such an approach with bitter dedication.

The essential conservativism of senior officials rests on a Burkean perception of the prison as an institution with a past, a present, and a future. It stands on a sense of the functional relationship of states of affairs at different points of time, a feeling for the tensions which enter into maintenance of a moving equilibrium, and the valid insight that any substantial change portends problems of order for the future. When the experienced official is unable to ignore the proposals of the research consultant, he is normally able to negate their force by compromising modifications elsewhere in the administrative system. The administrative resistance which a consultant is often inclined to attribute to stubborn ignorance or perversity is often the product of a more broadly based, if less articulate, theory of the system than his own.

If the general assignment of this program is translated into a search for the implications of administrative experience for a general social science, a relevant criterion becomes that of the capacity of any line of analysis to generate valid predictions. From that standpoint, the ability of the practitioner with his time perspective to anticipate problems implicit in change seems to exceed that of the research consultant with his structural approach. It is this gift which so often permits the senior administrator or politician to frustrate or exploit the predictable recommendations of a consultant to predetermined policy ends. The repeated exploitation of "experts" for politically predetermined ends in the story to follow comes as a painful shock to the ideal of a neutral, scientific competence. An arguable conclusion of this paper is that a structural analysis of an institution at one point in time, uninformed by a theory of institutional change, has only as much general intellectual significance as it has practical consequences.

Having considered various approaches to the search for significance above, the analysis of the case to follow will focus in some measure on three hypotheses which have been advanced in the effort to discover significance in administrative experience:

1. One hypothesis regards the administrative agency as an institutionalized, problem-solving system. Assuming that administration is an effort to control some set of events in order to secure certain desired consequences; action, when based on valid assumptions, should be instrumental to the ends desired. Hence, administrative experience should provide a test of the validity of assumptions being acted on in regulating any state of affairs. For example, the assumption that increased communication between two agency units will enhance co-ordination of their roles with regard to a prescribed end should be subject to empirical verification.

2. A second proposed hypothesis assumes that the design of a regulating agency is related to the nature of the phenomenon being regulated. Hence, an evaluation of administrative experience should provide a means for generating and testing hypotheses about the nature of any set of events being regulated. Applied to the specific context of correctional administration, this hypothesis might imply

a capacity to use experience as a basis for distinguishing "incorrigible" and reformable inmates or identifying the characteristics of the incorrigible.

3. A third hypothesis, one guiding much of the formal research on which this paper is based, is of a different character. It regards the correctional agency as an institution and a social system with energies and characteristics of its own, not as a problem-solving system operating at the behest of the state. Hence, for such purposes as the study of relationships between communications and authority, the prison may be considered as a society in microcosm and a source of insights into the nature of power structures in other settings.

The data on which the present analysis is based are drawn from observations, correspondence, conversations, public records, and intermittent periods of intensive study over a period of fifteen years. This extended period of observation is anchored at such points as two years of participant observation of Oahu Prison in 1945–47 and a year of concentrated research on its institutional culture and history in 1954–55. Of equal import to the analysis, however, is a carefully designed research study never executed at all. Earlier study had traced a disruptive process of administrative change to a point in 1955 at which authority had been re-established in a stable pattern extending throughout the structure of the prison community. In 1960, however, that pattern of authority collapsed in an explosive riot, and a study was formulated to explore the deterioration and failure of that system of social control.[1] Execution of that research, desperately sought by the senior career officials of the prison system, was forbidden by the cabinet official and the governor. All research access to the prison and parole systems was prohibited.

If administrative experience has intellectual implications, it has emotional implications as well. The prohibition of what seemed to be an intellectually significant line of inquiry transformed the author from a detached observer of obscure interactions into an outraged if unwilling participant in

---

[1]The earlier studies of the governing of men and comparative prison cultures were supported by a grant from the Doris Duke Foundation and by the Institute for Research in Social Science, at the University of North Carolina. Discussions of that work are available in a monograph, *Policy Change in Prison Management* (Government Research Bureau, Michigan State University, 1957) and in *The Prison: Studies in Institutional Organization and Change*, Donald Cressey, Editor (Holt, Rinehart & Winston, 1961). The projected study of the collapse of authority patterns within the prison was supported by a grant from the Social Science Research Council. The council graciously permitted, though it did not intend, the use of that grant to examine the larger administrative-political context after the technical project was forbidden, and responsibility for the present analysis lies entirely on the author.

a rising political storm. It transformed the research from a manageable, technical study of social process within the prison to an unmanageable inquiry into the complex political context of prison management and into the administrative logic of the decision to deny research. Reconstruction of the pattern of events within the prison in its crisis year of 1960 rests on little more than public testimony, institutional records, and the evidence of forty personal interviews at all administrative levels from the governor to parolees.

Analysis of the larger political context of prison management is a different matter. The hundred or more informants contacted with their varying perceptions of the case do not begin to represent a sample of the facets of the situation. The relevant data are, at once, too extensive and too private to permit even an effort at exhaustive accumulation. Hence, the search for a significant interpretation must take the form of exploring alternative theories in the hope of finding one consistent with a sequence of major events that are matters of public record. The fact of the author's emotional involvement with this case is undeniably evident in the pain and pace of writing these pages. The extent to which that involvement distorts, rather than motivates, the search for significance is a question and a caution submitted to the reader.

The set and sequence of events on which this analysis will focus can be outlined briefly here. A somewhat more extended treatment of background material will follow.

1. In January 1960, the Hawaii Prison System was transferred into a cabinet level Department of Social Services as part of a general reorganization of the executive branch following statehood. The first Departmental directive issued required that all information and press releases were to be sent over the director's desk.

2. Within three months, an employees' union emerged around internal personnel problems in the prison as a major factor in its administrative situation.

3. This was followed immediately by a brief sit-down strike by inmates for which no general set of grievances was ever advanced. The strike and a series of escapes extending back to the previous year became the occasion of a press campaign of protest against the prison management.

4. The late spring and early summer were marked by increasing intervention and a public overruling of career prison officials on administrative matters by the director of the department.

5. In July, the career officials drafted an administrative memorandum, later to become a matter of public controversy, to the director, citing instances of cabinet level interference in manage-

ment and stating that these were bringing matters in the prison to a dangerously explosive state.

6. Immediately after that note, a violent and destructive riot—the first in forty years—erupted in Oahu Prison, and the National Guard was called out to restore order.

7. Shortly thereafter, a highly publicized but professionally unknown "consultant" was employed by the director, without consulting career officials, to study conditions in the prison. The work of that consultant, assisted by investigators from the Attorney General's office, was issued to the press as a harsh, across-the-board denunciation of the prison staff.

8. Meanwhile, the aborted project for research on the collapse of authority within the prison was drafted on the mainland, cleared with top prison officials, financed by a research grant and, finally, prohibited by the cabinet official.

9. On the release of the consultant's report, the lay Parole Board, an administrative device designed to prevent political invasion of its domain, issued a public attack on the cabinet official for interference in parole and prison management, a defense of the prison staff and program, and a charge of "dictatorship and rising lust for power." This attack made public mention for the first time of the memorandum of July, warning of impending trouble in the prison.

10. After several action-packed days, top officials of the prison system joined members of the Parole Board in open rebellion against the director, charging, among varied particulars, the use of "third degree" methods in seventeen hours of intense, administrative pressure aimed at gaining a repudiation of the July memo. The outraged warden published his earlier memo in full and demanded an impartial study of the prison.

11. An interim committee of the House of Representatives, controlled by the Democrats, scheduled hearings on the matter, but the governor returned from a mainland trip in time to impose a temporary truce on the battle in his administration. By prohibiting all executive officials from testifying to the legislative committee, and by making promises of internal reform which are remembered differently by all conflicting parties, the governor let the air out of the scheduled hearings and regained an initiative to impose his own solution on the problem. The committee heard testimony from the acting chairman of the Parole Board who resigned in order to state his charges, but the issues were never joined and initiatives vanished by an Attorney General's ruling that called its legality into question.

Each of the above events except the second, the rise of the union, was reported in increasingly dramatic, front-page headlines, generating spasms of disorganized public agitation and protest as factors in the logic of further decision-making. In time the exercise palled on the public, and a further hearing in the next legislative session proved inconclusive. As the waves of public excitement slowly subsided from the explosion, the principal actors left the stage. The advice of the first consultant was adopted after three months with the dismissal of the deputy warden, the superintendent of Oahu Prison. Then, on the basis of recommendations advanced by a second consultant to the cabinet official, the warden was reduced in rank, by-passed in the chain of command, and, eventually, dismissed. Finally, as in the story of the gingham dog and the calico cat, the director was removed by the governor "with regret" on the grounds of a report submitted by a third expert of his own.

Thus the battle ended with no apparent victor left on the field, but the implications of the conflict remain at all levels of the process of government. The balance between custodial and rehabilitative values in prison management, the balance between political and professional roles in administration, and the balance between executive and representative powers in government have been shaped by the conflict around these events. The manner of its resolution has provided precedents for the emerging constitution of the future.

At any point of time in this period, and at any level of the administrative hierarchy, it would have been valid for research to report that authority was at a point of collapse, efficiency was minimal, morale was in a crisis condition, and rebellion was brewing. Further, it would be natural, at least, to fix responsibility for those conditions in legally accountable officials. That, however, is to attribute more force to acts of individual will than formal grants of authority can convey. A more adequate interpretation and significant understanding of these events may be provided by considering them in the perspective of time and in terms of the internal momentum of institutional behavior. Surely this series of events confronts an academic theory of social control with a challenge and an opportunity, for each of the events noted constituted a crisis in the system of government. The background of these crises is sketched below in the organic constitution of the past.

CONSTITUTIONAL CHANGE IN THE PRISON SYSTEM

In 1946, a new warden of the Hawaii Prison System inherited a prison government dominated by punitive concepts of reform and a purely custodial orientation. Its already obsolete physical plant was, even then, inadequate to the problem of security; and much of the process of social control had been delegated by a corruption of authority not uncommon in institutions of that type. Limited custodial forces and weak security equipment repressed serious disorder by enlisting tough and prison-wise senior inmates in the maintenance of a mutually tolerable *status quo*, gaining such assistance in exchange for privileges and informal authority.

Despite the myths and appearances of equality then, the resulting organization of the inmate community was a steeply graduated hierarchy of power and privilege, dominated by adjusted and confirmed old convicts. One inmate leader of the prison yard in 1946 banked an income of $8000 on the prison's official books entirely from earnings within the institution and was later convicted of income-tax evasion on that amount. That constitution of prison government produced a climate of repression and exploitation analogous to the culture of an extremely authoritarian state and hostile to the logic of moral rehabilitation, but it had obvious advantages and dominant roles for some elements of the prison community. These real advantages of the old system give a continuing appeal to the idea of a return to the "good old days" whenever problems emerge in an effort to operate the prison on different principles.

The new warden and the top-level staff which he recruited to the prison were unfamiliar with and shocked by the detailed processes of its government. Indeed, one of its working principles was that much of the operating detail of the old system should not be known to top officials—a principle familiar on other governmental levels. However, this new and largely inexperienced staff brought habits and expectations to the government of the prison which had devastating consequences for its traditional processes of control.

One of the first major acts of the warden, following futile efforts to be informed of practices within the institution, was to commission a study of the prison. (Perhaps a sign of vitality in any institution is a capacity to identify and resolve problems on the lowest operating level.) Although the report was used in the most generous manner possible, it led to the resignations of several custodial officers on grounds of long continued practices which, while functional in the context, were clearly illegal. The illegality of these shakedowns and sales of privileges was beyond doubt, but they had continued so long as to seem normal, and the dismissals remained a longstanding basis of discontent in the custodial ranks.

The suppression of these corrupt practices removed several crucial incentives from the processes of control. That, in turn, increased the burden on the punitive portion of the control system—the portion which consisted of repression, arbitrary force, and fear. However, at that juncture, the inexperienced staff formed a disciplinary committee to increase the quality of fairness and judicial concern for the rights of individuals in the process of punishment. This change decreased the arbitrary aspects of control through force—the "reign of terror" quality of previous sanctions which had made the security of the institution the highest law. Whatever their moral merits, the removal of corruption and the reduction of arbitrariness as methods of control had disturbing consequences. Institutional records show evidence of a widespread disorganization in the inmate community following a loss of status on the part of its old-convict leaders. Increases in the guard force and its training and strengthening of the physical plant were not sufficient to offset a wave of escape, violence, and internal tension at that time. Only the insulation from popular protest provided by territorial government and the grace period in which new officials are allowed to blame their mistakes on their predecessors permitted the survival of the reform group in the prison.

The impact of these early changes, by itself, illustrates certain conclusions which seem to have general import. *First*, the organizational structure of the institution is a complex of human energies and traditional roles in delicate balance, and ill-considered efforts to tamper with that balance are apt to release explosive results. *Second*, even in the authoritarian regime of the traditional prison—perhaps, especially there—a large part of the processes of social control were informal and internalized in the inmate body. The bulk of those coercing definitions which governed inmate behavior were communicated through their own peers and fears. Hence, the *third* conclusion is that control over inmates lies in the steel and concrete in which their energy is confined than in the direction which is given to that energy. If that is true of inmates, it is even more true of employees and the limited force of administrative sanctions. During the past fifteen years, there have been three waves of tension, violence, and escape at Oahu Prison; and these bear almost no relation to the number of guns, guards, or security facilities available there.

A New Direction: The early period of change and its consequences fixed conclusions of a different type in the minds of the now more experienced prison officials. Since corruption and terror seemed to be inevitable components of the old, authoritarian regime, they resolved that its punitive concepts had to be replaced with an entirely new philosophy and constitution of prison management. By 1950, the core of that philosophy had emerged from the values of the professional staff, and the direction of prison government began to take a revolutionary turn in contrast to the earlier phase of reform.

An attempt to summarize that revolution tends to deteriorate into cliches: rehabilitation instead of repression, leadership in place of dictatorship. It involved an effort to create an atmosphere within the institution which corresponded as far as possible with elements of the free society, and it encouraged the practice of responsible citizenship in place of the authoritarian submission which had prevailed. It included an effort to enlist the initiative and will of the inmates in the task of creating a healthy institution, in contrast with the repression of their initiative before. Finally, it involved the provision of institutional means to those ends which were quite out of character with the ways of life in the old prison.

The political circumstances of an appointive governor in the territory provided the conditions for such an administrative revolution. In the absence of an elective contest for the governor's post, there was little need to mobilize the resources of bureaucracy for political ends and the party in control of the executive branch had relatively little stake in the internal operations of the agency. Although the appointive governors in the past have been responsive to major political and economic forces in the territory, the absence of direct political responsibility permitted the executive to act as a buffer between bureaucrats and the mass public. Thus, in the absence of political channels for transmission of unsophisticated popular protests or motives for mobilizing those, experimentation in prison government by career officials was possible to an unusual degree. The old Department of Institutions, an agency incorporating diverse functions, placed responsibility and permitted freedom for the governing of its several divisions in the professional division heads. This permitted officials to execute a thoroughgoing revolution in prison management from 1949 to 1953 with enough sensitivity to the social consequences to moderate the shock of sudden change. In addition, this condition of a comparative political vacuum served to allow the conduct of intensive research and study of the prison community as a relatively self-contained interactional system or society in microcosm.

Although the Inmate Council and its committees, the industrial and education programs, and other devices for appealing to the initiative of the inmates in redirecting their lives had a dramatic, cumulative impact on the prison community, it was a false assumption of the program and research on it that the resulting social reorganization would be immediate and direct. In fact, change was mediated through a redefinition of social roles far more complex than expected, and a new order emerged only after a period of prolonged and intense social disorganization. As the differences between the old punitive and the new treatment-oriented direction went to all aspects of prison life, they sharply altered the role and status of elements in prison society and produced bitter periods of tension and conflict.

From a purely legal standpoint, the revolution in the prison would seem to have been completed when the professional staff published a new policy manual as the constitution of prison government. In fact, however, the revolution had barely begun. The direction of energies within the prison community was still governed in large part by habit and the roles which had been communicated in the past, and the patterns of communication through which controlling definitions were transmitted remained a monopoly of custodial officers and senior inmates. The incentives and a wider range of activity which came with new programs were employed by the custodial force to gain conformity and exploited by old inmates to restore their status in place of the privileges lost with the passing of corruption. The means by which the "word" was communicated to the inmate body insured that the word would remain what it had been in the past: "Do your own time and never talk to a screw."

A matter of pride in the old inmate community was its ability to resolve its own internal conflicts in its own ways. There was substantial truth in the inmate claim, "The cons run the joint." However, the cons ran it in a way consistent with the dominant custodial values of peace and order. The hatred and contempt for "rats" which was shared by the guard force and inmate society rested on a valid sense of the fact that open communication constituted a serious threat to the traditional social order of the institution. As long as the extended freedom of movement and contact provided by new programs were exploited to reinforce the traditional order of the institution, escape and internal conflict remained minimal. Official sanctions, while harsh and arbitrary in the old prison, had been relatively infrequent as the inmates retained initial responsibility for internal social control. While that old order prevailed, the security record of the prison in 1951 and 1952 was the finest established in many years, and the incorrigible unit remained closed for an extended period. The group of men released in 1953, however, made the poorest record of parole success of any group released in many years. As long as new activities were exploited for status by hardened, prison-wise old cons, they accomplished nothing of their intended rehabilitative purpose. In that period of internal peace and good will, it was only the treatment staff and its newly created programs in the industrial area that were moving in a new direction.

Arbitrariness in the management of the old prison had given experienced inmates an advantage in their ability to predict and explain the events of that hostile and mysterious environment. Using a "devil theory" to explain every unfortunate event as the work of "rats," old cons, like a primitive priesthood, based much of their status on an ability to provide coherent and psychologically satisfying explanations of official action. By focusing the characteristic hatreds and hostilities of the inmates on nonconforming individuals, these leaders were equipped with a powerful instrument of social control. The reduction of arbitrariness and secrecy in management and an enlargement of the range of functions and contacts open to inmates undercut the old leaders and permitted a new leadership to emerge which violated the traditional expectations of inmate culture.

Gradually, the newly created patterns of prison life began to have an effect. The attitudes of fairness and frankness maintained by the staff, the more judicial disciplinary procedures, and the provision of means for co-operative activity gave rise to a more open and complex pattern of life in inmate society. Those patterns and the lines of communication implicit in them began to focus in the treatment unit and to by-pass the monopoly of communication once enjoyed by the custodial force. Treatment officials grasped the initiative at the staff level in the definition of policy and as-sumed an increasing responsibility for the manipulation of incentives, using these to reward self-improvement rather than simply adjustment in the prison. A counterelite to custodial officers at the official level and to inmate leaders in the yard began to emerge.

The Crisis Barrier: By 1953, inmate society was being led in two contradictory directions by competing forces within both staff and inmate groups, and the era of good will was replaced by one of confusion and violence. On the guard force, the oldest employees continued in the tradi-tional direction out of a studied ignorance of new policy directives, from the inertia of intrenched habit and with a moral conviction that the new ways of dealing with criminals were improper and dysfunctional for the prison's legitimate ends. They were joined in these positions by senior in-mates whose overt contacts with the old guard indicated how the old myths of the inmate culture had been tarnished. As the professional staff, plus a growing number of inmates, moved in the direction outlined by new policy, each day widened a split, weakened communication of controlling defini-tions, and intensified a competition for authority until authority failed en-tirely. Although the leadership of both factions at all levels seems to have been responsible and sincere, the conflict, countercharges, and simple failure to be authoritative in the face of uncertainty cost each leadership control over irresponsible subordinates. A few custodial officers engaged in overt sabotage of the new program, and bands of reckless young inmates went out of control as they saw chances to take advantage of divisions of authority with exploitation and violence.

The resulting period of internal violence and escape (escape is often a response to intolerable conditions) demonstrated that the inmate com-munity had lost its capacity to resolve conflicts internally with its own re-sources. An inability of management to cope with the crisis through stand-ard security measures indicates a similar weakness in the administration. Every failure of security equipped an honestly disgruntled guard force with charges against the professional staff and increased its belief in the virtues of the "good old days." Finally convinced that there was no way to gain their point within the administrative processes of the prison system, now dominated by the professional orientation of the treatment staff, the "old guard" sought external support from political forces and found this from groups legitimately concerned with the security situation as well as from others seeking an issue to exploit. A legislative hearing in 1953 aired the complaints of disgruntled guards and inmates and, by giving authoritative expression to those views, brought the condition of the prison to a state of utter turmoil. (While the present paper is not prepared to speak to this point with confidence, it is suggested that prison life in those circumstances approximates Hobbes' state of nature and permits empirical verification of certain of his propositions. It may be hypothesized that the prison riot and, perhaps, a considerable amount of mob behavior reflects a quest for certainty and a demand for some controlling definition of a confused situation. It may be less a rebellion against authority than a demand for it.)

The challenge to the complex structure of authority within the prison left formal sanctions meaningless and required that conflicts be resolved by force at all levels. As legislative hearings continued, tensions increased until rival factions within the prison yard armed themselves for mob action. At one point, the staff was forced to mount a machine gun on the cell block roof to forestall an impending riot. With the collapse of those social controls inherent in habit, traditional role definitions and social structure, control of the prison was reduced to a dependence on naked force and physical equipment which is never enough.

This challenge to the administration, however, required the staff and the warden to take a high degree of initiative in the face of anarchy. It forced them to express and communicate the direction of the prison in terms so clear as to remove confusion for both the legislative and the inmate body. It forced the staff to define and reinforce its role in the prison community in a way which established its leadership and mobilized inmate commitment to the new goals. In the course of those activities, the staff established communication patterns in the institution which had a continuing force in transmitting definitions of the situation. While complex and multipurposed, a crucial aspect of those communication patterns lay in the fact that they served to identify problems early and to raise them quickly to a level for authoritative resolution. Without the support of such communication patterns, the nominal authority of position was meaningless.

By the time the legislative committee had considered the evidence, endorsed the new direction of the prison, and rejected the claims for the old, the crisis of social control had been met internally and the prison was moving coherently on its new course. In the two years that followed, escape and serious internal disorder declined again to negligible proportions and a perceptibly different social order emerged.

A number of mainland prisons attempted a transition to the treatment emphasis in the years after World War II, but a "crisis barrier" normally stopped those transitions short of effectiveness. Over fifty major riots swept mainland institutions in the period from 1950 to 1953, and the most common result was to generate political protest, reverse the transition in an emphasis on greater physical "security," and return to the safe, traditional, custodial system. "Rehabilitation" in many of those institutions was reduced to a morale-building function or to a sign on a door for public relations purposes. The inmates who enjoyed the greatest stake in the old prison had a capacity to ensure the continuance of the traditional system by creating disturbances in the face of change and generating demands for a return to the custodial emphasis. By successfully passing through its period of crisis without a destructive riot and by successfully resisting ill-articulated demands for reaction, Oahu Prison became one of the few such institutions in America to make its revolution, for a time, a meaningful and accomplished fact.

Study of the crisis within the prison generates conclusions which go beyond prison to social institutions of other types. *First*, the direction of human energies involves more than the giving of formal orders and commands; it involves the whole complex of processes by which roles are defined and definitions are communicated within the group. *Second*, because the giving of direction is so deeply interwoven with the whole system of social control, any effective change in the direction of an agency has seriously disorganizing consequences. *Third*, when patterns of communication fail to correspond to the structure of authority, a group is unable to resolve its problems internally and conditions of conflict emerge. It is natural for elements defeated in such conflicts to seek aid outside the system, and only the morale reflected in a binding institutional code prohibits such recourse in normal conditions. If external political forces are sought out by discontented elements within the prison, and such forces take the initiative from its officials in resolving internal problems, the institutional structure of authority breaks down. Because the prison contains elements anxious to exploit any weakness of authority, it is vital that prison officials retain the initiative in resolving internal conflicts.

When a year of intensive research was focused on Oahu Prison in 1954 and 1955, its management, its security record, and its climate for rehabilitation were exceptionally sound. There were problems, for a prison is essentially a wall built around problems, but the disaffected elements which remained at all levels seemed resigned to the main emphasis of the institution and had ceased to play a dominant role in its social life. The prison at that time was subject to congratulation by many observers on a number of its records and qualities, but two distinguishing characteristics stood out on examination.

1. In contrast with normal attitudes of extreme defensiveness in prison officials, the Oahu Prison staff maintained an exceptional ability to recognize problems, to accept a joint responsibility for those problems, and to concentrate its resources on their solution.

The ability to accept and profit from criticism was illustrated by a regular use of research and professional assistance.

2. In even more striking contrast with similar institutions elsewhere, the prison had displaced the traditional dominance of inmate society by crime-hardened recidivists and achieved a social climate favorable to co-operation and a high level of treatment activity based on voluntary participation.

By the end of 1955, a combination of active official leadership and constructive social pressure within the institutional community permitted the closing of the incorrigible unit again and a general reduction in the use of severe sanctions to coerce discipline.

The Recent Conflicts: Despite the prohibition of direct observation in the prison, institutional records and the full cooperation of many persons connected with the institution permit the recent conflicts in the prison to be viewed in a broader context of time and social process. That analysis provides a base from which to examine several hypotheses advanced to account for conflicts ranging from the prison riot to the insubordination of the prison's top officials.

The first of these hypotheses, that advanced by the director's consultants, attributes the series of disturbances to the drastic incompetence of the prison's career officials. The officials were charged with willful neglect of dangerously inadequate security measures and derelictions ranging across the width of the organization chart. A considerable accumulation of evidence—the growing incorrigible population, labor problems, the inmate strike and riot, and the open break with the director—demonstrates the failure of the career officials to resolve their problems with their own administrative resources in that period. Security measures were inadequate to contain the rising tensions within the institution. The predictable reaction of temporary consultants was to place responsibility squarely on the prison officials. That is, it was to reject the officials and, in the language of our first, more general hypothesis, to reject the assumptions on which the officials acted in the administrative process. However, this explanation seems inadequate to observers and employees who have watched the prison's record of progress over the years and seen it successfully break through the crisis barrier of its own administrative revolution. Viewed in the larger perspective of time, it seems necessary to concede some loss in the capacity of the prison staff to see and resolve internal problems, but it is also necessary to note differences in the nature of the problems faced and the manner in which they were posed.

On the side of the prison's failing administrative capacity, it is evident that the momentum and initiative which carried the staff through its early crisis period had declined in a later stage of consolidation. A decline in the vigor of staff leadership tended to resign initiative for the definition of the situation to custodial personnel—less eloquent or dedicated advocates of the new regime at best. Every three years, a majority of the inmate population is replaced by normal turnover, and new arrivals reach the prison with traditional expectations of its governing principle. Hence, controlling definitions of the situation must be transmitted effectively and continuously, and this accounts for the normal abdication of that function to old convicts. In recent years in Oahu Prison, traditional definitions and a hard core of older inhabitants regained some of their lost influence while inmate leaders with a commitment to the rehabilitative ideal lost in status and in their capacity to resolve conflicts in their society. This marks a weakening of forceful, official leadership. Gradually increasing failures in security and more frequent appeals to repressive force by inmates and officials indicate that leadership was failing to reach an expanding part of the prison population. This evidence, as always, supplied arguments for those who continued to favor the traditional, punitive approach. But the staff, confident that its record was sound and its revolution essentially secure, failed to recognize many of its problems and met others with explanations rather than solutions.

In this connection, as well as in conjunction with explanations which account for the conflict in terms of personality clashes, the role of one individual must be noted. The man who rose through the treatment ranks to the post of superintendent of Oahu Prison by 1955 was, as a subordinate, the most effective advocate of communication patterns which identified and resolved the problems of the institution. In his role of superintendent, however, he gradually became less receptive to the transmission of problems from below, limited the access of subordinates to the warden, and permitted the atrophy of various channels of communication which had marked the administration in its most vigorous phase. It is clear that discontent generated by unresolved problems was accumulating in the prison prior to the act transferring it into the Department of Social Services. It is not clear that management failures account for the intensity of the problems which followed.

During this time, the achievement of statehood placed the problems of the prison in a vastly more mature and different political context. Many of these differences are illustrated by a contrast between the processing of problems in 1960 and the handling of those in the crisis conditions of 1953. The territorial era, in which career officials could control the manner in which problems were presented and the means of their solution, was gone. The politics of statehood supplemented internal channels of communication with outside groups ready to seize on discontent and exploit that for political purposes. One of the political consequences of statehood and the nature of the governing coalition which resulted when labor threw its support to the Republican governor was to permit a union to represent the grievances of custodial employees in the prison. Although established just prior to 1960 in the institution, the union had few members and less influence until the Prison System was transferred into the Department of Social Services. After that time, it became a vital, if little noticed, factor in the series of emerging conflicts.

The prison officials resisted this external processing of institutional problems through the union on principle even after reorganization went into effect. Their refusal to confront the fact of the union, and the fact that union members enjoyed an advantage over them in direct, personal access to the cabinet level, betrayed a certain wooden-headed intransigence on the part of otherwise competent officials in the face of a vastly changed administrative and political situation. A series of private interviews with union guards, supplied the director with the bulk of those opinions, objections, and observations issued in the report of the consultant employed after the riot. In the public conflict which followed, that channel of communication kept the director informed of every move and tactic planned by the prison staff, and it constituted a central strand in the emerging pattern of power. One aspect of the significance of the union in the changed situation, in addition to its rapidly expanding membership roll, is suggested by the inmate sit-down strike, an unsophisticated borrowing of the union concept as a means of venting discontent. The strike illustrates the consequences of any intervention which may crystallize division in a prison staff.

An explanatory hypothesis frequently advanced for these conflicts at their outset was to call them temporary maladjustments occasioned by the readjustments required in the Reorganization Act. Because that explanation was issued by those who clearly desired to minimize the conflict, and because the situation deteriorated over so long a period, this hypothesis has gained little credence. Some evidence to the contrary may be implied from the fact that the prison officials involved in the conflict had served successfully under both Democratic and Republican governors before and had survived the transition from one to another. Another consideration is the fact that the reorganization mandated few specific changes and the director issued very few orders to implement it. By itself, the reorganization does not constitute a sufficient condition for the disturbances that followed. Although the movement of the Prison System into the department was a necessary condition for much of what followed, its effect must be interpreted in the larger context.

In light of unresolved and accumulating internal problems, the Reorganization Act had a potential for disorganization. Designed to effectuate a constitutional mandate for increased political accountability through executive control, the act generated doubts as to the responsibility of career officials. These doubts were in their own minds as well as in the minds of their subordinates. Because matters had not been going well in the prison, some staff members reacted to uncertainty by taking a narrow definition of their responsibility at a time when an aggressive assertion of responsibility was most needed. The director withheld approval of the policy and procedure manual of the prison which had been in force for years and refused to confirm existing arrangements pending further study. Thus, a spirit of uncertainty sapped the initiative of career officials at just the moment when the most vigorous action was required to make their authority effective. Under more favorable circumstances within the prison, its officials might have grasped an opportunity to enlarge their role by mobilizing professional and citizen support for their program. Instead they retreated to await an endorsement from above that never came.

Under those circumstances, the characteristic vigor of the director captured the initiative from the prison staff in a manner which had explosive consequences. It was this energy of the director and the fact that the conflict later deteriorated into a name-calling contest which gives rise to explanations of the entire series of conflicts as a clash of personalities. This hypothesis must be examined in detail.

Something of the character of the aging warden and his chief subordinates may be implied from the administrative history sketched above, for that group remained almost intact from 1950 on. Although physically small, the warden was a warm and forceful personality, generally respected in the institution and throughout the state. Over two-thirds of the prison's inmates presented a petition on his behalf when he was under attack, and his abrupt dismissal produced a spontaneous disturbance in the prison yard. A major premise of the warden's administrative philosophy was that of delegating responsibility and authority to create an institutional climate of cooperative problem-solving. Perhaps too much of that delegated responsibility and authority was assumed by the superintendent of Oahu Prison, a coldly efficient and dedicated man who became the primary object of attack by the director.

By far the most dramatic of the personalities was that of the director, a lady of amazing energy and personal force who had risen from humble origins to a dominant role in both the formal and the "kitchen" cabinets of the administration. Lacking a college or professional education, she had risen through party offices and had a demonstrated talent for political organization. Efforts to prevent her appointment as director of Social Services by inserting professional qualifications for that post in the Reorganization Act had been made by the Democrats in the House but rejected in the Republican-dominated Senate. Well back into the territorial era, she had advocated the necessity of supporting the oligarchical party with a popular base, and she had played a leading role in forging an alliance with organized labor that weighed heavily in the party's victory in the first gubernatorial election under statehood. Deeply identified with the lower classes and regarding herself as the spokesman for those classes and their welfare, the lady had uncontestable political claims to the post she received.

In her office, the director completely dominated her subordinates by physical vigor and force of character. The deputy director, an ex-newsman who had managed publicity for the governor's campaign, was reduced to a pale shadow of her personality. Her administrative character was marked by an acid contempt for pretensions of middle-class respectability, which she properly identified with the opposition party, and for empty and mealy-mouthed bureaucratic jargon. She was quick to use and proud to boast of direct lines of communication with welfare clients, working-class employees, parolees, prison inmates or their families, and the general public, but her flat refusal to be "trapped" in the stilted conventions of administrative discourse throttled communication with top-level career officials. Pre-empting all news releases from divisions of the department to her own office and constructing each story with a sensitive eye to its broader political implications, she cast the definitions of each agency's role in terms of the language and expectations of the mass public. These public definitions of the prison's role, circulated in the course of hostile press coverage of escapes, differed in tone and emphasis from the controlling definitions of the situation imposed within the institution by its professional staff. These alternative definitions, implying simplistic antitheses between the goals of security and rehabilitation among other things, provided standards for popular criticism of professional officials and bases on which to crystallize conflicts within the institution.

The problems of the institution were the problems of people. Simply by moving forcefully to resolve those problems while career officials waited in uncertainty, the director assumed the role of a partisan of discontented elements among the employees and was widely perceived within the institution as an advocate of all the values those elements expressed. Her active intervention in management details unwittingly encouraged every disgruntled faction to seek political relief. With the director's door and the public press open to hostile criticism of the prison officials, disaffected elements within the institution felt no necessity to use internal channels to communicate their complaints. Thus by-passed, the authority of the warden and the entire structure of formal and informal power which focused in him to transmit his definitions of the situation were visibly undermined. The thinly disguised spirit of insubordination expressed by guards who looked to the union and its contacts for relief was more visibly demonstrated by a number of inmates in the weeks prior to the riot.

Exhaustive efforts by all sides to find some preliminary conspiracy, some structure of leadership, or even plausible grievances behind the inmate riot have uniformly failed. Its instant stimulus was nothing more than a callous but petty order to confine a hysterical inmate issued by the superintendent, an event with a thousand inconsequential precedents in the administrative practice of the institution. But the hysteria of the single inmate became a mass phenomenon, a reckless, violent, destructive outburst involving over half the inmate body in arson and uproar. The outbreak was a senseless thing, not clearly directed at injury to the guards and involving not a single escape or apparent attempt at escape. One of the most difficult problems of interpretation, one that has generated conspiratorial theories of the event by both parties to later conflicts, was the failure of the guard force to put down the disturbance. It was not beyond the reasonable resources of a disciplined custodial force, and the failure of the guards to control the riot at its outset provided ammunition for later charges of incompetence and lack of preparation at all levels. The hypothesis of this paper, the explanation for the calling of the National Guard, is that the custodial force did not really try to quell the riot. It was as though they took the position that the superintendent, having started the trouble, could take care of it himself. The structure of effective authority over the guard force had collapsed as certainly as had the structure of authority over the inmates. That second failure can be seen as a consequence and a reflection of the first.

Although various efforts have been made for a variety of partisan reasons to interpret the riot as a calculated protest against prison conditions later judged inadequate, these seem to fail. It is interpreted here as the hysterical outburst of men who need some degree of security against a condition of anomie, against a condition in which they could not know who was in charge or where they stood, against a condition in which a controlling definition of the situation and the pattern for its transmission had failed. When that demand to know where authority lay was answered by the National Guard, the answer clearly implied that it no longer lay with the career officials of the institution.

If an explanation of the over-all case in terms of personality clashes is to hold at all, it must hold only for the period after the riot, for no clear evidence of hostility or animosity can be found earlier. At this point, however, the director perceived the previously ignored administrative warning as, at least, a calculated trick by the career officials to fix on her the responsibility for their own incompetence. As the conflict broadened later to involve her political opponents, the director came to think of the riot as possibly started or magnified as part of a broadly based political conspiracy to discredit her. At the outset, however, her response was quick and direct in publishing an "expert" study, fixing all the blame and laying charges of gross incompetence on the career officials. This was both a necessary defense and a preface to the dismissal of the officials, but it served as the immediate basis of an extended series of detailed administrative orders from the director's office. Ostensibly designed to tighten institutional security, the

list contained orders designed to neutralize the warden's role and con-
solidate operating authority in the director's office.

For the increasingly restless elements in the prison to see the officials
overridden and given all the blame for recent disturbances was more of an
invitation to anarchy than even a well-ordered prison can stand. Mounting
tensions required a continuous maintenance of intense security precautions
and produced an intolerable situation. The Parole Board opened an attack
on the director in the press. This was followed by a weekend of intense
pressure on the warden to repudiate his warning memorandum. At that
point, the warden engaged in his rebellion with public charges and a flat
refusal to accept certain of the orders issued. The revolt of the warden
and his top subordinates was addressed to the governor as much as to the
general public, for the warden had been unable to gain an audience with
the governor throughout the previous month. It was a desperate attempt to
recapture that initiative necessary to maintain his authority in the prison,
but it was more than that and less at the same time. In many respects, it
was as emotional, as unplanned, and as ineffective as the outburst of prison
inmates. It was a demand to know where he stood and to receive some
authoritative definition of the situation on which to act. Finally, like the
revolt of the inmates and that of the guards in similar circumstances, it was
an appeal from the administrative to the political sphere for support and
for a solution of unresolved problems. Its result was the governor's "un-
qualified endorsement" of the cabinet official.

The resolution of the conflict was long and painfully delayed. The
political position of the director at that time was such as to require her
endorsement, but the widespread, if temporary and disorganized, public
support for the warden was such as to make his dismissal then impossible.
The warden, who thought of himself as the only defense of a professionally
sound penology, refused to resign and abdicate his painfully constructed
prison program to the director's charge. The governor's refusal to permit
the officials to testify before the legislative committee constituted an assertion that the problems of the administration must be solved internally and
without the aid of the political opposition. His refusal to permit independent investigation or research in the prison or the Department of Social
Services is an extension of that stand. These acts, in themselves, did not
resolve the conflicts or define the roles of career and political officials in
terms which made resolution possible. The career officials were retained in
office until the public temper permitted their dismissal, but they were effectively by-passed by the construction of formal lines of communication and
command, concentrating or legitimizing the direct authority of the director's
office over the prison system.

One cannot entirely dismiss an explanation in terms of the clash of
personalities in this case, for the existence of persons with the courage and

vigor to play their roles in the conflict was one of its necessary conditions. Testimony given then and later at the director's eventual dismissal indicates a number of instances in which professional career officials had been displaced, repressed or humiliated by the energy of the director without resort to public conflict. The particular case has involved the confrontation of one role played with dynamic, aggrandizing energy with a second played with stubborn dedication. The assumptions of this paper are that an adequate understanding of the case requires at least a brief and superficial look at the stage and the situation which brought these roles into conflict.

In stable situations, it is possible to understand the major dimensions of institutional behavior with little reference to personality and individual motivation. Persons are normally responding to the settled demands of the situation and playing roles clearly defined by the nature, customs, and purposes of the groups in which they act. People are almost universally behaving in ways that are expected of them, and even aggressive, irrational behavior can often be explained in terms of role conflicts or contradictory expectations. Individuals are vastly different in personal characteristics, but a complex social institution incorporates a variety of roles, and complex formal and informal processes of selection combine to fill such roles with persons whose talent and temperament equip them to play traditionally defined parts. From this point of view, authority is seen as inherent in the processes by which controlling definitions of the situation are transmitted as premises in the logic of individual behavior.

It is unusual when a situation permits a person with rare resources of energy to reshape human institutions with a personal stamp. More often, society seeks in vain for a prince who does not come. The habits of subordination disqualify most men for leadership long before seniority places them in a position of power, and responsiveness to narrowly defined requirements is a habit which normally restrains the conduct of leaders within comfortable bounds. There are, however, times when institutions are in a process of change, when roles become uncertain and expectations confused, and dynamic individuals carve out a place for themselves consistent with their cravings. The Caesar or the Lincoln writes a page in the history of their societies because new roles are required in a state of uncertain transition and they have the will to define these. There are times when it is valid to say, with Egypt's Nasser, that there is "a role in search of a hero."

The condition of individualism placing its stamp on institutions is a condition of change which brings traditional expectations into question. People must doubt the usefulness or propriety of conventionally given definitions. In such conditions, the advantage lies with an individual who is unfamiliar with or prepared to disregard the conventional expectations. This is a quality of ruthlessness, a willingness to proceed without concern for the outraged sensibilities of others by virtue of a clear perception of a goal unseen by others. The warden, coming new to an unsettled prison situation in 1946, was such a person within the narrow confines of its institutional society. The explanation proposed here is that the director of the Department of Social Services was such a person, defining her own role on the larger stage of a society in transition to statehood.

This paper assumes that the several conflicts reported are not separate and disconnected events. Taken separately, they may be explained in terms of personality, the strains of reorganization, or administrative incompetence at various levels. Taken as a series, however, the conflicts ranging from the riot to the aborted clash between executive and legislative powers are consequences of statehood and a fundamental change in the constitutional system of social control in Hawaii.

The coming of statehood brought new opportunities and responsibilities into the total process of government. The opportunity to elect a governor, in particular, created a necessity for mobilizing political resources into an organization able to contest that election successfully, an organization far more substantial and centralized than those required for legislative district elections in the past. As a political organization emerges with sufficient power to be effective, as it did, that power becomes a factor in the environment of both political and administrative behavior. Control of the organization becomes an object of ambition to factions within the party, and the struggle for control, in turn, requires some type of organizational base, an organized popular following, business or labor support, or a segment of the bureaucracy. As a significant concentration of power, such organizations are forces to be checked, balanced, and incorporated in the complex framework of social control. Newly independent states elsewhere have often failed to constrain political forces unleashed by independence.

As indicated throughout the analysis above, the term "constitution" as used here applies to more than the legal formula assigning roles to agencies in the governmental process. Hawaii's formal constitution is quite standard except in its establishment of an exceptionally strong and centralized executive branch. Indeed, the provisions for a strong executive seem to assume the counterbalancing dispersion of power among organized groups in the society which have given rise to such provisions elsewhere. In a mature, pluralistic, interest group society, the various programs and agencies of government align themselves with or tend to fall under the domination of organized elements with a special stake in their activities, and a strong executive serves as a counterweight against that dispersion of responsibility. The distinctive characteristics of Hawaii's constitution of the present are not in its legal document so much as in the relative absence of a structure to extend the distribution of power throughout the society. Under these circumstances, the effective constitution of power is one in which the formal organs of government are organized to exercise powers conferred on them, a political organization has emerged to capture those offices, but those developments far outpaced the organization of interested publics to play their political role effectively.

As the legal skeleton of Hawaii's constitution takes on flesh, blood, and character in the definition of multitudinous details of the governmental process, the party in control of the executive enjoys an exceptional opportunity at this time to impose its will in the resolution of each uncertainty and to shape in detail the constitution of the future. This makes a virtue of uncertainty. The more extensive the climate of doubt as to the location of responsibility, the wider becomes the range of discretion to be exercised by political officials in view of political consequences. This is a concept which can account for a number of factors in the conflict in and around the prison system.

In the older states, it is not unusual to find a political organization or "machine" alert to exploit welfare agencies and their clienteles for partisan purposes. Law enforcement agencies lend themselves especially to such exploitation as a consequence of their internal discipline and extreme control over dependent persons. Thus, there is nothing unusual in the appointment of a highly skilled, political organizer to head the Department of Social Services or in systematic efforts at the concentration of power at the cabinet level in that agency. The distinctive characteristic of the recent transitional situation lies in the absence of internal checks and restraints on that concentration of power. An unusual feature of the case, in the absence of a system of social groups poised to exercise influence, was the exceptional power enjoyed by the few groups—the union, the director and her associates, and, eventually, those organized against her—organized for political action.

The failure of interest groups to keep pace with the organization of governmental and political machinery at the state level and to assume the role of an intervening force in the structure of social control produced a transitional period of "mass politics." This is witnessed by the temporary dominance of a "politics of personality" and the imposition of "mass values" as the controlling definitions of the correctional system. It is evidenced in instances of coercive force employed at various levels in the governmental process—use of the National Guard in the prison, the alleged "third-degree" methods of administrative problem solving, and the well-remembered threat of the director to "smash and destroy forever the professional reputation" of this author if he pursued his inquiry. Was the present case a calculated political raid on law enforcement agencies in the struggle for political power? Note the later reopening and resolution on obviously political grounds of a long-settled, administrative decision on the location of a $15 million new prison plant. Or was this series of conflicts only an incident in the emerging politics of statehood?

To return now to our more basic questions, what is the significance of administrative experience? On the evidence of the case reviewed, the answer would seem to be that significance depends on the interpretation given rather than the experience itself. A wealth of successful experience by the administrators of the prison described did little more than render them incompetent and helpless in the face of a changed situation. Their ethic of political neutrality led them to fumble away what, at one point, seemed an unbeatable political position from which to defend their role and reduced them to the position of dispensable eunuchs in the director's court. An unfailing political capacity to predict the conclusions of standard expertise in the present case permitted the regular employment of consulting research to perform the functions of "hatchet men" in the political process. Can academic analysis of administrative experience achieve results more significant than that? Three hypotheses have been advanced for analysis in terms of the present case.

1. The first hypothesis was that administrative experience should provide a test of the validity of assumptions being acted on in the regulation of any state of affairs.

One proposition flowing from this study is that assumptions which were highly effective for one state of affairs were associated with anarchy and disaster in another. Hence, if the hypothesis is to have meaning, the "state of affairs" must be read as the "affairs of the state." Thus defined, the term provides something less than a measurable referent for empirical analysis. Further, the present case indicates that the controlling premises of behavior in an institution are not those formally published but, rather, those effectively transmitted through a complex structure of authority, influence, and communication. Thus, the working assumptions of behavior vary through time, through different levels of the institutional hierarchy at a single time, and in the extent to which acceptance of a common, controlling definition of the situation prevails. Except in the most rare instances of harmonious unanimity, these assumptions defy discovery and specification as completely as does the state of affairs.

Another proposition of this study is that the capacity to give controlling definition to operating premises is intimately related to status and power. In any institutional setting where authority itself is a value, the capacity to define the premises of the behavior of others is an object of almost continuous conflict. It is the very essence of the "political." To consider the subhypothesis advanced in this connection, any assumption about administrative communications in a prison must be considered in terms of its implications for the communication of a controlling definition of the situation. The fact that the effective test of administrative assumptions is their political viability and contribution to institutional survival colors the manner in which they are defined at each level of the hierarchy. Hence, the assumptions of an administrative agency are not of the character of scientific hypotheses about natural events. They are value assumptions by virtue of the fact that they are political assumptions and subject to the limitation of scientific analysis as applied to propositions of that type. The first hypothesis is rejected.

(2.) The second hypothesis holds that analysis of administrative experience should provide a means for generating and testing hypotheses about the nature of any set of events being regulated. This was elaborated to suggest that penal administration might provide insights into the nature of criminals or incorrigibles.

There is a quality of obviousness about that proposition which must make it applicable to the management of inanimate materials. In theory, at least, the "success" of different problem-solving systems that are employed should provide insights into the nature of the problem. Unfortunately for this approach, the problem of social control is something that characterizes the society, not the criminal. Administrative solutions to the problems of social control are complicated by the fact that society becomes more outraged by a single prison escape than by fifty parole failures. It is possible to parole the incurable car thief but not the completely rehabilitated murderer, and the behavior of administrators, car thieves, and murderers in prison is guided by some degree of recognition of those premises. Administration must accommodate to the characteristics of the society as well as to those of the offender. That is the lesson learned by officials in the present case at their cost.

The cycles of incorrigibility and internal violence have waxed and waned in the prison studied with little reference to its formal structure as a problem-solving system. The cycles of violence have expanded at times beyond the capacity of the administrative mechanism to contain them. Speaking in general, prison administrations have been far more influenced and disrupted in recent years by changes in public expectations than by changes in inmates. This is true in spite of the classic apology for prison riots that holds, "We just are not getting the type of men we used to." The custodial institution is a social system in its own right. Any substantial change in the administrative system produces corresponding changes in the total institutional community and the roles which govern behavior there. It is futile to talk about alternative ways to govern the same inmate community. Governed differently, it becomes a different social system with different behavioral roles and different problems for its inhabitants and the society at large.

It must be emphasized that the prison is not administering criminals. It is administering society's sense of justice and executing a definition of right. Because the meaning of those terms is never clear and certain, it must emerge in the operating details of administration. The struggle to impose operating definitions of those terms or maintain the vital continuity of existing definitions makes administration a crucial part of a continuous political process and identifies the career administrator's vital stake in that process. For more than a generation, we have mouthed the truism that politics and administration are functionally inseparable, but its implications have not been adequately extended into analysis. One of its implications is that the administrative agency cannot be conceived of as a problem-solving machine at the service of some abstract state. On the contrary, the administrative system must be regarded as a part of the state, an extension of the state, a reflection of the state and a participant in the continuous process of giving definition to the law—to those propositions which enter as axioms into the logic of individual behavior. Thus, the second hypothesis must be rejected.

3. The third hypothesis considered the prison system as a society in microcosm and a source of insights into the nature of power structures in other settings.

On the basis of the case examined, it is suggested that the prison and administrative experience there can serve as a source of insights into certain problems. If it tells us little about the nature of criminality, it may suggest many things about the relationship of communication patterns to authority and power. Research in the prison in the present case has suggested constructs useful in the analysis of change in the state at large. There are times when it seems that the larger structures of power in society are reflected in the prison as though in a still pool. However, recent events betray the fact that our capacity to treat the institution as a society in microcosm was a temporary and transient circumstance. For a brief period of time in the territorial era, as a consequence of that political arrangement, it was possible to consider the prison as a self-contained pattern of interaction. With the politics of statehood, that opportunity was lost and the institution became a part of the larger political process. The third hypothesis holds, if at all, under exceptional conditions.

However, in both the state prison and the state at large, it seems that similar conditions produce similar consequences for individual behavior and the system of social control. Change or failure of a controlling definition of the situation—of a common sense of the constitutional order of life—produces anarchic consequences and provides a license for those with the will and the organizational resources to define the constitution of the future for themselves. In such conditions, force, aggressiveness, and fear replace habit and customary roles as the main resources of social control. The administrative life of those who fail to catch the tide of human affairs at those times promises to be poor, solitary, nasty, brutish, and short. If the scholar or the administrator is to know what the significance of such a case is, he must know what it is a case of.

Part III

TREATMENT IN INSTITUTIONS AND THE COMMUNITY

The initiation of effective modes of treatment both in the American and in other correctional systems has proved to be an exceedingly difficult task. Although the conditions of life in most correctional settings have improved a good deal in recent years, evaluations of new treatment programs all too often show that these programs have little if any impact on the attitudes and behavior of the offenders for whom they were designed. The reasons for the frequency of these failures are numerous, but several factors involved seem obvious. First, considerable attention has been focused on developing a more humane system of handling the offender population, but insufficient attention has been focused on making humanitarian advances that are also sound in terms of their rehabilitative potential. Second, despite the long-standing conviction on the part of many that offenders can be rehabilitated, we actually know pitifully little about the dynamics of the change processes by means of which the desired changes can be ensured. Third, both the public and the responsible legislative bodies continue to push for not only the punishment but also the rehabilitation of offenders even though the best available evidence strongly suggests that these two goals are probably not attainable within the same types of organizational structures. Fourth, given the dubious character of many of our criminal codes and the selectivity that has become so obvious in the determination of which types of offenders will be forwarded to the correctional system, it is not at all clear whether treatment as it now exists is even needed. If it is, in a pluralistic society such as ours few are confident that they can define exactly what it is that they wish to change the offender into. Finally, regardless of what is done within the correctional system, the means by which success and failure can be determined are unclear. How much change is required, for example, in order for a "success" to be claimed? Are the effects of programs designed for difficult cohorts of the offender population to be evaluated in a way unlike that for other groupings?

The list of reasons could of course be extended considerably, but that is not the point we wish to make in this section on issues and strategies of treatment. Instead, we wish to provide a brief sample of an increasingly large literature on the topic in order to demonstrate that the field of corrections is not as static and unchanging in its perspectives and approaches as one might be led to believe by the many critics of the system. Whether these ideas and programs continue to prove useful is not necessarily the most important consideration. What is at least equally important is that these selections show a healthy willingness to critically examine the present state of corrections and to move away from traditional practices when some reasonable departure from tradition seems to merit a try.

We have included in this section writings on such diverse areas as treatment theory in corrections—Don Gibbons; treatment programs for the special offender—David Petersen *et al.*; innovative programs for dealing with the juvenile delinquent—Roy Gerard and Marguerite Warren; conjugal visitation in prison—Columbus Hopper; short-term incarceration—Paul Friday *et al.*; and work release and other community-based programs— Serapio Zalba and H. G. Moeller.

14

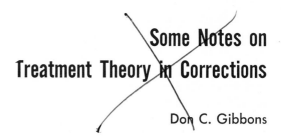

Some Notes on
Treatment Theory in Corrections

Don C. Gibbons

Some years ago Ernest Greenwood discussed some relationships between social science and social work.[1] In that essay he stated the ideal form
that a technology of social work should take. He indicated that social work
would operate with diagnostic typologies that define the nature of the problems for treatment. "Diagnosis" would then constitute a process by which
a given problem would be classified as falling within a type in the diagnostic
scheme. A well-developed practice field would also employ a typology of
treatment procedures linked to the diagnostic device. Together, these sets
of principles would constitute the "practice theory" of the field. Greenwood
also issued a call for collaborative research between social scientists and
social work practitioners which would be designed to convert social science
theory into practice theory. The end product of such research would be a
relationship between social science and social work similar to that between

From "Some Notes on Treatment Theory in Corrections," *Social Service
Review*, 36 (September, 1962), 295–305. Reprinted with the permission of The
University of Chicago Press.

---

[1]Ernest Greenwood, "Social Science and Social Work: A Theory of Their
Relationship," *Social Service Review*, XXIX (March, 1955), 20–32. See also his
"Attributes of a Profession," *Social Work*, II (July, 1957), 45–55.

medicine and certain fields of basic science, such as physiology, biochemistry, and bacteriology.

Correctional treatment of criminals and delinquents is commonly identified as a legitimate area of social work practice. Accordingly, Greenwood's analysis can be applied to corrections in order to indicate the direction in which that field should go if it is to become a technology based on scientific knowledge.[2] Thus, in a well-developed correctional profession, a diagnostic model or typology shared by all treatment workers would be applied to offenders. The determination of the "treatment problem" for any specific offender would involve locating that individual within a set of diagnostic categories. In turn, treatment would involve the manipulation of that person's behavior and attitudes in some manner specified within a body of statements of strategy or theory linked to the diagnostic typology. Further, the training of workers would include the communication of the diagnostic models and treatment principles to trainees.

At present, correctional work does not show this structure to any pronounced degree. Instead, what is now most characteristic is the use by treatment workers of crudely articulated behavioral theory which holds that most offenders are emotionally maladjusted and in need of intensive individual therapy. Such theory systematically ignores an abundant amount of sociological theory and research which indicates that many forms of unlawful conduct arise out of strains and defects in the social order, to which illegal behavior is a "normal" response. Although some of the work of such investigators as Cohen, Cloward and Ohlin, Sutherland, Sykes and Matza, and others has begun to creep into discussions of treatment, this material is not prominent in comparison to the mass of psychological material in correctional literature.

Moreover, it is not simply that etiological theory in corrections shows little sensitivity to sociogenic variables in deviant behavior. In addition, most current theory does not take full account of variations among types of offenders. There is mounting evidence to indicate that neither a psychogenic nor a sociogenic image of offenders is sufficient to encompass the variety of behavior patterns represented by the total population of law violators. A satisfactory description of offenders would involve the delineation of a number of criminal and delinquent types. Some of these patterns of illegal behavior are characterized by personality problems and other characteristics identified in psychogenic models, while others are not.

As for treatment techniques, the use of unshared and largely intuitive procedures by different workers is predominant. These tactics are frequently vague and ambiguous, even to the worker, and they are not based upon the

---

[2]For a discussion of some complexities involved in the professionalization of corrections which are ignored in the present paper, see Donald R. Cressey, "Professional Correctional Work and Professional Work in Correction," *NPPA Journal*, V (January, 1959), 1–15.

available empirical evidence regarding the nature of offenders.[3] Instead, they are compounded out of gross behavioral theories and speculative hunches arrived at by trial and error in the work setting.

In considerable part the use of crude behavioral theories and intuitive treatment procedures is a reflection of the kind of training characteristic of correctional workers. This is usually some kind of generic social work training. Unfortunately, generic principles of social work do not provide specific guides as to how the correctional worker should operate in particular situations. For example, consider the kinds of statements made about "relationship" as a key to effective casework. Doubtless the establishment of a relationship is important, but the really difficult questions have to do with the specific kind of relationship that is required in order to effect changes in criminal behavior, the techniques by which such a specific relationship may be established, and the special problems that arise in correctional settings in establishing treatment relationships. The literature is not particularly helpful on such points. In summary, generic principles applied to corrections do not indicate in any very precise way the tactics that can be expected to rehabilitate offenders.[4]

Diagnostic models are not usually involved in the training of correctional social workers. Trainees do not customarily come face-to-face with a solid body of information about the nature and etiology of criminality or the variations among offenders. Moreover, rehabilitative theory based upon diagnostic models is virtually nonexistent and is not part of correctional training. As a consequence, "treatment" is now largely a situation in which "someone does something to someone else."[5] That something which is done may or may not be related to the problems of the offender. Moreover, relatively little is known about the effectiveness of those things that are done in the name of treatment.[6]

Of course the preceding is an exaggerated description of the present state of affairs. Signs of progress in the direction of empirically sound and

---

[3]For a discussion of some deficiencies in current treatment theory, see Don C. Gibbons and Donald L. Garrity, "Some Suggestions for the Development of Etiological and Treatment Theory in Criminology," *Social Forces*, XXXVIII (October, 1959), 51–58.

[4]The following are representative cases of "generic" statements on treatment: Harleigh B. Trecker, "Social Work Principles in Probation," *Federal Probation*, XIX (March, 1955), 8–10; David Dressler, *Practice and Theory of Probation and Parole* (New York: Columbia University Press, 1959), pp. 124–70.

[5]Some evidence of the inadequacies of conventional social work training for corrections can be found in Lloyd E. Ohlin, Herman Piven, and Donnell M. Pappenfort, "Major Dilemmas of the Social Worker in Probation and Parole," *NPPA Journal*, II (July, 1956), 211–25.

[6]One brief résumé of the evidence on the effectiveness of treatment is found in Don C. Gibbons, "Comments on the Efficacy of Criminal Treatment," *Canadian Journal of Corrections*, II (April, 1960), 165–74. See also Daniel Glaser, "Scientific Evidence on the Prison Potential," paper delivered at the American Correctional Association Congress of Corrections, Columbus, Ohio, September 27, 1961.

effective correctional practices can be seen in recent issues of professional journals. Some analyses of treatment strategies[7] and some materials on delinquent and criminal typologies[8] offer encouragement. Also, some rather good research material is now accumulating on the effects of specific programs of treatment upon offenders.[9] Finally, there are a few state correctional systems in which research evaluation of programs has become a permanent part of operation. In California in particular, both the adult and the juvenile correctional systems are involved in the study of the impact of programs upon offenders, who are classified according to diagnostic devices developed there. No doubt much will be learned from such research.[10]

In spite of these promising signs, there is more that could be done in order to accelerate the development of sound correctional techniques and practices. It is the thesis of this paper that explicit attention should be given to constructing a clear, detailed, and comprehensive conceptualization of treatment based upon a set of empirically grounded diagnostic types. This theory would spell out those kinds of manipulation of the offender which are required in order to modify his behavior patterns so that he may become a law-abiding citizen. Such theory could be used in the training of correctional workers so that intuitive and unshared tactics might give way to standardized and describable practices.

This paper offers only a bare beginning in this direction.[11] The com-

---

[7]Some samples of recent statements on treatment which are guided by an explicit theoretical rationale are: Donald R. Cressey, "Contradictory Theories in Correctional Group Therapy Programs," *Federal Probation*, XVIII (June, 1954), 20–26; Donald R. Cressey, "Changing Criminals: The Application of the Theory of Differential Association," *American Journal of Sociology*, LXI (July, 1955), 116–20; Lloyd W. McCorkle, Albert Elias, and F. Lovell Bixby, *The Highfields Story* (New York: Henry Holt & Co., 1958); LaMar T. Empy and Jerome Rabow, "The Provo Experiment in Delinquency Rehabilitation," *American Sociological Review*, XXVI (October, 1961), 679–95; Richard L. Jenkins, M.D., *Breaking Patterns of Defeat* (Philadelphia: J. B. Lippincott Co., 1954).

[8]Clarence C. Schrag, "A Preliminary Criminal Typology," *Pacific Sociological Review*, IV (Spring, 1961), 11–16; Clarence C. Schrag, "Some Foundations for a Theory of Corrections," in Donald R. Cressey (ed.), *The Prison* (New York: Holt, Rinehart & Winston, Inc., 1961), pp. 346–57; Don C. Gibbons and Donald L. Garrity, "Definition and Analysis of Certain Criminal Types," *Journal of Criminal Law, Criminology and Police Science*, LIII (March, 1962), 27–35; Don C. Gibbons, "Problems and Prospects of Delinquent Typology," *Sociological Inquiry*, XXXII (Spring, 1962), 235–44; John W. Kinch, "Continuities in the Study of Delinquent Types," *Journal of Criminal Law, Criminology and Police Science*, LIII (September 1962), 323–28.

[9]See Gibbons, *op. cit.*

[10]For results to date, see California, Department of the Youth Authority, *Current Status Report of Research Activities* (Sacramento, 1961).

[11]The author is indebted to Peter G. Garabedian for a critical reading of an earlier version of this paper and for a number of suggestions which have been incorporated into this draft.

ments below include a discussion of several possible diagnostic models for adult offenders along with some statements about strategies for the treatment of the types specified in one of the models. However, this is only a first approximation of a developed body of treatment theory. For one thing, the business of articulating treatment hypotheses for a range of offender patterns is too complex to be accommodated within a brief paper. More important, it is not possible at present to specify in detail the complete list of behavior patterns which exist in the real world of offenders. However, if the development of treatment theory waits until a set of diagnostic types is produced in which the supporting evidence is overwhelming, it will wait forever. In addition, even though the present data are incomplete, more is known about criminal patterns than is sometimes recognized.

POSSIBLE DIAGNOSTIC MODELS

Where can suitable diagnostic models be found? This section considers two typologies that might serve as diagnostic models. It should be noted that this essay is restricted to treatment theory for adult offenders, although the basic view outlined here is relevant to juvenile delinquents as well.

One typology that has much to recommend it has been presented by Schrag,[12] who has summarized a sizable body of research data indicating that there are four patterns of inmate roles oriented around certain focal issues in the prison community. He identifies these as the "prosocial," "antisocial," "pseudosocial," and "asocial" role patterns.

"Prosocial" inmates are those who have committed violent personal crimes who have few prior criminal convictions, whose criminality is a response to situational stress, and who verbalize pro-administration norms in prison. "Antisocial" inmates show extensive delinquency records, recidivistic histories, and anti-administration attitudes. They are usually property offenders who regard crime as a livelihood. They tend to be products of criminalistic families who live in urban, lower-class neighborhoods. "Pseudosocial" inmates have been involved in subtle, sophisticated property offenses. They exhibit no delinquency record and have above-average educational and social backgrounds. They are frequently from parental backgrounds of inconsistent discipline and family disharmony. In prison they exhibit shifting loyalty attachments as they attempt to "work both sides of the street." That is, the pseudosocial inmate is the "politician" who operates as a manipulator of both the inmates and the administration. Finally, the "asocial" inmate exhibits a pattern of bizarre offenses, frequently ac-

---

[12]Schrag, *op. cit.*

companied by violence, high recidivism, and a history of early behavior disorders. He is egocentric, with poorly developed loyalty relationships to either inmates or administrators. He is a frequent troublemaker in the institution and is usually the product of a parental background of severe rejection.

Schrag's analysis is the product of research investigation rather than speculation. One major implication of this material is that the search for criminal types is worth pursuing, for it may be that role patterns observed in prisons represent situationally specific manifestations of variations among offenders which can be discovered in a variety of different settings, such as probation caseloads, prisons, and parole or other correctional situations.

One effort to define a set of criminal types not specific to any particular correctional milieu has been made by the present author.[13] This typology identifies thirteen offender types in terms of "definitional dimensions" of offense behavior, attitudes, and self-definitions. In addition, it specifies "situational correlates," or background characteristics for the defined types. No claim is made that this classification is inclusive of all adult criminals, but it is argued that it would include a sizable portion of the total population of offenders.

This is not the place for a detailed discussion of the derivation procedures by which this typology has been developed, but it should be noted that the typology has been drawn out of the existing research literature. For example, it includes as one type the "naïve check forger," defined in part in terms of characteristics identified in Lemert's investigation of naïve forgers.[14] On the other hand, limitations in the existing data have required that these statements about offender types be supplemented by intuitive "hunches" from case record material and elsewhere so that the empirical accuracy of some of the descriptions in the typology is indeterminate.

The comments about treatment strategies in the next section are organized around the second typology rather than around Schrag's categories. However, the two are related. For example, it is likely that the quasi-professional property offender and the joyrider–auto thief represent patterns that frequently emerge in antisocial inmates in prison. Similar relationships probably exist between other types in the two systems.

Although the complete typology includes thirteen patterns of offender behavior, some of these are of little importance in discussions of treatment, for they are infrequently found in the group of conventional offenders. These types are the "professional thief," the "professional 'heavy' criminal,"

---

[13]Gibbons and Garrity, *Journal of Criminal Law, Criminology and Police Science*, LIII, 27–35.

[14]Edwin M. Lemert, "An Isolation and Closure Theory of Naïve Check Forgery," *Journal of Criminal Law, Criminology and Police Science*, XLIV (September-October, 1953), 296–307.

the "upper-class fringe violator," and the "white-collar criminal." From this point on, this paper will omit consideration of these four patterns.

Space limitations preclude an extended discussion of the elements and variables in the typology, but in Table 1 the defining characteristics of the types are briefly indicated.[15] The prison role-type parallel of each pattern is indicated in Table 1.

DIAGNOSTIC MODELS AND
TREATMENT STRATEGY

The following comments constitute an initial attempt to specify some directions for treatment of the criminal types included in Table 1. The intent is to suggest directions for further development rather than to lay out a set of detailed recipes for treatment. In the interest of brevity, the discussion of treatment tactics is handled in two ways. First, summary analysis of treatment strategies for all of the types is presented in Table 2, in which some of the major dimensions or aspects of treatment are indicated and in which comments are made about different offender patterns. Second, some relatively detailed remarks are made about one of the offender patterns in order to illustrate treatment theory in greater detail.

Most of the dimensions in Table 2 require no explanation. However, the distinction between formal treatment and adjunct programs is not self-evident. By "formal treatment" is meant those programs directly aimed at modification of characteristics of offenders—such as unfavorable attitudes toward work or criminalistic self-images—which are responsible for deviant behavior. "Adjunct programs" are those parts of the correctional process which are not directed specifically at the modification of attitudes, but which do play an auxiliary role in rehabilitation. Vocational training is a case in point. Persons are not criminals because of a lack of job skills but rather because of unfavorable attitudes toward work. Treatment should be directed toward modification of such attitudes. However, those offenders who exhibit negative attitudes toward work frequently have poor work habits and are deficient in vocational skills. In such cases, vocational training could play

---

[15]For a résumé of the research data on which these types are based, see Gibbons and Garrity, *Social Forces*, XXXVIII, 51–58, and *Journal of Criminology and Police Science*, LIII, 27–35. This typology is obviously an oversimplification of the actual characteristics of offenders, for, as the typology is stated here, it does not provide categories for classifying actual offenders who exhibit versatile offense careers. Additionally, the statement of the typology in Table 1 is somewhat terse. However, there are difficulties which could be overcome in an extended discussion of typologies and treatment. The typology presented in Table 1 is detailed enough to serve the purposes of the analysis in this brief paper.

TABLE 1

Defining Characteristics of Offender Types

Type	Offense Pattern	Self-Definition and Attitude
Semiprofessional property offender (Antisocial)	Robbery, burglary, larceny, and allied offenses; unskilled repetitive crime with small profit	Self-definition as a criminal, but as a victim of society; hostile toward police and correctional authorities
Auto thief— joyrider (Antisocial)	Repetitive auto theft for pleasure; "car clouting" and other auto offenses for profit not included	Self-definition as a criminal, and as tough, manly; concerned with others' perception of him as a "tough guy"
Naïve check forger (Prosocial)	Passing bad checks, usually without skill; often passes checks while drinking	Self-definition as a non-criminal, and as a person burdened with personal problems
Embezzler (Prosocial)	Illegal conversion of property from a position of financial trust	Self-definition as a non-criminal, as different from "real criminals"; rationalizes acts as not really criminal
Personal offender ("one-time loser") (Prosocial)	Crimes of violence under situational stress — murder, manslaughter, assault	Self-definition as a non-criminal, but as deserving of punishment; no pronounced antisocial attitudes
Psychopathic assaultist (Asocial)	Offenses against persons or property or both, characterized by violence in "inappropriate" situations	Self-definition as a criminal, but as a victim of the treachery of others; views others as generally untrustworthy
Violent sex offender (Prosocial)	Sexual assaults upon physically mature females, characterized by extreme violence, mutilation, etc.	Self-definition as a non-criminal
Non-violent sex offender (Prosocial)	Sex offenses—such as child-molesting—usually with immature victims; statutory rape and similar offenses not included	Self-definition as a non-criminal; frequently rationalizes himself as Christian and his offense as not sexual but "educational"
Heroin addict (Antisocial)	Use of heroin or other opiate; property offenses as source of income for purchase of drugs	Self-definition as a criminal, but sees criminal status as unjust; holds that drug usage is a relatively harmless personal vice

TABLE 2

Treatment Dimensions and Diagnostic Types

Semiprofessional property offender

Formal treatment program	Guided-group-interaction form of therapy in group composed of other "antisocial," "right guy" offenders
Adjunct program	Vocational training or educational program
Goal	Modification of attitudes toward police, work, crime, and society; development of "prosocial" attitudes
Periods	Institutional group therapy carried on most intensively during last few months of incarceration and continued during parole
Frequency	Intensive in the pre-release period, with group meeting at least several times a week

Auto thief–joyrider

Formal treatment program	Guided-group-interaction form of therapy in group composed of other "antisocial," "right guy" offenders, but with some members who have been non-joyriders
Adjunct program	Recreational program with active participation in athletics
Goal	Demonstration of inappropriateness of "tough guy" criminal activity, aid to offender in developing a self-image which is tough and masculine but consistent with socially acceptable behavior
Periods	Same as for semiprofessional property offender
Frequency	Same as for semiprofessional property offender

Naïve check forger

Formal treatment program	Client-centered individual therapy, group therapy in groups composed of other forgers, or both
Adjunct program	Alcoholics Anonymous
Goal	Breaking down the offender's rationalizations for forgery, discouraging dependent behavior, building up a fund of acceptable solutions to problems
Periods	Intensive treatment if on probation or institutionalized, continued during parole, including group treatment, at least in part, and involvement in Alcoholics Anonymous during parole
Frequency	Several times a week

TABLE 2 *(continued)*

Embezzler

Formal treatment program .... Intensive treatment not usually required; superficial assistance from time to time from treatment workers; isolation from more criminalistic types of prisoners

Adjunct program .... Assignment to clerical or other service position in the institution

Goal .... Preservation of the offender's prosocial self-image and attitudes

Periods .... During parole some help in adjusting to altered social and economic status

Frequency .... Infrequent—once a week or less

Personal offender ("one-time loser")

Formal treatment program .... Similar to that for embezzler

Adjunct program .... Assignment to institutional position

Goal .... Similar to that for embezzler

Periods .... Intensive treatment during parole

Frequency .... Infrequent—once a week or less

Psychopathic assaultist

Formal treatment program .... Some form of group treatment combined with intensive psychiatric counseling

Adjunct program .... None specific

Goal .... Development of "normal" personality structure; resocialization of essentially undersocialized person, including development of loyalty attachments, role-taking abilities

Periods .... Intensive treatment during entire period of incarceration and parole

Frequency .... Relatively intense—several times a week

Violent sex offender

Formal treatment program .... Psychiatric therapy conducted by psychiatrist or clinical psychologist

Adjunct program .... None specific

Goal .... Modification of bizarre sexual orientations

Periods .... Intensive treatment during entire period of incarceration and parole

Frequency .... Relatively intense—several times a week

Non-violent sex offender

Formal treatment program .... Intensive psychiatric therapy, particularly at initial stage of incarceration; possibly supplemented with group treatment in group of other non-violent sex offenders at later stage of prison term

Adjunct program .... None specific

Goal .... Modification of offender's self-image of inadequacy and sexual impotency; breaking down rationalizations regarding deviant sex acts; directing offender to-

TABLE 2 *(continued)*

	ward more aggressive and dominant relations with adults, particularly with his spouse
Frequency	Relatively intense—several times a week
Heroin addict	
Formal treatment program	Individual therapy designed to deal with personality problems, along with guided group interaction designed to modify group-supported norms and attitudes regarding drug use and criminality
Adjunct program	Vocational or educational program
Goal	Modification of "antisocial" attitudes, particularly attitudes toward drug use, law enforcement agencies, and drug addiction treatment programs; reduction of severe personality problems
Periods	Individual treatment and withdrawal from use of narcotics during early period of incarceration; group treatment toward end of prison term and in parole period
Frequency	Relatively intense—several times a week

an important part in the rehabilitation of the individual, provided that he also undergoes attitude modification.

The discussion below, concerning treatment policies for "semiprofessional property offenders," is designed to indicate the kind of extended analysis that could be made about other types as well.

SEMIPROFESSIONAL PROPERTY OFFENDERS

Persons who exhibit repetitive careers of relatively unskilled property crime and pronounced "antisocial" attitudes are relatively common among offenders, particularly in correctional institutions. Such criminals are usually from urban, lower-income slum areas where patterns of criminality are widespread. They often show backgrounds of family neglect, unstable work records, juvenile delinquency, and involvement in frequent petty offenses.

In many programs, semiprofessional property criminals are placed in some kind of intensive, individual treatment on the assumption that they need "insight" into their "problems." A corollary of such treatment is that if he gets an understanding of his problems, the offender will then be able to behave in a law-abiding fashion. It might be that intensive individual therapy would improve the mental health of such offenders, just as some amount of psychotherapy might be beneficial to many law-abiding citizens, but it is unlikely that this is the most effective strategy for the treatment of semiprofessional property offenders. These individuals exhibit a well-developed structure of "antisocial" attitudes, including hostile views of the police, anti-treatment views, antipathy toward conventional work roles, and a sense of injustice which holds that they are the victims of a corrupt society in which everyone has a "racket." Moreover, these attitudes are group-shared and group-supported. They are, of course, the kind of attitudes specified in the inmate code as "proper." The treatment problem in the case of semiprofessional property offenders centers around the substitution of prosocial attitudes for the kinds enumerated above.

How is this to be accomplished? The most realistic strategy is probably a form of group therapy along the lines of "guided group interaction."[16] There the effort is made to change group attitudes by encouraging offenders to exert pressure upon each other to exhibit prosocial views. In such a program, the role of the therapist tends to be that of a kind of parliamentarian, rather than of a technical psychiatric expert who uncovers personality problems. In guided group interaction, an offender is likely to verbalize more acceptable attitudes as a result of peer group pressures rather than of "insight." In effect, the offenders in the therapy group represent both the patient and the therapist or agent of change.

Existing programs of this kind are most commonly found in institutions, rather than in probation or parole settings. However, the argument for group treatment should be equally valid for these other situations. It would be highly desirable to continue this form of treatment outside of the institution. Indeed, the major technique of treatment for parolees of the semiprofessional offender variety would be group therapy. In this instance, however, the optimal treatment recommendation may have to be tempered by other considerations. Many communities are not prepared to accept "novel" experiments which encourage fraternization among parolees, even though the assumed risks of such innovations may be grossly exaggerated in the public mind.

---

[16]Not everything now called group therapy would be included within the scope of group therapy as used here. That is, there are many programs called "group therapy" which are actually individual treatment in a group setting. In these the orientation is toward providing individual offenders with insight into deep-seated personality problems. The essential aims of such programs are the same as those of intensive individual therapy. Such programs should be distinguished from group therapy, in which principles of group interaction are employed for the purposes of changing behavior and in which treatment problems are seen as group-shared and group-supported.

For an incisive discussion of the confusion of different forms of group therapy, see Cressey, *Federal Probation*, XVIII, 20–26.

Many semiprofessional criminals exhibit extremely spotty work records, poorly developed work habits, and negative attitudes toward work. One part of the treatment problem involves changes in attitudes toward work, so that the offender will verbalize sentiments other than those implied in the statement that "only slobs work." However, it may be argued that attitude change alone will not be sufficient to insure parole success. Favorable work attitudes may not insulate an offender from illegal behavior unless he also has an opportunity to engage in non-criminal employment. On these grounds, there is much to be said in the case of semiprofessionals for vocational training as a valuable adjunct to treatment.

An additional, related point is that the combination of group treatment and vocational or educational training should be designed to adjust the criminal to the realities of life outside the walls. Offenders cannot realistically look foward to interesting, highly paid jobs upon release even when they have received vocational training. For some semiprofessional criminals, law-abiding jobs will not pay as well as crime, but such consequences as additional and more lengthy prison terms make the criminalistic alternative to law-abiding behavior unprofitable. It is this view of the choices open to the offender which must be made clear to him.

There is no claim that group treatment represents a cure-all. What is argued is that, relative to alternative forms of treatment, group therapy is likely to result in lower recidivism rates and better adjustment. Nevertheless, recidivism rates among semiprofessional offenders are likely to remain rather high regardless of the kind of treatment used. Numerous obstacles lie in the way of effective group programs in institutions, particularly in maximum security prisons. For example, the inmate social system is organized in such a way as to exert pressure upon inmates to exhibit consistently antisocial attitudes. The inmate group has effective sanctions which it can employ to force "deviant" inmates to behave properly, that is, to discontinue participation in treatment programs. One of two responses to these pressures is likely to occur. The inmate may withdraw entirely from therapy programs when faced with a loss of status among other inmates, or he may attempt to "beat the system" by entering into treatment in a kind of sham performance designed to "con" the administrators. Yet it is possible that the inmate system is not as consistently "anti-treatment" in organization as has sometimes been suggested in the literature,[17] and changes in the prison system might be effected to lessen the impact of associational patterns among inmates upon therapy. Nonetheless, such changes have yet to be developed and implemented.

---

[17]Stanton Wheeler, "Socialization in Correctional Communities," *American Sociological Review*, XXVI (October, 1961), 697–712; Peter G. Garabedian, "Western Penitentiary: A Study in Social Organization" (Ph.D. dissertation, University of Washington, 1959).

Another impediment to treatment in institutions is that administrators can provide few opportunities for inmates to practice prosocial behavior. Ideally, therapy should be accompanied by outside-the-therapy-group activities in which inmates are encouraged to act out law-abiding citizen roles. The possibilities for such activities in prison seem limited indeed.

A final difficulty with group treatment, or any other therapy with semiprofessional offenders, is that treatment does not alter the nature of the environmental pressures that contributed to criminal behavior in the first place. Instead, the parolee goes back into a community in which opportunities for work and other environmental problems continue unchanged. For this reason alone, extremely high rates of success cannot be expected. It may be that a drastic alteration in recidivism among lower-income, slum-area offenders depends upon some rather profound changes in the nature of American society.

SUMMARY

This paper has directed attention to deficiencies in the treatment theory with which correctional agents now attempt to rehabilitate offenders. The discussion has indicated that formalized diagnostic models are needed in order that a body of explicit and detailed statements of strategy specific to different problems of treatment may be developed. Several diagnostic models have been suggested, along with some terse statements of treatment strategy for various diagnostic types. The diagnostic models and treatment hypotheses presented here fall considerably short of ideal, but most of the correctional literature is even more inadequate. The purpose of this essay was to point to directions for further development. If the general argument has the result of stimulating more attention to problems of diagnostic typologies and treatment theory, the aims of the paper will have been accomplished.

15

The Federal Bureau of Prisons
Treatment Program for Narcotic Addicts

David M. Petersen

Richard M. Yarvis

Gerald M. Farkas

Following passage of the Narcotic Addict Rehabilitation Act (NARA) of 1966 by the 89th Congress, responsibility for the evaluation and treatment of selected narcotic addicts convicted of federal offenses (Title II of the Act) was delegated to the Attorney General.[1] The Bureau of Prisons of the Department of Justice was charged with the responsibility for implementing the Act and developing a treatment program.

The purpose of this article is to discuss the general philosophy and overall organization of the treatment program and to provide federal and state courts, probation authorities, federal, state, and local administrators, and professionals working in the area of narcotics addiction with information about the program.

From "The Federal Bureau of Prisons Treatment Program for Narcotic Addicts," *Federal Probation*, 33 (June 1969), 35–40. Reprinted by permission.

---

[1]Public Law 89–793, 89th Congress, H.R. 9167, November 8, 1966.

PREVIOUS TREATMENT OF PRISONER ADDICTS

Prior to the passage of the Narcotic Addict Rehabilitation Act of 1966, federal prisoner addicts who required treatment for addiction were sent either to the U.S. Public Health Service Hospital at Lexington, Kentucky, or Fort Worth, Texas.[2] O'Donnell reports in 1962 that federal prisoner addicts represented about half of the total patient population at the Lexington hospital on any given day.[3] Only a small percentage of the total federal prisoner addict population was at any given time selected for commitment to U.S. Public Health Service hospitals. Most federal prisoner addicts were committed to one of 27 federal correctional facilities for any of several reasons: failure of the staff to recognize the addiction; refusal of treatment by an inmate; and ineligibility based on security restrictions related to the nature of the offense or to prior criminal record. Inmates deemed insufficiently motivated for treatment were excluded.

In the main, the federal prisoner addict committed to one of the Bureau's institutions received no special treatment for his drug problem. No special programs existed either to identify or treat addicts committed to federal custody.[4] Withdrawal problems were rarely encountered since most of those persons committed to federal institutions usually had been withdrawn from drugs prior to arrival. Although there were no specific addiction treatment programs in the federal institutions, addicts were, as all federal prisoners are, eligible for the general treatment programs provided by the various institutions, including group therapy, long-term individual therapy, and vocational and educational training programs. But because of the inadequate staff-to-inmate ratios, resources could not meet overall treatment needs. Therefore, no specialized treatment program for narcotics addiction existed in the federal correctional system prior to the implementation of the Narcotic Addict Rehabilitation Act of 1966.

---

[2]The treatment programs at the U.S. Public Health Service hospitals at Lexington and Ft. Worth have previously been described. See James V. Lowry, "Hospital Treatment of the Narcotic Addict," *Federal Probation*, December 1956, pp. 42–51; John A. O'Donnell, "The Lexington Program for Narcotic Addicts," *Federal Probation*, March 1962, pp. 55–60; and Arthur K. Berliner, "The Helping Process in a Hospital for Narcotic Addicts," *Federal Probation*, September 1962, pp. 57–62.

[3]*Ibid.*, p. 55.

[4]For example, during the fiscal year 1964, out of a total of 1,297 narcotic addict prisoners committed to federal institutions, 858 remained under the custody of the Bureau of Prisons and the remainder were sent to Ft. Worth and Lexington. During 1968 sentenced narcotic drug offenders confined in federal institutions made up 13.9 percent of the total inmate population.

TREATMENT UNITS IN THE NEW PROGRAM

To provide direct services for selected narcotic addicts in the custody of the Attorney General, three institutions, initially, are receiving addicts. Each of these institutions is programmed to accept a maximum treatment population of 100 to 150. The institutions presently accepting addicts for treatment include the Federal Correctional Institution at Danbury, Connecticut (100 men from eastern areas), Terminal Island, California (100 men and 50 women from western areas), and the Federal Reformatory for Women at Alderson, West Virginia (100 women from eastern areas).

The NARA unit at Danbury began accepting patients on March 15, 1968, while the Terminal Island and Alderson units became operational in August of the same year. Unit staffing at each institution includes psychiatrists and psychologists, as well as social workers, correctional officers, medical technical assistants, and clerical personnel. The assistance of regular prison staff augments the staff of each NARA unit.

At present the Danbury unit is staffed by one psychiatrist, one psychologist, two social workers, four correctional counselors, one medical technical assistant, and clerical help. At Terminal Island the unit consists of one psychiatrist, one psychologist, three social workers, six correctional counselors, one medical technical assistant, and clerical help. The unit at Alderson includes one psychiatrist, two social workers, four correctional counselors, one medical technical assistant and clerical help.

The social worker-to-patient ratio at each unit institution is 1 to 50, and the correctional officer-to-patient ratio is 1 to 25 (considerably more favorable than usual ratios). All personnel assigned to the NARA treatment teams work exclusively within the NARA program, although psychiatrists and psychologists may provide some general consultation to their institutions. Each unit functions as a screening center for court referrals and also serves the function of a treatment unit.

ADMISSION POLICIES

Not all addicted individuals are eligible for treatment in the NARA program. Under the provisions of the Act, a person is to be committed to the custody of the Attorney General for an examination to determine whether he is a narcotic addict and is likely to be rehabilitated through treatment. This examination is to be completed within 30 days.

To be eligible for treatment under the provisions of NARA, a person must be habitually addicted to narcotic drugs as defined in federal law by section 4731 of the Internal Revenue Code of 1954. This definition of narcotic drugs includes opium and opium derivatives, both synthetic and natural. The selection of patients for treatment in the program is, in part, also determined by statutory requirement. Persons *not* eligible for treatment under the provisions of the NARA Act include:

1. Those charged with a crime of violence,
2. Those charged with unlawfully importing, selling, or conspiring to import or sell a narcotic drug unless the court determines that such sale was for the primary purpose of enabling the offender to obtain a narcotic drug which he requires for his personal use because of his addiction to such drug,
3. Those against whom there is pending a prior charge of a felony which has not been finally determined,
4. Those who have been convicted of a felony on two or more prior occasions, and
5. Those who have been civilly committed under the Act because of narcotic addiction on three or more occasions.

Looking beyond statutory requirements, there remains a need for adequate criteria for patient selection and disposition. It is clearly wasteful to select patients for whom treatment bears no promise of success. Such patients consume program resources which could otherwise be utilized by others. Moreover, they can have deleterious effects on other patients adequately selected for a program. Prior research has not given us the tools with which to determine which patients are most likely to be benefitted by treatment programs, nor are we adequately able to match specific program elements to particular patient needs.[5] Initially, individuals who are designated as addicted will be included in our treatment program except for the following:

1. Those whose sentences are determined to be too short to encompass the necessary treatment program envisioned,

---

[5] Promising research in differential treatment with juvenile and youth offenders utilizing typological approaches to differentiate inmates, staff, and correctional programs has been conducted by Marguerite Q. Warren, *et al., Interpersonal Maturity Classification: Juvenile Diagnosis and Treatment of Low, Middle and High Maturity Delinquents,* 1966 Edition, Community Treatment Project, California Youth Authority, Sacramento (Mimeographed); and Herbert C. Quay, "Personality and Delinquency," *Juvenile Delinquency: Research and Theory* (ed.) Herbert C. Quay (Princeton, N.J.: Van Nostrand, 1965), pp. 139–169.

2. Those whose physical or mental disability is such as to preclude their participation in a treatment program,
3. Those whose necessary treatment needs are not available and cannot be obtained, and
4. Those whose alien status would preclude their participation in an aftercare program.

Discretion in the determination of eligibility in these areas is left to the NARA staff at the examining institution. No attempt is made at this time to make selections based on criteria such as motivation, insight, and so on. All patients, except those excluded above, will be assumed to be equally treatable. Experience gathered from the administration of this program should help to establish specific criteria important to the selection of persons who will benefit most from treatment.

LENGTH OF TREATMENT

Under the provisions of the Narcotic Addict Rehabilitation Act, commitment for treatment of addiction provides that a prisoner may be kept under treatment for the full length of his sentence. However, adequate measurement of treatment success will generally require a period of post-treatment observation which will be facilitated where the period of treatment is shorter than the sentence. We estimate that the institutional phase of treatment will require about 1 year to 18 months. A minimum of 6 months of institutional care is required by the statute. Release under supervision to the community requires an assessment of readiness by the institutional staff and approval of this recommendation by the U.S. Board of Parole.

Criteria governing release of the patient from the institution must also be developed. Readiness for release from the institutional setting will reflect staff assessments of each patient's progress according to the following tentative guidelines:

1. Day-to-day institutional function,
2. Progress within the treatment program,
3. Freedom from addiction,
4. The development of an adequate aftercare plan, and
5. The subjective evaluations by the patient of his readiness for release, as well as the evaluation of staff and fellow patients.

These parameters will be studied to evaluate their real effectiveness in assessing readiness and will be modified and given weighted emphasis as future experience dictates. The period necessary for adequate postinstitutional treatment (aftercare) cannot yet be estimated accurately. By law, such care must cease at the time of expiration of sentence. Ideally, it will cease earlier to allow a period of posttreatment observation.

THE TREATMENT PROGRAM

The first phase of the treatment program at the institution begins with the evaluation period. Upon determination that treatment for withdrawal is unnecessary,[6] the patient is placed in an Admission and Orientation Unit. The time he will spend in this unit will vary from 2 weeks to a month. Once in this unit, he is required to participate in the institutional A&O activities along with regular institutional commitments. During this time he is seen by the NARA staff social worker, psychologist, and psychiatrist for purposes of beginning compilation of information relating to his past and current life. This information will be used to assess his current needs and also as research data. Recommendations to the court relating to the status of the addiction and the patient's suitability for treatment are prepared. At the same time, through a series of introductory lectures, the patient is familiarized with the NARA program, its aims, and its objectives.

Following release from the A&O unit, each patient is housed within a special dormitory group, an arrangement in which a number of NARA program patients live together among a larger group of nonprogram institutional commitments. During the remainder of the observation period, the patient participates in regular NARA group activities and is assigned to a temporary job pending the court's response to the recommendations of the evaluating staff. Patients found to be addicted and to be suitable for treatment begin treatment after the treatment program is formulated but prior to final court disposition.

The postevaluation treatment phase contains within it three program elements. The first of these is the involvement of the patient in the general institutional program. This aspect of treatment emphasizes vocational training as one of its major treatment thrusts. The patient is assigned to a job that is consistent with his current ability to handle tasks. Of central importance to his treatment is the working relationship between the patient's work supervisor and members of the NARA staff. Continuous feedback from the job supervisor about the patient's progress allows the staff to effect

---

[6]Previous experience at the U.S. Public Health Service hospitals has indicated that withdrawal of prisoner patients is seldom a problem. It is not expected that significant numbers of our patients will require medical treatment for withdrawal. See O'Donnell, *op. cit.*, p. 56.

changes and work out problems when necessary or suitable. As each patient's level of functioning improves, he may graduate to increasingly more sophisticated tasks until finally work-release programs, furloughs, and parole are employed in his treatment program. Programs of specialized vocational training will be employed within the institution and in conjunction with work release.

An important part of the general institutional program is in the area of education where major stress is placed on literacy and fluency in English. Attempts are made to provide education leading to a high school equivalency diploma, or at least improvement of the patient's educational level so that he can achieve his high school diploma following release under aftercare supervision.

All institutional facilities are available to each patient committed under the NARA. In addition to the specialized NARA staff, the patient has access to the regular hospital staff, including specialists in medicine and dentistry. Other facilities include recreational pursuits, religious activities, and special ongoing groups such as Alcoholics Anonymous and Addicts Anonymous.

The foregoing description of the treatment program is applicable to all NARA units. For convenience we shall later discuss the specialized treatment at the Danbury unit. Specialized treatment elements in the other two units parallel the Danbury program in scope but differ in some specifics.

 The second major focus of the treatment program is the specialized treatment provided patients by NARA staff members. The patient is placed in an ongoing psychotherapy group following evaluation. These groups meet twice weekly for 1½ hours. Each group has a maximum of 10 members. The groups meet once weekly without a therapist. The focus of group interaction and inquiry is on the nature of the maladaptive behavior of the group members.

Once placed in a group a patient generally is not transferred to another group. Provision for individual therapy can be made if necessary, but usually will not be employed. The possibility of individual psychotherapy is not totally excluded, but is not given special emphasis. However, where a patient feels that he has something of concern to him that he does not believe he can discuss in the group, he may seek a member of the staff if his dormitory group approves this measure. In the main, group psychotherapy techniques are emphasized.

The third major thrust in the overall treatment program is the activities centered around the patient's dormitory group. The dormitory group is arranged to confront the patient with a situation or hierarchy of ascending responsibilities and status. This includes such aspects of group life as task assignment, distribution of information, liaison with staff, and therapeutic assistant functions. Group living stresses the need of each group member to be concerned about all other group members and to be mutually responsible for all group behavior. Patients must not only behave in an acceptable manner, but also are expected to feel responsible for the behavior and progress of others.

On arrival at the institution, each new patient is greeted by those group members responsible for the greeting task and is assigned to a more senior member of the group who will function to help acquaint the new patient with the procedures and values of the group and to act generally in a "big brother" capacity. As a new patient progresses through the program, he gradually assumes similar responsibilities for other newly arriving patients.

Each group holds meetings 7 days weekly. Meetings include encounters similar to those employed at Synanon meetings,[7] group meetings to discuss group business, and seminars. The latter are of three general types:

1. Seminars dealing with the outside world which include such things as discussions of news, speeches by guest speakers, and so on,
2. Debates and public speaking exercises, both prepared and extemporaneous, and
3. Socialization seminars in which members are taught how to eat, dress for a job, and how to behave in social situations.

Group meetings are also held which include all NARA patients and all NARA staff. These meetings are generally concerned with the passage of information from staff to the group (staff policy announcements), from patients to staff, as well as exchanges of information between patients. The meetings are generally held weekly.

The treatment program is not a single program for all patients. Rather, there are a number of possible programs to meet the various needs of patients. The determination of which program a patient will follow depends partly on his needs, partly on his desire to participate in a program, and partly on the availability of resources.

AFTERCARE

After release from the institutional phase of treatment, the patient is provided with any additional treatment he will require in the community.

---

[7]Lewis Yablonsky, *The Tunnel Back: Synanon* (New York: The Macmillan Co., 1965); and Rita Volkman and Donald R. Cressey, "Differential Association and the Rehabilitation of Drug Addicts," *American Journal of Sociology*, September 1963, pp. 129–142.

Separation of aftercare from other aspects of treatment reflects the tremendous importance of aftercare in the total treatment program. Aftercare remains a key element upon which the treatment program is based. To be successful the program must possess the following qualities:

1. Intensity of service,
2. Continuity of service linking institutional and aftercare phases closely together, and
3. Individuality of service, that is, an aftercare arrangement capable of encouraging and nurturing individual relationships between counselor and patient.

The Attorney General has delegated to the Bureau of Prisons the authority to contract with community agencies and private individuals to provide specialized aftercare treatment services for those released to community supervision. The scope of these aftercare services includes counseling, group and individual psychotherapy, self-help ex-addict coordinated groups, emergency medical care for conditions arising from or related to addiction, urine testing surveillance, temporary housing assistance, and transportation, and where deemed appropriate, vocational and educational training.

At the present time all NARA patients released from the Bureau's institutions to community supervision are supervised by the Federal Probation Service. This plan calls for the supervision of patients by the probation officers, supplemented by whatever corrective counseling and other specialized services are needed by the patient and are available in the community. The responsibility for locating and evaluating potential participating aftercare agencies is shared by the Bureau of Prisons, the Board of Parole, and federal probation officers.

Since released patients are under the jurisdiction of the Board of Parole, the probation officer as the Attorney General's agent in matters pertaining to parole has responsibility for liaison with the agencies with whom contracts have been made and for determining that all of the conditions of release are met. The probation officer is the key person in the implementation of the aftercare program. Both he and members of the contract agency staff work as a team to achieve the congressional mandate for supervised aftercare.

The probation officers involved in this program are using different approaches to implement aftercare. As one example, the Los Angeles probation office is using a treatment team approach augmented by consultation services from the University of Southern California Institute of Psychiatry and Law. The team has six members, four of whom are probation officers. One probation officer conducts individual and group counseling for Title II releasees. This is his sole responsibility as an officer. He is assisted by a second probation officer who, in addition to his regular case-load, has the administrative responsibility for these cases and sees to it that all of the conditions of release are met. A third probation officer assumes the dual role of research consultant and family counselor. A fourth officer is a trained psychometrist. Additional members of the team include a psychiatrist and a Bureau of Prisons employment placement officer.

Each case received is assigned by the treatment team to one of four treatment groups, depending on the type and intensity of service needed. As the program progresses, comparative studies will be made to determine the effects of treatment.

NEED FOR RESEARCH

There have been no definitive studies to date that have provided satisfactory answers why some addicts are successfully treated while with others treatment fails. For this reason, the Bureau of Prisons program includes extensive systematic research to acquire "hard" data about all aspects of addiction. Present data about addiction are incomplete and are based primarily on clinical impressions and inadequately controlled studies. The research plans are designed to provide information about the addict group in the custody of the Bureau of Prisons which can be considered a controlled study group within which hypotheses and assumptions about all aspects of addiction can be evaluated. Efforts will be made to develop profiles of addict patients, to develop a typology based on such profiles, and to attempt to identify social, psychological, cultural, and situational factors which influence the genesis of the addictive process. Each treatment unit will provide an adequate setting within which to evaluate treatment approaches to addiction.

As indicated above, differences in specialized treatment elements have been built into each NARA unit in the hope of isolating and identifying effective treatment approaches. The research protocol will attempt to measure, for example, which forms of institutional and aftercare treatment will be most effective with different kinds of patients. There are limited data to suggest that supervision of patients after release produces lower relapse rates than does release without supervision.[8] However, what *kinds* of aftercare supervision and treatment work best with narcotic addicts largely re-

---

[8]Michael J. Pescor, "Follow-Up Study of Treated Narcotic Drug Addicts," Public Health Reports, Supplement No. 170, 1943, and Meyer H. Diskind, "New Horizons in the Treatment of Narcotic Addiction," *Federal Probation*, December 1960, pp. 55–63.

main unresearched. To provide basic data about drug addiction it is believed necessary that research proceed concomitantly with the ongoing treatment program. Certain decisions regarding treatment have been based at this stage on educated guesses. It is anticipated that information from the research thrust of the program will provide more reliable data on which to base program modifications.

Varying definitions of addiction will influence estimates of ultimate success. Dole and Nyswander measure success in terms of social performance, Lindesmith in terms of disappearance of feelings of craving, and so on.[9] Abstinence from drugs as a measure of successful treatment must be employed with care. A person who used drugs during the first 2 weeks after release, but never thereafter, would be reflected as having failed in treatment if total abstinence is the sole measure of success. The pattern of abstinence and drug use, then, is the more fruitful area of exploration. Abstinence alone represents only one possible measure of success and not necessarily the best one at that. If the individual remains abstinent, but at the same time makes no adequate marital or job adjustment and continues to engage in criminal activity, we have accomplished little. If addiction is replaced by incapacitating psychiatric symptomatology, we have likewise gained nothing. With this in mind, community adjustment, internal adjustment, and abstinence from narcotics (measured along a continuum) will be considered in the evaluation of treatment outcome.

---

[9]V. P. Dole and M. Nyswander, "A Medical Treatment for Diacetylmorphine (heroin) Addiction," *Journal of American Medical Association*, August 1965, pp. 646–650; and A. R. Lindesmith, *Opiate Addiction* (Bloomington, Ind.: Principia Press, 1947), p. 46.

16

Institutional Innovations
in Juvenile Corrections

Roy Gerard

The closing of the Bureau of Prisons' obsolete National Training School for Boys in Washington, D.C., provided an opportunity to which all correctional practitioners look forward—the chance to build a new institution based on the latest ideas in correctional design and treatment; an institution that would "graduate" law-abiding young citizens instead of potential recidivists.

Planning to replace the 100-year-old National Training School was actively begun in 1961. Morgantown, West Virginia, was selected as the site of the institution, the newest in the Federal Prison System.

One of three federal facilities serving youthful offenders,[1] the Center is the first in which architecture was especially designed to facilitate treatment for a youthful population. Opened January 14, 1969, the $10,250,000 Center is located in a natural amphitheater formed by the Appalachian foothills. It is less than a mile from Morgantown and about 3 miles from

From "Institutional Innovations in Juvenile Corrections," *Federal Probation*, 34 (December 1970), 37–44. Reprinted by permission.

---

[1]The other federal institutions for youthful offenders are the Federal Youth Centers at Ashland, Ky., and Englewood, Colo.

West Virginia University. The Center maintains close ties with the University faculty and students. The University has made its computer available to help keep track of a vast amount of data and records necessary to the operation of the institution's innovative treatment programs.

A minimum custody facility, the institution resembles a modern college campus and is a self-sufficient community. Four cottages, housing 55 youths each and two housing 30 in each, accommodate almost all of the Center's population. An additional cottage is used as a prerelease facility.

The housing units are grouped informally around a "community square" which includes the dining room, school and library, hospital, auditorium, gymnasium, chapel, vocational shops, and other service buildings. This complex of units contains most of the Center's formal training and re-education programs.

The treatment approach used at the Center differs considerably from traditional correctional philosophy.[2] The accent is on the individual, his needs and his potential. An "open" institution, the Center has no bars and no fences. The cottages' large, ceiling-high windows frame a peaceful vista of hilltops, trees and grass. In this relaxed atmosphere, tensions and pressures are eased. The Center's programs are open-ended; a youth can begin at his own level of capability and go as far as his determination will take him.

There are no external fences at the Center, neither are there the traditional internal barriers between inmates and staff. The students, as they are called, learn to communicate openly and freely and find that others, particularly the staff, will listen.

The institution's programs are designed to find new ways to reshape the behavior of delinquent youths. The techniques used are experimental in nature, but are based on carefully researched theoretical concepts. Potential commitments are screened to select those boys most likely to respond to the innovative programs. All designations to the Center are made at the Bureau of Prison's headquarters in Washington, D.C.

The 300 federal offenders who comprise the Center's population are 16 to 20 years old and generally come from the eastern part of the country. More than two-thirds are committed for driving a stolen car across a state line. Others are committed for forging government checks, stealing from the mails, "moonshining," and other federal offenses.

The program on which each new student embarks is individualized and flexible to meet his changing needs. It is carefully planned, however. Every possible area of institutional life is integrated and directed toward the treatment objective.

---

[2]A complete description of KYC treatment strategies is contained in "Differential Treatment . . . A Way To Begin," Robert F. Kennedy Youth Center, Morgantown, W. Va.

DIFFERENTIAL TREATMENT

The Center's correctional approach is based on the philosophy of "differential treatment." Under this concept, treatment programs developed for youths vary according to the boys' behavioral characteristics, maturity level, and psychological orientation. To evaluate these factors, the Center uses a typological technique developed by Dr. Herbert C. Quay, of Temple University, and first used experimentally at the National Training School.[3]

The methodology developed by Dr. Quay and his associates has been validated as statistically reliable. It identifies four dimensions of deviant behavior: (1) inadequate-immature, (2) neurotic-conflicted, (3) unsocialized-aggressive or psychopathic, and (4) socialized or subcultural delinquency.

Dr. Quay points out that these same dimensions occur not only in delinquent populations but also with "emotionally disturbed" and "normal" persons. The difference among these groups is quantitative—the "normal" individual either has lower scores on these dimensions or is more successful in controlling his undesirable tendencies.

The methodology for classifying offenders under a given behavioral category uses three thoroughly researched instruments[4] developed by Dr. Quay: (1) a 44-item checklist of behavioral problems, completed by correctional officer/counselors who observe the boy as he interacts with his environment, (2) a 100-item true-false questionnaire filled out by the boy himself, and (3) a 36-item checklist on the boy's life history, completed by a counselor from the presentence report.

The cottage staff plays a key role in the differential treatment approach. An employee is assigned through a technique of "staff matching" to the cottage program in which by temperament and personality he can be most effective. Another Quay instrument, the "Correctional Preference Survey,"[5] is used to help make the assignment.

---

[3]"Project R.E.A.D.Y.—Reaching Effectively Acting-Out Delinquent Youths," Bureau of Prisons, Washington, D.C., 1968: "The Prediction of the Institutional Adjustment of Four Subgroups of Delinquent Boys," H. C. Quay and R. B. Levinson, mimeo., 1967.

[4]Dr. R. Peterson, H. C. Quay, G. R. Cameron, "Personality and Background Factors in Juvenile Delinquency as Inferred From Questionnaire Responses," *Journal of Consulting Psychology*, Volume 23 (1959), pp. 305–399; H. C. Quay, "Personality Dimensions in Delinquent Males as Inferred From Factor Analysis of Behavior Ratings," *Journal of Research in Crime and Delinquency*, Volume 1 (1964), pp. 33–37; H. C. Quay, "Dimensions of Personality in Delinquent Boys as Inferred From the Factor Analysis of Case History Data," *Child Development*, Volume 35 (1964), pp. 479–484.

[5]"Correctional Preference Survey"—Preliminary Form (January 1968), mimeo., Robert F. Kennedy Youth Center, Morgantown, W. Va.

DIMENSIONS OF DELINQUENCY

The discussion which follows outlines briefly the characteristics of youths placed in each of the behavior categories, the type of employee most effective as a treatment agent, and the major treatment objective for each category:

BC-1: *Inadequate-immature.*—These students are described as being preoccupied, reticent, lazy, inattentive individuals who behave in childish and irresponsible ways. They are resentful and/or dependent in their relationships with adults and are easily threatened by peers. Treatment agents for the BC-1 youth are selected for their ability to be instructive, patient, reassuring and supportive. The major program objective is to establish a secure, nonthreatening environment in which "growing up" can be stressed.

BC-2: *Neurotic-conflicted.*—This youth demonstrates anxiety, depression, feelings of inferiority and guilt. He readily verbalizes his problems and shows some understanding of his behavior. He often is sorry for what he has done but is likely to do it again anyway. The treatment agent should be perceptive, sensitive, able to become personally involved with the youth, and provide understanding support while emotional conflicts are being resolved. Treatment emphasis is on helping the youth to increased self-understanding of his limitations, strengths, and potential.

BC-3: *Unsocialized aggressive or psychopathic.*—This group consists of aggressive, untrustworthy, manipulative individuals. They have a high need for excitement, reject authority, and frequently become the institution "troublemakers." The treatment agent should be toughminded, direct, and able to avoid being manipulated and to enforce strict adherence to rules. BC-3 youths need a highly controlled environment with a lively activities program to absorb their destructive energy. The behavioral objective is to teach them to conform, to accept responsibility for their own acts and to develop genuine, meaningful relationships with others.

BC-4: *Socialized or subcultural delinquency.*—This student has been involved in gang activities and adheres to the values and code of his delinquent peer group. He presents no serious personality problems and can make a suitable adjustment in the institution. However, he will support the gang position in any confrontation with institution authority.

BC-4 treatment agents must adhere strictly to a strong personal code to earn the respect of these students. They also must exercise firm control and be alert to the group's attempts at manipulation. The treatment objective is to help the youth change his gang-influenced value system and to teach him how to meet status and material needs in ways acceptable to society.

BC-5: *Subcultural-immature*.—During the institution's first few months, the research staff noted that some youths scored equally high on two behavior categories (BC-1 and BC-4). The staff's clinical judgment was that these youths shared more traits among themselves than with any other group. This, coupled with an administrative need for more equal distribution of population, led to establishment of the BC-5 behavior category. As with the other groups, they have their own cottage and their own treatment program.

The BC-5 youth presents a mixture of the behavioral problems of the BC-1 and BC-4. Somewhat socially inept and inadequate, the BC-5 youth seeks to meet his need for direction through attachment to a gang. However, he is not necessarily loyal to his peer group. The family of the BC-5 youth usually is severely disorganized, accounting for his distrust of authority figures.

"Strong" but flexible individuals who enjoy working with adolescents seem to work best with the BC-5 group. The youth should recognize the counselor as one who is interested in him as an individual and who is helping him to set limits rather than to restrict or punish him. Treatment programs for the BC-5 youths emphasize the development of positive, trusting relationships with adults and overcoming social learning deficits.

A youth admitted to the Center is assigned initially to the Admission and Orientation Unit of the Reception Cottage. There he is given extensive diagnostic tests to evaluate his educational, vocational, and medical requirements. After he has been under observation for about 2 weeks, the Behavioral Problem Checklist is completed by the Unit's specially trained Correctional Counselors. A youth who is difficult to categorize by the Quay tests, because of similar scores in two areas, will be assigned to a category on the basis of the clinical judgment of the psychologist who interviewed him.

COTTAGE STAFF

The Center operates a cottage-based treatment program. Each cottage is staffed by a cottage supervisor, an assistant cottage supervisor, two or more correctional officer/counselors and enough correctional officers to provide 24-hour coverage.

The positions of the cottage supervisor and his immediate assistant can be filled interchangeably by a caseworker or a correctional supervisor, depending on the experience of the personnel available. Customarily the caseworker is the cottage supervisor and the correctional supervisor is his assistant.

A shortage of professional caseworkers plus the extra casework services required for younger offenders led the Bureau of Prisons to train correctional employees as counselors, with gratifying results. At the Center correctional counselors are the prime treatment agents. They work under the supervision of the cottage supervisor and a professional consultant (psychiatrist or psychologist) attached to each cottage.

Correctional officers assigned to the cottages also counsel and train the youths and are important members of the treatment team. The officers rotate to assignments in other areas (control center, patrol, etc.) and must be highly trained and flexible.

CASE MANAGEMENT

The Center uses a decentralized case management approach to treatment programming. This assigns most decision-making concerning students to the cottage staff who are in the best position to make knowledgeable and timely judgments.

The responsibility for developing and implementing appropriate treatment strategies rests with the Cottage Committee (treatment team). The committee is made up of the cottage supervisor, the student's counselor, and an educational specialist. They determine such matters as educational and counseling goals, work assignments, and how soon the student is to be reviewed for parole.

Misconduct also is handled at the cottage level rather than by one central committee. The emphasis is on positive behavior, which is encouraged by rewards for good performance rather than punishment for lapses. Disciplinary measures available range from fines and loss of privileges to transfer to another institution. Action taken is related, not to the offense, but to the individual involved.

Responsibility for overall operation of the institution's cottage programs rests with the supervisor of case management. He is chairman of a Program Management Committee that also includes the supervisor of education, chief psychologist, and chief correctional supervisor. The group meets weekly to develop and interpret program guidelines and to review matters referred by the cottage committees.

Each youth at the Center is involved in responsibility for planning his own future. He is considered a full member of his treatment team and is expected to participate actively in designing his institutional program. Specific goals are established for the student by the Cottage Committee in three areas: education-vocational, cottage life, and work. The goals may vary from completing a course of study or qualifying for a high school equivalency certificate to staying out of some specific difficulty over a given period of time. The student also helps set the dates for periodic review of his progress and the setting of new goals.

BEHAVIOR MODIFICATION TECHNIQUES

Underlying the retraining approach at the Center is a procedure by which positive behavior is reinforced through use of external rewards. Reinforcement strategies are built into almost every student activity. The basic reinforcement devices are the class level system and token economy.

The class level system has proved to be one of the institution's most highly effective motivators of good behavior. By achieving progressively higher goals set by the cottage committee, youths can earn advancement from Trainee to Apprentice to Honor student. Living accommodations, work assignments, pay, clothing, and recreation improve with each class level.

Students usually progress from Trainee to Apprentice in 3 to 5 months and reach Honor status in from 5 to 8 months. They usually are ready for release in 10 to 12 months.

A second major reinforcer of positive behavior is the token economy system.[6] While this approach to retraining has been used successfully in other areas (mental health, retardation, emotional disturbance), its application in corrections has been limited. Consequently, its institutionwide use at the Center represents one of the more ambitious undertakings of this nature in the field of corrections to date.

Under the token economy, students earn points (1 point equals 1 cent) as they meet goals set in each program area (school, work, cottage life). The students use the points to "buy" a wide variety of goods and services available at the institution.

Each youth receives a weekly pay check, in points, based on staff ratings of his daily performance. The pay check again reflects the distinction made between class levels. Apprentices earn points at a rate higher than Trainees and Honor students earn at a rate higher than Apprentices. A student also may earn "bonus" points, awarded on the spot for certain kinds of positive behavior.

A student's institution expenses, including room rent, are deducted from his pay check. Trainees pay the least and Apprentices and Honor students pay more for their more desirable quarters. Fines, which are few, also are deducted from the pay check. Here, again, discipline is differentiated. A student in BC-1 may be fined 15 points for fighting while one in BC-3 may be fined 75 points for the same misbehavior. A fine for an Honor student may be up to three times that assessed a Trainee.

Students also can use their points to buy commissary, snack bar goods, and civilian clothing, and to participate in recreational activities. Points are not transferable from one student to another. They can spend only what they themselves earn. In effect, the point system teaches youths that if they want something, they must work for it.

PRERELEASE PROGRAM

A month to 6 weeks before release, Honor students can graduate to the Prerelease Cottage. This unit, which is primarily self-governing, houses youths from all five behavioral categories, brought together under the same cottage program for the first time since admission. Prerelease students are given the greatest measure of self-responsibility as a test of whether they are ready for release to the community. They do, however, retain some ties with their "home" cottage program, frequently serving as counselor-helpers with the newer students.

COUNSELING PROGRAM

Counseling is an essential ingredient in the Center's approach to reshaping behavior. While it is an ongoing feature of the daily cottage program, the most intensive counseling takes place during the evening and weekend hours.

The type of individual and group counseling provided varies with each behavior category.

The BC-1 student needs consistent daily contact with the counselor. Individual counseling sessions, which are held frequently, are short, casual, and usually relate to problem-solving. Transactional Analysis[7] is being introduced into this cottage as the primary treatment strategy.

Each week each BC-2 student is involved in a minimum of two group sessions, one individual counseling session and one Cottage Forum (Town Meeting). Role-playing also is used to explore conflicts and behavior problems.

---

[7]See "Transactional Analysis: A New Method for Helping Offenders," by Richard C. Nicholson, *Federal Probation*, September 1970.

Individual counseling is of limited use with the BC-3 student. Therapy programs involve the whole group and are action-oriented to supply the novelty and excitement sought by these youths. "Directed sociodrama" is conducted twice a week, with emphasis on making the youth aware of the effects his behavior has on others. A Town Meeting is held once a week.

The counselor holds short individual sessions with the BC-4 student at least once a week, working to instill pro-social values and attitudes. BC-4 students participate in Reality Therapy group sessions three times a week, and a 1-hour Town Meeting once a week.

Heavy emphasis is given to individual counseling for BC-5 youths to help them overcome immature behavior. Group involvement takes the form of role-playing (Modeling). A large group meeting and several small-group sessions are held weekly. The group approach stresses problem-solving within the environment of the cottage to replace "acting-out" behavior.

EDUCATIONAL-VOCATIONAL PROGRAM

For 6 hours a day, 5 days a week, the student is in school. The Center's vocationally oriented instructional program is designed to give every student basic educational skills, entry-level proficiency in a trade, and supportive academic and social education. Courses at the Center are ungraded and the student progresses at his own pace. The institution uses the "integrated curriculum" approach in which education and trade training are coordinated so that a youth may achieve the equivalent of a high school education as he gains vocational skills.

The center offers several general areas of academic instruction: remedial and intermediate reading and mathematics, general equivalency development preparation, and courses in social, cultural, intellectual and physical improvement (SCIP).

All programs in the Education Department are structured toward the achievement of performance objectives. However, expectations and teaching techniques vary with each behavior category.

The Cottage Committee and the student set educational and vocational priorities, based on the youth's needs and abilities. Specific, measurable objectives are agreed upon in writing, along with estimated completion dates. Here, again, the student finds that good performance pays. When he completes an objective, he is awarded a predetermined number of points.

An evaluation of 47 students on the California Achievement Test at the time of admission to the Center showed that their average median score was 8.7. At the time of release, less than a year later average median score was 10.1, reflecting a gain of 1.4 grades. In recent months, precision teaching was introduced in the basic mathematics area. Preliminary evaluation of this approach indicates that general mathematical ability can be raised four grades in a 6-week period for the average student.

Each youth at the Center completes an introductory course in each of the Center's three vocational clusters: Aerospace, Graphics, and Electronics. He then trains in depth in the specific technology he has selected (for example, power, wood and plastics, or metals, in the Aerospace Cluster). At the same time, he attends academic classes designed to help him understand the technical language in his books.

The Center uses the Modular Concept in its vocational training program. This system breaks down the complex study units into small segments which, when mastered by the student, come together to form a total learning experience. The student signs a contract with his instructor for each segment to be learned and receives points for successful performance.

RELIGIOUS PROGRAM

The Center has two full-time chaplains and a modern, uniquely designed chapel that readily lends itself to the requirements of all faith groups. People from the local community come to the ecumenical Sunday services, which feature folk masses and contemporary music. The chapel is at the geographic center of the campus and the focal point of much student activity.

Community volunteers have become an essential feature of the Center's treatment program. Recruited by the chaplains, more than 150 volunteers visit the cottages each week in what is called the "Life School Program." Over 70 percent of the volunteers are women and many are students from West Virginia University. All volunteers are screened and matched to the BC cottage they can work with best. About 95 percent of the cottage population are involved in a Life School activity.

The Life School Program has produced multiple benefits. Students retain their identity with the free community, learn social skills, and learn to form positive, trusting relationships. The community is becoming more involved in the Center's programs. Local businessmen sponsor a student Kiwanis Key Club, a Jaycee Chapter, and an Explorer Scout program.

STAFF AND TRAINING

The Center has a staff complement of 170 full-time employees, or about 1.6 students per employee. The largest department is Case Management, with 53.1 percent of all staff. It combines services other institutions normally assign separately to the Correctional, Classification and Parole, and Religion Departments. Their incorporation under Case Management serves to insure that the treatment and training philosophy will predominate.

Many staff members formerly worked at the National Training School. Over half, however, have been recruited from the local area and, for the most part, are new to correctional service. Before the Center received its first student, all staff received 88 hours of basic training and about 40 hours of specialized training by department. Those staff members initially assigned to work in the cottages were given further specialized training.

Currently, all correctional officer/counselors receive weekly training from the cottage caseworker or consultant (a psychologist or psychiatrist). A continuing inservice training program is necessary because of the newness of many staff members and the complex nature of the Center's program.

EVALUATION OF THE CENTER'S PROGRAM

Since the Kennedy Center is an experimental institution, the planning design includes provisions for extensive ongoing evaluation. The Bureau of Prisons' research staff is involved in a long-term study of program effectiveness. They will base their evaluation on data being compiled on (1) postrelease adjustment, (2) program costs, (3) custody and control, and (4) the quality of student life at the Center. Data obtained on the Center's students will be compared wherever practicable with control groups selected from inmates at the two other Federal Youth Centers and from nonfederal correctional and noncorrectional populations.

Among other research efforts in progress is a project under the direction of Dr. Robert Vinter of the University of Michigan School of Social Work. His study relates to organizational structure and should be completed this year.

As with any new undertaking, the breaking-in process at the Center has not been without problems to be resolved. Under the token economy system as originally designed, students earned far more than had been anticipated. This created a serious budgetary strain. It was resolved by cutting back on the points a student could earn, limiting the purposes for which points earned in the cottage could be used and eliminating bonus points to a large extent. Students were unhappy about the changes, but no serious behavioral problems developed.

The token economy has not been an easy system to operate. Without a dedicated staff and the West Virginia University computer to process a seemingly endless number of forms, it would have been quite difficult to meet the deadlines necessary to maintain the system on a current basis. Despite the problems encountered, the token economy has proved to be workable and well worth retaining for its positive effect on student performance.

Application of the BC typology is still in the experimental stage and conclusions regarding its effectiveness would be premature. An analysis[8] made by the Center's staff indicates that their BC classifications generally have been accurate. Many staff members believe the system has been effective in distinguishing among different types of students. Some, on the other hand, feel differences that appear to exist reflect response to staff expectations rather than actual differences among students.

The typology approach has made it easier to operate the institution. It gives structure to the programs and makes the staff feel more confident that they know what they are doing. The students also like the system, feeling more secure in the structured environment.

CONTROL MEASURES

The focus at the Kennedy Youth Center has been on treatment and training, rather than custody and control. Only one cottage, which houses the Adjustment Unit, can be said to have built-in security features. The reduced custodial concern seems justified for the type of offender handled at the Center. Student misconduct has not been a serious problem. There have been few instances of physical assault and little by way of homosexual threats or involvements. Contraband appears occasionally but is within controllable limits. Students who find contraband frequently turn it over to a staff member.

During the first year of operation 40 students escaped from the Center. All were apprehended, most of them within a short period of time, and several returned on their own. No doubt this number will increase as the Center reaches its capacity. Given the openness of the institution and the youthful age of its population, a certain number of escapes must be expected. However, escapes are taken seriously and are studied to try to reduce their incidence and develop more effective preventive techniques.

In the final analysis, the success or failure of the treatment program at the Kennedy Youth Center must be measured by its impact upon youth experiencing the program. A preliminary report prepared by Dr. Vinter revealed that 81 percent of the students regarded the Center as "a place that helps men (youth) in trouble."

---

[8]"Probability of BC Misclassification," mimeo., Robert F. Kennedy Youth Center, Morgantown, W. Va.

MODEL ROLE

In November 1969 President Nixon sent the Attorney General a 13-point program as a first step toward improvement of the Nation's correctional institutions. In the program emphasis is placed on improvement of the Federal Prison System so it will serve as a model for other correctional systems. The Robert F. Kennedy Youth Center is now serving as a learning laboratory for many correctional visitors, including an Institute sponsored earlier this year by the Law Enforcement Assistance Administration (LEAA) for representatives from seven regional areas. The Center expects to continue its role as a correctional innovator. If it can be demonstrated that releasees from the Center have lower recidivism rates and lead more productive lives in society than releasees from traditional correctional programs, the expense and effort put forth to achieve these results will be well worthwhile.

17

Differential Treatment of Delinquents

Marguerite Q. Warren

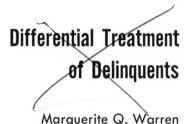

Beginning with the Community Treatment Project (CTP) in 1961, a number of experimental treatment projects for delinquents have developed around a theory of *differential* use of program elements. The question asked in this series of studies has been: What kinds of treatment programs conducted by what kinds of workers in what kinds of settings are best for what kinds of juvenile offenders? In order to approach these investigations, it has been necessary to have a way of classifying offenders, a way of classifying workers, a way of classifying treatment environments, and a way of classifying treatment methods. Assuming that one's goal is an overall reduction in delinquency, one can—with these various classification schemata —proceed to "match" treaters, environments, and methods with types of delinquents in a manner calculated to bring about the maximum positive impact.

RATIONALE FOR DIFFERENTIAL TREATMENT

One of the few agreed-upon "facts" in the field of corrections is that offenders are not all alike; that is, they differ from each other, not only in

From "The Case for Differential Treatment of Delinquents," *The Annals*, 381 (January 1969), 47–59. Reprinted by permission.

the form of their offense, but also in the reasons for and the meaning of their crime. Some individuals violate the law because the peer group on which they are dependent for approval prescribed criminal behavior as the price of acceptance, or because the values which they have internalized are those of a deviant subculture. Other individuals break laws because of insufficient socialization, which has left them at the mercy of any except the most protected of environments. Still others are delinquently acting out internal conflicts, identity struggles, or family crises. This list is, of course, illustrative, not exhaustive.

If one accepts the notion that offenders are different from each other in the reasons for their law violations, the implication follows that attempts to change the offender into a nonoffender will vary in ways which are relevant to the cause. Ideally, the goals of treatment will relate in some direct manner to the causes of the delinquency, and the treatment methods will relate specifically to the goals for the various offender subgroups.

The case for differential treatment was given support by two studies conducted in California during the 1950's.[1] In both of these studies, specific treatment methods—in one study, individual interview therapy and in the other, three types of group treatment—were found to be differentially effective with different types of offenders. Both studies showed that by lumping together all kinds of offenders, the beneficial effects of the treatment program on some individuals, together with the detrimental effects of the same treatment program on other individuals, masked and cancelled out each other. It is likely that, in many treatment studies, this masking effect has occurred because the data have not been viewed in sufficiently complex fashion or because the crucial dimension—the classification of subjects in a treatment-relevant way—was missing.

HISTORY OF DIFFERENTIAL-TREATMENT PROJECTS

The series of projects to be described have been jointly sponsored by the State of California and the National Institute of Mental Health. They all involve programs developed within the California Youth Authority, the state agency to which county courts commit youthful offenders who are beyond the handling capabilities of county probation departments. The target population of these studies may thus be described as serious or habitual delinquents.

---

[1] J. D. Grant and M. Q. Grant, "A Group Dynamics Approach to the Treatment of Nonconformists in the Navy," *The Annals*, Vol. 322 (March 1959), pp. 126–135; S. A. Adams, *Interaction between Individual Interview Therapy and Treatment Amenability in Older Youth Authority Wards*, Vol. 2, California State Board of Corrections Monograph, 1961, pp. 27–44.

Phase I of the Community Treatment Project has been operating now for more than seven years. This study, being conducted in California's Central Valley, involves a comparison of the impact of institutional and intensive community-based programs on particular subgroups of the delinquent population. The intake cases are first identified as eligible or ineligible for the community-based program. Approximately 90 percent of girls and 70 percent of boys have been declared eligible, with the primary reason for exclusion being assaultive behavior.[2] Eligible cases are then randomly assigned to institutional and community programs. The research design calls for following both those cases assigned to the traditional Youth Authority program (the Controls) and those cases assigned to the community program (the Experimentals) in terms of subsequent behavior in the community and in terms of personal and attitude change as reflected in psychological tests given before and after intensive treatment.

No assumption was made that either community or institutional programs would be preferable across-the-board. Instead, the questions asked were: For what kinds of delinquents is a community alternative to institutionalization feasible and preferable? What kinds of delinquents require or benefit from a period of incarceration? Findings have, in fact, shown a considerable advantage to the community-based program for all delinquent subtypes combined (that is, a comparison of total Experimental versus total Control cases), as indicated both in parole criteria and in test-score changes. However, there have been even more dramatic differences between the two programs when the various delinquent subtypes have been considered separately—several subgroups showing a large difference in favor of the community program, one subgroup showing a difference in favor of the institution program, and several subgroups showing contradictory evidence or minimal differences.

By 1964, the feasibility of treating a large proportion of the juvenile offender population in intensive community programs, rather than in institutions, was a settled issue. In addition, it was clear that the community program offered higher success rates than the traditional Youth Authority program. What was unclear—and what is, perhaps, unclear in all comparisons of one large, complex program with another large, complex program—was which particular program element or combination of elements accounted for the difference in success rates. For example, the differences in favor of the community program might be attributable to the particular treatment model being used, superior staff, differential decisions, specific community attitudes, simple avoidance of the institution, or numerous other

---

[2]Details about the characteristics of eligible and ineligible cases, as well as comparison of the Experimental and Control populations, are available in the numerous research reports of the project, obtainable from Dr. Ted Palmer, Community Treatment Project, 3610 Fifth Avenue, Sacramento, California.

factors. In an effort to sort out some of these factors, Phase II of the Community Treatment Project was begun in the San Francisco area. This experiment involves a three-way design in which two types of community programs are being compared with each other and with the traditional institutional program. One of the community units is based on the treatment model developed in Phase I of CTP (the Differential-Treatment Model), and the second community unit is based on a different theory and treatment model (Guided Group Interaction). Consistent with the study of *differential* impact, assessment of the three programs is being made with regard to the various delinquent subtypes, separately.

STUDY OF DIFFERENTIAL-TREATMENT ENVIRONMENTS

Beginning in 1965 and 1966, two projects were launched which had as major themes the study of differential *settings* or the attempt to develop treatment *environments* which are specific to the management and to the growth needs of specific subgroups within the delinquent population. The first of these projects was the Preston Typology Study.[3] Using an experimental-control design, delinquent youth of a given subtype were placed randomly in homogeneous living units (that is, only boys of one subtype in the unit) and in the traditional heterogeneous living units. The staff's task in the experimental units was to develop management and treatment techniques specific to the needs of the offenders in their particular living unit. The researchers' task was to describe the environment which developed in each experimental living unit, and to compare the impact of the program on experimental boys of a given subtype with the impact of the regular program on boys of the same subtype placed in the heterogeneous units.

The second study of differential settings involves the use of group homes for cases involved in the Central Valley units of the Community Treatment Project.[4] The development of intensive community-based programs made apparent the frequent necessity for out-of-home-placement resources. This need relates to the observation that some types of delinquents in some types of settings appear to have little or no alternative to

---

[3]C. F. Jesness, "Preston Typology Study: Final Report" (Sacramento, Calif.: Institute for the Study of Crime and Delinquency, in collaboration with California Youth Authority, 1968). (Mimeographed.)

[4]L. W. Look and M. Q. Warren, "Differential-Treatment Environments for Delinquents: Project Proposal" (Sacramento: California Youth Authority and National Institute for Mental Health, 1966). (Mimeographed.); see also J. W. Pearson and T. B. Palmer, *Differential-Treatment Environments for Delinquents*, California Youth Authority and National Institute of Mental Health Research Report No. 1 (Sacramento, 1967).

delinquency. For example, a child whose major way of relating to the world is conformity to the power which surrounds him may have little alternative to delinquency in a high-delinquency neighborhood; similarly, a child who is acting out a family problem may have little alternative to delinquency in his own home. These considerations have led to more frequent use of out-of-home placements in CTP than is typical of large caseload field programs. In addition to the size of the problem, differential-treatment thinking suggests that home atmospheres and attitudes which may be helpful to some kinds of delinquent youth may be nonhelpful or even detrimental to other kinds of youth. The goals of the Group Home Project then were to develop five types of group homes (four to six youths in each)—each home representing a range of environments specifically related to the growth and development needs of particular types of delinquent youth.

STUDY OF DIFFERENTIAL-TREATMENT MODELS

A further attempt to carry out the study of the differential impact of specific treatment methods on various subtypes of delinquents began in 1968 in the Northern California Youth Center Project. This program is being implemented in two institutional settings and is also based on organizations of the population into homogeneous living units by subtype. The Karl Holton School is developing its treatment program around behavior-modification (operant conditioning) principles; and the O. H. Close School, around transactional analysis principles.[5] As in CTP, Phase II, the question being asked is: Which treatment model shows the greatest payoff for each specific subtype of the offender population? An interesting additional complication in this institutional study relates to the question of what particular forms each theoretical model will take when applied to the various subgroups of the population.

MATCHING OF CLIENTS AND WORKERS

An area of study which runs through all of these projects involves the attempt to "match" clients and workers. There has long been clinical experience—and some research evidence as well—which suggests that few, if any, workers relate equally well with all types of youth or are equally comfortable with the range of treatment styles and stances required by the

---

[5]C. F. Jesness, "Differential Treatment for Delinquents in Institutions: Project Proposal" (Sacramento: California Youth Authority, Institute for the Study of Crime and Delinquency, and National Institute of Mental Health, 1967). (Mimeographed.)

full variety of offenders. Based on this premise, the Community Treatment Project began in 1961 to hire as workers individuals whose area of sensitivity, talents, and interests appeared to be "right" for given types of youth. An attempt was then made to develop for each worker a caseload made up of delinquents for whom the worker's "natural" style of relating and his areas of belief and concern seemed particularly appropriate. To the extent possible, homogeneous (by delinquent subtype) caseloads were built. Although these efforts at matching were at first based on intuition, interest in tying down the dimensions of worker and client crucial in the matching increased rapidly as the interactions among the treatment strategy, the worker's ability to carry out the treatment plan, and the youth's reaction to worker and plan became known. Research activity in this area increased rapidly.[6]

Matching has become an important program element in all subsequent projects mentioned here (with the exception of the Guided Group Program in CTP II which calls for heterogeneous groups). Although the data indicate the extreme importance of the matching factor in differential-treatment planning, the crucial experiment has yet to be conducted. Matching has been included in the various projects as one of *several* elements which were varied concurrently; thus, the unique contribution of the matching *per se* has not been studied extensively. A purposeful study of matching and mismatching is now in the proposal stage as one experiment of the Community Treatment Project, Phase III.

CLASSIFICATION OF DELINQUENTS

At the heart of all these studies of differential treatment is the classification of the target populations into treatment-relevant categories. The classification system utilized in all of these experiments is based on Interpersonal Maturity Level (I-level) theory.[7] The first application of the theory to the offender population began in the early 1950's in a study of military offenders (see footnote 1 in this article). A major elaboration of the Interpersonal Maturity Classification occurred in 1960–1961 with the beginnings of the Community Treatment Project.

The original theoretical formulation described a sequence of personality (or character) integrations in normal childhood development. This

---

[6]T. B. Palmer, *Personality Characteristics and Professional Orientations of Five Groups of Community-Treatment-Project Workers: A Preliminary Report on Differences among Treaters* ("Community-Treatment-Project Report Series," No. 1, 1967).

[7]C. E. Sullivan, M. Q. Grant, and J. D. Grant, "The Development of Interpersonal Maturity: Applications to Delinquency," *Psychiatry*, Vol. 20, 1957, pp. 373–385.

classification system focuses upon the ways in which the individual is able to see himself and the world, especially in terms of emotions and motivations; that is, his ability to understand what is happening between himself and others as well as among others. According to the theory, seven successive stages of interpersonal maturity characterize psychological development. They range from the least mature, which resemble the interpersonal reactions of a newborn infant, to an ideal of social maturity which is seldom or never reached in our present culture. Each of the seven stages, or levels, is defined by a crucial interpersonal problem which must be solved before further progress toward maturity can occur. All persons do not necessarily work their way through each stage, but may become fixed at a particular level. The range of maturity levels found in a delinquent population is from Maturity Level 2 (Integration Level 2 or I_2) to Maturity Level 5 (I_5). Level 5 is infrequent enough that, for all practical purposes, use of Levels 2 through 4 describes the juvenile delinquent population. It should be stressed that interpersonal development is viewed as a continuum. The successive steps, or levels, which are described in the theory, are seen as definable points along the continuum.

The elaboration that came with the development of the Community Treatment Project was based on the assumption that although a diagnosis of Integration Level (I-level) identified a group of individuals who held in common a certain level of *perceptual differentiation*, not all individuals in this group responded to this perceptual level in the same way. An attempt was then made to classify within each I-level according to *response set*. There appeared to be two major ways in which the Integration Level 2 (I_2) individual responded in his perceptual frame of reference. Similarly, there appeared to be three typical response sets among delinquent I_3's, and four typical response sets among delinquent I_4's. In this manner, the nine delinquent subtypes were identified. These nine subtypes were originally described—as part of the proposal for CTP, Phase I—by lists of item-definitions which characterize the manner in which the members of each group perceive the world, respond to the world, and are perceived by others. The description of the nine delinquent subtypes, with predicted most-effective intervention or treatment plans, combined to make up the original statement of the Differential Treatment Model.[8] This Model has been revised and expanded over the years of experimentation in CTP. The most recent edition in print was published in 1966.[9]

Brief descriptions of the three maturity levels (Integration Levels or

---

[8]S. Adams and M. Q. Grant, "An Evaluation of Community-Located Treatment for Delinquents: Proposal for CTP, Phase I," 1961. (Mimeographed.)

[9]M. Q. Warren, and the Community Treatment Staff, *Interpersonal-Maturity-Level Classification (Juvenile): Diagnosis and Treatment of Low-, Middle-, and High-Maturity Delinquents* (Sacramento, Calif.: Community Treatment Project, 1966).

I-levels), as well as the nine empirical subtypes, found in the juvenile delinquent population are given below:

Maturity Level 2 (I_2): The individual whose interpersonal understanding and behavior are integrated at this level is primarily involved with demands that the world take care of him. He sees others primarily as "givers" or "withholders" and has no conception of interpersonal refinement beyond this. He has poor capacity to explain, understand, or predict the behavior or reactions of others. He is not interested in things outside himself except as a source of supply. He behaves impulsively, unaware of anything except the grossest effects of his behavior on others.

Subtypes: (1) *Asocial, Aggressive* (Aa) responds with active demands and open hostility when frustrated. (2) *Asocial, Passive* (Ap) responds with whining, complaining, and withdrawal when frustrated.

Maturity Level 3 (I_3): The individual who is functioning at this level, although somewhat more differentiated than the I_2, still has social-perceptual deficiencies which lead to an underestimation of the differences among others and between himself and others. More than the I_2, he does understand that his own behavior has something to do with whether or not he gets what he wants. He makes an effort to manipulate his environment to bring about "giving" rather than "denying" response. He does not operate from an internalized value system but rather seeks external structure in terms or rules and formulas for operation. His understanding of formulas is indiscriminate and oversimplified. He perceives the world and his part in it on a power dimension. Although he can learn to play a few stereotyped roles, he cannot understand many of the needs, feelings, and motives of another person who is different from himself. He is unmotivated to achieve in a long-range sense, or to plan for the future. Many of these features contribute to his inability to predict accurately the response of others to him.

Subtypes: (3) *Immature Conformist* (Cfm) responds with immediate compliance to whoever seems to have the power at the moment. (4) *Cultural Conformist* (Cfc) responds with conformity to specific reference group, delinquent peers. (5) *Manipulator* (Mp) operates by attempting to undermine the power of authority figures and/or usurp the power role for himself.

Maturity Level 4 (I_4): An individual whose understanding and behavior are integrated at this level has internalized a set of standards by which he judges his and others' behavior. He can perceive a level of interpersonal interaction in which individuals have expectations of each other and can influence each other. He shows some ability to understand reasons for behavior, some ability to relate to people emotionally and on a long-term basis. He is concerned about status and respect and is strongly influenced by people he admires.

Subtypes: (6) *Neurotic, Acting-out* (Na) responds to underlying guilt with attempts to "outrun" or avoid conscious anxiety and condemnation of self. (7) *Neurotic, Anxious* (Nx) responds with symptoms of emotional disturbance to conflict produced by feelings of inadequacy and guilt. (8) *Situational-Emotional Reaction* (Se) responds to immediate family or personal crisis by acting-out. (9) *Cultural Identifier* (Ci) responds to identification with a deviant value system by living out his delinquent beliefs.

The delinquent subtypes, along with their code names and the proportions they represent in the CTP population, may be summarized as follows:

TABLE 1

Delinquent Subtypes: Code Names and Proportion of Population

Code Name	Delinquent Subtypes	Proportion of Population (%)
I₂ Aa	Asocial, Aggressive	<1
Ap	Asocial, Passive	5
I₃ Cfm	Conformist, Immature	16
Cfc	Conformist, Cultural	10
Mp	Manipulator	14
I₄ Na	Neurotic, Acting-out	20
Nx	Neurotic, Anxious	26
Se	Situational-Emotional Reaction	3
Ci	Cultural Identifier	6
		100

It is with respect to these nine delinquent subtypes that the various projects have sought differentially to define treatment goals as well as the various elements—environments, methods, worker styles—of the treatment strategies.

WHAT HAS BEEN LEARNED SO FAR

The series of studies on differential treatment of delinquents has produced a number of usable findings and products. These studies have contributed support to several program directions as well.

(1) A theory of personality and interpersonal development (I-level) has been elaborated. The theory provides a classification of offenders which can be reliably used and which has relevance to treatment-planning, goal-setting, and program-organization. I-level classification is now being used for all new intake into the California Youth Authority. A large number of other correctional agencies, both within and outside California, are also organizing parts of their programs around I-level and Differential Treatment concepts. The Center for Training in Differential Treatment has been established, having as one goal the development of training curricula for those agencies. The Training Center itself is a research project, investigating the ways in which training and consultation can support correctional agencies in their efforts to develop more rational and effective treatment programs.

(2) The operational feasibility of treating a large proportion of the delinquent population in the community, without prior institutionalization, has been clearly demonstrated. The community-based program appears to have its greatest advantages over the institutional program for the subtypes identified as: Acting-Out Neurotic (Na), Cultural Conformist (Cfc), and Manipulator (Mp). The Situational-Emotional Reaction subtype (Se) can be handled very successfully in the community program, although this group also does well following institutionalization. These four subtypes combined represent almost 50 percent of the population eligible for the community program. Evidence to date suggests that the Cultural Identifier subtype (Ci) may be more effectively handled in a program involving incarceration, although success of this group in the community program continues to increase each year while the success rate for Controls does not change. This subtype includes 6 percent of the population. For the three remaining subtypes,[10] the data do not, at this time, point to a clear advantage for either program. If recidivism rate alone is considered the most important of the criteria, then two of these three subtypes—Anxious Neurotic (Nx) and Asocial, Passive (Ap)—would have an advantage in the community program.

(3) The feasibility of developing a range of treatment atmospheres in group home settings has been shown. Four of the five theoretically defined group home environments have been located and/or developed with some degree of success. . . .

(4) Not enough follow-up data are yet in on CTP, Phase II, to indicate which subtypes have greater success in the Differential Treatment unit compared with the Guided Group Interaction unit. However, overall (for all subtypes combined) parole outcomes in the Differential Treatment

---

[10]Too few youths identified as Asocial, Aggressive have been declared eligible for the community program to make study possible.

unit in San Francisco are generally similar to those in the Central Valley units, suggesting that the success of the community program in Phase I was not simply the function of a particular location, community, or population. Early, but inconclusive, data do suggest that community treatment in a large metropolitan area may offer a greater opportunity structure than a smaller community—which is important for some subtypes—but may also represent a greater hazard in terms of peer pressure for delinquency—which is important for other subtypes.

(5) There is little support for the view that sheer avoidance of institutionalization *per se* explains the lower failure rates of CTP Experimentals. A direct test of random assignment of comparable cases to the institutional programs and to the regular parole programs has not been conducted. However, within the Control group, there are a number of cases who were returned directly from the Reception Center to their community without first having been sent to an institutional program. These cases, for whom institutionalization was simply avoided, have a somewhat higher parole-failure rate (57 percent at fifteen-month follow-up) than the Control cases who went through the institutional programs (48 percent failure).

(6) A product of the differential-treatment studies is a set of increasingly elaborate techniques and strategies for working with a delinquent population. Collectively, this set of techniques and strategies for each of the delinquent subtypes being treated in the community setting is referred to as the Differential Treatment Model, 1966 edition.

(7) As a result of the success of the Community Treatment Project, the California Youth Authority is now operating five in-lieu-of-institutionalization community units in addition to the four CTP units. In addition, the favorable experiences in CTP made a major contribution to the development of the Probation Subsidy Law, passed in the California legislature in 1965. It was apparent that, if intensive treatment conducted in the youth's home community could be successful when organized through a state agency, the same results might well be accomplished by the county probation departments without commitment of the youth to the state. The legislation calls for a maximum payment of $4,000 to a county for every criminal adult or young delinquent *not* committed to a state correctional institution but whose incarceration was expected on the basis of past performance. Quotas for individual counties have been established on the basis of past commitment rates, adjusted for anticipated county population growth. An important aspect of the Subsidy Law is that, in order to qualify for the funds, a county must not only reduce commitments but must also *define* a treatment program which has reduced commitments as a goal. Thus, for example, a county may not qualify by simply reducing probation caseloads; some further plan must be in evidence.

Forty-one of California's fifty-eight counties are now participating in the subsidy plan. Subsidy units in twenty probation departments have so far received training in differential treatment from the Training Center. During 1967–1968, the county earnings exceeded $9½ million. There are now a substantial number of empty beds in Youth Authority institutions for the first time in its history.

(8) Among the most clear-cut of the findings from the Preston Typology Study is that homogeneity (by delinquent subtype) in the living units of a training school consistently decreased unit-management problems. Significantly fewer serious rule-infractions and peer problems were reported in the experimental units. Transfers out of the living units for closer confinement were also fewer in the homogeneous units. Sufficient follow-up parole data are not yet available to indicate clearly the more long-range treatment impact of the experimental program. Some treatment-impact clues, however, are to be found in psychometrics and behavior ratings from early and late in the institutional stay. These measures show the greatest advantages of the Experimental over the Control program to be for the subtypes Manipulator (Mp), Cultural Conformist (Cfc), and Acting-out Neurotic (Na).

The impact of these findings on the agency is a general movement toward homogeneous living units in many of the institutional programs. Even though the final treatment-evaluation data are not in, apparently the management advantages are convincing. Many questions should still be raised in this area. Although, with present data, it is difficult to make a case for random heterogeneity, it may well be that *planned* combinations of the subtypes would have even more advantages than homogeneous units.

(9) The differential-treatment studies have given support to the view that treatment can usefully be conceptualized as a product of at least four major, coexisting interactions—interactions between type of program, type of treatment environment, type of client, and type of worker. The analyses of CTP data show the serious distortions introduced when viewing the target population as though it were a homogeneous collection of individuals. For example, in comparing the total Experimental group with the total Control group, one misses the information that, although the former has higher success rate than the latter, the Cultural Identifier group does better following incarceration. Additionally, a distorting factor is introduced by not taking type of worker into account. Thus, for example, Experimental cases who—on *a priori* grounds—were well-matched with their workers in CTP had a parole failure rate of 19 percent on a fifteen-month follow-up, while another group of Experimental cases who were not well-matched had a failure rate of 43 percent.

(10) Data from these studies indicate, not only that the treatment process with offenders must be viewed with a realistic degree of complexity, but also that the measurement of change must be viewed with the same complexity. Since the Differential Treatment Model specifies goals for each

of the subtypes, it is necessary to develop methods of measuring progress toward these specific goals, rather than to assume that certain changes always have a positive or negative meaning. Two examples may be given. Although increased conformity may be a goal generally hoped for in an offender group, increased compliance is a very negative sign in the subtypes identified as I_3 Conformist. Although one typically anticipates that increased self-acceptance will occur with improvement in treatment, there are several subtypes whose self-acceptance is already exceptionally high in comparison with other dimensions such as self-control, responsibility, and socialization. In this instance, hoped-for change could be defined as a better balance between self-acceptance and these other factors, perhaps even involving a decrease in self-acceptance.

(11) Program-assessment is complicated by still another factor which involves differential decision-making. In action-research programs such as those described here, it is impossible to conceal from decision-makers information regarding the Experimental or Control status of a particular case. The data suggest that this information does make a difference in actual decisions made by the Youth Authority Board. For example, Experimental cases in CTP tend more often to be restored to parole following an offense than do Control cases. Experimental workers more often than regular parole agents request a restoration of the youth to parole when some growth has been shown or when the worker believes that a change in treatment plan may make a major difference. The intensive work with the Experimental cases also makes more visible to the decision-makers the improvement in a youth (for example, school and job performance and attitudes toward authority figures) even when the change has not been sufficient to eliminate all delinquent behavior. Differences in restoration practice undoubtedly account for some of the success-rate differences. Complicating the picture still further, but to some extent equalizing the advantages for Experimental and Control groups, evidence is available that—because of the high surveillance rate on the Experimental caseloads—"hidden delinquency" (that is, unknown to the parole agent) is more frequent among Control cases.

ISSUES REMAINING

Many areas of the differential-treatment theme remain to be explored and further tested. Already mentioned is a purer test of the impact on treatment of matching and mismatching workers and clients. Beyond the exploratory studies, crucial tests of well-defined differential environments need to be run. Questions still need to be asked with respect to the kinds of youth for which treatment should preferably be started in the protection of a residential program. For example, there is a sizable proportion of various subtypes which do not succeed in present programs, either in or out of institutions. What kinds of treatment programs—in or out—can be developed for them?

Continued efforts to study this question are proposed as part of CTP, Phase III. CTP experience to date has suggested that the likelihood of achieving specified treatment objectives with certain offenders would be considerably increased if treatment were to begin, not within the community proper, but within a differential-treatment-oriented *residential* setting. The percentage for which the "treatment of choice" would begin in a residential program is estimated at from only 5 percent (for subtypes Cfm, Ap, and Se) to perhaps as much as 50 percent (for subtype Ci). In a complex Experimental-Control design, the Phase III proposal calls for utilizing a Differential Treatment Model within a community program and within both short-term and longer-term institutional programs to bring into sharper focus a number of issues: Which of the early goals in treatment with the various subtypes can be better achieved in a residential program and which in a direct community program? Which treatment goals for the various subtypes *must* be achieved in a residential setting in order to protect society and the youth as well? What varying periods of time in an institutional setting are necessary in order to achieve particular goals?

Many of these issues reflect the general "irrationality" of present correctional programs. Frequently, the decision regarding incarceration or not, as well as the decisions regarding *length* of incarceration, are made solely on the nature of the offense or on the basis of offense history. The decisions are made prior to (or even without) assessing the nature of the problem involved in a particular youth's delinquency, and without establishing the treatment goals on which later "rational" decisions regarding release should depend.

An example which illustrates the questionable "rationality" of present correctional systems is found in decision-making regarding which youths are eligible for direct release to community-based programs. The delinquents judged ineligible for CTP have been followed in terms of parole-success criteria on release from Youth Authority institutions. Compared with the Control cases, who also went through the institutional programs, the ineligible group has a much lower parole-violation rate (only 30 percent failure at fifteen-month follow-up compared with 48 percent for Controls). Although this information is not surprising, since other studies have shown assaultive offenders to represent a low-violation-rate group, the conclusion that the ineligibles represent a better-risk group for community programs than the eligible group seems apparent.

By and large, the ineligibility decision represents a response to perceived community objection to release of assaultive individuals. In questioning the rationality of this response, an assumption is being made regarding the hierarchy of goals for the correctional process. It is only if one assumes the primacy of the rehabilitative goal (that is, changing the offender into a life-long nonoffender or life-long noncost to society), that the decision to incarcerate the "good risk" offender appears "irrational." If, instead, one accepts the legitimacy of such goals as deterrence of others, punishment, or retribution, then this decision to incarcerate may seem more logical. Present-day public concern with "safe streets" adds to the pressure on decision-makers to incarcerate when in doubt. The differential-treatment programs have attempted to maintain a clear focus on the goal of rehabilitation with the consequent emphasis on moving as far as possible toward rational decision-making with that end in view.

CONTRIBUTIONS OF THE STUDIES

The series of studies in differential treatment have been rather successful in teasing out some of the many complexities which interact in the correctional treatment process. A beginning has been made in sorting out the differential contributions to success, or lack of it, made by offender characteristics, worker characteristics, treatment atmospheres, and treatment methods. Evidence that it is *only* a beginning comes from the ratio of questions answered to questions raised. Some information which is immediately usable in programming has been found. Some general program-direction has received support.

The model of action research which has been followed calls for two major strategies—a tied-down experimental-control design whenever possible so that some hard data are available *and* process-oriented exploratory research which permits the detailed viewing of the complexities and interactions among the treatment elements. A unifying theoretical orientation guides the exploratory research in the direction of systematic hypothesis development. In this manner, the second experiment grows logically out of the leads of the first, and the third out of the leads of the second.

To the extent that differential-treatment research has a claim to fame, it is, perhaps, best placed in the area of trying to pin down more precisely the ways in which specific elements of the correctional process are *aimed* at intervening in specific aspects of the delinquency and its meaning. From a program point of view, this theme takes the form of attempting to insert a greater degree of rationality in the effort to change offenders into non-offenders.

18

Conjugal Visitation

Columbus B. Hopper

Since conjugal visiting is a controversial subject, generally disfavored in American penal practice,[1] it is important that penal administrators and others interested in corrections have an understanding of the way the practice developed and operates in Mississippi. The purpose of this article, therefore, is to describe and discuss briefly the unusual practice of conjugal visiting at the Mississippi State Penitentiary. It is based on specific research I carried out at the penitentiary during September 1963 to April 1964.[2]

The Mississippi State Penitentiary consists of 21,000 acres of delta plantation land. The central plantation and the offices of administration are located at Parchman in Sunflower County in the Yazoo-Mississippi Delta. Parchman, as the institution is called, is one of the world's largest penal-farm or plantation systems. Since it is a plantation system, the buildings and other facilities differ from those at most state prisons in the United States. The buildings are of many different types: administrative, hospital,

From "Conjugal Visiting at the Mississippi State Penitentiary," *Federal Probation*, 29 (June 1965), 39–46. Reprinted by permission.

---

[1] See Joseph K. Balogh, "Conjugal Visitations in Prisons: A Sociological Perspective," *Federal Probation*, September 1964, pp. 52–58.
[2] The complete report may be seen in Columbus B. Hopper, "A Study of Conjugal Visiting, Social Organization, and Prisonization in the Mississippi State Penitentiary" (unpublished Ph.D. dissertation, Florida State University, 1964).

barns, storehouses, cotton gin, equipment sheds, and repair shops. Other large buildings are found in the 16 inmate camps which form the basic organizational structure of the penitentiary.

Each camp at Parchman is a separate community within the plantation, under the supervision of a sergeant responsible for all phases of the camp's operation. An individual camp consists primarily of a large rectangular building for the detention of inmates. The buildings, made of brick, are built and maintained by prison labor. The one-story camp buildings are designed so that on an average 60 inmates may be housed in one wing. In each wing there are no partitions or cells separating the prisoners; they are housed in congregate quarters with electric lights, running water, showers, and toilet facilities. Some of the camp buildings are surrounded by wire fences; most are not.[3] The inmates sleep in beds arranged in the pattern of a military barracks. Each wing is ventilated by about 10 windows covered by bars. A hall, dividing the wings of each camp building, leads to a central dining room which also serves as an educational and recreational room where movies are shown once every 2 weeks. A kitchen, in which inmates assigned as cooks prepare food under the supervision of the prison dietician, is connected with each dining room. Each camp has a concession stand and each wing a television set which inmates may watch in their spare time. The number of inmates housed in a single camp is never large. While one or two confine 200 inmates, a few have less than 100, and two less than 50. The camps are segregated for the white and Negro races. Generally, a total of approximately 2,100 inmates are confined in all camps combined.

The institution is a productive plantation, not only producing all food and clothing used by inmates, but sometimes also showing a profit on its products. The work of the plantation is allotted by camp and varies somewhat with the season of the year. The work may be planting, gathering, canning, slaughtering beef or hogs, or whatever chore may be most urgently needed at any particular time. Since cotton is the major crop grown, much of the work for most inmates, especially in the fall, centers around the production of this crop. Although cotton is the chief source of income for the institution, income is also derived from the sale of other crops as well as livestock.

During the period from July 1, 1961, to June 30, 1963, the total cash receipts for the penitentiary products were $2,027,619 while the total expenses for the same period were $2,502,642.[4] Although largely self-

---

[3]Whether a camp has a fence around it depends mostly on the location of the camp. Camps located near the highway have fences; those located out on the plantation generally do not have fences.

[4]*Biennial Report of the Superintendent and Other Officers of the Mississippi State Penitentiary, July 1, 1961, through June 30, 1963.*

supporting, the institution is financed by the State and all profits of the penitentiary are turned in to the State treasury.

GENERAL VISITATION PROGRAM

A distinguishing feature of the penitentiary in Mississippi is its visitation program. Parchman apparently has the most liberal visitation program of any state penitentiary in the United States. The institution not only emphasizes bringing visitors into the prison, but also allows the inmates to keep contact with their families by leaving the prison themselves. In a survey carried out in 1956, for example, Parchman was the only prison among 47 surveyed which permitted inmates to make home leaves for other than reasons of emergency.[5] Under the existing leave program at Parchman, called the "Holiday Suspension Program," each year from December 1 until March 1, selected inmates who have been in the penitentiary at least 3 years with good behavior records may go home for a period of 10 days. During 1963, out of 275 inmates released on holiday suspension, only 3 did not return voluntarily.[6]

All visiting by the inmates' families occurs on Sunday afternoons; inmates may receive visits from their families each Sunday. Although visiting hours do not begin until 1 o'clock in the afternoon, the visitors usually begin arriving at any time after midmorning. They come mostly in private automobiles, although some come by bus and taxi. The visiting hours are from 1 o'clock until 3 o'clock except on the third Sunday in each month when they are from 1 o'clock until 5 o'clock. The third Sunday is called "Big Sunday" because of the longer visiting hours; this is the time when the largest number of visitors come. On a "Big Sunday" there may be as many as 300 or more visitors.

While waiting until the visiting hours start, the visitors wait in their cars parked on the sides of the highway in front of the administration building. As the visiting hours draw near, they drive in the main entrance and clear themselves with a guard. After a brief inspection of the car, consisting usually of the guard's looking into the car and recording the number of the license plate, the visitors drive by the administration building, past the hospital, and out on the plantation to the camp that houses the inmate they wish to visit.

---

[5]Eugene S. Zemans and Ruth S. Cavan, "Marital Relationships of Prisoners," *Journal of Criminal Law, Criminology and Police Science*, Volume 49, 1958, pp. 50–57.

[6]*Biennial Report of the Superintendent and Other Officers of the Mississippi State Penitentiary, July 1, 1961, through June 30, 1963.*

On arrival at the camp the visitors must undergo another inspection by the camp sergeant or the guard on duty at the entrance of the camp grounds. This inspection is more rigid than the inspection at the main entrance, particularly if it is the first time a visitor has appeared at the camp. The visitors must identify themselves, and if requested, submit to being searched. The guard looks into the car trunk, and records the visitors' names. If the visiting hours have begun, he admits them into the camp area, and informs the inmate concerned that he has a visitor or visitors. The inmate then is allowed to come out of the camp building unguarded, receive his visitors, and visit with them anywhere within the camp area.

The grounds around each camp building are extensive enough to allow inmates and their visitors room enough to be by themselves, considerably removed from other inmates or staff members. The penitentiary provides tables and benches for inmates and their visitors. When the weather is warm, the grounds around a camp building, although less crowded, look somewhat like a city park on a Sunday afternoon. People sit on blankets eating picnic lunches; others sit on benches in the shade of trees, while others walk around. One may even see a boy and his father having a game of catch with a baseball, or children playing by themselves on swings or slides.

The penitentiary allows all members of an inmate's family to visit him, except in the case where a member of the family had one time been incarcerated in Parchman. Since released inmates are not allowed to return for visits to other inmates, a member of one's own family may not visit if the member himself has formerly been an inmate. Otherwise, however, members of an inmate's family are allowed to visit him, every week if they desire. For the married male inmate, the visiting freedom means that he may see his wife in private. He may go with her to a private room in a little building on the camp grounds and have coitus. Parchman is the only penal institution in the United States which has publicly announced such a practice. The conjugal visit is considered to be a part of the family visitation and home visitation programs. The family visit is emphasized at Parchman, and the conjugal visit is believed to be a logical part of the visiting program.

INFORMAL DEVELOPMENT OF CONJUGAL VISITS

The conjugal visiting privilege has developed informally in the Mississippi State Penitentiary, and it is still best described as an informal, unofficial practice. That is to say, the beginning of the practice may not be determined from the existing penitentiary records and that it still does not have legal notice or control. In fact, until the last camp was built,[7] funds were not allocated for the program. Records are still not kept as to whether an inmate uses the privilege, nor does an inmate have to make application for it or hold any particular grade as an inmate.

At the time of this study, no employee at Parchman remembered when the penitentiary did not allow conjugal visits. Most of the employees believed that the practice had been in existence since the penitentiary was first opened in its present location.[8] One man who had been employed intermittently at the penitentiary for over 35 years and who lived near the penitentiary and had knowledge of it even before his employment, said that the privilege was allowed to his own knowledge as long ago as 1918.

While the practice has apparently been in existence for many years, it has only recently developed into a somewhat systematic program, and especially since it has begun to get publicity.[9] In earlier days of conjugal visiting at Parchman the practice was confined largely to the Negro camps. Moreover, there was little or no institutional control over the privilege. A sergeant of a Negro camp said, for example, that when he became sergeant of his camp in 1940, conjugal visiting was being practiced but no facilities were provided. The usual practice, he added, was for an inmate to take his wife or girl friend into the sleeping quarters of the inmates and secure whatever privacy he could by hanging up blankets over beds. Upon gaining control of his camp, the sergeant allowed the inmates to construct a small building for conjugal visits. He has continued to allow the inmates in their spare time to construct such buildings or add to them. At the time of this study, his camp had three separate conjugal visiting houses, each containing several rooms.

The buildings used for conjugal visits are referred to by the inmates and staff as "red houses." No employee contacted at Parchman remembered the origin of this term. Apparently the first building provided for the visits was red in color, and inmates in talking about it spoke of it as the red building or house. Most of the existing red houses are simple frame constructions with about five or six rooms, although some have as many as 10. The rooms are small and sparsely furnished; in each is only a bed, a

---

[7]The last camp built was the first offender's camp, opened only in the fall of 1963.

[8]The Parchman plantation was first used by the state as a penal farm in 1900. For a history of the various periods in the history of penology in Mississippi, see Paul B. Foreman and Julien R. Tatum. "A Short History of Mississippi's Penal System," *Mississippi Law Journal*, Volume X, 1938, p. 256.

[9]See C. Knight, "Family Prison: Parchman Penitentiary," *Cosmopolitan*, March 1960, p. 62; and Ernest A. Mitler, "Family Visits Inside a Prison," *Parade*, May 17, 1959, p. 8. The first and most significant professional notice of the practice was at the Fourth Southern Conference on Corrections at Florida State University, in 1959. The Superintendent of the Mississippi State Penitentiary at that time appeared on the program and discussed the practice.

table, and in some a mirror. A bathroom which the wives may use is located in each building.

Since the red houses have been built in an unsystematic and unplanned manner, through accommodative relationships between the individual camp sergeants and his inmates, they are not standard in appearance. Nor do they have the quality of workmanship found in the other penitentiary buildings. They do not, on the average, present an attractive or even presentable appearance. Their condition, however, has begun to show some improvement in the past few years.

Each camp sergeant usually referred to a feature of the red house in his camp to which he himself had contributed in its development. One mentioned having put a new roof on his red house; others spoke of painting, adding new rooms, or acquiring new furnishings for the rooms.

The only conjugal visiting facilities at Parchman planned and specifically provided by the penitentiary are those at the first offender's camp, opened in 1963. The planning and institutional construction of the conjugal visiting facilities at this camp denote a significant point in the development of conjugal visiting at Parchman; they represent institutional acceptance of the conjugal visit as an important phase of the general visitation program. In this camp the red house was included in the camp plan from the beginning, and it is made of the same brick and other materials as the main camp building itself. The main camp building is joined on one side by a chapel, and a few yards in back of the two is the red house. The rooms in this red house are larger than the ones in the older buildings. They are also more attractively designed, furnished, and decorated.

The conjugal visiting program at Parchman should, in fact, be considered to be still in a developmental stage or process. It is likely that the practice has only begun to take on the pattern that it will take in the future. Although it has been going on for many years, only recently have the staff members begun to speak of it among themselves. Whereas for many years they felt the practice to be something that should not be mentioned, they now speak of it with frankness and even pride.

EVALUATIONS BY CAMP SERGEANTS

In attempting to obtain the most meaningful evaluation of the program by the institutional staff, attention was directed to the camp sergeants. The position of camp sergeant is one which requires the individual to have constant association with inmates. He lives a very short distance from the camp building and is, in fact, on duty 24 hours a day. The average sergeant spends at least 12 hours a day with his inmates. He knows each inmate personally, his hometown or community, and other members of his family.

It is the sergeant's duty to censor the mail of each of his inmates, that which he writes as well as that which he receives. All disturbances and problems among his inmates come to the sergeant's attention, and are usually settled by him. If an inmate has a problem he takes it to his sergeant.

Furthermore, when a member of an inmate's family comes to the penitentiary with a problem concerning an inmate, he is referred first to the camp sergeant. Consequently, the camp sergeants come to know the inmates, their problems, and their behavior much more thoroughly than do the other staff members. In the case of conjugal visiting, the camp sergeants are the only employees who know which inmates do and do not have the visits. Inquiries dealing with staff members' evaluations of the influence of the conjugal visiting program were directed, therefore, to the sergeants of the 14 camps which have conjugal visiting privileges.[10]

Each camp sergeant was asked questions relating to the homosexuality, discipline, work, and cooperation of his inmates. Each was also asked what if any problems had developed relating to the conjugal visits, and what changes he would like to see made in the program as it was being practiced. The first question concerned the extent of homosexuality in their camps. While it is impossible for a camp sergeant to have accurate knowledge of the extent of such behavior, the sergeants were asked on the basis of incidents of it coming to their knowledge to rate homosexuality in their camps as a very big problem; definitely a problem; a small problem; or a very small problem. Of the 14 sergeants, one rated homosexuality a very big problem; six considered it definitely a problem; five said it was a small problem, while two considered it to be only a very small problem.

When asked to compare the extent of homosexuality among their inmates who had conjugal visits with that of those who did not, 11 said those receiving conjugal visits engaged in much less. The remaining three said inmates receiving conjugal visits engaged in a little less. All agreed that those receiving the visits engaged in less homosexuality.

In comparing disciplinary problems presented by inmates, six said they could tell no difference in their inmates in this regard. Four said that those having conjugal visits gave them much less trouble, and four said they gave a little less trouble.

When asked to compare the willingness to work of their inmates, five believed those receiving conjugal visits were much better in this respect. An additional five said those receiving conjugal visits were a little better workers, while four said they could tell no difference. When asked about the overall cooperation of those receiving conjugal visits as compared to other inmates, three reported no difference. All the others, however, stated that

---

[10]The maximum security unit does not have the privilege, nor do the female inmates housed in a small camp near the hospital.

they could definitely say those receiving conjugal visits were more co-operative.

The sergeants were also asked what they believed to be the most helpful aspect of the conjugal visiting program. One sergeant said the work of the inmates was most importantly influenced in his judgment; four felt the visits were most helpful in producing cooperative attitudes in general among inmates while two others suggested the reduction of homosexual behavior. Seven of the camp sergeants, however, believed the most helpful aspect and the chief purpose of the visits was to keep marriages from breaking up.

When asked if the program caused any extra work for them, 12 of the 14 asserted it did not. They said, rather, that they had to be on the job all of the time anyway. On the other hand, one believed the practice actually saved him work in some instances. The freedom of visiting privileges in general, he added, kept the prisoners' wives and other family members from worrying so much and making inquiries about them. When an inmate and his wife can see each other in private, talk freely, and even have inter-course, he said, they do not have to come to him often for help or informa-tion. Speaking of this he said:

> Most problems the inmates have are concerned with worry about their families. And most people who come to the penitentiary are concerned about how the inmate is getting along, how his health is and so on. The best thing I can do is to allow them to see each other and judge for themselves. A common thing in prison is for a married man to worry about his wife, whether or not she still loves him and is faithful to him. One visit in private with her is better than a hundred letters because he can judge for himself.

Two sergeants of Negro camps, however, indicated that the program caused them extra work in ascertaining whether a woman was the wife of an inmate. Although the sergeants of the white camps said they did not allow a woman to visit an inmate unless she had official proof of their mar-riage, the Negro camps still present problems in this respect. Since many Negro inmates in Mississippi have common-law marriages, which the peni-tentiary wishes to respect, the sergeants have to question the female visitors and try to determine whether the visitor and inmate have actually been living as a married couple. Often, one said, he checked with one or two people in the inmate's home community as additional proof of marriage. While he admitted that several of his inmates probably received visits from women to whom they were not married, even by common law, he did not believe that many of his inmates did so because most of the women who visited also brought their children with them.

The other camp sergeant who spoke of problems involved in screening out the unmarried female visitors said that at least on one occasion to his knowledge, a prostitute had slipped by his screening and spread venereal disease among several inmates. He also mentioned that several wives of inmates had become pregnant. He did not say that the wives becoming pregnant had caused any trouble at the penitentiary, but mentioned it as a problem associated with conjugal visiting.

All of the sergeants of camps having conjugal visits said that the facilities provided for the visits should be improved. Not a single sergeant rated his red house as being in satisfactory condition. Even with neglected facilities, however, all sergeants enthusiastically supported the program as being of basic importance in their camps. Each believed that the program should, in general, be continued as it was being practiced. The changes they felt would be desirable related to the adequacy of the buildings. All said that they needed larger and more attractive red houses which would afford more privacy and a more pleasant atmosphere.

Except for the two who complained of the work and problems involved in screening wives, the sergeants felt that the informal administration would curtail the freedom and privacy of the visits which they believed to be the most important aspects of them.

INMATE OPINION

A question of importance concerning conjugal visiting is: "How do the single inmates feel about married inmates having the conjugal visiting privilege?" Since the program of conjugal visiting is intended only for married inmates, it is a categorical privilege which the majority of inmates do not have. It might be, for example, that the unmarried men in the institution feel that the penitentiary is unfair in its treatment of inmates. If this were the case, then one would expect that a program of conjugal visiting would, as some writers suggest,[11] cause more tension and conflict than it would reduce. To obtain some indication of this problem, a questionnaire was submitted to a total of 1,600 inmates. Of this number, 822 were unmarried and not receiving conjugal visits; 464 were married and receiving conjugal visits, while the remaining 314 were married but were not receiving conjugal visits.[12]

An item in the questionnaire was directed to unmarried inmates and stated as follows: "If you are unmarried, do you resent married inmates having the conjugal visiting privilege?" The possible answers were: "yes,"

---

[11]See Paul W. Tappan, *Crime, Justice and Correction.* New York: McGraw-Hill Book Co., Inc., 1960, p. 680.

[12]The sample studied comprised 76.0 percent of the total inmate population.

"very much," "yes," "a little," and "no." The response indicated that the great majority of unmarried inmates did *not* feel resentment over the privilege being granted to married men. Of 822 unmarried inmates responding to the question, 737, or 89.6 percent percent, answered that they felt no resentment; a total of 85 inmates, however, did report resentment, 58 replying "very much" and 27 replying that they felt a little resentment.

The fact that very nearly 9 out of every 10 unmarried inmates did not indicate resentment suggests that for most inmates a pattern of relative deprivation operates within the institution in regard to conjugal visits.[13] Apparently most unmarried inmates identify with other unmarried inmates and view a married inmate and his wife very nearly in the same way unmarried individuals do in a free community. Of several unmarried inmates talked to by the researcher, not one said he felt any resentment toward the staff or other inmates concerning the visits.

Since the embarrassment associated with and the obviousness of sex in conjugal visits have been objections to the practice,[14] two items in the questionnaire were directed toward these aspects. The inmates who received conjugal visits were asked the following question: "If you engage in conjugal visiting, has any other inmate ever acted in any way disrespectful to your wife?" Of 462 inmates answering the question, only 18, or 3.9 percent, replied in the affirmative. When asked if the visits were embarrassing to them, 42, or 9.1 percent, replied in the affirmative. When asked if they believed the conjugal visits were embarrassing to their wives, however, 87, or 18.8 percent, answered that the visits were embarrassing to their wives.

The inmates who received conjugal visits were also asked to choose from among several items the one for which they believed conjugal visits to be most helpful. The items from which they had to choose were as follows: keeping marriages from breaking up; reducing homosexuality; making inmates more cooperative; helping rehabilitate inmates; making inmates easier to control; or making inmates work harder. As a final choice, the inmates could choose to mark that the visits were helpful for all of the above equally. As may be seen in Table 1 of the 464 inmates responding to the question, 234 believed that conjugal visits were most helpful in keeping marriages from being broken. It is interesting to note that the inmates, as did the sergeants, ranked the preservation of marriages as the most important function of conjugal visiting.

The majority of the inmates using the conjugal visiting privilege did not believe that the facilities provided for the visits were in satisfactory condition. When asked to rate the buildings provided for the visits, only

---

[13]For a discussion of "relative deprivation" see Samuel Stouffer, *et al., The American Soldier*. Princeton, N.J.: Princeton University Press, 1949, Volume 1.

[14]Zemans and Cavan, *loc. cit.*

152 out of 464, or 32.7 percent, rated them as being in satisfactory condition. Most of the inmates who were talked to about the red houses complained that the rooms were too small and that the buildings were in need of repairs.

IMPORTANCE OF SMALL CAMPS

The fact that so few inmates reported embarrassment and so few problems have been encountered despite neglected facilities, is perhaps best explained by the small size of the inmate camps and the informality and freedom small numbers allow. In an inmate camp at Parchman housing only 150 men, the number of visitors coming on a single day is never large. It is easier to evolve and maintain a working system of interpersonal relations, generally, when numbers are small. In conjugal visiting, small numbers are basic for sex activities are the most delicate of human activities.

Although the practice of conjugal visiting at Parchman has begun to be a recognized, institutionally supported program, informality is still stressed in its operation. Inmates are not specifically encouraged or discouraged to use the privilege. They simply use the privilege if they wish to do so. The wives are not informed officially that they are allowed to make conjugal visits. The individual inmate is responsible for answering any questions his wife may have about the privilege.

The penitentiary provides no contraceptive devices for the inmates nor does it require their use. If an inmate and his wife wish to use contraceptives, the wife must provide them.

The freedom and informality of conjugal visiting at Parchman are

TABLE 1
Rating of the Helpfulness of Conjugal Visits, by Inmates
Receiving Conjugal Visits

For which of the following do you believe conjugal visits to be most helpful?	Number	Percent of Total
Total	464	100.0
Keeping marriages from breaking up	234	50.4
Reducing homosexuality	75	16.2
Making inmates more cooperative	19	4.1
Helping rehabilitate inmates	19	4.1
Making inmates easier to control	39	8.4
Making inmates work harder	10	2.2
Helpful for all equally	68	14.6

further revealed by the fact that the inmates themselves are responsible for the orderly operation of the red houses and for cooperation in the use of them. No time limit is imposed by the staff of the institution on the time an inmate and his wife may stay in a red house. The inmates are left to use their own judgment. They know how many inmates have wives visiting on a single day, and know that when there are few visitors they may stay longer in the red house. In camps having a fairly large number of men receiving conjugal visits, systems have been worked out by the inmates to avoid embarrassment in determining whether a room in the red house is being used. The usual procedure is to erect a board in the front of the building that indicates which rooms are and are not empty. Each room is numbered and its number is written on a piece of wood or some other material suitable for a marker. A string or chain is then attached to the marker and it is hung on the board. Before an inmate and his wife go into the building, they select a room, remove the marker from the board, and take it with them into the room. An inmate may thus determine whether the red house has rooms available simply by walking by the board. This procedure helps prevent embarrassment arising over such things as knocking on doors, standing in line, and other such incidents likely to be of concern.

In leaving the inmates alone without formal rules and regulations, the penitentiary has forced the inmates to cooperate with each other if they are to have the conjugal visiting privilege. Thus, the inmates cooperate in several ways. By informal agreement, married inmates whose wives are visiting are left to themselves in one area of the camp grounds. Inmates not having wives or whose wives do not visit, do not go near the areas in which the red houses are located. Inmates often cooperate by watching or attending to the children of a couple in a red house. Above all, the inmates cooperate by being respectful and courteous to each others' wives.

The conjugal visit at Parchman is not a privilege granted specifically for good behavior. The inmates in the maximum security unit do not have the privilege nor do women inmates have it.[15] All married inmates in the other camps, however, have the privilege. While the privilege is not granted for good behavior within an individual camp, inmates whose behavior presents a persistent problem are often removed to the maximum security camp for a few days. If an inmate attempts to escape, refuses to work, or attacks a guard or another inmate, he will generally be placed in a cell in the maximum security unit until he indicates that he is willing to abide by the farm camp rules. Actually, very few inmates are removed from the regular camps for disciplinary reasons. In October 1963, for example, there were only 13 inmates confined in maximum security, and two of these were on "death row" awaiting execution dates.

---

[15]In October 1963, there were 63 women confined in the women's camp.

The attitude of the staff at Parchman toward conjugal visiting privileges is that a man and his wife have the right of sexual intercourse, even though the man is in prison. Inmates are eligible to receive conjugal visits upon commitment as soon as they are assigned to a camp. No special counseling is given to an inmate using the privilege nor is any extra requirement made of him. He is like any other inmate except that he and his wife take part in the conjugal visiting program.

If a married inmate at Parchman does not use the privilege, it is generally because his wife does not live close enough to visit him, he and his wife are not getting along well, or they simply do not choose to use it. Most married inmates not using the privilege or using it rarely fall into the first category. These are the inmates whose wives live at such a distance that visiting is expensive and time-consuming. Since many wives work, if they live two hundred miles or more from the penitentiary, a visit generally means travelling overnight and considerable expense as well as a loss of a day's work.

The second reason why a married inmate may not use the conjugal visiting privilege is because he and his wife were not getting along well before his incarceration. Inmates serving a sentence for nonsupport, for example, are usually in this category. A few inmates also told me that their wives engaged in conjugal visiting on their first incarceration but that on their second commitment they did not.

Other inmates do not use the privilege because they or their wives do not wish to do so. This may be because children, parents, and other members of the family always come with the wife to visit, or it may be because they are embarrassed by the poor facilities generally available. At any rate, when married inmates do not use the conjugal visiting privilege, it is not because they are different in their offenses or general conduct within the prison.

CONCLUSION

The development of conjugal visiting in the Mississippi State Penitentiary has not been due so much to the individuals or officials involved as to the social and physical organization of the penitentiary itself. It is believed there are general and specific features of the structure and organization of the penitentiary in Mississippi especially amenable to its development. The features believed important in its development are: the rural environment in which the penitentiary is located, the plantation life the penitentiary follows, the small semi-isolated camp organization of the institution, the economic motives of the penitentiary, and the segregation of the Negro and white races within the prison.

The conjugal visit in Mississippi seems, above all, a manifestation of the rural emphasis on the stable family. Mississippians are, and always have been, a rural people. Although the percentage of people living in urban places in Mississippi has been increasing, the rate has been slow. The census of the population in 1960 showed that only 37.7 percent of all Mississippians lived in urban places. Until 1950, more than 80.0 percent of the people of Mississippi lived in rural communities.[16] The influence of the rural environment upon marital and familial relationships is well known, and the stability of the rural family is a widely accepted fact.[17] As a union of husband and wife, parents and children, the rural family is much more closely integrated and more permanent than the urban family, and in comparison with other social institutions, the role of the family is much more important in the country than in the city. A prison in a rural culture in which both staff and inmates have a high regard for the stability of marriage is more likely to make efforts to safeguard a marriage even though the husband is imprisoned than a prison in an urban setting.

Not only does the penitentiary allow wives to visit husbands, but it also allows all members of the family to visit and allows the family to visit as a group in private. The high regard in which rural Mississippians hold the family has not only been a factor in the development and operation of conjugal visiting within the prison, but also is important in making the practice acceptable to the general public and officials of the State. The fact that the practice of conjugal visiting is believed to help in keeping marriages and families from breaking up helps the people of Mississippi not only accept the practice but also gives them pride in it.

The small, semi-isolated camp structure was favorable to the development of conjugal visiting in part because it simply increased the probability of its development. Instead of being one big central prison, Parchman is several different prison camps, most of them separated by several miles. More importantly, however, the small number of inmates housed in each camp reduces security precautions a great deal. It also allows a camp sergeant to know his inmates well and to develop primary relationships with them. The fact that a sergeant knows an individual inmate and his wife is very helpful for the conjugal visit for it means less formality in the reception of wives and in security precautions. The small camps present wives with a less rigid and more informal situation than would a large prison. As a result, they are able to relax and are not constantly reminded of the prison setting of the visit. Such an atmosphere allows wives to keep their self-respect and to have the feeling that the visit has been a private one.

---

[16]John C. Belcher and Morton B. King, *Mississippi's People*. University, Mississippi: Bureau of Public Administration, University of Mississippi, 1950, p. 13.

[17]See Paul H. Landis, *Rural Life in Progress*. New York: McGraw-Hill Book Co., Inc., 1948, p. 319.

Since segregation of the races is a general feature of the social organization of the State of Mississippi, the functioning of the conjugal visiting program at Parchman is also dependent upon the segregation of the Negro and white races within the penitentiary. While this factor might be of no importance in a prison in a state having successful integration of the races generally, there can be little doubt of its significance in Mississippi. Segregation of the Negro and white races in Parchman precludes conflict of the races in the most carefully guarded aspect of their interaction—that of sexual behavior.

The fact that conjugal visiting in Mississippi developed in an unofficial, unplanned manner as an accommodative adjustment does not necessarily mean that it is undesirable; it merely shows the magnitude of the problem of sexual adjustment in penal institutions. It is to be expected that penal institutions will, when the relationships between the inmates and staff become accommodative or cooperative, for whatever motivation, turn attention to sexual problems of inmates. The practice of conjugal visiting at Parchman reveals such relationships. With adequate facilities, careful selection, and appropriate counsel, it is possible that the conjugal visiting program in Mississippi could be developed into one of the most enlightened programs in modern corrections.

19

Shock Probation:
A New Approach to Crime Control

Paul C. Friday

David M. Petersen

Harry E. Allen

A convicted felon in the United States is faced with two possible "treatment" dispositions—the court may place him on probation or sentence him to an institution. The process involved in determining which alternative is employed is not always clear, but it is assumed to depend upon the nature of the crime, the circumstances and characteristics of the offender.

Criminologists and the courts see definite advantages and disadvantages to each alternative. Incarceration first serves to protect the society; it isolates the offender, takes him out of circulation thereby reducing his opportunities to commit his crime again and subsequently reduces community anxiety over his presence. It may also fulfill punitive (atonement), therapeutic, or preventive objectives (Johnson, 1968:281). In addition, incarceration may function to deter others from committing the offense, provide a setting where "rehabilitative" therapy may be employed and rein-

From "Shock Probation: A New Approach to Crime Control," *Georgia Journal of Corrections*, 1, No. 1 (July 1973), 1–13. Reprinted by permission.

force cultural norms and values by demonstrating the absolute power of the State.

Probation, on the other hand, is designed to keep the offender in the community and not isolate him from his family and the influence of noncriminal values. It attempts to avoid many of the perceived disadvantages of incarceration such as the exposure of the naive offender to more sophisticated and hardened criminal elements or the increased bitterness and negativism associated with the deprivation of liberty.

Neither incarceration nor probation by itself may be a viable or effective approach to crime control. Incarceration may reach a point of diminishing returns. Studies have indicated that communities spend enormous sums of money keeping offenders imprisoned longer than is necessary; so long, in fact, that the chances of any rehabilitation are decreased. The findings of a California State Assembly Report emphasize the absence of a positive correlation between time served in prison and subsequent criminal conduct (California State Assembly, 1968:31–32).

In Florida following the 1963 U.S. Supreme Court decision in the Gideon case, 1,252 felons were summarily released long before their normal release dates. The Department of Corrections matched 110 of these early releasees with comparable offenders who served their full terms and found that 28 months after release, 13.6 percent of the Gideon group had returned to criminal activity in contrast to 25.4 percent of the full-term releases (Florida Division of Corrections, 1966). Similar results of reduced sentences were also reported from the State of Washington and California (Joint Commission on Correctional Manpower and Training, 1970:60–61).

It is difficult to assess the results of probation studies because of the numerous imponderables involved, but claims of success are relatively high. Whether due to the selection process or the possible self-correcting nature of many of the clients, probation as an alternative has been supported. Empirical studies of the effectiveness of probation have generally demonstrated claims of a 50–90 percent "success" rate (Dressler, 1969:262–267). In a summary analysis of eleven probation studies since 1920, England (1957) found four indicating 80–90 percent adjustment during the probation period, five with 70–80 percent, and two reporting 60–70 percent. Caldwell looked at post-probation success after eleven years for Federal probationers in Alabama and found that 83.6 percent committed no new offense (Caldwell, 1951:10).

Despite the relatively high "success" rate, probation may not be the appropriate sanction for all offenders. There still remains a group of 10–50 percent of those probated who do not succeed. These "failures" may have needed the prison experience, treatment, or supervision; their experiences and backgrounds may have required more structure and supervision, not minimal contact.

COMBINED INCARCERATION AND PROBATION

There is an alternative to the prison versus probation dilemma; this is to incarcerate the offender for part of his sentence, suspend the remainder, and place him on probation. Such a procedure is a judicial decision, not one made by a division of correction or parole board. This option exists in modified form in Sweden, Denmark, Federal courts in the United States and in the States of Ohio, Maine, California, and Wisconsin.

The split sentence attempts to combine the advantages of probation with some of the advantages of incarceration. On the one hand, it attempts to avoid the long-term prison commitment and subsequent hardening of attitudes, while at the same time providing constant supervision for short period of time. Moreover, it is intended to impress the offender with the hardships and psychological problems of isolation and prison life.

The advantage of combining incarceration with probation is debatable. One argument *for* such a practice is that institutionalization may be to the inmate's advantage. Incarceration provides the opportunity to evaluate the needs of the offender in more detail and helps him utilize training and other educational services provided by the prisons. Correctional personnel may better be able to determine the needs of the individual while, at the same time, providing the authorities with greater control over him and consequently, providing greater protection for the society (Master, 1948:40).

Another advantage of a mixed or split sentence is to "shock" or "jolt" the individual into a realization of the realities of prison life through the experience of imprisonment (Jayne, 1956:319; Kaufman, 1962:8; Hartshorne, 1959:10). For example, the United States provision under Public Law 85–741, 85th Congress, 72 Stat. 834, provides a minimum sentence of six months to be served in a county or local jail instead of federal or state institutions. This permits the offender to remain in his local community and close to his family while, at the same time, experiencing the negative aspects of incarceration.

Those opposed to mixed sentences argue that a person is either eligible for probation or he is not; prison and probation are dichotomies and cannot and should not be mixed (Campbell, 1960:12; Chandler, 1950:44; Report of the Committee on Probation, 1948:6). One spokesman for this position has pointed out ". . . that once having determined that a person can be trusted to remain in the community and can benefit most under community supervision, no appreciable benefits can be derived from committing to a short period of incarceration. . . . (Barkin, 1962:12)."

In addition, the argument is made that mixed sentences "contaminate" the individual and any chance he might have of rehabilitation. This argument suggests that any time spent in an institution is disruptive of normal therapeutic efforts which might be made in a more open setting (Chandler, 1950:44, Kaufman, 1962:8). Besides, short-term stays may even harden attitudes, expose the individual to more criminals, and make him resentful, feeling that he has served his "debt" (Chappell, 1947:32; Scudder, 1959: 12; Chandler, 1950:44).

A third argument against mixed sentences is more abstract than the first two, but along the same lines. It is held that to mix sentences is to act contrary to the stated purpose and objectives of probation; jail time is inconsistent with the philosophy of probation (President's Commission on Law Enforcement and Administration of Justice, 1967:34–35). Probation is viewed as non-punitive and any use of prison makes the work of probation officers more complex and, in the long-run, may defeat the purpose of community supervision (Scudder, 1959:12, Chappell, 1947:31). The purpose of probation is to avoid incarceration, not be a supplement to it.

Most of the debate on mixed sentencing has occurred in the United States, but as far as we know, there exists no empirical research in this country to support or reject the practice. Experimental programs have been set up to test split sentence effectiveness in Sweden, France, Norway, and the Netherlands (European Committee on Crime Problems, 1967:17–18), but statistical or empirical results are incomplete.

Christiansen and Bernsten in a study conducted in Denmark looked at short-term prisoners who were randomly placed in an intensive socio-psychological treatment group and control group. They concluded that short-term incarceration may be effective as a sanction, but only under special circumstances, for certain types of offenders, and when it is utilized as the first step in the process of resocialization (Christiansen, 1971: 291). While they did not draw any conclusions regarding the effectiveness of short-term incarceration except that the incidence of recidivism increased with the length of sentence, they did state that non-institutional treatment should be utilized if at all possible since the individual can remain in the community, maintain contacts with his family, retain his job, and avoid some of the stigma of institutionalization (Christiansen, 1971:295). This conclusion in the main supports the findings of the Small Committee of Research Workers of the Council of Europe who concluded that non-institutional commitments should be attempted and where incarceration is required, that it should be applied to only certain types of offenders, but those types are not specified (European Committee on Crime Problems, 1967:84).

Hartshorne (1959:11), a federal judge in the United States, concluded from his experiences in sentencing that such a practice of imposing short-term prison treatment should be applied only when probation is not applicable. He notes two conditions when split sentences should be used: (1) when probation is not sufficient on the merits of the case (i.e., the nature of the crime and the societal reaction to it), and (2) when the individual has already demonstrated that he has violated a probation order. In sum, previous research does not enable one to draw any definite conclusions regarding the use of split sentences as a correctional tool.

SHOCK PROBATION: THE OHIO EXPERIMENT

In July, 1965, the General Assembly of the State of Ohio passed a law providing for the early release from prison of convicted felons by placing them on probation. This law, Ohio Revised Code, 2947.06.1, made any felon eligible for early release provided he had not committed a non-probationable act in the State of Ohio. The law has become known as "shock probation" and is basically intended as a treatment tool and as a compromise between the advantages of incarceration and of probation. The procedure provides, according to the Ohio Adult Parole Authority:

1. a way for the Courts to impress offenders with the seriousness of their actions without a long prison sentence,
2. a way for the Courts to release offenders found by the institutions to be more amenable to community-based treatment than was realized by the Courts at time of sentence,
3. a way for the Courts to arrive at a just compromise between punishment and leniency in appropriate cases,
4. a way for the Courts to provide community-based treatment for rehabilitable offenders while still observing their responsibilities for imposing deterrent sentences where public policy demands it, and
5. . . . it affords the briefly incarcerated offender a protection against absorption into the "hard rock" inmate culture (Denton *et al.*, no date: 1).

Unlike the federal split sentence provision, shock probation is not part of the original sentence. According to the law, the offender is sentenced to a correctional institution (not a jail as with the federal statute) for his crime and must file a petition to the court to suspend further execution of the sentence no earlier than thirty days nor more than sixty days after the original sentence date.[1] Until the court acts upon the petition, which must be within ninety days, the defendant does not know what the length of his institutional stay will be.

---

[1] Actually, early release may also be granted by the judge upon his own initiative.

RESEARCH ON SHOCK PROBATION

The authors recently completed a research project designed to evaluate the effectiveness of the shock probation law. The sample design included all persons granted shock probation from three of Ohio's seven correctional institutions during the first full year of this legislation, 1966, and all those granted shock probation during 1970. This group is compared with a control group of persons who were eligible for the act under the Ohio law during the same period, but were not granted it. The control sample was selected by taking each eligible case before and after each shock probation case as listed in the institutional admissions record log. The study was centered in the two youth facilities (age range: 16–30) and the only female institution in the Ohio Penal System. The total sample included 1,043 cases. The number of cases placed on shock probation in 1966 was only 83; our sample was 61, or 73.5 percent. In 1970, 632 individuals were released under this legislation; our sample was 485, or 76.7 percent.

The study utilized institutional case records; all data relating to background characteristics, offense, prior record, institutional behavior, and so on were recorded for both the sample of shock probationers and the institutionalized controls. In addition, for each case, evidence of "current status" was recorded indicating whether the individual was currently on parole, on probation, successfully completed probation or parole, or failed and reincarcerated.

The effectiveness of the shock probation procedure is somewhat difficult to ascertain, particularly since 87 percent of the males and 90 percent of the females released during 1970 are currently on probation. Therefore, data regarding the outcome, or more specifically, rearrest or reincarceration, is known for only about 13 percent of the 1970 males and 10 percent of the females. Data are available for all 1966 releasees, but the total number of cases is very small.

The measure of success or failure used in this study was whether the individual was rearrested for an offense and returned to the institution or rearrested and declared a probation violator and not returned. While we provided for the possibility of rearrest without reincarceration, no such cases were found in our sample.

Table 1 shows the distribution of shock probation success and failure cases for males and females for both years. For those released in 1966, success is approximately 85 percent. This figure is close to, but slightly lower than, the official estimate of 90.2 percent issued by the Adult Parole

TABLE 1

Present Disposition of Shock Probation Cases for 1966 and 1970,
Males and Females

Sex and Year	Currently on Probation		Successes		Failures		Total	
	N	Percent	N	Percent	N	Percent	N	Percent
Males, 1966	0	—	46	85.2	8	14.8	54	100.0
Females, 1966	0	—	6	85.7	1	14.3	7	100.0
Males, 1970	385	87.3	12	2.7	44	10.0	441	100.0
Females, 1970	40	90.9	1	2.3	3	6.8	44	100.0
Total	425	77.8	65	11.9	56	10.3	546	100.0

Authority[2] or the 91.1 percent figure previously published (County News, 1970:12).

No conclusion can be reached regarding the 1970 releasees, although 10 percent of the males have already been determined to have failed and only 2.7 percent have been classified as successes and released from supervision. The figures for the females are 6.8 and 2.3 percent respectively.

Because of the small sample size over the two years studied, and because the relative difference in rates of success and failure for males and females is negligible, to facilitate analysis all successes and failures for both years were combined in order to determine what characteristics appeared to be related to success or failure. Subsequent control for both years of the sample and sex demonstrated no significant difference.

VARIABLES ASSOCIATED WITH "SUCCESS" UNDER SHOCK PROBATION TREATMENT

Those variables related to successful completion of probation after a period of short-term incarceration are in most cases the same variables associated with successful completion of regular parole (Dressler, 1969; Glaser and O'Leary, 1966:5–24). Age and personal background characteristics appear to differentiate between the groups better than most other variables (see Table 2). Clearly, the older a person is when incarcerated,

---

[2]We are grateful to Mr. James H. Calhoun, Ohio Adult Parole Authority, for providing us with this data. It should be noted, however, that the data provided is based upon voluntary reporting of the various probation departments in the 88 counties of Ohio and the exact nature of their accuracy is unknown to us.

TABLE 2

Success or Failure on Shock Probation by Age at Penal Commitment

Success-Failure	<17 N	Per-cent	18–19 N	Per-cent	20–21 N	Per-cent	22–24 N	Per-cent	25+ N	Per-cent	Total N	Per-cent
Successes	1	10.0	16	47.1	20	62.5	14	56.0	14	73.7	65	54.2
Failures	9	90.0	18	52.9	12	37.5	11	44.0	5	26.3	55[a]	45.8
Total	10	100.0	34	100.0	32	100.0	25	100.0	19	100.0	120	100.0

[a]Age at commitment was unknown for one subject.
$x^2 = 12.394$ $p = < .02$
Coefficient of Contingency = .31

the better his chances are of falling into the success category; 73.8 percent of all successes were over 20 at the time of their commitment. As a point of contrast, of all persons under 17 at the time of penal commitment, only 10.0 percent ($N = 1$) succeeded, whereas 73.7 percent of those over 25 ($N = 14$) succeeded. Statistically, the relationship between age and success was significant at the .02 level.

In addition to the age of the offender, other personal conditions appear to affect subsequent reincarceration. For example, the presence or absence of a previous police record by another member of the offender's family was significant at the .02 level. Regarding parent or sibling criminality, some 76.8 percent ($N = 43$) of the successes had no other member of their family with known police records. Of those who did have a family member in trouble, only 37.1 percent ($N = 13$) succeeded.

Regarding the individual's own criminality, the greatest percentage of successes had no known juvenile record and had only one or two prior misdemeanor or felony convictions as an adult.[3] What is important here is to note that having had *no* prior record was not a guarantee of success. This is perhaps due to the selectivity process involved in issuing a shock probation order by the court. Since shock probation is not a first offender act, only 9.2 percent of all shock cases studied had no known prior record; of those for which outcome was known ($N = 11$), only 18.2 percent successfully completed probation. On the other hand, 68.7 percent ($N = 46$) of those with one or two priors succeeded, while 38–42 percent of those with a larger number of priors succeeded (see Table 3). In this sense, shock probation seems to be most effective for those who have had some previous

---

[3]Given the institutional records used and the discrepancy between States regarding offense classification, it was not possible to distinguish between felony and misdemeanor cases.

altercation with the law, but have not become part of the "serious" criminal element.

Finally, success was most often found among those who had some outside attachments or commitments which created demands for non-criminal behavior. Those, for example, who were married and had dependents were more likely to succeed than the single, unattached offender. Marital status was significant at the .01 level and most significant for the 22–24 year old group. Some 73.7 percent (N=28) of the married group succeeded where 45.1 percent (N=37) of the single group succeeded. Single included the never married, widowed, and divorced. No linear relationship was found between the number of dependents and success, but rather, success was most probable for those with 1–3 dependents. Those with less and those with more were more likely to fail. This indicates, along with marital status, that external commitments may generate a sense of responsibility or other commitments of conformity. If the number of dependents is low, there appears to be little such impact; when they are high, the burden may be too much. More research is needed in this area to determine the most functional amount of commitment necessary to impede rearrest.

Offense did not prove to be a significant variable relative to success except for violations of the State narcotic laws. The difference was not statistically significant, however. Only 38.5 percent of those convicted of narcotic violations were in the success category; 50–60 percent successes were recorded for personal, property, or fraud violators. No explanation can be offered, but such a finding may reflect the nature of the narcotic violator as different from "traditional" offenders—the nature of the sub-culture to which he returns, the temptations to recommit his act, and the relative ineffectiveness of conventional imprisonment in the treatment of this offender.

Finally, it should be noted that a number of variables were tested

TABLE 3

Success or Failure on Shock Probation by Prior Adult Arrests

Success-Failure	None		1–2		3–5		6+		Total	
	N	Per-cent	N	Per-cent	N	Per-cent	N	Per-cent	N	Per-cent
Successes	2	18.2	46	68.7	10	41.7	7	38.9	65	54.2
Failures	9	81.8	21	31.3	14	58.3	11	61.1	55[a]	45.8
Total	11	100.0	67	100.0	24	100.0	18	100.0	120	100.0

[a]Prior adult arrest record was unknown for one subject.
$x^2 = 14.607$ $p = < .01$
Coefficient of Contingency = .33

which showed little or no difference between the successes and failures. Variables such as race, social class, father's occupation or education, I.Q., legal residence, or previous employment were of little value in distinguishing between the groups.

CONCLUSION

One must, of course, recognize the limitations of the data just presented, but they do indicate that shock probation as a mechanism of crime control does hold some promise. It is not clear whether the procedure is more effective than probation alone, but as a technique, one cannot dismiss a success rate of 85 percent. The 1966 sample, the first year the law was implemented, may be biased and the 1970 sample may be incomplete, but the indication is that success and failure are not evenly distributed. Instead, success is concentrated in that group for which the law intended—the young, but not juvenile, the previously convicted, but not hard core, offender. In short, it appears this is the offender most in need of the short-term prison experience and the potential "shock" value of such an experience.

We would suggest that our data and findings should be considered preliminary. For more definitive results, we would recommend further research with a larger sample size at some future date after more time has elapsed since release of the 1970 cohort. What is also needed is research which is capable of comparing the "success-failure" rates of straight probationers compared with shock probationers. Further, a research design is required which explores in detail the selection process which determines who gets shock probation. And finally, one needs to investigate what aspects of incarceration, if any, actually affect the variables which indicate success. It may be entirely a delusion to believe that the effects of incarceration are operating at all. Perhaps, the external personal, social, and criminological characteristics of the offender account for all of the variance and success or failure is solely a function of those variables.

We are in a position to argue that if incarceration is used as a mechanism of social control, that for certain offenders its use be limited in time. Short-term incarceration coupled with the supervision of probation appears to not only be effective, but humanitarian as well. For those with the characteristics given above, it is also probably a very good risk. We would caution, however, that shock probation requires a much more thorough-going empirical analysis and interpretation, particularly as its use begins to expand throughout the correctional system.

REFERENCES

BARKIN, E. N., "Sentencing the Adult Offender," *Federal Probation*, 26 (1962), 11–16.

BATES, S., "When Is Probation Not Probation?" *Federal Probation*, 24 (1960), 13–20.

CALDWELL, M. G., "Preview of a New Type of Probation Study Made in Alabama," *Federal Probation*, 15 (1951), 3–12.

CALIFORNIA STATE ASSEMBLY, *Deterrent Effects of Criminal Sanctions*. Sacramento: Assembly of the State of California, 1968.

CAMPBELL, W. J., *Probation and Parole, Selected Readings*. New York: John Wiley and Sons, Inc., 1960.

CHANDLER, H. P., "The Future of Federal Probation," *Federal Probation*, 14 (1950), 41–48.

CHAPPELL, R. A., "Federal Probation Service: Its Growth and Progress," *Federal Probation*, 11 (1947), 29–34.

CHRISTIANSEN, K. O., "Non-Institutional Care of Offenders in Practice: The Danish Experience," *International Annals of Criminology*, 10 (1971), 283–309.

COUNTY NEWS, "Shock Treatment Revisited," *County News*, November 1970, pp. 12f.

DENTON, G. F., J. M. PETTIBONE, and H. WALKER, *Shock Probation: A Proven Program of Early Release from Institutional Confinement*. Columbus, Ohio: Adult Parole Authority. (mimeo)

DRESSLER, D., *Practice and Theory of Probation and Parole*. New York: Columbia University Press, 1969.

ENGLAND, R., "What is Responsible for Satisfactory Probation and Post-Probation Outcome?" *Journal of Criminal Law, Criminology and Police Science*, 47 (1957), 667–76.

EUROPEAN COMMITTEE ON CRIME PROBLEMS, *Probation and After-care in Certain European Countries*. Strasbourg: Council of Europe, 1964.

———, *Short-term Methods of Treatment for Young Offenders*. Strasbourg: Council of Europe, 1967.

FLORIDA DIVISION OF CORRECTIONS, Impact of the Gideon Decisions upon Crime and Sentencing in Florida: A Study of Recidivism and Socio-Cultural Change. Research Monograph #2, 1966.

GLASER, D., and V. O'LEARY, *Personal Characteristics of Parole Outcome*. Washington: U.S. Government Printing Office, 1966.

HARTSHORNE, R., "The 1958 Federal Split-Sentence Law," *Federal Probation*, 23 (1959), 9–12.

JAYNE, I. W., "The Purpose of the Sentence," *NPPA Journal*, 2 (1956), 315–19.

JOHNSON, E. H., *Crime, Correction, and Society.* Homewood, Ill.: Dorsey Press, 1968.

JOINT COMMISSION ON CORRECTIONAL MANPOWER AND TRAINING, *Perspectives on Correctional Manpower and Training.* Washington: Joint Commission on Correctional Manpower and Training, 1970.

KAUFMAN, I. R., "Enlightened Sentences through Improved Technique," *Federal Probation*, 26 (1962), 3–10.

MASTER, J. M., "The Relation of Judicial Selection to Successful Probation," *Federal Probation*, 12 (1948), 36–41.

PRESIDENT'S COMMISSION ON LAW ENFORCEMENT AND ADMINISTRATION OF JUSTICE, *Task Force Report: Corrections.* Washington: U.S. Government Printing Office, 1967.

REPORT OF THE COMMITTEE ON PROBATION WITH SPECIAL REFERENCE TO JUVENILE DELINQUENCY, *Federal Probation*, 12 (1948), 3–9.

SCUDDER, K. J., "In Opposition to Probation with a Jail Sentence," *Federal Probation*, 23 (1959), 12–17.

20

Work Release—
A Two-Pronged Effort

Serapio R. Zalba

In contemporary America, two positive purposes guide the societal response to deviant behavior: protection of society-at-large and rehabilitation of the transgressor. How rationally these goals are pursued is another matter. Taking them as given, we may ask, in respect to the hundreds of thousands of our fellow citizens sent to jail each year, "What should we do that will afford us protection against their antisocial acts and yet will rehabilitate them so that they can be happy (for their sakes), law-abiding (for our sakes), and productive (for both our sakes)?"

The work-release program (also called *work furlough, day parole, out-mate program, private work-release, intramural private employment,* and *semi-liberté*),[1] which combines incarceration in the local jail with work on regular jobs in the community, is an attempt to meet the above requirements.

The question of how the offender can make best use of his time is basic. More often than not, the answers to it have typified the confusion and

Reprinted with permission of the National Council on Crime and Delinquency from *Crime and Delinquency*, October 1967, pp. 506–12.

[1]Stanley E. Grupp, "Work Release and the Misdemeanant," *Federal Probation,* June 1965.

conflict of a society that wants rehabilitation but is still struggling with its impulses for vengeance.

As early as 1873 the Wisconsin State Board of Charities and Reform expressed its concern about the lack of constructive programming for its county-jail inmates in the following declaration:

> Here are scores and hundreds of men, some of them young and in vigorous health, who are compelled to spend from a few days to a year, and sometimes two years, in absolute idleness, while the taxpayers of the various counties are supporting them.
>
> What a waste of labor! What an injury to the men themselves to keep them in a state of enforced idleness! What an unwise expenditure of public funds to support healthy, able-bodied men in such idleness![2]

This criticism of local correctional practice is still valid today, despite the long experience in this country (since 1913, when the first enabling legislation was passed in Wisconsin) with day parole of county-jail prisoners so that they might pursue regular employment in the community.[3] Although work-release has existed in the United States for over fifty years, a trend toward its wider adoption has developed only recently. Of the twenty-four states which were utilizing the concept in 1965, nineteen had adopted it after 1956. It was not until 1965 that Congress passed legislation authorizing work-release programing for federal prisoners.[4] And official adoption of the work-release concept in a state does not necessarily mean actual statewide use. For instance, in California, considered by some to have one of the more active programs, only five of the fifty-eight counties have put work-furlough programs into operation.

The basic meaning of the work-release approach was expressed as follows by Wisconsin State Senator Henry Huber, the father of the idea:

> Committing a man to jail with nothing to employ his time defeats the ends of humanity more often than advancing it by depriving his family of its breadwinner. Under the proposed [work-release] law he is shown the error of his ways, given his sentence, and kept employed so his family is not reduced to want.[5]

Traditional incarceration punishes both the offender and society. The offender loses his freedom and his job, and he may also be fined; society is required to pay the cost of his keep, treatment, and supervision, and it

---

[2]"Private Employment for County Jail Inmates," State Department of Public Welfare, Division of Corrections, Madison, Wis., 1957.

[3]*Ibid.*

[4]Edward V. Long, "The Prisoners Rehabilitation Act of 1965," *Federal Probation*, December 1965. At least twelve other countries have some equivalent to work-release; see Grupp, *supra* note 1.

[5]*Supra* note 2.

may also have to support his family through public assistance of some kind[6] in addition to incurring losses to the economy in manpower, buying power, and taxes.

The psychological losses are equally damaging. Prevented from supporting his family financially, he is also deprived of the normal parental role and cannot support it affectionally.[7] Withdrawing the opportunity and responsibility for performing the major adult-role tasks in our society is not a constructive act, yet it is the most frequent official response to crime in the U.S. today.

The social-psychological and the economic aspects of work-release are intimately related;[8] both must be considered in evaluating it as an alternative to traditional incarceration.

CORRECTIONAL TREATMENT

Some external control, such as institutionalization, is frequently necessary for the person whose previous behavior has been extremely unacceptable or unpredictable, especially if he has a prior history of physical violence. At the same time, along with attempts in the protected and structured environment to inculcate new patterns of social behavior and personal adjustment to social norms, he needs the opportunity for practicing adequate social performance in the "real" outside world. Ultimately the resocialization of the offender will be hampered unless adequate opportunities for appropriate social performance and autonomy of action are provided before he is finally released to the free community through discharge or parole.

Most correctional programs, however, follow the course of either complete incarceration or relatively free life in the community and ignore another alternative—the use of institutional social control and noninstitutional life at the same time. The socialization process followed in our society in the rearing of children makes use of both components. The child spends part of his time in a structured, institutional, supervised setting, at home with his parents, for example, and part of the time away, with peers, in the neighborhood, playgrounds, etc.

It is in this respect that the work-release plan makes a therapeutic

[6]Pauline Morris, *Prisoners and Their Families* (London: George Allen & Unwin, 1965); Serapio R. Zalba, *Women Prisoners and Their Families* (Los Angeles: Delmar Press, 1964).

[7]Columbus B. Hopper, "Conjugal Visiting at the Mississippi State Penitentiary," *Federal Probation*, June 1965.

[8]S. M. Miller, "Poverty and Inequality in America: Implications for the Social Services," *Child Welfare*, November 1963.

contribution by releasing the offender from the county jail to go to work on a regular job in the community but to return to the institution at the end of the working day. *Some* needed institutional control is provided, and, concurrently, *some* opportunity is given to the offender to perform in socially desired roles and ways in the free community.

WORK-RELEASE PROGRAMING

The following description of typical work-furlough programs is based on those in Wisconsin and in Marin, Orange, and Santa Clara counties in California.[9]

Most programs are for misdemeanants sentenced to county jails.[10] The misdemeanant may be specifically committed to the program by the sentencing judge, may be placed on work-release by a county parole board, or may be automatically eligible for it (as in Wisconsin) if sentenced to "hard labor."

The offenses committed by work-release prisoners cover a wide range. The most common are nonsupport, driving with a revoked license, and drunk driving, but some programs place offenders convicted of narcotics violations, burglary, armed robbery, and even sex crimes, thus emphasizing the individual's potential for adequate performance on the work-furlough program rather than the specific crime committed.

If the furloughman already has a job, he continues his employment, leaving the jail during his working hours and returning after work. If he has no job, an attempt is made to find one for him. In some cases men are released from the jail to seek employment. In Marin County, 65 percent of the furloughmen retained the jobs they had before being sentenced; 30 percent worked on jobs found for them by the staff; 5 percent were self-employed.

Some furloughmen hold a number of part-time jobs or may even hold a full-time job *and* a part-time job. In a very few cases, an offender with limited employability—for example, a deteriorated chronic alcoholic—may be allowed to take work almost on a volunteer basis and accept donations

---

[9]*Supra* note 2; "Wisconsin Jails 1952–1962, A Decade of Progress," State Department of Public Welfare, Madison, Wis., 1962; Walter H. Busher, "Dividends—Furlough Style: The Work Furlough Program in Marin County," Marin County Probation Department, San Rafael, Calif., 1962; Memo of 7-28-65 from Walter H. Busher to John D. Kavanaugh and George Gaehle, Marin County Probation Department; David R. McMillan, "Work Furlough for the Jailed Prisoner," *Federal Probation*, March 1965; letter of 11-9-65 from V. A. Verhurst, Detention Supervisor, Wisconsin Division of Corrections; letter of 11-3-65 from Joseph R. Silver, Executive Director, Northern California Service League.

[10]The maximum county-jail sentence for most misdemeanors in most states is one year.

for his labor, the major benefit lying in performance of a useful activity rather than in financial gain to the offender or the county.

Payment is generally in accord with current rates paid to others on similar jobs in the same company and the same community. Labor in Wisconsin and California is highly unionized, and union scales are generally adhered to. The average wage of Huber Law participants in Wisconsin is reported as $20 a day. There is always the possibility that unscrupulous persons administering work-release programs will conspire to provide labor at less than current market wages for a fee or kickback. It is usually avoided by giving the worker the right to change jobs or quit if he feels he is being exploited. Some sheriffs in Wisconsin set a $1 minimum hourly wage for work-release employment.

Transportation to and from the job can be a source of difficulty, but the offender's ingenuity and desire generally triumph over often awkward circumstances. Some furloughmen walk to work, some ride a bicycle, and some are picked up at the jail by the employer and driven back after work.

Programs differ in the amount of responsibility given offenders in handling their own earnings. In Wisconsin the furloughman's earnings are paid directly to the sheriff's department for fiscal management. In contrast, in Marin County the paycheck is turned over directly to the worker, who then cashes it and brings to the work-release officer the amount agreed upon for reimbursement to the county for his keep, payment of fines and restitution, and family support (unless he sends his support directly to the family). Personal expense money is kept by the furloughman, and the balance is held in trust pending final release from custody. The amount charged to furloughmen for keep, or administrative costs of the program, varies from program to program. In Wisconsin the charge ranges from $1.50 to $3.23 a day.

During his nonwork hours the furloughman generally remains in the jail, but the administrator of the work-release program has a great deal of latitude: he may allow him to attend night classes in the community, go for medical or psychiatric treatment, etc. If the furloughman works near his family home, he may be allowed to eat his lunches there and pick up his personal laundry. This allows for some maintenance of family contact and solidarity.

RATE OF USE

The geographic areas included in this study vary greatly in the extent to which they use work-release. The most recent data available (see Table 1) show that Marin County had a rate of 1.54 furloughmen per 100,000 population, while Orange County, almost five times as populous, had an average rate of only .24 per 100,000. (Comparative arrest and incarceration rates for the various jurisdictions were not available to the writer.)

EARNINGS AND DISBURSEMENTS

In Wisconsin, furloughmen earned a total of $2,800,000 during the years 1955 to 1960; the sum in 1960 was $633,000. In Marin County, the annual average for the years 1959 to 1965 was $46,000; in Orange County, the annual average for the years 1962 to 1964 was $122,000. In Santa Clara County, the total earned by persons in the program in eight years (1957 to 1965) came to over $1,375,000, averaging $486 for each furloughman; the total earned in 1965 alone was $243,000.

The disbursement of funds varies from program to program. The major categories of disbursement are (a) reimbursement to the county for partial cost of room and board and administration of the program, (b) family support, (c) personal expenses, (d) fines and restitution, and (e) savings kept for the prisoner until his release.

As can be seen in Table 2, the major item of disbursement from earnings is family support. From a rehabilitation point of view this is desirable: responsible performance of the parental and adult roles is a major objective of the program. The proportion of earnings allocated for this purpose ranges from about one-third (in Wisconsin) to about two-thirds (in Orange County).

The second largest item is reimbursement to the county (for keep and administrative costs of the program). From a rehabilitation point of view this is also desirable. Some advanced European correctional institutions and programs—e.g., Holland's Van der Hoeven Clinic—require the inmate to work and pay for his keep *and* the cost of his psychological treatment.

TABLE 1
Number on Work-Release

Political Unit	Population[a]	Number of Furloughmen per Year	Rate per 100,000 Population
Marin County	146,820	226[b]	1.54
Santa Clara County	642,315	583[c]	.91
Wisconsin	3,951,777	2,281[d]	.58
Orange County	703,925	168[e]	.24

[a]1960 census [b]1963–64 [c]1965 [d]1960 [e]yearly av. 1962–64.

TABLE 2

Disbursement of Work-Release Earnings

Political Unit	Total Earnings	Family Support	Reimbursement to County	Personal Expense	Fines & Restitution	Savings & Misc.
Wisconsin	$633,000	36%	27%	5%	14%	18%
Santa Clara County	$243,000	44%	25%	15%	1%	15%
Marin County	$ 46,000	51%	20%	11%	6%	12%
Orange County	$122,000	68%	17%	?	?	?

Personal expenses and fines and restitution play a less important part in the program. Savings held in trust for the furloughman until his release are important from a rehabilitation as well as an economic point of view. Everyone working in correction is well aware of the social and psychological problems faced by the offender released from an institution with little or no money. The releasee is much better prepared to face the stigma and readjustment problems that will confront him if he is bolstered by adequate funds and has a job awaiting him.

FAILURES

Work-release programs are not free of failures. Though the vast majority of furloughmen respond positively to the trust placed in them, some escape, and some violate other rules. Escape rates vary from less than 1 percent (Orange and Marin counties) to 12 percent (Milwaukee County, Wis.).[11] Those furloughmen removed from the program for violation other than escape were involved in such behavior as drinking, returning to the jail late, etc. Escapes and violations of institutional rules occur, of course, even in counties without work-release programs.

A TWO-PRONGED EFFORT

Walter H. Busher, work-release administrator for Marin County, offers the following cautions to a political jurisdiction considering the development of a work-release program:

---

[11]Eighty percent of the Milwaukee escapees were apprehended and returned to jail.

TABLE 3
Work-Release Escapes and Violations

Political Unit	No. of Furloughmen	Escapes No.	%	Violations No.	%
Orange County	350	1	.3%	18	5.1%
Marin County	450	3	.7%	40	8.8%
Wisconsin (except Milwaukee County)	2,082	37	1.8%	36	1.7%
Milwaukee County	576	71	12.3%	87	15.1%
Totals	3,458	112	3.2%	181	5.2%

1. Do not institute a program unless the sheriff is willing to assure his fullest cooperation.

2. Do not expect existing staff to absorb the program into the existing workload.

3. Require regular reports from the program's administrator.

4. Do not expect the program to reach full bloom suddenly.

5. Do not become panicked by the first adverse experience.

6. *Finally, do not let the attractive financial aspects of the program— which can be considerable—overshadow the fact that a work-release program is basically a device to strengthen society by improving the quality of citizenship of some of its members.*

Even while urging caution, Busher reports great enthusiasm for the program in his area by the offenders and their families, the probation department, jail personnel (who often seek jobs for the furloughmen *on their own time*), the courts, and the unions. The majority of the furloughmen are wage-earners (90 percent in Marin County) rather than salaried employees; most of the furloughmen in the highly unionized geographic areas discussed in this paper are union members.

An unexpected outcome of some programs has been that, as the judges have become more and more aware of the practicability of releasing offenders under supervision, they have placed larger numbers directly on probation rather than committing them to jail. The work-release program in Marin County, for example, is becoming smaller and smaller—paradoxically, a sign of its success.

Widespread interest in the "halfway house" concept is evidence that we are aware of the difficulties of re-entry into the free society from institutional life. We now face an equally important issue: man cannot be separated from the economic life of his society without loss to both himself *and* society.

Work-release has demonstrated that it can provide (a) institutional supervision and (b) opportunity for offenders to perform the major societal economic roles. It thus offers a two-pronged effort to deal with the rehabilitation of offenders.

21

The Continuum of Corrections

H. G. Moeller

There are growing indications of the need for a thoroughgoing reassessment and realignment of correctional services in the United States. For fifty years, there have been continuing efforts to build, strengthen, and develop the three principal components of the correctional system. Probation, institutional services, and parole have, typically, grown concurrently, and frequently have been actively in competition for scarce resources. In some few instances, notably in the state of Wisconsin, the interdependence of these services has been recognized in the creation of organizational structures for the coordination of services. But, as the President's Commission on Law Enforcement and Administration of Justice (National Crime Commission) has emphasized, the criminal-justice system in the United States is badly fragmented. The extent of the fragmentation is reflected in our inability to accumulate even the most rudimentary base-line statistical information on the work-load of the correctional agencies and services of the country.

IMPACT OF STUDIES BY NATIONAL COMMISSIONS

The National Crime Commission has focused attention upon the application of systems analysis to the study of corrections within the broader framework of the administration of justice. Growing out of the work of the

From "The Continuum of Corrections," *The Annals*, 381 (January 1969), 82–88. Reprinted by permission.

Commission has come the enactment of the Omnibus Crime Control and Safe Streets Act of 1968. Under its provisions, funds will be made available to states and to local governments to develop comprehensive law enforcement plans. In the development of such plans, an opportunity will present itself to examine the kinds of correctional services needed at each important decision-point in the criminal-justice process. Such planning must achieve a more rational approach to the allocation of resources to make certain that services are integrated and that the various options available to the decision-maker are appropriately used. Correctional planning will encompass every activity impinging on the offender from his introduction into the system until his discharge. It will seek to create a continuum of services related to his needs from the time of his arrest to his eventual reintegration in society.

Those who do the planning must take into account the fact that there have been many significant developments in correctional practice which have blurred the sharp lines of jurisdiction which hitherto existed between probation, institutional services, and parole, and which in themselves forecast the possibility of a new alignment of services. The introduction of institutional work-release programs; the experimentation with community-treatment centers; the emergence of community-based institutions; and the increasing use of institutional furloughs have, singly and in combination, introduced new dimensions to correctional practice, and provide a strong rationale for organizational change.

These new correctional tools have not been introduced independently of other major developments within the larger society. One of the most important influences contributing to the change was the work of the Joint Commission on Mental Illness and Health, which began in 1955. The Commission's findings, published in 1960 in its report *Action for Mental Health,* provided for that field a blueprint which furnished important guidelines for the development of new services. It was this report which articulated the importance of assisting the patient to maintain himself in the community in a normal manner: to minimize the regressive effects of institutionalization and to provide a wide range of supportive aftercare services—day hospitals, night hospitals, aftercare clinics, rehabilitation centers, work services, former patient groups, and the like.

The Commission's insistence on a broad range of community services to reinforce aftercare of mental patients had obvious implications for the correctional system. Before 1960, corrections had developed no substantial aftercare services and had limited access to community resources supportive to the needs of the probationer or the parolee. In many instances, such care has been difficult to obtain because of restrictive intake policies or practices of welfare agencies, or because these agencies assigned a higher priority to helping nonoffenders.

Recently, agency policies have been broadened and eligibility standards modified to expand the range of services available to the offender
group. For example, the Rehabilitation Services Agency of the Department
of Health, Education, and Welfare has increasingly made resources available to offenders. The Department of Labor has mounted a new program
which will assure manpower-training services for offenders who are among
the hard-core unemployed, as well as specialized programs of employment
placement. New community mental health services which are in the process
of development have shown special interest in the organization of programs
supportive of the needs of persons under probation and parole supervision.

The availability of new public services to the offender, of which those
cited represent only a few illustrations, has been matched by other developments in the private sector of the economy. Work opportunities for the
probationer and the parolee in private industry are increasingly available.
The National Association of Manufacturers has publicized the importance
of work-release programs. Industry has co-operated with correctional authorities in introducing into institutions training programs specifically designed to provide the offender with skills which are scarce in the labor
market. An ever widening range of training opportunities in the community
are being opened to offenders.

COMMUNITY-BASED PROGRAMS

These developments, hastily sketched, provide the background within
which the new continuum of correctional services remains to be developed.
Concurrently with the changes described, corrections has developed new
community-based programs. The introduction of the community treatment
center, or halfway house, in its present form, is less than ten years old, and
the possible uses of such centers have scarcely begun to be explored. The
conceptual framework for the centers was clearly expressed by the Corrections Task Force of the President's Commission on Law Enforcement and
Administration of Justice:

> The general underlying premise for the new directions in cor-
> rections is that crime and delinquency are symptoms of failures and
> disorganization of the community as well as of individual offenders.
> In particular, these failures are seen as depriving offenders of contact
> with the institutions of society that are basically responsible for as-
> suring the development of law-abiding conduct.
> The task of corrections therefore includes building or rebuild-
> ing solid ties between the offender and the community, integrating
> or reintegrating the offender into community life—restoring family
> ties, obtaining employment and education, securing in the larger

sense a place for the offender in the routine functioning of society. . . . This requires not only efforts toward changing the individual offender, which has been the almost exclusive focus of rehabilitation, but also the mobilization and change of the community and its institutions.[1]

If the offender can be positively motivated to learn new skills and to develop new and positive social relationships, the task which remains is to provide a linkage with a noncriminal environment. This is a task which he usually cannot handle by himself. The new assignment for corrections is to open doors to services which, in the past, have been denied to offenders or which they may not have known about. Such an undertaking is more than the creation of formal working relationships between the correctional service and business, industry, organized labor, civic groups, churches, schools, and other community agencies. It requires the correctional service to develop the knowledge and skill to assist the offender to avail himself of the array of services to gain the continuing support he needs to maintain himself in the society. Another way of saying this is that many offenders need help in finding access to the opportunity structure which they have previously lacked or have been denied.

A major function of the community center, as now designed, is to provide a residential setting, to which offenders may be referred after release from the correctional institution. The center mediates those services needed by the offender restored to society. The resident of such centers also receives from their staff day-to-day assistance in facing the crises arising during his effort to make adjustments to his job, his responsibilities to his family, and his duties as a citizen. The main thrust of the center must be outward. It is not a sanctuary providing the insulation of the traditional institution. Rather, it provides planned access to situations in which the resident can test his skills and measure his expectations against reality.

During the last five years, the numbers of such community-based programs has grown steadily. The organization of the International Association of Halfway Houses took place in 1963. This Association now boasts a registry listing some two hundred public and private facilities, other than those for alcoholics and mental patients. This number will expand rapidly as states implement recently enacted legislation authorizing the creation of such facilities.

The community centers which have been developed so far serve primarily the needs of offenders released from institutions. But the optimism which has surrounded the development of these facilities has stimulated interest in the creation of other models. There has been some experimenta-

---

[1]U.S., President's Commission on Law Enforcement and Administration of Justice (National Crime Commission), *Task Force Report: Corrections* (Washington, D.C.: U.S. Government Printing Office, 1967), p. 7.

tion in the use of centers for the study and diagnosis of persons awaiting sentence; there are some indications that such service to the courts can help improve decision-making in the imposition of sentence. Another potential use of the center would be to provide supportive services to probationers who, for want of a satisfactory probation plan, might otherwise be committed to an institution. Legislation is currently pending in the Congress which would permit the use of centers operated by the Federal Bureau of Prisons for some classes of probationers. Other jurisdictions are using centers as resources to which parolees under supervision are referred for re-planning as an alternative to parole revocation.

Experience with the use of centers for transitional support of offenders foreshadows the coming of the model community-based correctional institution which was projected by the Task Force on Corrections of the National Crime Commission. This model would provide an alternative to conventional imprisonment. Its program would rely almost exclusively upon existing services in the community. Community agencies would assume the tasks of training, education, and resocialization. As in existing models, the institution staff would identify both the individual needs of the resident and the community services related to his requirements. The staff would induce him to use community resources and would encourage him to assume personal responsibility for his choices and decisions. Work in the development of the design of a community-based program is already well advanced. With funds provided by the Ford Foundation, the State of California has invested several months in the design of such a project, which the California Youth Authority will implement.

Work-Release Legislation

Work-release, or community work programs have already profoundly affected traditional correctional regimes. These programs trace their origin to the 1913 statute in Wisconsin which authorized judges and magistrates, in co-operation with sheriffs in charge of local jails, to impose conditional sentences for specified misdemeanors. The purpose of the law was to enable offenders to work on their jobs in the community while serving short sentences in jail. In 1957, North Carolina adapted the principles of the Wisconsin statute to felony offenders, under limited conditions. Maryland and Michigan subsequently enacted similar laws. In 1965, Congress enacted the Federal Prisoner Rehabilitation Act which included provisions for work-release, short-term furloughs, and transfer of adult offenders to community-treatment centers.

Twenty-five states have adopted work-release legislation during the last three years. In several jurisdictions, the management of the program is the exclusive responsibility of the department of corrections. In others, the affirmative recommendation of the sentencing judge or the concurrence of the paroling authority is required. The most flexible statute enacted was that adopted by the Congress of the United States, and several states have used it as a model. The statute provides:

> The Attorney General may extend the limits of the place of confinement of a prisoner as to whom there is reasonable cause to believe he will honor this trust, by authorizing him, under prescribed conditions, to . . .
> 1. visit a specifically designated place or places for a period not to exceed thirty days and return to the same or another institution or facility. An extension of limits may be granted only to permit a visit to a dying relative, attendance at the funeral of a relative, the obtaining of medical services not otherwise available, the contacting of prospective employers, or for any other compelling reason consistent with the public interest; or
> 2. work at paid employment or participate in a training program in the community on a voluntary basis while continuing as a prisoner of the institution or facility to which he is committed, ...
> The willful failure of a prisoner to remain within the extended limits of his confinement, or to return within the time prescribed, to an institution or facility, designated by the Attorney General, shall be deemed an escape from the custody of the Attorney General.[2]

The Congress clearly intended that work-release be a correctional tool to be administered on a selective and informed basis by the executive branch of the government. The program is not a substitute for probation or parole. Nor is it designed as a part of an internal system of punishment and reward. While it provides offenders with an opportunity to contribute to the support of dependents, it was not intended as an obligatory means of offsetting the costs of public welfare payments to families. It will succeed to the extent that it is used for specific purposes and as a means to achieve the correction of the offender. Work-release is oriented toward the offender's discharge. It may provide a prerelease transitional experience leading to increasing levels of skill and personal responsibility. It affords an opportunity to test new work skills in the community. It may supplement institutional educational and training programs. The participant may contribute to the needs of dependents or save a nest egg for release. Sometimes his earnings may be used to make restitution or pay debts. His response to the program can provide the paroling authority with a practical measure of his readiness for release. Finally, the program can reduce the risks and

---

[2]U.S., Congress, House, Public Law 89–176, 89th Cong., 1st Sess., 1965, H.R. 6964 to amend Section 4082, Title 18, U.S.C.

fears both of the offender and of the community during the critical period of adjustment immediately after imprisonment.

There are a number of side-benefits accompanying a well-managed work-release program in a community which has been adequately prepared to participate. The time and care devoted to the preparation of the community is of critical importance, as is the willingness of the correctional service to keep the community fully informed of the program outcome. As he becomes directly involved with offenders on their jobs and in training situations, the informed citizen develops a better understanding of their problems and their potentialities. He also becomes more supportive of correctional efforts. So far as the offender is concerned, work-release provides him with the opportunity to associate with stable fellow workers and to gain their acceptance on his own merits. These associations contribute to an improved climate for the ultimate reintegration of offenders into the community.

Short-term Furloughs

The furlough is another approach to the extension of the limits of confinement. The federal statute enumerates several specific purposes for which unsupervised absences from an institution may be authorized. Serious family emergencies, the search for work, and medical services not provided by the institutions are specified as legitimate purposes for furloughs. But the law recognizes other "compelling reasons consistent with the public interest." So far, the use of the authority by federal institutions has been limited to the functions specifically enumerated in the law. The community centers, however, take advantage of the provisions of the furlough statute to enable residents who have demonstrated their stability to spend additional time with their families during the period immediately before their discharge. Wider uses of the furlough provisions remain to be explored as correctional managers gain greater experience with them.

PROGRAM-EVALUATION

The extent to which these measures have contributed to the correction of the offender and his reintegration in society remains in doubt. Despite the general enthusiasm with which the National Crime Commission applauded the establishment of new community-based programs and encouraged their extension, there is little hard evidence that any of the programs have achieved the objectives which have been sought. The lack of such data is partly a function of the short period of time in which these programs have been in operation. It is also a function of the lack of resources for program-evaluation existing across the entire spectrum of correctional activity. One small fragment of research growing out of the Bureau of Prisons' community-center experience may have significance. It suggests that among offenders who have been selected for centers in the past, certain groups of participants appear to achieve higher levels of success in the program and after return to the community. The finding is one which must, for many reasons, be accepted as tentative, but it tends to give added importance to the recent efforts in the Federal Prison System, and in some state systems, to develop diagnostic typologies with which the relevance of specific program strategies may be tested. As in other correctional systems, work has been in progress for some months in the Federal Prison System to computerize information about the prison population to provide a more adequate base for the study of the results of program-participation. The collection of data on the outcome of community-based programs is proceeding concurrently and will eventually provide a base for the critical evaluation of the new correctional methods.

Despite the absence of validated findings, the experience of the Bureau of Prisons encourages the hope that the community-based programs can contribute to the reduction of recidivism among a substantial proportion of participants. Program-managers observe higher levels of job stability among former work-releasees. Center-directors, through their informal intelligence systems, report generally high levels of success among offenders who have developed meaningful ties in the community, but there is also a general feeling of discouragement about the lack of success with rootless nonresidents who are referred to centers in the absence of other resources. Nonetheless, there is a continuing need for data to assist the manager in identifying the groups for whom the community programs have the greatest value.

The numbers of participants in the Bureau's community programs indicate what may occur when states implement the new statutes which have been enacted. Between October 1965 and March 1968, nearly four thousand inmates were involved in work- and study-release programs. Of this total, 65 percent successfully completed their programs. The gross earnings accumulated by the participants totaled $3,814,384. The daily average number of work-releases is now approximately five hundred, while the number of residents in community centers during the course of 1968 will exceed 1,200. Thus, a program which began with three small community centers in 1961 has increased until the projections for the current year indicate that some 14 percent of all federal releasees will have been participants either in work-release or community-center programs or both.

ASSIGNMENT OF RESPONSIBILITY

As community-based correctional programs have been launched in various jurisdictions, issues have inevitably arisen about where they properly "belong" in existing organizational structures. Protagonists for probation and parole, the traditional community-oriented correctional programs, have sometimes insisted that they should be assigned the responsibility for the new services. In a few instances, the situation has been compromised. Some states, as indicated earlier, have divided responsibility for the administration of work-release between institutional and paroling authorities. In a few jurisdictions, both probation and parole authorities are busily developing plans for the independent establishment of community-treatment centers.

Unfortunately, this debate regarding the assignment of responsibility for the administration of community correctional services ignores the central question: How does the local community or the state organize its resources to assure the delivery of appropriate services to the offender regardless of his legal status? Are the distinctions between the needs of probationers and parolees so sharp that a separate system of services is required by each group? What really distinguishes the needs of the probationer or the parolee from those of the committed offender for whom the limits of confinement have been extended? Correctional planners must address these questions in designing a comprehensive system of correctional services.

One group of planners, the New York's Governor's Special Committee on Criminal Offenders, published a preliminary report in June 1968. The report proposes the organization of postadjudicatory treatment services on the basis of the function to be served—rather than upon the basis of labels used for court purposes. It recommends the administration of all services to individuals convicted of antisocial behavior through a single unified agency—a Department of Rehabilitative Services. It proposes to eliminate probation, correction, and parole as separate concepts. It recommends the organization of treatment services to permit a person's program to be carried out on a continuum from adjudication to discharge, whether field supervision or confinement, or both, are used in the program.

In New Jersey, a Joint Legislative Committee to Study Crime and the System of Criminal Justice has also issued a recent report. This study recommends the creation of a New Jersey Department of Criminal Justice which "will span the entire system" of criminal justice. The report proposes that "all convicted offenders, adult, juvenile, male, female, long-term, short-term should be held or supervised under the custody of the Commissioner of Criminal Justice." The report adds: "With great administrative flexibility he could develop a wide range of different facilities to meet the individual needs of programs best for the offender, and they could be moved between them as desired."

Both reports suggest major departures from existing organizational arrangements, and it is not the purpose of this paper to argue the merits of the recommendations contained in either. Rather, they represent examples of a continuing and necessary effort to realign correctional services in ways which will make it possible to exploit the opportunities now available to corrections, to make effective use of community resources and services in the reintegration of the offender into society.

Part IV

FUTURE DIRECTIONS
FOR CORRECTIONS

In the preceding sections of this anthology we have attempted to provide the reader with an overview of the central issues and problems now confronting the American correctional system. Obviously, we have had to be selective in determining which of the many potential articles would be appropriate for those readers who lack previous exposure to the correctional literature and who are not yet thoroughly familiar with the methodological and statistical techniques that are characteristic of much of the contemporary writing in this area. Still, we trust that the point is clear that those involved in correctional work are not without their critics, nor are they necessarily unresponsive to many of the criticisms they have received. On the contrary, evidence indicates that correctional policies and practices are changing more rapidly today than at any other time in recent history.

As we have already noted, the fact that change is taking place should not be considered either a strong or a weak point until the form and direction of the change becomes somewhat more apparent. Thus, in this final section we have chosen articles by two of the leading authorities in the field, Norval Morris and Daniel Glaser. Morris's review of the current status of corrections in Sweden is of particular interest to those who correctly perceive the possibility of profiting from the experiences of others in the design of changes in our own system. Glaser, on the other hand, provides an outline of the directions in which American corrections appears to be moving.

22

Lessons from
the Adult Correctional System of Sweden

Norval Morris

The police court, the local jail, and the penitentiary provide insights into the brotherliness and decency of a country's social system. Visit the art galleries, the cathedrals, the fountains, the squares, try the restaurants, and inspect the shops, and you will have certain social soundings. Examine how a society handles its poor, its sick, its old, and its antisocial and asocial discordant elements, and you will have quite others. My tastes turn to the latter type of tourism and in particular to criminological and penological wanderings.[1] This preference led to my spending 2 months in Sweden visiting their correctional institutions and agencies, talking with their staffs and many of their prisoners who are English speaking (and they are numerous), questioning those responsible for probation and parole supervision, and collecting statistical and descriptive materials on their system.[2]

From "Lessons from the Adult Correctional System of Sweden," *Federal Probation*, 30 (December 1966), 3–13. Reprinted by permission.

[1]This has certain collateral merits. There is an international brotherhood of prison administrators who most generously facilitate travel for those whom they will accept as members; transport is efficient, and the food is quite excellent.

[2]A declaration of interest is appropriate. The author was for these 2 months a guest of the Swedish Government; his judgment is peculiarly seducible by the charm, kindliness, and generosity of Swedish hospitality and a critical eye may have failed. His conscience is clear; but judge for yourself.

This should be sufficient for a broad overview of a correctional system; it is not, however, anything like adequate for a responsible description of such a system. For this and other reasons, no attempt is made here to offer any rounded description of the Swedish adult correctional system. The purpose is rather to examine certain organizational methods and practical techniques applied in Sweden with a view to assessing their transatlantic exportability, now or in the future. The focus is candidly reformist. The question posed is: What practices in the Swedish adult correctional system merit emulation in this country and adaptation to our different correctional problems? Or, put more succinctly, how can the Swedes help us to escape from our correctional cultural cocoon?[3]

Sanford Bates, of vast experience in American corrections and with wide international perceptions, recently suggested that "America has set the example . . . in several important innovations and developments in our correctional system"[4] and listed, as such, probation, parole, some indeterminacy in sentencing, the juvenile court, the youth court, inmate classification within correctional systems, open institutions, and the prison camp program. It is an impressive list and by and large well justified, though there are dangers of chauvinism in such claims, for in this field historical firsts are rarely easy to establish.[5]

There is a history of international borrowing of correctional ideas, and it is a process to be encouraged. The problems of crime and the treatment of criminals differ widely between cultures, being set deep into the political, social, and economic structure of the country, frequently precluding any direct emulation of correctional organizations and methods. On the other hand, themes, ideas, and techniques often are entirely capable of adaptation to cultures other than those which produced them, and underlying principles and broad objectives frequently merit consideration for emulation in other and different societies.

Comparative studies are particularly important to us at the present time when the field of corrections in the United States is in such a state of ferment. We are doubtful of our inheritance, skeptical of many of our methods, appalled by the size and diversity of the problems we face, and cognizant of the lack of knowledge with which we work, yet it is also a time of great hope. There is a sense of increasing empathy towards one's

---

[3]John P. Conrad's *Crime and Its Correction*, University of California Press, 1965, is the leading text for those who wish to break their cultural chains and desire comparative understanding of the direction and speed of penal reform in this country.

[4]"Anglo-American Progress in Penitentiary Affairs" in *Studies in Penology*, edited by Manuel López-Rey and Charles Germain, Martinus Nijhoff, The Hague, 1964, p. 43.

[5]For example, the open institution claim. I am an Australian. My country *started* as an open institution. And we immediately began a "working out" plan called the "ticket of leave" system!

fellow man, even the criminal; a desire determinedly to avoid needless suffering, a willingness to experiment, a general striving towards improvement. We have an Attorney General of the United States who presses his far from unimaginative director of the Federal Bureau of Prisons to experimentation and even more rapid development—surely a Gilbertian reversal of traditional roles. And in state after state the old hard-nosed, tough warden, who knew that nothing could be done, gives way to energetic realist-reformers. At such a time it is particularly important that we seek to learn the lessons of corrections in other countries.

Sweden is no place for the enthusiastic penal reformer. As William Hazlitt observed, "Those who are fond of setting things to right, have no great objection to seeing them wrong."[6] But the persistent reformer who sees things wrong within his own state may gain from seeing the avoidance of many of these evils in Sweden. Exorcising some of these evils may be facilitated by comparison with one of the most humane correctional systems in the world and one which has achieved close links with the community which supports it.

GENERAL BACKGROUND

Books like Marquis Childs' *Sweden: The Middle Way*, and the general interest in the United States in the pattern of life in Sweden, have made commonplace some knowledge of the political, social, and economic structure of Sweden, some understanding of its high standard of living and of its well developed social welfare system. The national background can, I believe, be assumed, and we can turn to a general description of the correctional program in Sweden as a prelude to considering some of the specific lessons that may be learned from it.[7]

The population of Sweden slightly exceeds 7,700,000. The correctional institutions at present hold, in round numbers, 5,000 prisoners of the age of 18 or above. There are also nearly 3,000 persons of that age range on aftercare supervision. Further, about 15,500 persons within this age group are on probation. These figures reflect a crime rate, and cer-

---

[6]*Characteristics: In the Manner of Rochefoucault's Maxims*, 1823, p. 148.

[7]One praising Swedish social organization frequently meets these replies. Is theirs not a sexually immoral society? Is their suicide rate not indicative of a deep social malaise? In the post-Kinsey age I doubt the differences between societies in any measurement of sexual high-frequency and high-fidelity. And concerning suicide rates, it seems to me that the published figures measure differences in honest compilation of figures rather than differences in the incidence of this behavior. We struggle with success at several levels not to classify our suicides as suicides; the Swedes do not. The alleged differences in sexual morality and suicide seem to me more likely to measure the degree of social frankness than the different incidence of the behavior.

tainly an imprisonment rate, appreciably lower than that which obtains in this country.[8] It is not my present task to speculate on the reasons for these lower rates but it is at least worthy of mention that they are in part a function both of shorter sentences and of a much less moralistic criminal code. It has often troubled me that the country which proclaims the highest moral standards in its criminal law, the United States, seems to have the largest problems not only in attaining those very standards but with the remainder of its criminal law also. Gambling, sex, narcotics laws of quite amazing virtue, all largely unenforceable, are to be found in this country but to nothing like the same extent in Sweden, nor indeed elsewhere in Europe or throughout the British Commonwealth.

Putting such large speculations aside and returning to correctional problems, not only do the Swedish courts try to avoid committing offenders to penal institutions but when imprisonment is the sentence, the terms of years imposed also are short in comparison with those obtaining in the United States.[9] The prison administrators further try to minimize both the actual terms served and the amount of social isolation and separation that is involved in a prison sentence. For example, of the 5,000 prisoners, over one-third are at any one time held in completely open conditions.

Finally in this numbers game, it is important to stress that the 5,000

---

[8]These figures are also reduced, in comparison with other countries, by the commitment to mental hospitals in Sweden, under civil process, of a group of persons who in our system would be committed to prison.

[9]Comparative statistics is an elusive exercise; but the following figures give some support to what is an observable difference. *National Prisoner Statistics*, published by the Federal Bureau of Prisons, in 1960 reported that the average time a prisoner served before he was released from a state institution in this country was 2 years and 4 months. Compare this with sentences imposed in Sweden in 1964. In that year 10,535 prisoners were received into Swedish prisons on fixed prison sentences. Their division by duration of sentence was:

Sentence Imposed	Total	Percent of Total
All Cases	10,535	100.0
Under 2 months	3,208	31.0
2 months to 6 months	3,973	38.0
6 months to 1 year	2,261	21.0
1 year to 2 years	887	8.0
2 years to 4 years	168	1.0
4 years to 10 years	30	0.3
10 years and over	8	0.08

These figures do not include 692 preventive detainees who, in 1964, were serving sentences of preventive detention—the internment group. This is an indefinite sentence with a minimum term of between 1 and 12 years fixed by the court; they are held in practice for an average of 5 years. These figures also are skewed by their inclusion of what would be part of the grist of the mill of the local jail in this country. The pattern of appreciable shorter sentences nevertheless starkly emerges. (The above figures are extracted from *Kriminalvarden*, 1964, published by the Department of Official Statistics, Stockholm, 1965.)

prisoners also include nearly 500 persons detained pending trial. The fact that less than 500 persons are at any one time detained in jail awaiting trial is a remarkable tribute to the Swedish police and judicial systems. If you doubt it, visit the local jail nearest you and reflect that the Swedish 500 are drawn from a population of 7,700,000. This number does not include people arrested and held in custody by the police; however, police custody is limited to a maximum of 4 days, after which the offender must be brought before a court and if further detained can only be detained in facilities provided by the correctional system—he then falls within the 500. But the lessons here are not for corrections; they are lessons for a judicial system which the lawyers most urgently should learn in this country.

Pervading the Swedish social and political system is a high level of respect for individual human rights. It is also a very polite society in which citizen treats citizen and the state treats its citizens with punctilious respect. These attitudes lie deep in Swedish social organization and are in no way abandoned when the citizen becomes a criminal or a prisoner. Thus, section 23 of the law on Treatment in Correctional Institutions, 1964, the first general provision on the conditions of imprisonment, provides that "An inmate shall be treated with firmness and determination and with respect . . . injurious effects of the loss of freedom shall be prevented as far as possible."

This humanitarian and egalitarian attitude is indeed the mainspring of the whole correctional system, an explanation of both the low incidence of imprisonment and of many of the conditions and practices within the prison system. This attitude is both its strength and a key to some of its weaknesses. This is what moved Karl Schluyter when, as Minister of Justice in 1932–1936, he laid the foundations of the modern Swedish correctional system; and it seems to me to be the main motive of the energetic and imaginative leadership now given to that system by its present, internationally esteemed Director-General, Torsten Eriksson. The predominance of humanitarian and human rights purposes also in part explains some of the weakness of the system—staff training is far from well-developed and that which exists is at a low level of technical sophistication, reliance being placed very heavily on the personality and decency of the staff member with insufficient attention being given to his training.[10] Research is exiguous and little indeed is known of which treatment methods work better with which categories of offenders; again, the motivation of the system is human respect, not empirical or clinical perceptions.

The prison administrator and the prison officer in Sweden has this advantage over his colleague in many other countries: Swedish citizens

---

[10]On July 1, 1966, the Swedish Legislature provided the legal basis and financial authorization for a much expanded and ambitiously designed staff training program.

generally are intensely proud of their social welfare system. More and more they take their very high standard of living for granted and express pride in their country in relation to its care for the sick, incompetent and discordant elements within it. When they turn to the international field their national amour-propre is likewise expressed in terms of extensive technical and financial contributions to the developing countries and to the United Nations. The Swedish citizen not connected with prison work will, at the dinner table, express pride in the Swedish correctional system; this is hardly a common experience at the American dinner table. And his satisfaction is not in any clinical skills that the system mobilizes or in its effect on recidivist rates, but rather in the fact that the Swedish criminal or prisoner still remains a Swedish citizen meriting respect, continuing properly to enjoy a quite high standard of living, and remaining a part of the community.

Examples of this attitude are frequently to be found in the press, where the prisoners' complaints to the Ombudsman[11] often receive considerable press attention. The community appears to be interested in and to take seriously complaints by prisoners which would not in this country merit protracted attention within the walls and certainly would receive no consideration whatsoever outside. This sometimes borders on the extreme. While I was in Sweden, for example, a complaint to the Ombudsman by a group of inmates in open institutions that the guards were occasionally at nights shining flashlights into their cells to make sure that they were still there, and that this was a serious interference with their right to a good night's sleep, was taken quite seriously by the press. The prisoners argued that if they were trusted in open institutions they had to be trusted completely. Torsten Eriksson had no great difficulty in satisfying the Ombudsman of the need to confirm the continued presence of the prisoners, even in open institutions, and that this was no interference whatsoever with their decent treatment; but the point remains. The complaint was not treated frivolously by the press; it was thought of as a serious issue. The community generally has pride and a sense of responsibility for conditions in their prisons to a much larger degree than in this country and to a larger degree they have given up retributive punitive attitudes. These sentiments are brought to this work by the prison officer who sees a Swedish quality of firm, decent, respectful, and polite treatment between individuals as properly determining his attitude and behavior towards the inmate. It is a great

---

[11]"Since 1809, an officer of the highest rank and authority the Ombudsman . . . has been elected by Parliament, invariably from among the most prominent members of the Bench, to exercise surveillance over the way in which public authorities respect the freedoms and rights of the citizens . . . Every citizen is entitled to address his complaints to [the Ombudsman] . . . . No special requirements as to form need be followed, and no complaint is dismissed without investigation." *Legal Values in Modern Sweden*, Folke Schmidt and Stig Strömholm, p. 5 (Stockholm, 1964). See also "The Swedish Justitieombudsman" by Walter Gellhorn in 75 Yale L. J. 1 (1965).

asset, substantially diminishing the alienating and prison subculture creating processes that are to be found so often in other countries.

SIZE OF INSTITUTIONS AND STAFF-INMATE RATIO

The largest prison in Sweden is Långholmen in Stockholm. This is a traditional cellular prison with a daily average population of 620 in the summer of 1965. Långholmen dates from the early 1850's, is overcrowded (its population occasionally exceeding 700, in an institution designed for 450) and is soon to be abandoned. The Karolinska Institutet maintains a 60-bed psychiatric clinic, built in 1932, in the grounds of Långholmen prison which provides extensive and highly efficient diagnostic services to the courts and the prison authorities. If Långholmen were characteristic of the Swedish prisons there would be few lessons for us in them; even though by American standards it is a small prison. By Swedish standards it is absurdly large. On the day I went to Långholmen the next most populous prison in Sweden was that at Malmö, in the South, with a population of 241 inmates.

These statistics tell a story of determinative significance for the system and spell out a lesson that one hopes will ultimately be learned in this country. For the 5,000 prisoners in Sweden there are at present 88 prisons. With a range and diversity of small prisons and with an institutional staff in excess of one member of staff for every two prisoners, with small institutions and small groups of prisoners, it has proved possible to set up a correctional institutional system which avoids the mass anonymity characteristic of the penal system in this country, and which largely avoids the hot-house growth of the evil subculture which has characterized our correctional efforts.

This lesson from Sweden is one that we already know, but it is underlined by the Swedish practice. Our institutions are grossly too large. Sweden has avoided the mega-institution; we should abandon it. There is little point in arguing the merits of this; few will disagree. It is a question of ignorance and tradition masquerading as political and social priorities; the readers of *Federal Probation* need no persuasion of the many advantages of smaller institutions. With small institutions, much else that we all seek to achieve in our correctional work is possible; with the mega-institution, little is possible.[12]

---

[12]Wandering around a Swedish prison and talking to a member of the prison staff, at the level of deputy warden, I heard him launch into a bitter criticism of the central correctional administration in Sweden for not appreciating the need for small

WOMEN STAFF

Women are found to be working not only in institutions for younger offenders in Sweden but also throughout their adult correctional system. I do not mean working only in the front offices outside the security perimeter; I mean within the walls and within the cell blocks. And there are women governors of prisons for male prisoners. Only in Långholmen, of the institutions I visited, is there the sense of an exclusively male society. Monasticism is avoided even in the main long term institution of Hall which is the central prison for the internment group, who are the persistent and professional criminals; it is likewise avoided for the 18- to 21-year-old group of vigorous males, and indeed when I visited the institution of Mariefred, holding such offenders, the warden was a woman. The advantages of our learning this lesson from Sweden are obvious, women bring a softening influence to the prison society, assisting men by their presence, to strengthen their inner controls, through a variety of deeply entrenched processes of psychosocial growth.

What are the disadvantages or risks involved in emulating this sensible plan, which would be sensible even did we not face chronic staff shortages? I suppose the risks or disadvantages are four-fold: Loss of discipline, a barrage of obscenity, sexual assaults, and successful courtship by those we too often see as pariahs. The first I doubt, the second is a matter of staff training, the third is not a serious threat, and the fourth is to be occasionally expected and welcomed. One would not isolate a woman or women members of staff amongst a large number of recalcitrant hostile male prisoners; the main custodial staff should remain male as it is in Sweden. The lesson is clear and is that women should be employed within the correctional institution for those skills in psychology, casework, administration, and counseling which they can offer as well as men, and nothing but advantage to the entire correctional system will ensue.

AN INTEGRATED REGIONALIZED
CORRECTIONAL SYSTEM

Under the administrative control of the Ministry of Justice, the correctional administration is responsible for the integrated but regionalized

---

institutions. I laughed. He was offended. I asked him what he meant by a small institution. He said, "one with a population of approximately 40 inmates." I tried to make my peace with him by assuring him that I had had exactly this conversation with many prison officers in the United States who spoke in exactly the same terms, but who advocated prisons 10 times as large as he was demanding!

system of corrections throughout Sweden. There are approximately 3,600 employees of the correctional administration, not counting the volunteers who do the actual work of supervision in the community.

Correctional work is regionalized into five geographic groups and into three special problem groups. Each geographic group provides a central prison and a range of classificatory and treatment institutions, prerelease centers and hostels, and extra-institutional facilities. There are, in effect, five operatively distinct correctional systems in Sweden, handling all problems of detention prior to trial, probation, imprisonment, parole, and aftercare in their regions. The three specialist groups—youth, women, internment—are not regionalized in this fashion. The institutions and facilities for the 18- to 21-year-old group are administered as a nationwide system as are the facilities, institutional and within the community, for women offenders and for offenders sentenced as habitual or professional criminals to indeterminate commitment. Conditional and final release under the indeterminate commitment is under the control of an internment board presided over by a judge or retired judge of the Supreme Court, and with four other members, including a senior lawyer, a member of parliament, usually a psychiatrist, and the director general of the Correctional Administration.

Considerable effort is made to delegate powers to the five regional correctional systems, and substantial authority in relation to the date of conditional and final release of inmates is given to local supervisory boards. There are 47 supervisory boards in Sweden, each serving one or more trial court districts, and responsible for recommending the parole of prisoners in its district. Parole is for 1 year or the unexpired portion of the sentence, whichever is longer.

The total cost of this unified, regionalized correctional system of Sweden, in 1965, was approximately 200 million Swedish kroner; that is, about $40 million. Of this sum, 90 million kroner ($18 million) was applied to staff salaries. These costs cover the 15,500 probationers, 5,000 prisoners, and 3,000 parolees.

Such an integrated, regionalized correctional system is, of course, not unknown in this country. The Wisconsin system comes to mind as such an organizational structure.

One of the currently contentious issues in the organization of corrections in the federal system in the United States is whether the federal probation and parole services should be joined with the Federal Bureau of Prisons and the Federal Parole Board in a single department administratively responsible to the Department of Justice. Unification and regionalization at the federal level, and in a country the size of the United States, raise problems of great complexity, with political and jurisprudential penumbrae which at present I would prefer to avoid; let me therefore suggest only some of the advantages of the Swedish unified and regionalized structure for a state as distinct from a federal correctional system.

The advantage of unification of institutional and extra-institutional processes, of some coherent single administrative structure of probation, prison, and parole, flows essentially from the fact that the link between institutional and noninstitutional correctional processes grows closer and requires overall planning. The prison is now rarely thought to provide an independent, self-contained correctional process; it is seen by all who hope that it will rehabilitate as involving a gradual release procedure and an effective aftercare program all linked into a single rehabilitative plan. And even effective probation is coming to be seen as requiring some institutional supports in an appreciable proportion of cases. The probation hostel may be necessary for some cases; institutional control of leisure in community treatment centers may be needed for others.

And so prison, probation, and parole grow closer together and structurally intertwine. The prison may be required as a base from which the prisoner goes out to work; a halfway house may be used as a release procedure; and aftercare will always be closely linked with the prison program and should provide a continuum of planning and execution of the prisoner's rehabilitative plan. It is hard to provide such continuous institutional and postinstitutional correctional processes, and such institutional and contemporaneously noninstitutional processes (halfway house, working out, community treatment center, probation hostel) unless there is the closest of ties between those responsible for these various services.

Continuity of treatment plan and execution is necessary as a release procedure; but it also proves necessary when we apply more effective control mechanisms in our aftercare processes, for this reason: At present when a prisoner on parole breaks a condition of his release, the choice facing the correctional authorities is too limited. He can be warned, or he can be taken back into custody. Just as we are developing "halfway-out" houses as release procedures so should we, as does Sweden, develop "halfway-in" houses to provide for those released prisoners who require a period of closer control than can be given when they are relatively free on parole but who do not need to be sent back to prison. This group may not be large, but it is appreciable, and again there is a happy confluence between better rehabilitative processes and less cost.

Another advantage of unification of correctional service should be mentioned. It has long seemed to me that the prison warden, to be entirely effective in his job, should not only be informed concerning probation and parole work but also should have had a period of active involvement in casework in the community. Likewise, it seems to me, the senior probation or parole officer should have had institutional experience if he is to be most effective. This theme is accepted within the Swedish correctional system, and no one reaches a high position in that system without a variety of work experiences both within and outside the walls. Again the theme of the continuum of treatment services is stressed by the very structure of those services.

So much for the value of unification in a state system. Regionalization needs little justification. It carries forward the theme of avoiding enterprises too large for any single man to have reasonably close and detailed acquaintance with their workings. And there is also in Sweden the advantage, in a community less mobile than that of the United States, of linking the correctional system, in each of the five regions close to the needs, opportunities, and social attitudes of the particular social group in which the offender lived and will live; regional differences require appropriate differences in correctional systems. Finally and obviously, regionalization greatly facilitates maintaining closer ties between the prisoner and his family, by visits and furloughs, than would be possible were correctional administration in Sweden not regionalized in this way.

PRISON INDUSTRY

An aphorism frequently heard in the prison administration of Sweden concerning their work program is: "First build a factory, then add a prison to it." Prisoners work a 45-hour, 5-day week from 7 in the morning to 5 in the evening with 1½ hours for lunch; the able-bodied idle prisoner is rare in Sweden. A few inmates, of course, are employed on maintenance work, but the atmosphere of all the industrial prisons is close to that of a factory. And even many of their very small open institutions are also industrial. One finds institutions of 40 inmates living in lightly built and unlocked and unfenced facilities in which about half the inmates will be engaged in farm work and half will be running a small timber-yard or carpentry workshop. The industries range from small, almost village industries, to substantial mass-production factories. The machine shop industry provides 500 jobs, the wood industry 850, and the garment industry 850. These are the major products, but there are also large laundries and substantial boat-building and prefabricated house building activities (200). Indeed, for the 5,000 prisoners, 2,500 jobs are available within various types of industry, while roughly 1,000 are employed in farming and forestry activities.

The correctional administration is one of Sweden's largest rural land owners, with 6,500 acres of farm land. The building industry is of importance, prison labor having recently been used to build several open institutions. There still remain tensions between employers and trade union organizations as to the extent to which prison building should be done by prison inmates for the larger closed and complex institution, but for the smaller open institutions the battle is won and they are largely the product of inmate labour.

The lesson here is one that needs little underlining. Everyone informed on corrections in this country sees idleness as a serious threat to any aspirations we may have. We all know that we face joint opposition from employers and trade union organizations. I would hope that everyone appreciates that this opposition lacks principle and is unjust. It is based on the unacceptable premise that when a person is convicted of a crime and sent to prison he ceases to be a citizen.[13]

The value of the produce of the Swedish correctional system of last year was 60 million kroner ($12 million). It seems to me that the stress on production sometimes involves a sacrifice or neglect of vocational training. This may be erroneous judgment and may well fail to take into account the high and universal standard of general education in Sweden together with the value of on-the-job training. It also probably insufficiently allows for the lesser vocational training opportunities when sentences are so very much shorter both in maximum term imposed and in actual time served than in the United States.

The average wage of the prisoner in industries, farming and maintenance in Sweden is one dollar per day. The institution of Tillberga, however, within the eastern institutional group, is the first of a series of six institutions of a new character. It is the largest open institution in Sweden, with a population of 120; but unlike most open institutions it is not organized even in part as a farming or forestry camp, but rather entirely as a factory. It consists of three "houses" proximate to a large factory for the manufacture of prefabricated houses and also for a certain amount of machine shop work. It has a staff of 44, of which 18 are guards while 13 work in the factory and 13 in administration. Most of the 120 inmates are short-term prisoners who come direct to the institution without escort from the courts. Many of them are sentenced for drunken driving and, as is the Swedish practice, have been committed to prison for a short term. Most are under 25 years of age.

When I visited Tillberga, the plan was to pay the prisoners the ordinary ruling wage in the community for the type of work that they do; the inmates would pay for their room and board at Tillberga, the remainder of the funds being their own as if they were working at large in the community. They would not pay for the guards. This is surely proper; like other people they pay income tax and as citizens they must make a contribution, as we all do, to the costs of prisons. It is improper, simply because they are prisoners, that a larger cost for prisons should fall upon them than on the rest of us. Prisons exist for us quite as much as they do for prisoners.

---

[13]The contrary argument is "unfair competition." Perhaps the unexpected but just solution is for prisoners to remain or to become union members, their interests vigorously protected by their union!

It will be years, I suspect, before we will be experimenting with the full wages prison in this country; but the logic behind it is compelling and it is only a question of time surely before the advantages to the community and to the prisoners that such a system offers for certain classifications of prisoners bring it into existence. The experiment at Tillberga is an important pathfinder.

ASPTUNA AND RESEARCH

Chapter 28, section 3, of the Penal Code of Sweden, which became effective on the first of January in 1965, provides that, "If the defendant is 18 years of age or older, the court may, if it has been deemed necessary for his correction or for some other reason, order that the probation shall include treatment at an institution. Such treatment shall continue for at least one and at most 2 months depending on decisions made as it progresses."

The first section of the Code represents Sweden's emulation of some lessons learned from the United States, particularly from institutions that have followed the path blazed by the State of New Jersey in the Highfields experiment. Sweden has built four 40-bed institutions for male offenders; one 15-bed institution for women is planned. It is intended that selected probationers shall be sentenced under this provision of the Penal Code to spend between 1 month and 2 months in such an institution being involved in group therapy, and in a settling-down, motivating, and planning period before they serve their 3-year probation term in the community. Like all other Swedish prisons which I visited (other than Långholmen), the institution at Asptuna, which is one of the four built pursuant to section 3, Chapter 28 of the Penal Code, is attractive in design and comfortable in its living circumstances. Inmates do not merely sit about in guided group interaction and in planning their probation experience; there is an active industrial program occupying their energies for 45 hours per week. These are vigorous young men who must be kept actively employed.

Overall, it is obviously an excellent plan and the Swedes are wise in having learned it from this country and in having so intelligently modified it to their own needs; but I would like also to draw from Asptuna a negative lesson that we might learn from the Swedish correctional system—a lesson of what we should not do.

When I visited Asptuna, the young and intelligent superintendent, having informed me in detail of the background of the institution, of the organization of its program and the group discussions and industrial activities that were daily pursued, then told me that this was a research demon-

stration project. I asked him how he would know if the project had succeeded, how discover if the experiment had demonstrated anything? He
replied, conscious that he was being facetious, that if they had 80 percent
success in terms of avoidance of recidivism he would regard that as a
successful experiment. Acting the graceless guest, I pressed him on this and
urged him not to be so confident of my ignorance. At length he agreed
that the recidivism rate itself would very likely give no guidance whatsoever on whether this had or had not been a successful experiment. He
agreed that if the selection process were such as to send to Asptuna young
offenders that were so promising that they were unlikely later to be involved in crime, that the 80 percent success might indicate an appreciable
failure of the institution; they might well have had 85 percent success if
they had been left alone.

In truth, no matter what the recidivism rate, it will throw little light on
the success or failure of the experiment. The offenders were selected for
Asptuna at least partly on the ground that the courts regarded them as less
likely to relapse into crime than those committed to prison. The failure
rate of a group like this under previous treatments was not known. The
classification and selection procedures may well influence the rate of
recidivism more than the treatment method itself; at least it is impossible to
disentangle the relevance of each. A very low recidivism rate may *not* be
desired. What we may prefer is a reduction of recidivism rates among
defined categories of offenders with known recidivism rates, and the experiment of Asptuna may be better attuned to the treatment of those who *do*
present a serious threat of future criminality rather than to those who do not.

If every correction experiment is not to be regarded as a success by
its innovators in Sweden as elsewhere, we must test it critically by methods
capable of guiding future correctional developments; experiments should be
capable of failure! The methodology of such research is now well-known to
us and there is no excuse in Sweden or elsewhere for our investment of
men, money, and materials in projects like Asptuna without any concomitant methodologically sound evaluative research.

In terms of research, we do not have lessons to learn from Sweden;
they have lessons to learn from us. Only quite recently have criminological
studies commenced at the university level in Sweden and the interest in
critical evaluation of correctional methods is still dormant. Sweden would
be an ideal country in which to develop criminological and correctional
research, since very soon they will be excellently equipped for the coordination of social information about all their citizens. Every citizen now has his
own individual nine-digit number made up of the last two digits of his year
of birth, two digits expressing the month, two the day of his birth, and
three digits completing his number by reference to his position amongst all

babies born on that day (odd numbers for males and even numbers for females!).

All social welfare information from Sweden is now being coordinated for every person around his own number, and all such information is being processed for the computers. There is, in other words, a far-reaching movement of high technical competence towards the amassing and effective processing of a great deal of statistical information concerning the population of Sweden in all their contacts with official and quasi-official agencies of the state; but there yet remains insufficient guidance at the technical level, in relation to criminology and penology, for the information which is now accumulating to be structured to produce the maximum gain of knowledge to guide social action in the prevention of crime and treatment of offenders. It is paradoxical how remarkably imaginative and creative the Swedes have been in correctional work in relation to the relative backwardness of their statistical information and research activities, particularly research evaluative of their wide and interesting range of correctional methods.

FURLOUGHS, VISITS, AND SEXUAL RELATIONSHIPS

My first visit to Swedish prisons was in 1955; I well remember my shock at Hall prison on seeing a prisoner's motorbike on which daily he went out from the prison to work on a nearby farm. The Huber law in this country and its gradual expansion from Wisconsin through federal and state correction systems is one of the brighter spots in corrections and the Swedes have few lessons to teach us on this theme other than that the system works well in their country also. However, in another process which allows prisoners to leave their prisons for defined periods, they do indeed have a lesson we should learn—the furlough system.

Furloughs for prisoners were introduced in Sweden in 1937. At first they were restricted to cases of serious illness or funerals of close relatives or comparable emergencies and to prerelease employment interviews; that is to say, they were restricted in exactly the same way that the current federal legislation[14] is restricted. I hope that it, too, will burgeon as has the Swedish practice. From open institutions Swedish prisoners now get home every 3 months after a fixed proportion of their sentence has been served; from closed institutions they get such home leave every 4 months. The minimum term they must serve before their first furlough ranges from 6

---

[14]The Prisoner Rehabilitation Act, 1965: Public Law 89-176, 89th Congress, H.R. 6964.

months to 3 years, the latter being the first possible furlough for a prisoner serving a life sentence. The duration of their first furlough is normally 48 hours plus traveling time, while subsequent furloughs are for 72 hours plus traveling time. At present, nearly 8,000 furloughs are granted each year.

Let me not conceal the difficulties that this system is facing. There was an escape rate of approximately 8 percent.[15] How seriously one is going to regard this, and whether one will reject such a system because of such an escape rate, is a matter of one's judgment of social policy. It should be remembered that all these prisoners are in any event going to be released and that furloughs are not given to prisoners who are regarded as actively and currently dangerous, and further that furloughs are better than any other method for maintaining the prisoner's ties with his family and the community in which he will be discharged to live.

Prior to and as a condition of being granted his first home leave, the prisoner will make a leave plan in consultation with a social worker. If he is to visit his family, a social worker will visit them and plan the leave with them also. This is obviously one valuable means of achieving our often expressed hope for continuity between treatment within the walls and on subsequent parole. Home leave compels both institutional and community planning for each prisoner; further, if he conforms on leave, his own sense of capacity for subsequent conformity is strengthened; if not, the parole board's inclination to avoid his premature release is informed and strengthened.

The advantages of this system are as obvious as are its risks; the question is one of social tolerance. And as I have suggested, the Swedish community is proud of its correction system and is willing to tolerate an appreciable escape rate as a part of the rehabilitative process they see their prisons as serving.

This should be said, however. One important consequence of the furlough system is the gross reduction of the problem of homosexuality within Swedish prisons. Small institutions and the attitudes and programs I have sketched are important factors in minimizing this problem; so also is the general attitude toward sex in Swedish society. But furloughs obviously diminish libidinal pressures for the inmates and lessen the likelihood of their homosexual expression. Visits also have this effect in many Swedish prisons.

Not in the central prisons in each region, like Långholmen, or Kumla (their most recently constructed, electronic, tunneled, TVed, space age,

---

[15]Furloughs normally are timed to end at the hour the institution closes for the night. If the furloughee has not returned by then, he is recorded as an "escapee." A majority of escapees are in reality merely late or late and alcoholic returns. The Swedes also register one gallant group as "an abuse of furlough"—those who return on time, drunk.

industrially sophisticated security prison) but in the other smaller and open institutions which make up the staple of the Swedish prison system, the regularity of and rules concerning visits also achieve the twin results of helping to preserve familial ties and of minimizing psychosexual aberrations. Visits are allowed weekly in most institutions. In several institutions the prisoner keeps the key to his own cell.[16]

In many institutions, wives and girl friends are allowed to visit prisoners in their cells—the conventions of privacy are not officially prescribed, but they are observed. I report a frequent practice, not an official rule. If you contemplate the transatlantic exportability of this practice to the American mega-institution, you will pause indeed; but in the institutional setting of the small Swedish prison, the female visitor, drinking coffee in the small mess halls which form part of each small cell block,[17] and visiting her husband or boyfriend in his cell does not seem at all surprising.

PROTECTIVE CONSULTANTS

In mid-summer 1965, there was a daily average of approximately 18,000 adult offenders under noninstitutional correctional supervision in Sweden. Of these, approximately 15,500 are what we would call probation cases and the remainder are on parole from institutions.

Conditional sentences and parole were introduced in Sweden in 1906, with the work of supervision being undertaken by volunteers in the local community where the offender lived. This voluntary supervision system still obtains, there now being more than 10,000 such supervisors supported by a complex system of 47 supervision boards, each under the chairmanship of a judge or lawyer. The boards have discretion concerning the conditions on probation or parole, variation of those conditions, and termination of supervision orders. They have power, in appropriate cases, not only to terminate probation orders but also to extend them for a period of a further 2 years, the normal supervision order being for a 3-year term. Between the supervision boards and the volunteers stands a professional staff of 150 protective consultants and assistant protective consultants.

This system has the advantage of mobilizing the interest of many thoughtful people throughout Sweden as supervisors. Since the Middle Ages, lay assessors of this type "have constituted a democratic stronghold

---

[16]The staff have, of course, master keys, but each prisoner's cell is lockable against other prisoners' keys.

[17]The lesson of avoiding central dining halls for the entire prison has, of course, been learned throughout Europe and the British Commonwealth; it is an amazing perseveration that they are still being built in this country.

at the very heart of Swedish public life."[18] The program brings them deeply into the total correctional system since the system is, as we have seen, unified and regionalized. It tends also to maximize the local community's interest in and support for the probationer and ex-prisoner. Some of the supervisors are professionally trained in the social sciences; many are school teachers; they carry caseloads of two or three (though there seem to be occasional cases of abuse in the system with some lawyers carrying rather larger caseloads of their own clients!). The protective consultants provide the presentence advice and also administer and control the system, introjecting a professional casework element into some cases, and advising the volunteers in crisis or different supervisory situations.

This system is not offered as a lesson in itself for our emulation. It seems to me to have certain lessons for us but not to be worthy of copying. It does have the advantage of involving senior members of the local community in the corrections system, of mobilizing those responsible elements in the community for the assistance of the probationer and the ex-prisoner; its main disadvantage is one that permeates corrections in Sweden—it provides little technically skilled social casework assistance to the offender, and there are certainly cases where such is needed.

In this country the historical progression has been clear and steady: With the development of social work training and the realization of the different demands of skilled casework, the volunteers have been supplanted by full-time paid and (in an increasing number of systems) trained caseworkers. The discourse has taken on the quality of choice—which do we want? What can we afford? This is, in my view, a mistaken choice, and that is why I would seek to draw a lesson from the Swedish practice. The problem is not one of choice, but of the effective deployment of the strengths of each.

Too often in criminological discussions we talk of "the criminal," "the juvenile delinquent," "the prisoner," our stereotypes masking almost the same diversity among offenders as exists among people generally. The correctional needs of one are not those of the other. The voluntary probation officer with a caseload of two or three can do better work with some probationers and some parolees than can the trained professional with his usually heavy caseload. By contrast, the problems which beset some probationers and parolees demand a skill in casework in their treatment which it is unrealistic to expect of the untrained, no matter how dedicated his purposes or how sterling his character.

The problem of classification is thus a serious one, but one that we cannot burke. Numbers and finances are forcing us to the difficult task of

----

[18]*Legal Values in Modern Sweden*, Folke Schmidt and Stig Strömholm, p. 9 (Stockholm, 1964).

classification, of building a system in which the professional and the volunteer both have their roles. The professional will clearly carry the burden of the presentence investigation and of advice to the courts; but the work of the volunteer in Sweden, and in many other countries, should be a stimulus to our developing supervision systems which can maximize the advantages and skills of each in relation to the needs of their clients. Some offenders will require the technical skills of the caseworker; some will best be supported by the volunteer supervisor; and a few may require both at different times during the period of his supervision. That both groups are needed is clear; what is unhappily less clear is which types of offenders respond to the supervisory and supportive skills of each but it is certainly not beyond our methodological competence to find out.

There is this lesson, then, in the Swedish system of supervisory boards, protective consultants, and volunteers which I must underline. It brings the community into the total correctional system.[19] The volunteer through the protective consultant establishes contact with the prisoner he will probably be supervising when he is discharged, he visits him and becomes to a degree a part of the institutional correctional system. It is an important method of lessening the banishment, the social isolation of the institution. And the prisoner will have been tested in regular furloughs before he is placed under supervision; it will be known to him, to the protective consultant, and to his supervisor, that he has a job and somewhere to live, and that determined efforts have been made to preserve such familial and social ties as he had.

CONCLUSION

Correctional systems reflect social systems; their development is limited by social and political attitudes. Yet there is an interaction here, too. The creative correctional administrator also can influence social and political attitudes towards prisons and prisoners. In this dynamic relationship, the Swedish experience has been most fortunate. Mr. Kling, the Minister of Justice did not exaggerate when he asserted at the opening session of the Third United Nations Congress on the Prevention of Crime and Treatment of Offenders, in Stockholm in 1965, concerning the correctional system in Sweden and the public's attitude to it, that "nowadays there finally exists, rather generally, public support for the desire continually to improve methods of treatment and that aggressiveness toward criminals has declined in our country and has been replaced by a common interest in how to shape

---

[19]For a thoughtful evaluation of the Swedish probation system, see John Conrad's *Crime and Its Correction*, pp. 26–29 (University of California Press, 1965).

treatment in the best possible manner so that the convicted offender may become a good citizen after serving his punishment." And the Minister was not expressing a pious hope; rather, he was describing the most significant factor in the development of the Swedish system.

These, then, are, in my view, some of the main lessons Sweden has to teach the American penal reformer. I have omitted mention of the many lessons for the lawyer and legislator: Their day-fine system which realistically adjusts the fine to the economic circumstances of the offender; their rational practice in relation to the defense of insanity to a criminal charge which avoids and with social advantage, the philosophic quagmire in which we struggle; the expedition of their criminal law processes; and the simplicity and clarity of their Penal Code of 1965.[20] The eulogy could continue but is excessive already. Further, the task facing the Swedish correctional authorities is less burdensome than ours—they have not known war for 150 years, theirs is a prosperous, homogeneous society lacking subcultural conflict and with a highly developed, community-accepted social welfare system. Even so, in the application of the social sciences, in the mobilization of the skills of the psychiatrist and psychologist to those aspects of classification and treatment in which they should play an important role, in their staff training and correctional research activities, they lag behind many less prosperous correctional systems. The lessons of effective treatment of the psychologically disturbed criminal and the inveterate recidivists are to be learned in Denmark, not Sweden; and there is much that Swedish corrections could gain from this country—particularly from some of our better probation and parole systems, and our developing efforts at research to evaluate our prevention and treatment methods. But why try to turn the discussion into a Correctional Olympics? The point is made—comparative corrections is of importance to penal reform and Sweden is a highly valuable contributor to the pool of shareable knowledge and experience.

---

[20]See Professor Ivar Strahl's introduction to *The Penal Code of Sweden*, translated by Professor Thorsten Sellin and published by the Ministry of Justice, Stockholm, 1965.

23

The Prison of the Future

Daniel Glaser

The prison of the future will differ drastically from today's prison, if it is rationally designed for goals which already are generally accepted. There goals are:

1. to evoke in offenders an enduring identification of themselves with anti-criminal persons;
2. to enhance the prospects that released prisoners will achieve satisfaction in legitimate post-release activities.

The pursuit of these two goals, in the light of today's common knowledge about criminals, would lead one far from traditional approaches to prison design and management. Already, there are signs that such movement has begun.

One of the most immediately evident differences between tomorrow's prison and that of today will be in location. The prisons of the future will be located in the communities from which most of their inmates come. This means that most prisons will be in metropolitan areas.

A home community location will have many advantages for a prison. It will simplify the staff's task of knowing both the anti-criminal and the criminal and disorderly personal influences in the community which affect their prisoners. It will permit a graduated release of inmates on a trial basis, for visiting prospective homes and seeking or even filling jobs in the community, prior to receiving complete freedom. This graduated release also will protect society, by providing a better test of the risks in releasing a man than can be had either by observing him only in a prison, remote and different from his post-release life, or by releasing him to traditional parole supervision, where his contacts with his parole agent are few and brief. Such graduated release also will permit the inmates to solve their social and economic problems piecemeal, reducing their prospect of finding themselves in desperate straits soon after they leave the prison, from having to face all their post-release problems at once. Finally, the predominantly urban location of tomorrow's prison will facilitate recruitment of superior employees, both line staff and part- or full-time specialists (e.g., teachers and physicians), for there will be a larger pool of potential employees within commuting distance of the prison.

The short-sightedness of current prison labor legislation will eventually be recognized. Therefore, in addition to their new locations, prisons of the future will have many program features distinguishing them from today's prisons. Prisons will operate industries and services comparable to those in which there is post-release employment opportunity for the prisoners. Also, any inmate who engages in the activities considered optimum for his rehabilitation, including school assignments, will get some financial compensation. This will be at a variable rate, to offer incentives for increased diligence and responsibility, and thus, to provide prior to release that sense of achievement which comes from truly earning rewards. An appreciable portion of these earnings will be deposited in a savings account, for gradual use by the inmate during his parole, based on a budget developed during his confinement, but subject to later revision, with consent of the parole staff.

The prison of the future will have extensive links with community organizations. Churches, social and fraternal organizations, service clubs, hobby groups, professional or trade associations, as well as societies and persons aiding each other in the control of vices (e.g., Alcoholics Anonymous), will participate in the prison more actively than heretofore. This is in addition to the great encouragement of visiting by non-criminal relatives and friends of the inmates. Many of these outsiders will be actively involved in prison treatment programs, and in the institution's social and recreational life.

The staff of the prison of the future will not have many of the sharp distinctions now characterizing prison employees. Whatever their job classification, they all will be treatment personnel, and all will also be concerned with maintaining whatever level of custody proves necessary. The prison staff may even include some ex-prisoners, who have demonstrated clear rehabilitation, and whose crime and reformation experience gives them unusual counseling propensities. Most of the parole supervision staff probably will have offices adjacent to, or in, the scattered urban prisons.

While there may be some formal group counseling programs, most of the treatment impact will arise from the face-to-face relations of line staff with small groups of inmates in the course of routine work, study, and play activities. The line staff will also be intimately involved in the diagnostic decisions of prison management on such matters as the custodial security required for each inmate, the optimum program for his rehabilitation, and his readiness for gradual release; the traditional central classification committee, limited to top institution officials, will be a thing of the past. Most group decisions seriously affecting the place or program of an inmate's imprisonment will be made in groups comprising the staff who know him best.

To facilitate this kind of program, the prison of the future will be small. There will be many institutions, of diverse custodial levels, within any metropolitan area. There will also be a few in rural locations for inmates of that background. Location may not be so critical for prisons to hold offenders considered so highly committed to crime or seriously disturbed as to long be dangerous. However, all inmates will be housed, for an appreciable number of months before their release, in an institution near their release destination, to procure the diagnostic and treatment benefits of community contact and graduated release.

The small institution will reduce the necessity for regimentation, and increase the extent to which most of the staff know most of the inmates on a personal basis, and know each other well. The prisons of the future, because they will be small, can be highly diverse, both in architecture and in program. For example, a graduated release establishment, or other prisons in which custodial security is not a difficult problem, may house as few as fifteen or twenty men, and can be located in large YMCA-type hotels, in sections of a low rental apartment development or in an ordinary family-type house. Where custodial security is needed, for society's protection and to prevent concern with escape from distracting inmates, custody will be achieved by having continuously connected or yard-enclosing buildings, or by having only a single edifice, so that there are few points of possible exit. Custodial emphasis can then be mainly peripheral and invisible; it will impose few restrictions on inside activities. The entire institution generally will house less than one hundred inmates, plus whatever school, work or other facilities are appropriate for the inmates housed there.

There will be less emphasis in the prison of the future on separating inmates by age than now prevails in prisons. The bulk of felony arrestees have long consisted of persons in a period of transition from childhood to adulthood. Their crimes express their prolonged difficulties, as youth, in trying to pursue independent adult roles. It is in this socialization sense, rather than in biological traits, that many offenders can be considered immature. This socialization immaturity is protracted when their social contact is primarily with persons of their own age. Older unadvanced offenders will certainly be better influences on youthful inmates than their delinquent age peers, for the most criminalized of the latter tend to set the standards of accepted behavior when they are in homogeneous age-groups. Tomorrow the most delinquent youthful inmates will be scattered and isolated from each other insofar as possible. Staff will be oriented to maximize the rewarding contact of such prisoners with those inmates least vulnerable to deleterious influence, and most likely to have a long-run anti-criminalizing effect.

In the prison of tomorrow there will be much concern with utilizing the personal relationships between staff and inmates for rehabilitative purposes. This means varying staff modes of interaction with inmates according to the individual inmate orientations towards staff. Thus, the manipulative or aggressive inmate will be met with firm but fair reactions, making violence or fraud unsuccessful, but rewarding legitimate effort. The dependent or neurotic inmate will receive acceptance and ego-support, but with encouragement of self-analysis and self-reliance. Most counseling will not be in formal programs, although these will exist; counseling will occur mainly as it is evoked by problem-revealing events in institutional life, as well as by discussions of the inmates' future plans. This means that both group and individual counseling will involve primarily the line staff, rather than clinical specialists; the latter, neither now, nor in the future, can be sufficiently numerous to be the major source of direct treatment influence on most of the nation's confined criminals.

It should be stressed that most efforts at personality influence of staff on inmates will not be considered as ends in themselves, but as means toward achievement of the two basic purposes cited in opening this paper: evoking identification of offenders with anti-criminal persons—such as staff—and increasing inmate capacity for success in maintaining satisfactory personal relationships with anti-criminal persons, in legitimate employment and other pursuits after release. The major focus in inmate-staff relationships, therefore, will be the staff's contribution to the inmate's development of a conception of himself as opposed to crime, and accepted and successful in a non-criminal life. Many types of personality may make these shifts without profound change in other aspects of their basic modes of psychological reaction.

The prison of the future will only evolve fully in the form described here, as the society of the future changes. This will be reflected in a growing interest of both government, and private groups and persons, in assisting their fellow men, not just with kindness, but with understanding. This means that research will be an integral part of the administration of the prison of the future. The research will include both routine monitoring of the effectiveness of ongoing operations, in terms of their relationship to post-release criminality, and controlled experiments for testing new measures.

If punishment is ever justified in future prison management, it will be only because of objective demonstration that for certain people, and under certain circumstances, it promotes an enduring change of behavior. In this sense, it will be a dispassionate negative reaction to proscribed behavior, administered within legal controls, and in conjunction with positive reactions to favored conduct. Of course, any restriction of freedom for inmates considered dangerous is inherently punitive. However, punishment beyond the minimum restriction essential for custodial purposes will only be imposed deliberately if its merit can be scientifically demonstrated in a given case, and it will then be subject to tight controls.

The prison of the future described here is not really so far away. We already see it foreshadowed in such enterprises as the Federal Pre-Release Guidance Centers, the Work Release programs of the North and South Carolina and Maryland prisons, and the Community Treatment Centers which the California Youth Authority has experimentally substituted for training school commitment from the Sacramento and Stockton areas. We see all of these features even more developed in new types of community institutions for treatment of mental disorders; most features of prisons once characterized mental hospitals, but the latter changed first, in many respects, with prisons following later. This sequence of change is likely to recur in the future, but as it does, the difference between a mental and a criminal commitment will be further reduced: both will be oriented to preparing their subjects for as safe and quick a release to the community as possible, yet both will continue to have custodial concerns.

The prison of the future, clearly, will be part of a society in which rationality is institutionalized, and goodness, truth, and beauty are cardinal goals. Such a society cannot be realized instantaneously. It has been evolving gradually, at least since the Enlightenment, but with many temporary delays and regressions. It will evolve more rapidly and with less interruption, the more clearly we envision it, the more adequate we comprehend the problems confronting its achievement, and the more diligently we work to procure it.

shaving cream
phone bill
Debbie
getting to 40s